109014

DATE DUE			

Written under the auspices of the
Center of International Studies
Princeton University

Also by Henry Bienen:

Tanzania: Party Transformation and Economic Development, 1967
and 1970

Violence and Social Change, 1968

Kenya: The Politics of Participation and Control, 1974

Editor and coauthor of:

The Military Intervenes: Case Studies in Political Development,
1968

The Military and Modernization, 1970

With David Morell:

Political Participation under Military Regimes, 1976

ARMIES AND PARTIES IN AFRICA

by Henry Bienen

AFRICANA PUBLISHING COMPANY

NEW YORK   LONDON

A division of Holmes & Meier Publishers, Inc.

Published in the United States of America 1978 by
Africana Publishing Company, a division of
Holmes & Meier Publishers, Inc.
30 Irving Place
New York, New York 10003

Great Britain:
Holmes & Meier Publishers, Ltd.
Hillview House
1, Hallswelle Parade, Finchley Road
London NW11 ODL

Copyright © 1978 by Holmes & Meier Publishers, Inc.

LIBRARY OF CONGRESS CATALOGING IN PUBLICATION DATA

Bienen, Henry.
    Armies and parties in Africa.

    Includes index.
    1. Africa—Politics and government—1960–
2. Africa—Armed Forces—Political activity.
3. Political parties—Africa.   I. Title.
JQ1875.A1B53   1978   322'.5'096   77-11796
ISBN 0-8419-0359-X
ISBN 0-8419-0386-7 pbk.

MANUFACTURED IN THE UNITED STATES OF AMERICA

Contents

To my sister, Sue Bienen Pearlman
and
To my brother, Richard Harrison Bienen

PREFACE

Armies and Parties in Africa is based on articles and essays written between 1966 and 1977. These articles and essays have been edited and occasionally altered slightly, but they have not been revised.

Chapter 1, "Introduction," has not been published previously, although parts of it rely on a paper I presented at the Department of State in February 1977, on "Military Regimes in Africa." Chapter 2, "The Ruling Party in the African One-Party State: TANU in Tanzania," is reprinted from the *Journal of Commonwealth Political Studies* 5 (November 1967); 214–230. Chapter 3 was published as Chapter 4, "One-Party Systems in Africa," in *Authoritarian Politics in Modern Society: The Dynamics of Established One-Party Sysems,* ed. Samuel P. Huntington and Clement H. Moore, pp. 99–127 (© 1970 by Basic Books, Inc., Publishers, New York). Chapter 4, "Political Parties and Political Machines in Africa," appeared in *The State of the Nations,* ed. Michael Lofchie, pp. 195–216 (Berkeley and Los Angeles: University of California Press, 1971. Copyright © 1971 by The Regents of the University of California; reprinted by permission of the University of California Press). Chapter 5, "Party Politics in Kenya," is culled from Henry Bienen, *Kenya: The Politics of Participation and Control,* pp. 66–130 (Princeton, N.J.: Princeton University Press, 1974. Reprinted by permission of Princeton University Press). Chapter 6, "Foreign Policy, the Military and Political Development," was first published in *Foreign Policy and the Developing Nation,* ed. Richard Butwell, pp. 69–111 (Lexington: University of Kentucky Press, 1969. Copyright © 1969 by The University of Kentucky Press. Used with permission of the publishers.) Chapter 7, "Public Order and the Military in Africa," is from *The Military Intervenes,* ed. Henry Bienen, pp. 35–69 (New York: Russell Sage Foundation, 1968. Copyright © Russell Sage Foundation. Reprinted by permission). Chapter 8, "Military and Society in East Africa," was first published in *Comparative Politics* 6, no. 4 (July 1974): 489–517. Chapter 9, "Military Rule and Political Process: Nigerian Examples," was first published in *Comparative Politics,* January 1978. The background notes to Chapters 9–11 partially rely on Henry Bienen, "Transition from Military Rule: The Case of Western State Nigeria," *Armed Forces and Society* 1, no. 3 (Spring 1975): 50–65. Chapters 10–11 include some material that was first published in *Soldiers and Oil: The Political Transformation of Nigeria,* ed. Keith Panter-Brick (London: Cass and Co., 1978). These chapters also include unpublished work. Work in Nigeria was carried out in collaboration with Martin Fitton, then a colleague at the University of Ibadan. I solely am responsible for all the written work. Chapter 12, "Conclusions: Transition from Military Rule," relies on Bienen, "Transition from Military Rule," in *Armed Forces and Society* (cited above) and on new work. I am grateful to all journals and publishers for permission to reprint.

I benefited from comments on the Nigerian materials made by Keith Panter-Brick of the London School of Economics, Ruth Collier of Indiana University, Grady Nunn of the University of Alabama, Robert Tignor of Princeton University, and Colin Leys of Queens University.

Many American and African institutions have helped my work. The University of Chicago first enabled me to go East Africa. The Rockefeller Foundation supported research in Kenya and Nigeria. Princeton University, with its generous leave policy and congenial climate for research, furthered my efforts in many ways. The Center of International Studies in Princeton's Woodrow Wilson School, ably directed by Klaus Knorr and then by Cyril Black, and administered by Jane McDowall, facilitated research. When I was Chairman of the Department of Politics at Princeton, my administrative assistant, June Traube, freed me from many tasks. I spent the most enjoyable of years, 1976–1977, at the Center for Advanced Study in the Behavioral Sciences, where I was partially supported through National Science Foundation funds. I am grateful to the staff of the Center, especially Kay Jenks, and to the Center's Director, Gardner Lindzey.

I am also very grateful to the various African universities and colleges that provided me with intellectual and physical homes between 1963 and 1974. Makerere University, Uganda; Kivukoni College, Tanzania; the University of Nairobi, Kenya; and Ibadan University, Nigeria, were places whose hospitality I enjoyed. I am, as always, grateful to the many Kenyans, Ugandans, Tanzanians, and Nigerians who took the time to talk with me and share their views. I am happy to acknowledge my appreciation to colleagues, friends, and teachers who interested me in comparative political analysis and whose own broad interests in social and political analyses have informed me. I hope my work has done them the credit they deserve as teachers. Among the many people who helped along the way, I want to single out the following teachers to whom I owe a special intellectual and personal debt: Jeremy Azrael, Bert F. Hoselitz, Leonard Binder, Morris Janowitz, Arcadius Kahan, and the late Tom Fallers at the University of Chicago; Leopold Haimson, formerly at the University of Chicago, now at Columbia; David Apter, formerly at the University of Chicago, now at Yale; and, above all, Aristide Zolberg, University of Chicago, and Colin Leys, Queen's University, Ontario. My greatest personal debt is to my wife, Leigh Buchanan Bienen, from whom I always learn when I am willing to listen.

PART I
Parties

Chapter 1
Introduction

Analyses of African politics that were undertaken during the late 1950s and up to the mid-1960s often focused on political parties. Many of the studies of African countries looked at the role of a particular party or different parties in the political system.[1] Some of the most influential collections of essays were those that were concerned primarily with parties.[2] The emphasis on parties was understandable, because the first wave of "new" African states gained independence in the late 1950s and early 1960s under the aegis of a national movement that turned itself into a ruling party. However, the fact that parties *could* be studied also influenced scholars of African politics. I argue in chapters 2 to 4 that because parties were in place and visible when scholars went to Africa to do political studies and because party leaders were available for interviews and party documents could be studied and party ideology could be traced and explicated, there was a tendency to overstate the importance of African parties in their countries' political lives.

There was also, perhaps, the feeling on the part of political scientists that parties were appropriate institutions to rule the newly independent states. The military regimes in Latin America had been thought of as authoritarian and corrupt. African parties promised to have some popularity and some internal democracy. They had grass-roots organizations so that views could come from the bottom to the top and a different style of rule from that of the colonial administration could be effected.

As the 1960s progressed, it was clear that not all ruling parties were popular; some did not have grass-roots organizations. Both new studies of whole political systems and studies of party operation in localities called into question earlier views.[3] And, of course, militaries replaced party rule in both single-party and multiparty systems.

It is not surprising that in the 1970s writing on African politics has come to be dominated by studies of military intervention and studies that correlate variables pertaining to characteristics of armed forces, such as size or level of professionalization, with variables such as income levels, size of country, and urbanization. Less frequently, writings on African militaries deal with performance of regimes in power; here, too, the studies tend to utilize aggregate data from different countries rather than take the form of the in-depth case studies carried out on African party systems. Where empirical work is done that describes the organizational features of individual militaries or that examines the relationships of armed forces and society in a given country, the work tends to rely less on intensive interviewing than did the earlier studies of political parties. And there is less analysis of the ways in which militaries actually function as compared to previous analyses of the operations of parties.[4]

Of course, it is difficult to study armies and to interview officers. Thus it is sometimes necessary to study the military from afar or indirectly when on the ground. One way to do indirect study of the military is to examine civilian roles and attitudes in military regimes. Chapters 9 to 12 do this with Nigerian materials. Preferably, we should also examine how civilian institutions function under military regimes. We should be concerned with how the social and organizational characteristics of armed forces organizations relate to the political and institutional structures of society if we are going to try to explain types and processes of military interventions in politics and military performance during military and civilian regimes.

We should be asking: What kinds of changes have taken place in society prior to formal military rule; how did these changes affect the military's position in society with respect to other institutions or with respect to social and ethnic groups? Questions concerning the scope and direction of social change, economic development, and political participation under military takeover must be raised, too. When we deal with these questions, we study not the military in society but rather military-civilian relations.

One reason why there remains so much to be learned about civilian-military relations under military regimes is that much more attention has been paid in the last decade to military intervention, and to the military as a putative modernizer, than to the way that civilian elements, both individual and institutional, enter or reenter a political process that has been dominated, at least ostensibly, by the military.

Although we should not stay focused on military interventions, it is of some use to go back to military interventions in order to try to understand possibilities for civilian-military relations in specific contexts and the ways in which different kinds of transitions from military rule may evolve. When we understand the reasons for specific military interventions and as we explore the links between the military and other political institutions and groups, we can better assess the future evolution of armed forces in society and can better judge the militaries' capacities to deal with specific problems. The factors that explain military intervention also help reveal the limits of the militaries' political capacities and the constraints on transition from military rule. Even if we have no general theory to explain military intervention, a dissection of the specific components of an intervention may reveal the potentialities for the kind of rule that the intervening military will exert. At this point, we cannot say that large-scale armed forces intervene more than small-scale ones or that presence or absence of "mass" parties before military intervention is a distinguishing variable. Algeria, Mali, and Ghana had supposedly strong parties. *Ex post facto* they always appear weak after we see the military intervene. Similarly, it is often argued that civilian elites who gave way to the militaries suffered from loss of legitimacy. But if legitimacy or strength of party are to be distinguishing criteria, they must be measured independently of the fact of military intervention. Nor can we say that armies with weak professional ethos intervene. There have to be independent measures for professionalization in armed forces apart from their reluctance to intervene.

We can agree with Zolberg that it is difficult to sort out the relationship between military motives for making a coup and military intentions about rule.[5] Indeed, both may change during the coup process. Nonetheless, it is relevant whether or not the military has a specific program for rule or whether it reacts out of fear for its own prerogatives or whether it simply makes demands for more resources. Chapter 6, "Foreign Policy, the Military, and Political Development: Military Assistance and Political Change in Africa," looks at the impact of external resource flowing to African militaries at an early stage of their development. Whereas Chapter 7, "Public Order and the Military in Africa: Mutinies in Kenya, Uganda, and Tanganyika," looks at initial interventions.

We can think about military intervention in terms of three rough phases that are defined perhaps more by the different political contexts in which the military operates than by factors peculiar to the military's own organization. Indeed, although military factionalism is one internal factor that is a critical element in the different phases, it must itself be seen as an outcome of the interactions between the military and civilian politicians and bureaucrats and more broadly as an outcome of the military's interactions with social and ethnic groups.

There is an initial stage during which the military may for the first time make overtly threatening demands on the government of a new nation; it may settle conflicts between civilian contenders or it may itself take over the government. Tropical Africa now presents us with many examples of this phase. The next phase can be considered one in which there is a struggle for stability after the seizure of power. The criteria for inclusion in this category are (1) a regime dominated by the armed forces, (2) a military leadership that has a great deal of continuity with the original leaders of the coup, (3) a situation that has not been characterized by a number of coups and countercoups. Thus, we are still dealing here with a first generation of military leaders although some change in the top leadership may take place.

The third of our rough phases is institutionalized intervention. Latin America, and increasingly Africa, presents us with examples. Here the military cannot bring about political stability and it cannot give up aspirations to rule. Military coup may become the accepted way of getting political change for groups within the armed forces, for certain civilian leaders, and for citizens who remain bystanders to coups. Dahomey, now Benin, Congo-Brazzaville, Sierra Leone, and Nigeria have all had at least three successful coups since their independence. Not all these coups had similar natures or effects. Some can be explained largely in terms of internal army politics. Others had sweeping consequences for centralization of power and interethnic relations, especially the 1966 Nigerian coups. The point is that the coup has become the vehicle for bringing abut both narrow and broad changes.

In each of the three interventionist phases, militaries have different immediate political problems. In the first, they must pick up the political pieces left by civilian regimes or by their own coup and must find allies among, and support from, political groups. In the second, they must build support, reach down into society, and maintain military cohesion. In the third phase, the militaries are split, by definition, and yet they must maintain some autonomy from civilian groups and keep military disputes within bounds if they are to survive as corporate groups.

Of course, these phases are analytical ones. In the real world, situations may be blurred. After one intervention, an armed force may move quickly into a relationship with its society that could be characterized as institutionalized intervention. This process of institutionalized intervention is especially interesting for thinking about problems of transition from military rule. Institutionalized intervention is a situation either where coup faction succeeds coup faction or where periods of military rule and civilian rule alternate. During the military periods, there are strong pressures for return to civilian rule, whereas during the civilian periods, everyone keeps looking over his shoulder to see whether the men in green or khaki are heading for the radio station, post and telegraph, and presidential or prime ministerial residences.

In these cases of institutionalized intervention, which can be seen in Argentina, Peru, Pakistan, perhaps Nigeria now, the following features appear. Social forces in a country can be characterized as what Huntington calls "massive." That is, levels of political participation are high and political strife between class groups or regional ones is very intense in periods of military and civilian rule. Indeed, military intervention can be understood as an attempt to choke off political participation. In Africa, class conflict is rarely so well defined, but ethnicity provides a substitute massive social force. And military intervention has sometimes taken place in the name of confining ethnic tension, although military intervention and rule has exacerbated it in Nigeria in 1966 and Uganda in the 1970s.

After intervention, the military is typically split over the question of continued military rule. Some military elements feel that the goals of the coup have been attained when a specific regime is brought down, for example, the Goulart regime in Brazil, the Nkrumah regime in Ghana, the second Margai regime in Sierra Leone. Others feel that the military must undertake a sweeping reconstruction of social, economic, and political life. Still other military men believe that it is too dangerous to abdicate to civilians, either because dominant civilian forces they oppose will once again come to the fore, or because they fear that their own privileges will not be maintained under a civilian regime. But military benefits is an issue susceptible to being bargained out between the military and civilians. More critical perhaps is the fear on the part of military figures that old scores will be settled if certain civilians get back in. Where the military has engaged in violence against civilian opponents, the fear of this settling of accounts is intensified. Where the military has engaged in a great deal of internal violence, those elements that have emerged on top will be extremely reluctant to give up the direct levers of physical control.

So far I have been using the term "the military." And throughout this book, the term reappears as a kind of shorthand phrase. However, one aim of this study is to show that the taxonomic dichotomy between military and civilian regimes will not stand. We know that there are political systems in which civilian supremacy is clear, where the military operates under civilians whose own power does not depend on the armed forces but where the armed forces have a great deal to say about both domestic and foreign policy formulation and even implementation and where the military takes up important shares of the society's resources. Both the United States and the USSR are examples. We know that there are societies in which the regime is a military regime in name but in which all government is highly limited in its scope and where central government does not much affect political life except in a capital city and a few towns. We know that there are civilian regimes that seem increasingly to depend on the military or a part of it for their continuation in power, perhaps China during the Cultural Revolution. The alliance may be between traditional elite and army or between party and army. The lines between the latter two may be very blurred, as for example when the army and party were forged out of the same experience in China during the 1920s and 1930s. There may be a narrow civilian leadership operating on top of a basically military regime. Or there may be a military regime of sorts operating on top of a civil service regime. This would describe many African countries. And within the latter type, there are many gradations and a good deal of flux in the determination of power between military, police, civil sevice, and civilian politicians.

Some militaries both "in" and "out" of power have tried to carry out nonmilitary functions in a wide range of social and economic fields. Civic action programs have existed in Indonesia and the Philippines, for example. In Latin America, civic action programs often have been seen explicitly as counterinsurgency programs. In Africa, both ruling and nonruling militaries often have been highly resistant to civic action programs.

All this has been by way of saying what is obvious. Military-civilian relations range across a wide spectrum with regard to relative power positions. There is variability with regard to military functions in both military and civilian regimes conventionally denoted. The reasons for military intervention are various, and the military's performance in power is affected by the type of initial interventions, by the power of social groups to aid or impede the military, and by the military's own internal characteristics.

Some of these hybrid political-military systems are very vulnerable to interest-group pressures. The level of political participation and the kinds of civilian organizations that continue to exist are important factors in making a judgment about the nature of military-civilian relations. Nigeria and Ghana are military governments with strong civil service components that both "make" and implement policy. In some military regimes, civilian organizations can exert pressures, and political groupings are near the surface. Argentina has been an example of a country in which military rule has been lengthy and at times pervasive but in which political participation has been high even under military rule, and political parties, trade union organizations, and mass movements have continued to be important throughout periods of military rule. We shall see that in Nigeria, civilian politicians remained active under a military regime.

In some military systems, the rule of law as expressed by a free, or relatively free, judiciary and due process continue to be factors for those who contend for present or future power. There are military regimes in which people can speak their minds. And there is no lack of regimes in which systematic torture and arrest occur without redress. There are, of course, regimes that are arbitrary but that are not systematic about repression through their own lack of organization and cohesion—for example, Uganda. There are military regimes in which at various times military personnel have tried to fill many roles in society, as, for example, when Ghanaian officers were appointed to run public corporations and boards and were even appointed to run enterprises.

Whether or not it matters if a regime is headed by a military man or men is a matter of investigation. We have to ask "matters for what?" We are concerned with how decisions are made and implemented, with the ability to get compliance for decisions, with amounts of centralization of authority, with the emphasis certain decision makers give to growth or redistribution policies. But we cannot take for granted that once we know whether a regime is a military one or not we have a good grasp of the answers to these questions. We can, of course, hypothesize that military regimes have certain characteristics that lead to certain regime outcomes, although cross-national studies have not established particular hypotheses for most of the concerns listed above.

Indeed, as empirical work is done on armed forces organizations, we begin to demystify the term "the military." We must subject the military to the same concern for finding internal factions, ethnic splits, generational gaps, functionally based division, and hierarchically based conflicts that has characterized the study of parties and civil services.[6] As work proceeds on African militaries, information is accumulating on individual armed forces. At the same time, typologies are proliferating once again in the study of African political systems. Whereas the first typologies in the study of independent African states were framed around the nature of party systems, typologies of civil-military relations are now the basis for defining regime types. Note that the new typlogies are usually not based on the organizational features of militaries per se; nor are they based, as in Huntington's work, on the kinds of societies in which militaries operate,[7] but they are based on civil-military relationships. Thus Luckham's case study of the Nigerian military stresses the interaction of political and organizational variables and creates a typology based on the kinds of boundaries that exist between military and civilian institutions.[8]

Praetorian states are said to have fragmented boundaries. There are splits and factions in the armed forces, and civil-military coalitions abound.[9] Similarly, Cox, in his case study of civil-military relations in Sierra Leone, shows the interaction of civilian and military politics. He outlines the ways in which relationships change over time. First, civilians in Sierra Leone try to politicize the military. The latter is already full of factions and personal cliques. The conflicts in military and civilian society work in on each other. New conflicts open up in the military and go beyond those of rank and personality or different educational and career backgrounds. And military conflict exacerbates civilian cleavages.[10]

Although both the new case studies and the new overviews stress civil-military relationships as the focus for analysis, increasing attention is being paid to personal or idiosyncratic factors inside armed forces organizations. Commentators are arguing that although we must retain concern for the militaries' organizational and social characteristics, we will not understand military politics if we do not look at personal factors. The argument is made that military politics cannot be deduced from organizational features any more than military politics can be deduced from broad social characteristics within a society.[11] It will not perhaps surprise firsthand observers that both military intervention and military rule in Uganda or the Central African Republic have something to do with the personality and motives of Idi Amin and Jean-Bedel Bokassa.

The new typologies, which sometimes describe themselves as being concerned with military styles or modalities of rule, try to take into account the personal factor or more generally try to account for the motivation of segments of officer corps. To give an example. Claude Welch has a typology of radical and conservative military regimes. He believes that variations in the large-scale characteristics of society, for example, the size of middle classes, wealth, and urbanization, matter. So do variations in strength of military and civilian institutions and in the levels of participation in society as a whole and within institutions. These variations create different constraints on the military. But the individual predilections of military leaders play a central role in determining the style of the regime.[12] Decalo goes further and argues that national differences between the systematic outcomes of regimes tend to fade into insignificance, at least statistically; what can be differentiated are styles of rule.[13]

Welch believes that conservative military regimes are more likely to emerge in African states with medium rather than low levels of political participation. Where there is an urban middle class that can articulate its concern, for example, Ghana or Nigeria (or presumably Kenya if it has a coup), the military is more likely to look for and need civilian allies, and these allies constrain military actions. But when one is dealing with as many factors as the new typologists throw up, prediction of military outcomes is difficult. For if, as Welch says, radical military regimes are more marked by junior officers coming to power who are relatively well educated by the standards of the particular officer corps in question and also if such regimes are more likely to appear in African states with low levels of political participation, what happens when such officers appear in societies with larger middle classes and more economic development?

Typologizing is easier for those who stress the styles of military leaders as the distinguishing variable. These styles are what matters, because the ecological constraints do not allow the different rhetorics to be translated into coherent social and economic programs. For such analysts, military regimes may be more or less brutal, arbitrary, or foolish, but the social, political, and economic levers do not exist for systematic social transformation in any case.[14]

Many of the new directions in work on African militaries are useful. The concern for doing empirical work in order to test generalizations; the suspicion of typologogies based on organizational theory that postulated that all militaries have certain characteristics that differentiate them from other organizations; the emphasis on personal factors given the frequent small-scale, incoherent, fragmented nature of African militaries; and above all the insistence on looking at civil-military relations make sense to me. Yet I find I depart from the new consensus in ways that are not trivial. I also find that there are some particular aspects of military rule that have been touched on recently but perhaps not given enough attention.

Table 1

Countries That Had Experienced Military Takeovers by June 1977

Country	Date of Independence	Date of Successful Coup(s)
Benin (formerly Dahomey)	1960	Oct. 1963; Nov. 1965; Dec. 1965; Dec. 1967; Dec. 1969; Oct. 1972.
Burundi	1964	Nov. 1966; Nov. 1976
Central African Republic	1960	Jan. 1966.
Chad	1960	April 1975.
Congo (Brazzaville)	1960	Aug. 1963; Aug. 1968.
Ethiopia	Not under colonial rule	Sept. 1974.
Ghana	1957	Feb. 1966; Jan. 1972.
Malagasy Republic	1960	May 1972.
Mali	1960	Nov. 1968.
Niger	1960	April 1974.
Nigeria	1960	Jan. 1966; July 1966; July 1975.
Rwanda	1962	July 1973.
Sierra Leone	1961	March 21, 1967; March 23, 1967; April 1968; Oct. 1969.
Somali Republic	1960	Oct. 1969.
Sudan	1956	1958; 1969; July 19, 1971; July 22, 1971
Togo	1960	Jan. 1963; Jan. 1967
Uganda	1962	Jan. 1971
Upper Volta	1960	Jan. 1966; Feb. 1974
Zaire	1960	Sept. 1960; Nov. 1965.

When we look at African military regimes, we see a wide variety of systems. As of mid-1977, almost half the black African states had experienced periods of military government (see Table 1). During these military regimes, there have been unsuccessful coups that we know about in Ghana, Benin, Chad, Nigeria, Sudan, Burundi, Uganda, Malagasy Republic, Ethiopia, Togo, Congo (Brazzaville). There were also unsuccessful coups during periods of civilian rule in some of these countries, just as there have been unsuccessful coups or mutinies in a number of the regimes that have not experienced military rule (see Table 2). Furthermore, within civilian systems there has been a great deal of variability in the importance of armed forces, from the low end of the scale in Gambia, to civilian regimes where armed forces evolved as part of the ruling civilian structure (Mozambique), or where they have been extremely heavy actors in determining the outcome of civilian political struggles (Kenya).

Table 2

Countries Remaining under Civilian Rule since Independence

Country	Date of Independence	Date of Unsuccessful Army Coups or Army Mutinies That Have Become Public*
Angola	1975	1977
Botswana	1966	
Cameroun	1960	
Equatorial Guinea	1968	
Gabon	1960	1963
Gambia	1965	
Guinea	1958	
Guinea-Bissau	1974	
Ivory Coast	1960	
Kenya	1963	1964
Lesotho	1966	
Liberia	1847	
Malawi	1964	
Mauritania	1960	
Mozambique	1975	1976
Senegal	1960	
Swaziland	1968	
Tanzania	1961	1964
Zambia	1964	

*There have been palace coup attempts with little or no military involvement in Lesotho, Senegal, and Guinea.

There has also been a great deal of variability between countries, whether ruled by militaries or civilians, with regard to the size of armies as a share of total available manpower (see Table 3) or with regard to the rates at which armies have expanded in size or shares of GNP that they consume (see Table 4).

Table 3

Comparisons of Military Manpower

Country	Total Regular Armed Forces			Para-military and Police Forces		1970 Estimated Military-Age Population (18-45)	1970 Regular Armed Forces as Percent of Military-Age Population
	1967	1970	1974	1970	1974		
Benin	1,400	2,250	1,530	2,000	1,000	427,000	0.5
Boswana				1,000		108,800	0.09
Burundi	950	1,600		900		585,000	0.3
Cameroun	3,000	4,350	5,500	6,800	10,000	969,000	1.15
Central African Republic	500	1,100		2,000		300,000	0.4
Chad	700	2,650	4,100	4,650	6,000	560,000	0.5
Congo (Brazzaville)	1,300	2,200	5,100	2,350	3,900	130,000	1.7
Equatorial Guinea				1,000	20,400	49,300	0.2
Ethiopia	35,000	45,400	44,570	28,000	37,600	4,165,000	1.76
Gabon	300	1,050		1,750		70,000	1.5
Gambia				150		61,200	0.024
Ghana	9,000	15,900	17,700	21,500	3,000	1,709,000	0.9
Guinea	3,000	5,400	5,500	8,500	8,000	628,000	0.9
Ivory Coast	3,600	4,500	3,450	2,550	3,000	722,500	0.97
Kenya	4,775	5,400	7,430	11,500	1,800	1,795,000	0.3
Lesotho				1,325		117,300	1.12
Liberia	3,580	4,150	5,170	6,750	1,300	226,000	1.8
Malagasy Republic	2,800	4,500	5,170	6,500	1,300	1,050,000	0.4
Malawi	850	1,150	1,600	3,000		748,000	0.55
Mali	3,500	3,650	3,650	2,500	2,700	855,000	0.4
Mauritania	1,100	1,530	1,000	1,300	1,110	204,000	1.38
Niger	1,500	2,100	2,100	1,900	1,400	660,000	0.3
Nigeria	11,500	63,500	250,000	25,000		13,375,000	1.2
Rwanda	1,500	2,750	4,000	1,200	400	610,300	0.64
Senegal	4,700	5,850	5,300	4,850	1,600	690,000	0.8
Sierra Leone	1,360	1,600	1,600	1,400		500,000	0.3
Somali Republic	9,500	12,000	23,090	9,500	3,500	505,750	4.25
Sudan	18,500	27,450		11,000		2,639,250	1.45
Swaziland				700		70,550	0.01
Tanzania	3,000	7,900	14,600	12,500		2,210,000	0.92
Togo	1,100	1,250	100	1,100		280,000	0.5
Uganda	5,960	6,700	21,000	7,000		1,905,000	0.4
Upper Volta	1,700	1,800	2,050	2,650	2,100	950,000	0.2
Zaire	32,000	38,250	50,000	20,000	12,000	4,000,000	1.0
Zambia	3,000	4,400	5,800	6,250	1,200	731,000	1.45

Source: Figures for 1967 are from Charles Stevenson," "African Armed Forces," *Military Review* (March 1967): 18–24; 1970 figures are from Richard Booth, *The Armed Forces of African States* (London: Adelphia Paper No. 67, 1970); 1974 figures are from *The Military Balance—1974–75* (London: International Institute for Strategic Studies, 1975).

Table 4

The African Military Balance as of July 1976
(*Denotes Military Regime as of 1977*)

Country	Total Regular Armed Forces
Angola	30,000
Benin*	1,530[a]
Burundi*	1,650
Cameroon	5,600
Chad*	4,700
Congo*	7,000
Ethiopia*	50,800
Gambia	
Ghana*	17,600
Guinea	5,750
Ivory Coast	4,100
Kenya	7,600
Lesotho	
Liberia	5,220
Malagasy Republic*	4,760
Malawi	2,300
Mali*	4,200
Mauritania	4,750
Mozambique	unknown
Nigeria*	221,000
Niger*	2,100
Rhodesia	9,200 + 2-6000 Territorial Army
Rwanda*	3,750
Senegal	5,950
Sierra Leone	2,145
Somali Republic*	23,050[a]
South Africa	51,500
Sudan*	43,500[a]
Swaziland	
Tanzania	14,600
Togo*	2,250
Uganda*	21,000
Upper Volta*	3,050
Zaire*	43,400
Zambia	7,800

Source: International Institute for Strategic Studies, *The Military Balance,* 1976–77, London.

[a]Figures are for 1975

Table 5

Defense Expenditures

Country	Defense Expenditures as a percent of GNP	
	1967	1974
Benin	2.5	
Burundi	.7	
Cameroun	2.7	
Central African Republic	2.2	
Chad	2.4	
Congo (Brazzaville)	4.7	6.0
Equatorial Guinea	—	—
Ethiopia	2.9	3.2
Gabon	1.7	
Gambia	—	—
Ghana	2.0	.8
Guinea	4.3	
Ivory Coast	1.3	
Kenya	1.4	1.8
Lesotho	—	—
Liberia	1.4	
Malagasy Republic	1.7	
Malawi	.8	
Mali	3.5	
Mauritania	3.4	
Niger	2.4	
Nigeria	1.6	7.3
Rwanda	2.3	
Senegal	3.1	
Sierra Leone	.8	
Somali Republic	5.0	5.1
Sudan	4.4	6.2
Swaziland	—	—
Tanzania	1.0	2.4
Togo	—	—
Uganda	2.9	2.7
Upper Volta	—	—
Zaire	5.9	3.5
Zambia	2.4	3.9

Source: Figures for 1967 are from Donald Morrison et al., *Black Africa: A Comparative Handbook* (New York: The Free Press, 1972), as found in Samuel DeCalo, *Coups and Army Rule in Africa* (New Haven, Conn.: Yale University Press, 1976) pp. 10–11. While the figures from Morrison and Charles Stevenson, "African Armed Forces," *Military Review* 47 (March 1967): 18–24, do not differ much in size of armed forces, they differ very much on defense spending as a share of GNP. I have used Morrison for all countries in 1967, except for Sudan, the figures for which are from Stevenson. For 1974, figures are from the *Military Balance—1974–75* (London: International Institute for Strategic Studies, 1975).

Yet, despite the range of variation between militaries and despite our inability to explain large amounts of variance between governmental performance and social indicators by dichotomizing civilian and military regimes or even by measuring strength of armed forces within a society,[15] I want to argue, too, that we should hold on to the idea that a military regime is not "just another" African regime, although it is clear that there are important differentiations between military regimes. There may be military characteristics, responses, orientations, and patterns of decision making that do not show up in cross-national analyses. That is, we may be able to capture some elements of military rule in Africa that are consequential, but we may not be able to see these elements in every case of African military rule, and we may not be able to see them via aggregate data such as growth rates, GNP, rate of urbanization, and literacy.

Contemporary militaries, no matter how small, faction ridden, or heterogeneous, are, as Stepan asserts, situational more than class elites. "That is, the military's corporate and individual power, status, and material well-being depend upon its relationship to a strong and relatively stable state structure."[16] No matter how imperfectly armed forces are insulated from other groups in society, no matter how much they in fact get infused with society's divisions, by their own self-definition, armed forces purport to be corporate bodies. That is, they have a concern for their own distinctiveness whether or not that distinctiveness exists in fact.

Military personnel worry about the issue of corporate identity. The prerequisites and power of militaries depend on their asserting, and making good on, claims to control over the means of violence in society. The justification for such claims has to do with the military as the corporate embodiment of the means of coercion of the state. For both ideological and practical reasons, militaries look askance at well-armed gendarmeries, private armies, and bodyguards and at attempts by civilians or officers to divide and rule them.

The state has not been taken all that seriously by analysts of Africa because its instruments are weak, because independent states have existed for only a short time, because no nation is said to exist underneath the state to give it content and meaning, and because social classes are not often clearly formed. But it is precisely because of the as yet unformed nature of social classes in Africa that the state is an independent factor.

African officers have rarely told us much in writing about their views of the state. They have not emerged as theorists of the state, even when they have taken radical stances, although language about the state has appeared in Marxist-Leninist form in Ethiopia and Congo (Brazzaville). Militaries in power have been hampered by lack of sophisticated knowledge about the relationships of social groups to the state and of civil servants to the military. Nor have African militaries always been cognizant of the real constraints on state power.

African officers who have adopted radical stances have not typically worried very much about the tactics and strategies of radical movements.

They have worried about the tactics and strategies of coup processes. But because African officers do not have to mobilize and organize constituencies to seize power, they have not thought much about mobilization and organization of constituencies after the seizure of power. They usually seek to demobilize segments of the population and to remain cut off from constituency groups.

Once the military is in power, of course, revolutionary change, indeed, any kind of rule, must be related to constituency and organizational concerns. It is no accident that those revolutionary movements rooted in military or military/party organizations that did have theorists of the revolutionary process—the Chinese and Vietnamese—were ones that ruled parts of countries before their overall victory. Revolutionary tactics and strategies emerged over a fairly extended period of time out of administration of territory. Regular army officers who carry out coups may in fact do radical and transforming things in Africa but perhaps more by inadvertance than by conscious design. Or they may pull down a structure in place—the cutting of the knot—which is a highly transforming act. This happened in Nigeria when the military decreed the end of the four regions and the creation of a new multistate structure. It happened in Ethiopia as the army removed the emperor and dismantled some state and quasi-state structures. It happened in Uganda when Amin expelled the Asians.

It is easier, however, to expell and pull down than it is to constuct new ties and continue to transform in some structured fashion. Indeed, most African armies are content to use the state against society in order to stay in power, or one army faction may use the state against another faction of the army. They are content to use the state to expropriate resources from society. They are engaged in primitive capital accumulation (and sometimes not much more.) African armies also try to use the state to maintain the army's corporate identity; the state may do so either by excising part of the armed forces or by delivering up the pie to keep the army happy. Indeed, one of the things that often allows African armies to be content with their own corporate prerequisites and to permit civil servants to operate within broad guidelines set by the military is that there is no attack on the legitimacy of the state structure as there is in Latin America. In short, there is no radical challenge to military rule.

True, demonstrations in the street may occasionally bring down a military, as in Sudan in 1964, or trade unionist and/or civil servants may withhold support, but the real pressure on the army for a return to civilian rule is from internal fragmentation of the military. Armies in Africa have not faced radical challenges, and so they have not expanded their roles. Civil servants, those other successful claimants to state power in Africa, have not challenged armies. And it is clear, as in Nigeria in 1975, that active collaboration of civil servants with military personnel has made them vulnerable to purges.

I am suggesting that African militaries have usually had a limited view of the way in which they will use state power. Their main concern has been to maintain, if possible, corporate solidarity and prerequisites. This has not always been possible. Seizing state power proves dangerous even as it gives advantages. Pressures work in on the military. Some officers feel unhappy about their roles, what their communities may be getting, about the army's very control of the state. The more the military is forced to make political decisions, the more difficult it is to maintain corporate solidarity. Yet this solidarity is necessary to the military whether it is in or out of power. Whenever the military engages in social transformation without prior internal agreement on programs, chain of command fractures; corporate solidarity goes out the window, as was the case in Ethiopia. The only way to maintain military cohesion in this situation is by means of frequent purges of opposition within the army. The way to deal with generational differences, different views of the role of the army, personality differences, and different ethnic origins is to create cumbersome representative committees for decision making.[17] But the principles of chain of command and decision by committee do not work well together; instability is built in.

When officers are given functional responsibilities for ministries or territorial responsibilities as governors of states, the problem of chain of command is complicated again. Nigerian military and police officers served from 1967 on as appointed heads of the Nigerian states. They were ex officio members of the Supreme Military Council, the governing body. Not all heads of the individual states were of general rank. Thus, anomalies in chain of command and executive responsibility came about. Governors of the states no longer serve ex officio on the Supreme Military Council.

Of course, the greatest problem for chain of command comes when junior officers or noncommissioned officers carry out coups, particularly coups against senior officers. In such cases, we usually see either a reassertion of rank even when senior officers were not involved in the original coup—for example, Ironsi in Nigeria, Ankrah in Ghana, Gowon in Nigeria—or rapid promotion—junior officers become senior in rank, as happened in the case of Qaddafi in Libya and Traore in Mali. If the reassertion of rank is not clearly established, as has been the case in Ethiopia since General Andom failed to be able to assume real power and then was killed, and if rule by committee or inner committee persists, instability and fragmentation also continue.

Unfortunately, we know rather little about the nature of decision making inside the collective bodies that the military establishes. Bebler tells us that, for a time at least, the Sierra Leone military functioned in British cabinet fashion with collective responsibility. Civil servants were present when their responsibilities were discussed, but they also left the room during the discussion of certain other matters.[18] It would be fascinating to have information on the deliberations of the old Provisional Military Administration Council in Ethiopia. Perhaps they would remind us of discussions among the military Soviets in 1917. But the Soviets were overarched and controlled by the Communist (Bolshevik) Party in the Soviet Union. In Ethiopia, an army talks about creating a party. A party is not discplining an army. In Chapter 9, in a study of cabinet government in a Nigerian state under military rule, an attempt is made to illustrate aspects of decision making during a military regime.

As we explore civilian-military relations, and as we look at transitions from military rule, which we explicitly do in Chapter 12, we come back again to parties in African political life. We have to analyze political networks when we look at civilian-military relations, and we must understand these networks in terms of their evolution from civilian to military regimes. Part I of this book sets the stage both chronologically and analytically for Part II. For party rule precedes military rule in Africa; party rule provides the context for the evolution of armed forces, the context in which takeovers took place. And, facts of African political life that condition and constrain party rule remain relevant during the period of military rule. After a military takeover, the low-income and largely agrarian-based economies do not disappear. Ethnically split societies are not consolidated with a wave of the gun. Problems of establishing authority, of gathering power, still obtain. For to wield power unchecked by opposition and unrestrained by formal and informal rules is not the same thing as centralizing power and radiating authority outward and downward into society. A military in power still has to contend with central and local factionalism and with civilian elites and civilian demands.

Thus, it is imperative to examine party politics in Africa in order to understand military politics. It is also necessary to examine party politics because military rule may prove to be short-lived in certain countries. Periods of military and civilian rule will alternate. And, even under military rule, politics continues. Party elites may not vanish, and party organizations at the local level may continue to exist in surrogate forms.

Chapter 2–5 examine party organizations generally but also with special reference to Kenya and Tanzania. These chapters are presented in the sequence in which they were written. The arguments follow from each other: the nature of one-party rule, party machines, party factionalism, and generation of support for regimes through limited competitive party politics.

Chapters 6–12 argue that military rule in Africa is a limited rule and that armed forces have a hard time performing many functions parties performed and continue to perform in some countries.

Chapters 9–11 suggest that "military rule" is a term that needs redefining. In the Nigerian context, these chapters ask: What political networks exist outside the military and in what ways do they relate to the military's own factional alliances? How do civil servants fit into these civilian and military networks? However, the questions are dealt with partially. They can be answered only on the basis of empirical research still to be undertaken. That they are pertinent questions should be clear from what we have been able to discern by this enquiry into civilian-military relations.

Notes

1. For example: Aristide Zolberg, *One Party Government in the Ivory Coast* (Princeton, N.J.: Princeton University Press, 1964); Zolberg, *Creating Political Order* (Chicago: Rand McNally, 1966); Henry Bienen, *Tanzania: Party Transformation and Economic Development*

(Princeton, N.J.: Princeton University Press, 1967, 1970); Herbert Weiss, *Political Protest in the Congo* (Princeton, N.J.: Princeton University Press, 1967); John R. Cartwright, *Politics in Sierra Leone 1957–1967* (Toronto: University of Toronto Press, 1970); Ruth Schachter Morganthau, *Political Parties in French-Speaking Africa* (Oxford: Clarendon Press, 1964); Richard Sklar, *Nigerian Political Parties* (Princeton, N.J.: Princeton University Press, 1964). There were books that spent a good deal of effort explaining the workings of parties but also examined other institutions—for example, Crawford Young, *Politics in the Congo* (Princeton, N.J.: Princeton University Press, 1965). There were also books that dealt with parties but whose primary focus was on elites and role changes—for example, David Apter, *Ghana in Transition* (New York: Atheneum, 1963); and Martin Kilson, *Political Change in a West African State* (Cambridge, Mass.: Harvard University Press, 1966).

2. James S. Coleman and Carl Rosberg, Jr., eds., *Political Parties and National Integration in Tropical Africa* (Berkeley and Los Angeles: University of California Press, 1964); Stanley Diamond and Fred Burke, eds., *The Transformation of East Africa* (New York: Basic Books, 1964); Gwendolen Carter, ed., *African One-Party States* (Ithaca, N.Y.: Cornell University Press, 1962).

3. Studies of the operation of parties in a particular region or locality include: Nicholas Hopkins, *Popular Government in an African Town* (Chicago: University of Chicago Press, 1972); Joel Samoff, *Tanzania: Local Politics and the Structure of Power* (Madison: University of Wisconsin Press, 1974); Colin Leys, *Politicians and Policies* (Nairobi: East African Publishing House, 1967); Maxwell Owusu, *Uses and Abuses of Political Power: A Case Study of Continuity and Change in the Politics of Ghana* (Chicago: University of Chicago Press, 1970); Goran Hyden, *TANU Yajenga Nchi: Political Development in Rural Tanzania* (Lund: Uniskol, 1968).

4. Perhaps the most comprehensive case studies of African armies are Robin Luckham, *The Nigerian Military* (Cambridge: Cambridge University Press, 1971); Thomas S. Cox, *Civil-Military Relations in Sierra Leone* (Cambridge, Mass.: Harvard University Press, 1976); Eboe Hutchful, "Military Rule and the Politics of Demilitarization in Ghana, 1966–1969" (Ph.d. diss., Department of Political Economy, University of Toronto, 1973); Samuel DeCalo, *Coups and Army Rule in Africa* (New Haven, Conn.: Yale University Press, 1976). Other case studies include: N. J. Miners, *The Nigerian Army 1956–1966* (London: Methuen, 1971); Robert Pinckney, *Ghana under Military Rule* (London: Methuen, 1972). There are also studies that compare African militaries: Anton Bebler, *Military Rule in Africa* (New York: Praeger, 1973); Ernest Lefever, *Spear and Sceptre* (Washington: The Brookings Institution, 1970). And there are studies that discuss militaries in Africa with reference to data from different armed forces: Ruth First, *Power in Africa* (New York: Pantheon, 1970); Michael Lee, *African Armies and Civil Order* (London: Chatto and Windus, 1969); Daniel LaTouche, "Process and Level of Military Intervention in the States of Tropical Africa" (Ph.D. diss., University of British Columbia, 1973); and Claude Welch, ed., *Soldier and State in Africa* (Evanston, Ill.: Northwestern University Press, 1970).

5. See Aristide Zolberg, "The Military Decade," *World Politics* 25, no. 2 (January 1973): 309–331.

6. This discussion takes from Henry Bienen and David Morell, "Transition from Military Rule: Thailand's Experience," in *Political Military Systems*, ed. Catherine Kelleher (Beverly Hills, Calif.: Sage Publications, 1974), pp. 3–6.

7. Samuel P. Huntington, *Political Order in Changing Societies* (New Haven, Conn.: Yale University Press, 1968).

8. Luckham, *The Nigerian Military*.

9. Robin Luckham, "A Comparative Typology of Civil-Military Relations," *Government and Opposition* 6, no. 1 (Winter 1971); 5–35.

10. Cox, *Civil Military Relations in Sierra Leone*.

11. Decalo, *Coups and Army Rule in Africa*, forcefully argues these points.

12. Claude E. Welch, Jr., "Radical and Conservative Military Regimes: A Typology and Analysis of Post-Coup Governments in Tropical Africa" (Paper delivered at the 1973 Annual Meeting of the American Political Science Association, New Orleans, September 1973).

13. Decalo, *Coups and Army Rule in Africa,* p. 241.

14. Ibid.

15. For examinations of military performance in terms of aggregate data indicators see, among others: R. D. McKinlay and A. S. Cohan, "A Comparative Analysis of the Political and Economic Performance of Military and Civilian Regimes: A Cross-National Aggregate Data Study," *Comparative Politics* 8, no. 1 (October 1975): 1–30; R. D. McKinlay and A. S. Cohan, "The Economic Performance of Military Regimes: A Cross-National Aggregate Data Study," *British Journal of Political Science* 6, pt. 3 (July 1976): 291–310; R. D. McKinlay and A. S. Cohan, "Performance and Instability in Military and Non-Military Systems," *American Political Science Review* 70 (September 1976): 850–864; Robert W. Jackman, "Politicians in Uniform: Military Governments and Social Change in the Third World," *American Political Science Review* 70 (December 1976): 1078–1097. Jackman reanalyzed the data used by Eric A. Nordlinger, "Soldier in Mufti: The Impact of Military Rule Upon Economic and Social Change in the Non-Western States," *American Political Science Review* 64 (December 1970): 1131–1148. Nordlinger, in turn, used data from Irma Adelman and Cynthia T. Morris, *Society, Politics and Economic Development: A Quantitative Approach* (Baltimore: The Johns Hopkins Press, 1967). For other analyses of policy output see Phillipe C. Schmitter, "Military Intervention, Political Competitiveness and Public Policy in Latin America: 1950–1967," in *On Military Intervention,* ed. Morris Janowitz and Jacques Van Doorn (Rotterdam: Rotterdam University Press 1971), pp. 425–506. See also Phillipe C. Schmitter, ed., *Military Rule in Latin America: Function, Consequences and Perspectives* (Beverly Hills, Calif.: Sage Publications 1973). Also on Latin America, see Arthur K. Smith, "Public Policy Impacts of Military Rule in Latin America: A Comparative Analysis of Military and Civilian Regimes" (Paper presented to the Annual Meeting of the American Political Science Association, Chicago, 1974), and R. Neal Tannahill, "The Performance of Military and Civilian Governments in South America, 1948–1967," *Journal of Political and Military Sociology* 4 (Fall 1976): 233–244.

16. Alfred Stepan, "Inclusionary and Exclusionary Military Responses to Radicalism: With Special Attention to Peru" (Paper prepared for Workshop on Radicalism and the Revolutionary Process, Research Institute on International Change, Columbia University, May 1975).

17. For Ethiopian examples, see W. A. E. Skurnik, "Revolution and Change in Ethiopia," *Current History,* May 1975, pp. 206–210.

18. Bebler, *Military Rule in Africa.*

Chapter 2

The Ruling Party in the African
One-Party State: TANU in Tanzania[1]

Discussion of one-party states in Africa has tended to swing from one extreme of interpretation to the other, as is common when analyses are undertaken of phenomena about which knowledge is difficult to come by and hard to organize. Studies of particular countries in depth, including politics outside the capital cities, have been rather rare. There have been some useful collections of essays which have presented material from various African countries, and there have been a number of wide-ranging and provocative articles. But we are only beginning to accumulate the necessary monographs which will allow us to formulate general propositions about African one-party systems in particular and African politics in general.

Perhaps the cart was put before the horse. In order to handle a large number of systems and to make African data meaningful for the comparative study of developing areas, typologies were devised for African politics which were neither descriptive of real systems nor of much heuristic value. At first a dichotomy was proposed between single- and multiparty systems. Observers were struck by the fact that competitive party situations seemed to survive after independence only in a few places where federal or quasi-federal arrangements provided regional strongholds of governmental power for opposition parties.

Then distinctions were made among the one-party systems themselves, as it was clear that the number of parties was far too simple a criterion upon which to decide whether or not a system was democratic or anything else about it.

One of the first differentiations among one-party states was made by Ruth Schachter Morgenthau when she proposed "mass" and "patron" parties as categories of analysis.[2] The way that elites related to nonelites, and the ideologies of elites, were to be treated as the crucial variables. This analysis rested on the view that mass parties reached out for all the citizens in the community in order to represent, lead, and rule them. Relative to patron parties, they had an articulated organization and institutionalized leadership. Less worked out in Morgenthau's analysis was the question: how successfully do mass parties represent, lead, and rule their constituents and society as a whole? In 1961 it was really not possible to say. In most of the West African states ruled by a single party, independence had been only recently achieved. And in East Africa independence had come to Tanganyika alone. It was clear that some parties lost their vigor almost on attaining independence; but there was not yet much experience of *ruling* single parties.

In the first years of the 1960s the typologies constructed for African politics became more and more focused on the notion of "dynamism." "Revolutionary centralizing systems,"[3] "revolutionary mass movement regimes,"[4] "mobilization systems,"[5] were all essentially defined by the characteristics of party systems. They were contrasted with "pragmatic-pluralistic"[6] or "consociational"[7] types. The inventors of these typologies did not insist that one kind of regime would necessarily modernize a country more than the other, but they did see the revolutionary and mobilizing systems as monopolizing legitimacy; demanding commitment and fulfilment from individuals; reaching people through hierarchically organized parties.

It soon became clear that something was wrong with the images these typologies conveyed. The dynamic parties were not getting their economic programs across. Growth rates were not rising precipitously in Mali, Ghana, Guinea, or Tanganyika. The Ivory Coast economy was growing faster And, as research was done outside the capital cities, it also became clear that the one-party revolutionary systems were not managing affairs well at local levels either.[8] Central party organs were not exacting the responses they wanted from regional and district party bodies. Plans and commands made at the center did not get implemented. Perhaps we should have been able to work this out deductively.[9]

In fact it should have been obvious that the apparatus of modern political life, on both the "input side" (parties, interest groups, voters, economic institutions) and the "output side" (bureaucracies, development corporations, legislative bodies, judiciaries, parties) were not very significant for large numbers of citizens. Many Africans operated in subsistence agricultural sectors; they were producing for or buying in markets only infrequently. Many did not vote in the elections which established majority parties (and still do not). Elections that were won by the "mobilization" parties were often participated in by less than half the potential voters.[10] Central and local government officials tried to widen the tax base and expended tremendous energy to collect taxes; but even now the bulk of the population in many African countries pays only local taxes or cesses; many people pay no tax at all either because of exemptions, avoidance of registration, or the absence of any cash income.[11] Whether indigenous traditional institutions were comparatively weak or strong, neither personnel nor programs always existed to replace them.

In fact, the characteristics attributed to political systems in Africa were often based on the images that African parties wished the world to see. But it cannot be taken for granted the explicit ideologies in African states have descriptive relevance, and the few people who articulate these ideologies may not even be very close to the center of power within the party.[12] The aspirations that certain elites have to transform their societies through a single party which penetrates all communities and social structures, and which mobilizes a society's resources, may or may not be significant.

A further, though related, problem is that typologies may be based on relatively formal structures, i.e. they relate to real phenomena but they are limited to an account of how they *would* work if they worked according to the normative expectations of the elites. They are not dealing with an empirical study of processes. They do not tell us the nature of relationships within the party, nor how the party relates to society as a whole and not merely to the modern, urban, or town sectors.[13] We cannot tell from them whether or not normative expectations which may be stated in explicit ideologies at the center are shared throughout society.

The need was therefore to focus on political structures, and parties in particular, without assuming that they operated uniformly, or with uniform effect, throughout the societies or the states in which they were found. But as soon as it began to be appreciated that national institutions, including ruling parties, were not operating in the same way in towns and countryside, or not operating everywhere in society, or being permeated by traditional patterns, assertions began to be made that the so-called African one-party states were better described as "no-party states."[14]

The argument for this designation can be briefly stated. Nationalist movements became parties of independence and then parties of rule in Africa. But as the victorious parties formed governments, they lost functional relevance and coherence.[15] The growth of state agencies proceeded, and party functions atrophied. "The party became largely an agency of the governmental bureaucracy or, at the expense of its rank and file, in certain cases it became a mere extension of the personality of a strong president or prime minister. No matter what roles parties have been assigned, almost everywhere in tropical Africa—whether in single-party, multi-party, or non-party states—they perform few."[16]

One could point to a number of developments in support of this argument. Party leaders have become heads of state. They have not only formed governments but have also not drawn sharp distinctions between their party, the state, and the nation. Rulers have relied on the civil service since civil servants are ordinarily better equipped for the problems of government than party cadres. Party members of influence and/or ability have entered government not only at cabinet level but also in the regular civil service. For example, TANU (Tanganyika African National Union) leaders in Tanganyika became permanent secretaries and foreign service officers, and district party secretaries occasionally became civil servants in the regional administration. Across Africa, party agencies such as youth wings, student groups, and para-military wings have been transformed into adjuncts of state control. They have often been governmentalized in order to ensure their loyalty to government leaders who could not rely on party mechanisms for this. The major decisions on development policy, the drawing up of five-year plans, programs to attract foreign investment, establishing proposed rates of growth and means of financing plans—all these decisions have more often been taken in councils of state than in party caucuses or congresses or even in national executives and central committees. Foreign advisers may have much more to say about these matters than ostensibly important party figures.

And if anyone could still doubt that parties no longer had primacy and centrality in African politics, the termination by the military of party rule and party existence in a number of African states could be cited.[17] Most of these states did not have socalled mass or mobilization parties. Nigeria's parties, however, were thought to have at least some of the characteristics of ruling single parties in Ghana, Guinea, Mali, and Tanganyika. They were easily overthrown by a few thousand men. Observers of the military in new states believed that strong and authoritarian ruling parties would not be so easily displaced by military intervention.[18] Yet the TANU Government had its authority successfully challenged by one battalion of the Tanganyika Rifles in 1964; less than a thousand men were able to bring the Government down, had they so wished and had the British refrained from intervening.[19] Above all, the Convention Peoples Party offered no resistance to the Ghanaian army. It is rather the disappearance of the CPP with no apparent ripples which is the striking fact of Ghanaian politics since January 1966.

When all this has been said, the idea of the "no-party state" is not a satisfactory tool for the analysis of African politics, any more than the idea of authoritarian and dynamic mass parties. It is based on a description of those aspects of African politics which are most visible to outside observers. This is the politics of the capital city; of the "modern" sectors; of institutions which can be "seen" (because they have chains of command, rosters of personnel, constitutions which define their structure and goals) and can be "heard" (because we can more readily interview party officials and civil servants). The pendulum has swung too far away from the importance of party in African political life and from the empirically established importance of individual parties in specific polities.

I cite some examples from TANU for their own sake and because they may be suggestive of the role that African ruling parties are playing in other single-party systems.

TANU in Tanganyika[20]

On the eve of Tanganyika's independence, the then Publicity Secretary of TANU, Kasela Bantu, wrote a pamphlet called *What TANU Is and How It Works*. He was trying to describe this national movement to an overseas audience and to non-Africans in Tanganyika. The aims and organization of TANU were also being explained to its own members. The politics of Tanganyika have been marked by such attempts to define new roles for

TANU and to establish the identity of the ruling party. Is it paradoxical that a national movement having become a ruling party should worry so much about its purpose and place within the nation? It is, at any rate, essential to recognise that leaders and followers alike are still asking: "What is TANU and how does it work?"

Posing the question in this way presupposes that TANU is an integrated party, with a defined structure, and a defining ideology, and thus we must merely find out how this entity functions. However, when we begin to examine the way in which institutions that meet in Dar es Salaam and the regions and districts work and interrelate we find a number of paradoxes.

TANU is the only political party in Tanganyike *de jure* and *de facto*. TANU has been able to make sure that all organized politics take place within the framework TANU sets. Thus political competition takes place within TANU institutions, be it elections to the National Executive Committee or elections to the heralded National Assembly of 1965. This is no small achievement. It alone would give the lie to the idea of a no-party state. The party here sets the rules for political participation. And, as we shall see, it also confers legitimacy. It faces no organized interest groups that it does not ostensibly dominate. Functional organizations are linked to it, e.g., the National Union of Tanganyika Workers. The highest-level leaders are not being challenged for their positions within the party. TANU is, indeed, hierarchically organized and led by what has come to be loosely designated a "charismatic" leader. The President of the United Republic of Tanzania, Julius Nyerere, is the President of TANU.

And yet Tanganyika is not really dominated by a national TANU elite. That is, the central leaders who reside in the capital city—Dar es Salaam—and who fill the high Government and TANU posts, often holding both simultaneously, do not make their will felt through the pyramid structure of the party. TANU is still a party where the relationships between the center and the organizations outside Dar es Salaam are posed as problems for the leaders. A number of interrelationships exists: between the national and the local units directly; between the center (TANU Cabinet, Central Committee, National Headquarters staff, and the National Executive Committee which has a heavy regional and district representation) and regional and district organizations[21]; and between TANU and associated organizations (the trade union movement, the cooperative movement, the Tanganyika African Parents' Association). TANU, in practice, reflects the lack of integration in society at the same time as it must serve as an instrument for bringing about integration. No central institution exists which could possibly direct or coordinate the thousands of TANU-elected and -appointed officials who operate outside the capital. The National Headquarters staff has only a handful of full-time paid officials. There is no filing system which might allow any official to know where TANU members are located. All these illustrations are cited to show that Tanganyika is far from being ruled by a monolithic party from the capital city. It is ruled partially and intermittently by the ruling party.

This is partly a matter of the organic evolution of the party. For a number of reasons decentralized forms of party organization inherited from the period of the anti-colonial struggle have not been overcome. TANU was the *first* national political party, formed out of the Tanganyika African Association (TAA) which began some time in the late 1920's as an association of government servants—junior officials and teachers—but which began to reach the small towns and rural areas after World War II.[22] TANU inherited the existing local organizations of the TAA, tribal unions, and cooperative societies.[23] However, when a new constitution was adopted and a new organization came into existence on 7 July 1954 in Dar es Salaam, TANU inherited not only a nucleus of existing branch organizations but also a tradition of local control, poor communication between branches, domination of a political movement by town-based people, and a lack of clearly defined aims. The local TAA groups and tribal unions often expressed parochial sentiments. Some of this localism has persisted in TANU's own structure.

There was, moreover, no serious obstacle in the way of the formation of a national movement. Tanganyika did not have large, centralized chiefdoms which might have become the focus for ethnic nationalisms.[24] Most of the large tribes are recent federations. They are not historic kingdoms with strong central rulers. For examples, the Sukuma, the largest tribe in Tanganyika, constituted about 12 per cent of the more than eight and a half million people in the 1957 census. This is not very much less than the 16 per cent of the population the Baganda are in Uganda. But, unlike the Baganda, the Sukuma peoples had a segmentary traditional system that did not lend itself to being made the focus of ethnic nationalism.[25]

Tanganyika has been cited as a case of extreme tribal fragmentation because over 120 tribes have been recorded in the census. But there were also positive factors making for national unity. The slave trade, besides disrupting most of the traditional social systems it encountered, spread the Swahili language inland from the coast and Swahili was fostered as a *lingua franca* by the Germans' use of Swahili-speaking agents. The slave trade also led to some amalgamation of peoples and thus may have facilitated the acceptance of leadership by people of differing tribes. One may even cite as a manifestation of a protean national unity the opposition to German rule which led to the Maji-Maji revolt of 1905.[26]; disruption of the traditional ruling systems and weakening of chiefs by the very use of indirect rule on the part of the British colonial administration. And although Tanganyika is not urbanized, even by African standards, there did exist towns, albeit small, within many of the rural areas dominated by particular tribes. Thus TANU was able to use *wageni,* or strangers who were not from the tribe of the area but who lived in the towns there.

In the towns there developed what can usefully be called a Swahili political culture. Swahili itself was important not only as a *lingua franca* which allowed TANU officials to be posted anywhere in the country, and so attain some independence of local factions; but it was also an important component of a Tanzanian identity. It has become associated with TANU and with a life style. The Swahili way of life involves having "a conviction of one's superiority which is shown by preferring to speak Swahili, . . . involvement in the affairs of a minor settlement . . . where possible, and a minimum involvement in the affairs of one's local community."[27] It involves the possibility of being a petty official in TANU, "with opportunities for making speeches and telling other members of the community how they must improve themselves and mend their ways."[28] Above all, it stands for life in the towns.

TANU is both a carrier of this culture and an expression for it—for all that it attempts to organize and represent rural areas. Most TANU leaders at national, regional, and district levels have lived, as adults, in the towns. The branch chairmen and secretaries aspire to be in the towns. Thus, although TANU has fed on rural discontent and absorbed tribesmen in their tribal unions and was itself drawn into the countryside as an instrument for voicing that discontent, it has been appealing to antithetical cultures. Thus many real and potential tensions exist within it. TANU's scope has been its source of strength and weakness. It grew rapidly, but has co-existed with a host of traditional authorities and local leaders.

Another reason why the TANU regional and district organizations did not dominate the countryside is that success in political competition did not require it. Since TANU was never opposed by a vigorous opposition, discipline was seldom needed in order to win elections. TANU did not have to centralize to gain power over indigenous opponents. It acquired a monopoly of politics because other African political organizations either did not attempt to become national, and did not have the political bases to do so (for example, the Bahaya or Wachagga tribal unions), or were weak splinter parties from TANU (e.g., the African National Congress led by Zuberi Mtemvu and the People's Democratic Party led by C. K. Tumbo). As a result TANU has often had little direct impact upon the lives of people outside the minor towns and settlements.

The dominant single party thus became a grouping of organizations functioning under known national leaders. As it grew, it became looser, not more disciplined and monolithic. It politicized ethnic groups and embraced an increasingly heterogeneous body of individuals and associations.

It was neither able to direct internal party affairs through an institutionalized TANU center nor to build such a center (or strong TANU local organizations) through the use of government machinery or patronage. Moreover, periods of development which have unfolded over a more lengthy period in other ex-colonial countries have been telescoped in Tanganyika. The political movement was formed, became the ruling party, and embarked on a major Five-Year Plan, all within ten years. Thus there was little time to confront the organizational deficiencies (which are after all the very crux of the matter) of the past. Furthermore, the low levels of economic development and the large share of the subsistence sector as a percentage of total output have persisted. TANU has not yet been threatened by economic interest groups, although it has had difficulties with the trade unions both before and after governmentalization of the unions. The absence of other strong, organized economic interest groups allowed TANU rulers a breathing space; but it also meant that such interest groups could not be used as instruments through which to rule.

How does such an organization survive, then, given its own weaknesses and the context in which it operates? How can we speak of the reality of the party state?

The Party State

In Tanganyika it is the relative weakness of structures which is striking, not their relative strengths. Yet to say that TANU is a party without a powerful center and that it rules Tanzania partially is not to maintain that party functions are atrophying nor that power and prestige are gravitating away from the party to somewhere else—state agencies or interest groups. These are also weak, for that matter. But, to put it positively, Tanzania is a party state. TANU performs important functions. Power does not reside somewhere within a polity waiting to be parcelled out to various structures. Power must be created by structures through a dynamic process and TANU is engaged in this process.

TANU's very looseness works to maintain party rule in Tanganyika. TANU's non-central bodies are oligarchical but they are internally competitive.[29] Different elected and appointed hierarchies exist within them. Party secretaries in the regions and districts, who are also heads of government in regions and districts, and are called regional and area commissioners, are able to prevail only through a process of compromise and consensus. They do not rule by fiat. They are not political bosses who tightly control either TANU-elected officials—district councillors, TANU chairmen, MPs, delegates to the National Executive Committee and the National Conference—or civil servants from central ministries who work within their jurisdiction. Functions are still very diffuse and this reflects the actual diffusion of authority among many people both in and out of TANU in the countryside.

In order to stay in touch with branch organizations, TANU regional and district secretaries must travel. Communications are poor and distances great. Thus the secretaries are constantly in motion. They are usually unwilling to delegate the running of district TANU headquarters to deputy secretaries, just as they are unwilling to leave the countryside to elected TANU officials. The solution arrived at is ingenious though not efficient in terms of utilization of human resources. Everyone travels at once and often together. And when members of the TANU "team" travel they do much the same things—appear on platforms together, making essentially the same speeches which exhort people to achieve goals set by leaders. There is a feeling of safety in numbers. Individuals reassure each other by their presence. Also, no one likes to be left out of these *safaris.* Not being on stage could be construed as a loss of status. And because there is fragmentation of authority, it is sometimes necessary for TANU chairmen, and secretaries, and civil servants to appear before people are convinced that the TANU organization is serious about a particular matter. This is becoming less true as the party secretaries/government commissioners who have been appointed since 1961 consolidate themselves in the regional and district TANU organizations. But since there is frequent posting of commissioners from district to district, or from district to some post in Dar es Salaam, and since the elected officials have independent leases of power, few area commissioners are able really to dominate their district TANU organization.

Many of them do not have the necessary skills to direct the activities of civil servants, and in fact they are enjoined not to try.[30] Nonetheless, the very weakness of the civil service outside the capital means that TANU officials and members perform governmental functions and legitimate the acts of the civil service. A traveller going from one district to another may find TANU members manning a road block. They may be checking for illegal movement of some commodity. Or they may be checking to see if individuals have paid their taxes. These duties devolve on TANU organizations because there are just not enough civil servants at the local level. Many districts do not have representatives of certain ministries at the district *boma* or headquarters. At a meeting of civil servants and TANU officials the difficulty of collecting taxes comes up. Someone suggests that TANU help collect taxes. The suggestion does not always come from a TANU officials; it may well come from a civil servant.

Civil servants, too, have been recruited to the posts of area and regional commissioners.[31] But most of these posts are still held by those who were TANU secretaries before independence. And the appointment of commissioners in 1961 was designed to emphasize that since TANU was the Government there should be political heads of regions and districts.[32] The idea was to bring a TANU presence to government in the regions and districts. Although there was never any exclusiveness about TANU in terms of ideology or membership categories, civil servants were debarred from joining TANU under a colonial ordinance which was allowed to stand until 1964. One of the aims of opening TANU to the civil service was to strengthen TANU as well as to make civil servants politically sensitive to TANU, and to abolish distinctions between them. Nyerere had always seen the distinction between politicians and civil servants as artificial even when he was upholding the British model of a neutral and apolitical civil service.[33] He has conceived of nation-building in Tanganyika as a unity by amalgamation, not unity by cutting out offending parts. The aim has been to create a synthesis of party and state—a synthesis which has its living embodiment in the commissioners who became head of party and state in the districts and regions.

Where civil servants *have* had administrative and technical skills they have still relied on TANU people to "put across" their programs. This brings us to TANU's critical function in Tanzania. Many functions that TANU and civil service bodies together carry out are economic, and it is around economic tasks that an attempt is being made to strengthen, or build for the first time, state and party structures.

It is not true, as one of Tanganyika's expatriate planning experts appeared to think, that Tanganyika has a "disciplined and dynamic party" whose machinery can be utilized to the maximum in achieving economic goals.[34] But whether dynamic and disciplined or not, TANU had to be used in the effort to meet pressing problems because it had local bodies, even if they were not ideally obedient nor universally close to the grass roots, which could at least try to reach ordinary people both to disseminate goals and to organize efforts.

Many people are strongly attached to TANU, even if they disagree with their local TANU structures. The party still retains its legitimacy as the fighter for independence. This is a function of the still short time since independence. For many people, though not for all, of course, TANU provides an "ought" component to an order.

There are also practical advantages to be gained from giving support to the party. Although local party organizations and the center have not had much patronage to dispense, money and status do attach to being an officeholder through TANU, and the party can also help determine who will get a salaried job, and influence the settling of old scores. Being a TANU activist or supporter gives one leverage for fighting battles over land rights or debts.

For leaders also, TANU legitimates rule. They can justify their own orders as TANU orders. Their responsibilities are derived from TANU positions, or from being given government posts by TANU. Many such posts are in fact filled by the personal appointment of the President. But he himself stresses the TANU origins of authority. Aside from the formal responsibilities that political heads of departments or regions and districts have for specific administrative and economic duties, it is often the authority of a TANU politician which enables him to get a hearing for civil servants and to support them as they explain their programs.

We could establish without much difficulty that economic policy has been ratified rather than made by central TANU organs. A few TANU Government leaders, in conjunction with expatriates in the planning and economic ministries, formulated the Five-Year Plan.[35] Nowhere in the Five-Year Plan were regional and area commissioners mentioned. With few exceptions, neither the Five-Year Plan nor regional plans mentioned TANU. However, information essential for plan formulation and implementation was gathered by TANU development committees. And above all, the conditions which make civil servants depend on TANU determine the nature of TANU's own contribution to implementing development programs.

The fact that tasks are not easily separable into component parts is related to the nature of local societies. Development does not consist in deciding to have a new well in a village and then telling technical personnel to construct the well. The decision to have a well, getting villagers to accept the location of the well, and having villagers themselves carry out much of the construction work and co-operate with technical specialists are all a matter of political concern. Thus it is crucial to the development effort that TANU makes available numbers of men who primarily make speeches and travel around bringing people into contact with centrally or regionally established goals.

Speech-making, arranging meetings, and employing persuasion not unmixed with compulsion are familiar tasks for TANU people. Local self-help and development projects provide a focus around which TANU can be organized. TANU is given something to do which it can do and which is useful. The hope is that TANU will also tighten its control over localities by popularizing and implementing local development programs.

It does not always work out this way. Local self-help projects have more and more given way to centrally determined pilot projects and "villagization" schemes, and TANU-sponsored projects sometimes prove to be failures or mistakes. Still, it remains TANU's job, together with community development personnel, to make connections for people: if you want this you must do that. Very often, Government cannot supply what is wanted and so it says: "You must do this and then by your efforts you can get a number of valued things." Not everyone is willing to strike this bargain. Individual perceptions of gains and effort are variable.

This applies to TANU people also. Not all TANU activists, let alone those who call themselves TANU supporters, opt for "modernity." It would be a mistake to conceive of a backward countryside seeded with TANU carriers of modern patterns of living. All the seminars, meetings, and exhortations that civil servants and TANU people are involved in giving are aimed, after all, at other civil servants and TANU people and not at the population at large. When individuals in a certain district are recalcitrant about doing something Government wants done, it would be not unusual to find them led by someone who calls himself a TANU leader.

It remains an open question as to what and how much the TANU Government can enforce. It was reaction to enforced change against the British which swelled TANU's following. Regional and district leaders seem aware that in some places communication has already broken down between villages, district, regional, and central authorities. They are aware of the costs involved. But they cannot abandon trying to impose their will on the country- side. For without reaching the villages, Government remains essentially confined to a few urban centers and towns. This was understood by Julius Nyerere when he said: "Others try to reach the moon. We try to reach the villages."[36] This aim is notoriously difficult to achieve. The institutional innovations which have been constructed so that TANU can become a "two way all-weather road between Government and the people"–the development committees, party cells, TANU-associated groups—can all become ritual forms without any content. But at their best, these institutional devices can become important and they are very much the manifestation of the "party state."

In writing of TANU's "legitimizing" function, I have tried to keep within the limits of the impressions I have formed in the course of field work in various districts of Tanganyika, but this is an aspect that needs further discussion. When it is argued by proponents of the no-party state analysis that ruling single parties are losing their functions it is sometimes acknowledged that they still have symbolic meaning. But we cannot take for granted that particular parties do in fact have "symbolic" meaning for citizens, any more than we can accept at face value the claims of leaders that the "ideologies" are the ideologies of party and citizens. But symbolic meanings are very important. Elites consciously try to define formulae by which they can justify their positions and through which they can bridge the gap between themselves and nonelites. If the formulas are accepted and if individuals identify with the institutions which put them forward, a reservoir of legitimacy exists which can be exploited for rule. This reservoir can run dry when elites become ineffective or coercive or as new bidders for power make claims on the loyalties of citizens. Nonetheless, when a radical transformation of society is undertaken or desired by ruling elites, formulas must be found which not only permit development but which provide an "ideological grease" for development.[37]

In Tanzania various leaders have begun to challenge Julius Nyerere's formulae, although a battle of ideas has not been fully joined. Where Nyerere speaks of African Socialism, others refer to scientific socialism. Nyerere wants to preserve the bonds of traditional community in order to bring about modernity, and he sees TANU as the carrier of both modern and traditional values.[38] Others see a contradiction between tradition and change; for them, traditional ties must be broken by a strong party. The pages of the TANU paper, *The Nationalist,* have sometimes expressed the belief that only through social conflict will backwardness be overcome. For some ministers and TANU middle-level leaders (junior ministers, commissioners, national headquarters officers) Nyerere's ideas have been too gradualist, too gentlemanly, and unsuited for rapid social and economic change, although Nyerere is not personally criticised or directly contradicted.[39] Mixed in with differing views of social change is a desire for more action and drama—and perhaps more assertion of authority—than Nyerere's formulations entail. And the political aspirations of newcomers to power, Zanzibaris and middle-level leaders in particular, lead them to search for their own formulae to legitimize their aspirations and provide them with ideologies to bind their followers.

If TANU is in fact a party without strong central organs and a party which is a congeries of regional, district, and subdistrict organizations which communicate with each other and with Dar es Salaam intermittently, then no single TANU ideology will be likely to reflect the outlook of the whole organization. Nor does any mechanism exist whereby an ideology could be imposed over those who call themselves TANU. There is no means for those in power within TANU to institutionalize their view of reality and to enforce this view within their own organization. There is not even a mechanism through which all TANU members can be constantly kept in touch with a political ideology. Certainly there is no reason to believe that people either in TANU or in Tanzania at large will spontaneously embrace an ideology simply because it is promulgated by leaders. Thus it is a mistake to identify the ideas of one man, Julius Nyerere, as the belief system of a whole party which attempts to promulgate them throughout society.

Entrance into TANU becomes increasingly a *sine qua non* for being part of the nation. At the same time, the search for TANU's identity goes on. This search is inextricably linked to a definition of the "Tanzanian way" and to the idea of a Tanzanian nation. This idea is not static. It emerges as a response to unforeseen events, like the mutiny of the Tanganyika army in 1964 which called forth an effort to incorporate the military and civil service into TANU so that they too could be "part of the nation" and thereby become politically reliable.[40] The idea gets defined consciously in Presidential speeches and documents of state and party, e.g., the *Report of the Presidential Commission on the Establishment of a Democratic One-Party State,* the new TANU Constitution, and the Arusha Declaration. The style and content of these documents and the emergence (or failure to emerge) of an ideology of development are important, because it is through the process of defining political formulae and establishing them as legitimizing doctrines that the gap between elites and non-elites begins to be closed.[41] The most recent attempt to create a frame of reference for looking at problems and for creating a political program to deal with problems is the Arusha Declaration of January 1967. In this document the TANU National Executive Committee resolved that leaders of TANU and Government should divest themselves of share holdings, directorships, multiple salaries, and rentals. While asserting a policy of self-reliance and self-sacrifice for the population at large, the NEC at the same time called for the end of privilege for leaders.

It is an empirical question as to whether or not the Arusha Declaration, or any particular doctrine, does legitimize and whether or not ideologies effectively link leaders and followers. In Tanzania there is a concern to create a working ideology and differences between various ideologies do matter. They matter not because we can understand systems in terms of ideologies propounded by leaders and publicists but because the success or failure of political formulae are crucial to the integration process.

Conclusions

It is tempting to generalize about the political systems of Africa. We can establish many "facts of life" which are indeed common to many of them in terms of their resources, *per capita* incomes, relative shares of subsistence and monetary sectors, and so forth. And we can show that the structures of most African economies have worked against the formation of disciplined and centralized parties and have precluded totalitarian or "revolutionary centralizing" systems. But we do not have to assume that these economic factors determine political development, although we must recognize that they act as constraints on political possibilities. It is important to explore the kinds of political organizations that can and do live in various economic settings. It is also necessary to show the interaction between political organizations and the economy.

Thus it is necessary to ask: Among other things, what kinds of political leadership exist? What values and programmes are espoused? Political leaders do not sit back and wait for enough economic development to take place to change the social structure and enable them to control their organizations. They are active agents in the process of making change, even when they may be inactive leaders. it makes a difference whether or not leaders are realistic about their ability to enforce close control within the party. There are elites who try to be coercive when they can succeed only in being repressive. And it matters if the party attempts to become an agent for economic change even when the party is too weak and loose and has too few resources to tackle developmental problems effectively, because it is in the process of attempting to change the economy that the party's internal organization evolves.

African one-party states are not bound to become more centralized, any more than economic development is bound to occur. The conditions for decentralization or for the disappearance of parties are already at hand. The military can intervene; the parties can disintegrate in face of overwhelming social, economic, and political problems. But the remaining ruling single parties have real roles to perform. Neither military forces nor civil services are likely to make up in force and effectiveness what they lack in legitimacy and political knowhow. Public order and political participation, which are pre-conditions for economic development and are the essence of political development, are not going to be guaranteed by the removal of parties.

We must now explore the remaining single ruling parties to find out how they differ in terms of political functioning and what their prospects are for continued existence. Indeed, we may have to hurry before we have no phenomenon to study. But it is too soon to proclaim the no-party state as ascendant throughout Africa, and it is very questionable whether when such regimes come about they will survive even as long as the party-states of Africa.

Notes

1.   For a fuller treatment of TANU see Henry Bienen, *Tanzania: Party Transformation and Economic Development* (Princeton: Princeton University Press, 1970).

2.   R. Schachter Morgenthau, "Single Party Systems in West Africa," *The American Political Science Review* 55 (1961): 294–307.

3.   J. S. Coleman and C. Rosberg, Jr., *Political Parties and National Integration in Tropical Africa* (Berkeley and Los Angeles: University of California Pres, 1965)

4.   R. Tucker, *Soviet Political Mind* (New York: Frederick A. Praeger, 1963), "On Revolutionary Movement Regimes," pp. 3–19.

5.   D. E. Apter, *The Political Kingdom in Uganda* (Princeton: Princeton University Press, 1961), pp. 22–24.

6.   Coleman and Rosberg, *op. cit.*

7.   Apter, *op. cit.*

8.   Discussions with Ernest Benjamin and Nicholas Hopkins, who worked in Ghana and Mali respectively, have corroborated my own research in Tanganyika.

9.   Aristide Zolberg has argued deductively to this conclusion using David Easton's concept of "authoritative allocation of values" to show that "modern" institutions deal with only a portion of total allocative activity and that the remainder must be allocated by other means, by other structures. Cf. "The Structure of Political Conflict in the New States of Tropical Africa," paper

delivered at the Annual Meeting of the American Political Science Association, 6–10 September 1966 in New York. See also his *Creating Political Order* (Chicago: Rand McNally, 1966).

10.   The Tanganyika African National Union (TANU) won a large majority of the votes cast in the 1960 election, but the 885,000 registered voters represented about half the estimated potential voters. And since less than one-seventh of the registered voters actually voted, the voting electorate was a small percentage of the possible one. In the Presidential election Nyerere received over 1.1 million votes to his opponent's 21,276. The total vote was less than a quarter of the potential electorate. TANU claimed a membership at the time which was greater than Nyerere's vote. The more than 2.5 million votes cast in the Presidential and National Assembly elections in Tanzania in 1965 represented a marked increase. However, about 50 percent of the possible electorate was voting. Dennis Austin shows similar figures for Ghana in his *Politics in Ghana 1946–1960* (London: Oxford University Press, 1964), p. 174, where the Convention People's Party received about 15 percent of the total potential vote in elections in 1954 and 1956. Zolberg, *op. cit.,* refers to similar phenomena in Guinea and Mali.

11.   The nonmonetary sector still accounts for more than a third of Tanganyika's total Gross Domestic Project (or £200 million out of £600 million). Ninetyeight percent of the population pay taxes only to district councils, who levy a tax of about 1 to 3 percent on the income of all adult males. But it is estimated that 15 percent of all males are escaping registration for taxation before official exemptions begin. See E. Lee, *Local Taxation in Tanganyika* (Dar es Salaam, 1964). Of course, taxes are hard to collect where communications are poor, means of coercion slight, and habits of this kind of payment not ingrained.

12.   For example, the ideologues of *Spark* in Ghana or *The Nationalist* in Tanzania certainly did not determine state policy, nor were they often influential in the councils of the CPP or TANU.

13.   The aforementioned authors are themselves conscious of these questions. In fact, their typologies are designed to seek out the data that will tell us how much tactical flexibility parties have, or how hierarchical is authority. See Apter, *op. cit.* Nonetheless, the typologies are dependent on formal structures and political rhetoric rather than hypotheses about party function, insofar as they purport to describe concrete African systems.

14.   For a discussion of this issue, see my article "The Party and No-Party State: Tanganyika and the Soviet Union," *Transition 3* (Kampala, 1964): 25–32.

15.   R. I. Rotberg, "Modern African Studies: Problems and Prospects," *World Politics* 18 (1966): 571. See also I. Wallerstein "The Decline of the Party in Single Party States" in J. LaPalombara and M. Weiner (eds.), *Political Parties and Political Development* (Princeton: Princeton University Press, 1962).

16.   *Ibid.*

17.   See H. Bienen (ed.), *The Military Intervenes: Case Studies in Political Development* (New York: Russell Sage Foundation, 1967).

18.   W. Gutteridge, *Armed Forces in the New States* (London: Oxford University Press, 1962), p. 67; M. Janowitz, *The Military in the Political Development of New States* (Chicago: Chicago University Press, 1964), pp. 29, 103; F. Green, "Towards Understanding Military Coups," *Africa Report* 2 (1966): 10–14; E. Shils, "The Military in the Political Development of New States," in J. Johnson (ed.), *The Role of the Military in Underdeveloped Countries* (Princeton: Princeton University Press, 1962).

19.   See my "National Security in Tanzania After the Mutiny," *Transition* 5 (Kampala, 1965): 39–46.

20.   I refer mainly to Tanganyika rather than Tanzania because most of my remarks pertain to preunion Tanganyika and to mainland Tanzania only.

21.   There are seventeen regions and sixty districts in Tanganyika, excluding Zanzibar and Pemba. The districts are the old colonially demarcated administrative units. A district is often around 6,000 square miles, although it may be as small as 1,000 square miles. District capitals sometimes have less than 1,000 people. The regions have been increased in number since the

colonial period. Regional headquarters are towns which are usually around 10,000 in population although Mwanza has more than 20,000 and Tanga more than 50,000. No region, and not even many districts, are homogeneous with regard to tribe, although some areas have a dominant tribal population. The towns are invariably ethnically heterogeneous.

22.   See R. A. Austen, "Notes on the Pre-History of TANU," *Makerere Journal* 9 (1964): 1; and G. Bennett, "An Outline History of TANU," *Makerere Journal* 7 (1963): 1.

23.   TANU's spokesmen now trace TANU's roots to the TAA and the cooperatives, denying a share in the parentage of the party to tribal unions, which are described as being tribalistic and disruptive of national unity. But the tribal unions fed on reactions against the British efforts to enforce unpopular agricultural policies, just as the TAA did. And TANU was able to use the discontent organized by the tribal unions and to absorb some of their members and local bodies.

24.   See Harvey Glickman, "Traditionalism, Pluralism and Democratic Processes in Tanganyika," paper presented at the Annual Meeting of the American Political Science Association, Chicago, 9–12 September 1964, p. 4.

25.   See D. E. Apter, *op. cit.* For materials on the Sukuma, see Hans Cory, *The Ntemi: The Traditional Role of a Sukuma Chief in Tanganyika* (London: MacMillan, 1951), and Hans Cory, *The Political System of the Sukuma* (London: Oxford University Press, 1953).

26.   See Julius Nyerere's "Foreward" to K. M. Stahl, *Tanganyika: Sail in the Wilderness* (The Hague: Mouton and Co., 1961), pp. 6–7. Also Daudi Mwakawago, "Growth of Nationalism in Tanganyika," *Mbioni* 2 (Dar es Salaam, November, 1965): 5.

27.   Alison Redmayne, "Preliminary Report on a Hehe Community," East African Institute of Social Research, 1962 Conference Paper, p. 8.

28.   *Ibid.*

29.   When special TANU district electoral conferences met to select candidates to run for Parliament in 1965, the votes were often split among seven or eight candidates or more. Rarely did any one candidate win more than 50 percent of the votes. Only 33 out of 180 final candidates polled more than 50 percent in the selection primary among TANU district leaders.

30.   See the Tanganyika Government's Staff Circular No. 14 of 1962.

31.   A number of TANU leaders have had a say in the appointment of commissioners. But President Nyerere has had to approve appointments, and appointments have been made from his office at certain times.

32.   In the first batch of appointments for regional commissioner, six of the then ten TANU provincial secretaries and two provincial chairmen became regional commissioners. Three of the ten provincial secretaries and five of ten provincial chairmen were to become area commissioners. (Province was the preindependence designation for region.)

33.   See Julius Nyerere, *Democracy and the Party System* (Dar es Salaam, n.d.) p. 26. When Nyerere told civil servants to keep out of the political arena in 1960, he was trying to insulate them from politics and from local TANU organizations as much as warning them off. Many civil servants were still expatriates who were vulnerable to attack. See Nyerere's Circular Letter No. 1, 1960, reprinted in *Transition* 1 (December 1961): 23–5.

34.   G. Karmiloff "Planning Machinery and its Operation in Tanganyika," Public Policy Conference No. 1, Kampala, October 1963.

35.   See my paper, "The Role of TANU and the Five-Year Plan," presented to the East African Institute for Social Research Conference, Kampala, 1964.

36.   Tanzania is not made up of compact villages. People live mostly in small settlements often spread out over a wide area. Thus it is physically hard to reach people.

37.   Alexander Gerschenkron has noted thrusts of development in Russia, Germany, and France being accompanied by specific ideas about the cause and cure of backwardness, which are worked into ideologies of development. See *Economic Backwardness in Historical Perspective* (Cambridge, Mass.: Harvard University Press, 1964), pp. 22–6. See also Mary Matossian, "Ideologies of Delayed Industrialization," *Economic Development and Cultural Change* 6 (1958): 217–28.

38. President Nyerere's ideas have been expressed in the aforementioned *Democracy and the Party System.* See also *Ujamaa: The Basis of African Socialism* (Dar es Salaam: Tanganyika Standard Ltd., 1962); *TANU Na Raia* (TANU and the Citizen) published in Swahili (Dar es Salaam: TANU Press, 1962); and President Nyerere's Guidelines to the Presidential Commission on the One-Party State published in *Report of the Presidential Commission on the Establishment of a Democratic One-Party State* (Dar es Salaam: Government Printer, 1965), pp. 1–5.

39. See, for example, pieces signed ''A Critic'' and ''A Contributor'' in *The Nationalist* 28.6.65, p. 5, 29.6.65, p. 6, 18.6.65, p. 6, and 19.6.65, p. 6. See also Mr. Kassim Hanga's Address to the National Assembly published in *The Nationalist* 2.7.64, and Mr. A. M. Babu's ''Tanzania Pointing the Way to Wealthy Economy,'' *The Nationalist,* 4.5.65, p. 5.

40. See my ''National Security in Tanzania after the Mutiny,'' *loc. cit.*

41. See L. Binder, ''National Integration and Political Development,'' *American Political Science Review* 58 (1964.)

Chapter 3

One-Party Systems in Africa

Introduction

Various typologies have been constructed for the study of African politics, in order to differentiate party systems. However, what might be called sub-system variables which pertain to political parties have usually been omitted in the more general formulations of political types. This chapter is an attempt to come to grips with the meaning of one-party systems in Africa by shifting attention to factors of party operation, to the techniques for maintaining and exerting political power. This involves being more specific about political organizations and organizational techniques in Africa than the typologies have heretofore been—typologies which distinguish between mobilization and consociational systems,[1] or revolutionary-centralizing and pragmatic-pluralist systems,[2] or even between mass and patron parties.[3] It also involves shifting to a different language than the one employed by the creators of these and other typologies for African politics.

The language of description, definitions, and typologies has had a peculiar importance in the study of African politics precisely because we have not had a great deal of evidence at hand about the workings of political parties. If we knew a great deal about political organizations in Africa from empirical studies, we could define parties in terms of a number of categories and then throw the specific parties into the various bins. But we would know, to begin with, that the bins were relevant because their relevance would have emerged out of the accumulated studies. The problem is that analysts have operated in somewhat of an empirical vacuum and the typologies they have constructed have been designed to seek out what was important about political organizations in terms of a wider set of questions for the society as a whole, for example, questions about mobilization of resources, control networks, economic development. But difficulties have been evident in moving from a concern with, for example, a *single* party as a defining variable, or the ideology of a given party, to outcomes for economic development, when we do not know how the parties operate at the grass roots or in the society as a whole. Moreover, typologies have had a tendency to be used (often by other than their creators) to explain political phenomena when they were meant originally as classificatory schemes. Somehow, it is assumed that the definitions actually explain. The rather sterile debates about democracy and one-party government in Africa or about economic development and single-party rule reflect both the aforementioned empirical vacuum and this tendency to move from definitions to explanations.

It is striking how dependent the typologies of one-party systems in Africa have been for their language, images, and variables on characterizations of communist or socialist parties, and in particular how derivative they are from a particular model of the Communist Party of the Soviet Union.

David Apter borrowed from Philip Selznick the concept of a mobilization system as one in which a party or regime engages in drastic and thorough reorganization of the society. The latter's work on the organizational weapon was concerned with studying Bolshevik strategy and tactics.[4] Another typology was designed by a specialist in Soviet politics to come to grips with the revolutionary nationalist regimes in order to compare them with communist regimes. I refer to Robert C. Tucker's revolutionary mass movement regime under single-party auspices, which he called the "movement-regime."[5] Tucker stressed revolutionary dynamicism as a basis of differentiation among types; he warned against trying to differentiate types primarily in organizational terms—a warning that was not heeded, at least by political scientists concerned with Africa. Henry Bretton, for example, noting that Ghana might pass through a pronounced non-democratic, "in all probability authoritarian-totalitarian regime" said that the form might be not only Marxist but fascist, although in a modified form "making allowances for organizational deficiencies."[6] Organizational deficiencies are themselves the crux of the matter; organizational forms are not.

Tucker did not address himself to specific African cases in any detail at all. Nor did other specialists on the Soviet Union or communist systems apply their analyses to Africa, although there has been much discussion of African socialism, Soviet theories of "national democracy," and Soviet models for economic development.[7] Rather, what happened was that a generalized image of the Communist Party of the Soviet Union (CPSU) was brought to the study of African one-party systems, perhaps because they were, after all, one-party systems and the CPSU has been the most prominent, salient, long-lived one-party system going. There is a certain irony that those aspects of the CPSU which were contained in the totalitarian model—monolithic organization, hierarchical authority, organizational weapon in a word—were brought into the literature on African politics through typologies just when the totalitarian model was itself being called in question by analysts of the Soviet Union. A revisionist literature on Soviet politics is now stressing the prevalence of cliques in the system, the porosity of political structure in the system, the problem of extending central control to the peripheries, the existence of diversity of institutional forms at the local levels.[8]

It would not be earth-shaking to point out that cliques, family circles, and factions have abounded in African one-party systems, including the so-called moblization ones as well as the parties of notables or patron parties although the idea has been resisted by some analysts and some African leaders as it was resisted by analysts of China's and the Soviet Union's communist parties. Once we would have said that all African one-party systems have factions, and even gone so far as to say that all are in some respects parties of notables, we would not have said either enough or the most useful things. We do not want to be guilty of overhomogenization here.

Relative dominance of the soon-to-emerge-victorious nationalist movements over rival organizations differed greatly between countries. One-party states emerged in places where, on the basis of electoral performance, it looked as if at least a two-party system was being institutionalized in the terminal colonial period—for example—Mali and Ghana.[9] Thus we cannot infer one-party dominance back into the nationalist movement period for all the systems which became independent under the aegis of a single party that identified itself with state and nation. We now have studies available which show how marginal advantages were used to consolidate one-party rule and which try to specify at what point in time and why a particular nationalist movement won out.[10]

The one-party systems that did emerge at independence were subsequently compared in terms of the differing party organizations by which the systems were defined. One such differentiation among one-party states was Ruth Schachter Morgenthau's categorization of "mass" and "patron" parties.[11] Professor Morgenthau noted that in 1956 the *Union Soudanaise* in Mali and the *Parti Démocratique de Guinée* (PDG) in Guinea defeated patron parties based on "chiefs," and that the mass parties consolidated their electoral victories as soon as they were in a position to do so.[12] Professor Morgenthau, however, did not stress the marginal advantage of the mass parties. Rather, her political history unfolded as a contest between modern-izers and traditionalists, although it did not specify as a necessary outcome the victory of mass parties (which after all were not victorious everywhere, for example, the Sawaba Party in Niger), and it did doubt whether the distinction always remained valid after independence.[13]

The time variable is very relevant but not primarily because the popularity of given parties peaked near independence and then fell. It is important be-cause given the short time that individual parties have been dominant, including a period in the pre-independence period, say from 1956 for the PDG in Guinea and, from 1958 for the Tanganyika African National Union (TANU), and from 1956–1966 for the Convention Peoples Party (CPP) in Ghana, and given their resources in terms of tasks to perform, time has been very short for African parties.

The typologies that proliferated in the 1960s for African political systems have been misleading for reasons other than neglect of a time factor. I have argued in other chapters, that, for all the concern for elaborating a number of distinguishing variables, the characteristics attributed to political systems in

Africa were often based on images that African parties wanted to convey to the world and themselves.[14]

I am aware that analysts of African parties have been conscious of the "inexhaustible mixture" of differentiating elements. Nonetheless, the very existence of the typologies avows that their creators believe the units are not *sui generis* and are subject to useful generalization. And despite my awareness of dilemmas encountered in classifying complex political phenomena in Africa, I think the criticisms stand. Let us briefly consider other typologies.

The work of Coleman and Rosberg on "revolutionary-centralizing trends" and "pragmatic-pluralistic patterns" as two general tendencies in uniparty or one-party dominant states has ideology as its first differentiating factor. (Ideology receives the most elaboration of all the differentiating factors in terms of categories and subcategories.)[15] Other major differentiating factors are popular participation, and organizational aspects. Parties are classified according to tendencies. The dominant parties in African states representative of the revolutionary-centralizing trend are said to be preoccupied with ideology, the content of which is programmatic and transformative regarding the socioeconomic modernization of contemporary society. They also tend to be ultrapopularistic and egalitarian, and stress participation in affairs of party and state. Organizationally, it is said, the parties tend to be monolithic and centralized.[16]

This categorization is not derived from the ways parties work. It is an example of the aforementioned reliance on normative and formal structural differences. These normative and formal differences may be important, but this has to be shown. We must make the same demands here with regard to stipulating institutional arrangements, i.e., constitutions, that are made in critiques of "formal-legal" studies in comparative politics of Western European countries and the United States.

The same criticism applies to David Apter's typologies of "mobilization" and "consociational" systems.[17] Apter states that a mobilization system usually contains a party of solidarity, which either monopolizes power openly or in other ways makes all other groups dependent on it. The party network is, in effect, the structure of the new society. As he elaborates the system with reference to Africa, the party in the mobilization system demands fundamental commitment on the part of the individual; it can make quick changes in its alliances and alter its goals and targets. Power usually resides at the top of the organization, generally in a single leader who monopolizes legitimacy. The party or state will most often act on grounds of expediency and necessity, using ideology to give perspective and justification for what appears necessary. Thus hierarchical authority, claims for total allegiance, appearance of tactical flexibility, and party links to and domination of functional organizations and political groups seem to define the party of solidarity in the system.[18]

Of course, this typology is designed to help seek out the data that will tell us how much tactical flexibility parties have, or how hierarchical authority is. Nonetheless, this typology is dependent on formal structures and political rhetoric too. What we want to find out is how the central and local institutions work and how homogeneous or heterogeneous the one-party systems are. As we find out that the one-party systems even have a great deal of formal diversity of structures at local levels and that central organs cannot exact desired responses from regional and district bodies, we realize that there has been a focus on parties as if they were coterminous with the societies or territorial entities they purport to rule. If, in fact, all political parties in Africa have great difficulty in radiating out central authority, if authority is widely diffused, if one-party systems are vulnerable to military takeover, if power is dispersed, then it is not useful to pose a consociational model where authority is pyramidal (dispersed and shared between constituent units and a central agency) as compared to a mobilization system's hierarchical authority. If African countries are plural societies in the extreme, then is it heuristic to pose a consociational model where there tends to be a system of loyalties functioning on various levels as against the demand for total allegiance of the mobilization system's party? And what sense is there in postulating a unitarism of political organization when the local party organizations may constitute a political opposition to the center (as Apter himself has argued, the CPP's constituency organizations did in Ghana),[19] or when this local organization shows deflection from the center's commands (as I have argued for TANU)?

Now the inventors of the categories "mass," "revolutionary-centralizing" and "mobilization system" did not insist that such parties as characterized these systems would necessarily best modernize a country or best solve the problems of ethnic heterogeneity. Indeed, Morgenthau noted that conflicts among ethnic groups were often sharper in mass than in patron parties, since "mass parties made a continuous attempt to propagate modern values and diminish the weight of ethnic exclusiveness," and were egalitarian by policy.[20] Moreover, she stated that mass party leaders sometimes institutionalized ethnic differences and played the ethnic arithmetic game.[21] For her, however, mass parties tried to blur the ethnic distinctions, although they sometimes failed.[22] Apter did not argue that a mobilization system would always be optimal for modernization but only that it was most successful in establishing a new polity and converting from later modernization to industrialization. In fact, his modernizing autocracies and neomercantilist societies were optimal political forms for long-term modernization and for the conversion from early to late stages of the modernization process.[23] Still, the very terminology shows that the revolutionary-centralizing, mobilization, and mass-party systems were seen as being more dynamic and tougher. But it is precisely this presumed strength that must be questioned, for this strength was thought to rest on the party's organizational coherence, which in turn rested on a mass base. Thus, the mass party was thought to be linked to the countryside and able to exert itself there.

There has been a seeming paradox in the treatment of leadership and party in Africa, for the application of the concept of charisma to the political analysis of African states has occurred for the mass single parties, not the patron ones, and the connection between personalism and mass popualrity has been remarked abut much more in analyses of so-called mass parties than of so-called patron ones. Discussion of politics in Ghana, Guinea, Mali, Tanzania has often been in terms of the political thought and personal characteristics of Nkrumah, Toure, Keita, and Nyerere.

Ghana's Convention Peoples Party qualified as a mass party in Morgenthau's typology, and it was to Ghana that Apter strikingly applied the concept of charisma in order to explain institutional transfer from the colonial to the independent regime in terms of Nkrumah's leadership.[24]

And yet this is paradoxical when we consider that patron parties, after all, are supposed to be parties of personalities.[25] When Thomas Hodgkin and Morgenthau discussed mass parties they stressed differentiation, strong articulation, organization in general, or what could be called relative institutionalization as compared to what were variously called patron,[26] elite, or cadre parties.

Morgenthau explicitly states that mass parties had comparatively institutionalized leaderships, although these were not always collective leaderships. Patron parties had essentially personal leadership, although the mass party in the Ivory Coast, the *Parti Démocratique de la Côte d'Ivoire* (PDCI) after 1952 had essentially personal leadership too.[27] And the *Mouvement de l'Evolution Sociale de l'Afrique Noire* (MESAN), which dissolved opposition parties in 1962 to become a ruling single party in the Central African Republic, has been described by one commentator as having broad popular support but being a personalistic organization.[28] It is at least terminologically strange that discussion of charisma centered on mass parties and their leaders and personalistic parties were not seen as having charismatic leaders.[29] But even more important is the peculiarity that the relatively institutionalized parties were seen as having charismatic leaders (this was particularly true for analysis of politics in Ghana and Tanzania), while charismatic leadership is by definition not institutionalized, although the leader's popularity may enhance the party's short-term strength. Granted, the term "charisma" was loosely applied to African leaders so that any popular leader with visibility and flamboyance came to be called charismatic.[30] Still, there is an anomaly in analyses that stress the mass characteristics of parties that reach out for a whole population through articulated organizations and analyses of charismatic leadership where the leader's direct ties to the population are stressed and his personal qualities rather than organizational ones are emphasized. (I do not want to explore the problems of the idea of charisma here but am interested in pointing to an anomaly in the writings on one-party systems.)[31]

What I am suggesting is that there was an assumption made that political structures, "mass" parties in particular, operated uniformly throughout their society at least at the time of independence. Those like Professor Morgenthau who saw a conjunction of national and party communities were emphasizing the absence of overt opposition. They saw popular regimes at a particular point in time. But this did not establish the nature of the relationships between party and society or within the party; it did not establish that parties were operating the same way in towns and countryside or operating everywhere in society.

If there was an exaggerated perception of the strength of some ruling single parties in Africa in the early 1960s, 1964–1965 marked a watershed in both the political history of Africa and the creation of typologies to encompass African politics. By 1964 most of the countries of tropical Africa were independent. When Zambia became independent at the end of that year, there were left the white minority-dominated regimes of southern Africa and the soon-to-become-independent Gambia and the enclaves within South Africa. However, 1964 was the last year of civilian rule in a number of African states. True, armies had intervened in the politics of independent African prior to 1964. From independence in 1960, the *Armée National Congolaise* had been prominent in Congolese politics; there were abortive coups in Ethiopia and the Somali Republic the same year. And the military was to be a factor in the Senghor-Dia conflict in Senegal in 1962 as it had been in the Senegal-Soudan breakup in 1960. In 1963, the military overthrew civilian regimes in Togo and Dahomey and was involved in negotiations on a new government after the fall of Youlou in Congo-Brazzaville. Also in 1963, there was a mutiny in Niger, but this was unsuccessful and civilian rule was restored in Dahomey too.[32] In 1964, army mutinies broke out in the East African countries (Uganda, Kenya, and Tanganyika), and there was a revolution in Zanzibar. However, no military regimes emerged.[33] It was in 1965 and 1966 that military coups swept civilians from office in Algeria, Congo (Leopoldville, now Kinshasa), Dahomey, Central African Republic, Upper Volta, Nigeria, Ghana, and Burundi. (There were also abortive coups in Togo and Congo-Brazzaville.)

These coups narrowed the universe of one-party systems in Africa for Algeria, the Central African Republic, Upper Volta, Ghana, and the northern and eastern regions of Nigeria were all one-party systems that could have been put in various categories. Ghana's Convention Peoples Party qualified as a mobilization or mass typology, as did the *Front de Libération Nationale* in Algeria; the *Union Démocratique Voltaique* was considered a patron party.[34] Just as the military coup in the Central African Republic removed a one-party system that might not have fit unambiguously into the mass-patron category, so the Nigerian military revolt removed two one-party dominant regimes that gave some difficulty in classification. The Northern Peoples' Congress (NPC) was not the only party in northern Nigeria. In the 1961 regional election, the NPC won close to 70 per cent of the votes and 130 out of 170 seats in the regional assembly.[35] There were other contenders, among them the Action Group and an alliance between the Northern (now Nigerian) Element's Progressive Union and the National Convention of Nigerian Citizens (NCNC). In the 1964 federal election, the NPC won by an increased margin.[36]

As C. S. Whitaker described the NPC, it is a party which after 1952 passed to the control of persons loyal to and dependent on the emirate bureaucracies of northern Nigeria. Membership in the northern House of Assembly became part of the patronage system of emirs.[37] Yet, "clearly the NPC could not have remained dominant in an era of democratic elections of its support had been limited to a coalition of minority interests. The requisite mass support has been enlisted through appeals that make use of both associational and communal principles of participation on the one hand, and of both modern and traditional sentiments on the other."[38] In a complex situation, clients transfer their dependence on persons—their allegiance to individual, traditional patrons—to the modern party of their patrons.[39] Organizationally, the NPC party authority is decentralized, a fact which reflects the traditional status of emirates as virtually autonomous states.[40] Yet the NPC strives for a mass following and wants to push down to the village level. It is able to do this by using the administrative apparatus of traditional emirate units. The NPC has a set of constitutional arrangements that establish a National Working Committee, annual conventions, annual elections of party officers, and so forth. Many of these arrangements establish structures similar on paper to those of TANU, the PDG, and the CPP. There are also ancillary bodies for youth and women, and trade unions, as there are for so-called mass parties. The constitutional arrangements would not be much of a guide to the practice and operation of party organs, but neither would they have been for TANU or the CPP in the past. The NPC, then, partakes of features of both "mass" and "patron" parties; it is a traditionally oriented party with wide support.

The NCNC has been the dominant party in the eastern region of Nigeria. It has been described as having undergone a transformation since elections in 1951 from a national front of affiliated groups into a political party in a stricter sense.[41] It too would be put in the mass party category. While many authors have noted the dependence of the NCNC on affiliated organizations, and especially Ibo ethnic associations, one recent paper has gone so far as to argue that ethnic associations in one county council area performed many of the functions normally assumed by political parties because the monopoly of the NCNC rendered the party unsuitable as an organizational base through which to compete for scarce economic resources and political offices. The clan became the group through which participants in the political system acted, and the party emerged as a holding company for ethnic and clan organizations.[42]

As the military successfully intervened against political party rule, analysts again had to ask themselves what kinds of political animals these parties were. I have tried to suggest the complexity of the party situations and the variety of kinds of parties vulnerable to military intervention in this brief reference to the party types that the military replaced.

In order not to overhomogenize African politics, which is tempting to do when one is aware of significant economic constraints on the development of political structures, we need much more work on the operation of single parties at the grass roots and middle levels.[43] It is not really possible to say that the "staying power of single parties seems to be a function of the explicitness of an ideology, the degree of national isolation, and the degree to which the party concentrates on mobilizing and training middle cadres as agents of the center"[44] when we do not know how ideologies elaborated at the center are received, and when we do not know how middle-level elites function. Waller-stein maintained, "Today [1961–1965/] the party is an effective organism of power to some extent in some states, for example, Guinea, Mali, Tanzania and Tunisia, and irrelevant in many others."[45] But is party irrelevant when it does not quality for being mass or mobilizational or even single-party in the system?

All this is not to say that we should stop searching for crucial variables across systems and cease asking general questions. And of course we must try to keep refining our definitions of one-party system and try to assess the importance of the existence of one-party systems. We do want to know whether it matters if a system is *de jure* or *de factor* single party and we want to know whether it matters if a country has a one-party dominant system or is ruled by a party without any other party opposition. We want to know whether it does make a difference to the operation of a single party within a unit that it also operates within a larger unit where it contends with other parties. There are a number of such cases. Tanzania is a *de jure* one-party system but TANU operates in mainland Tanzania, and the Afro-Shirazi Party operates in Zanzibar. Similarly, when East and West Camerouns were linked, the smaller unit kept its separate single-party structure; this was true in Somalia too.[46] The one-party dominant regimes of Nigeria were also linked in a federal system. And in the Congo, at the end of 1963, some provinces had a dominant party.[47]

It is of more than passing interest whether or not a party becomes dominant through electoral manipulation, through bludgeoning its opponents with force and/or patronage power at its disposal, or whether it has direct and vast electoral support.[48] There is a rather vast literature on European and Amer-can parties that has addressed itself to the questions: Are one-party systems a different breed of animal from competing parties' systems? What is the importance for a party configuration of registration laws, electoral districting, and the various ramifications of elections in general? There has been much speculation in the discussion of African parties about the former question, but, on the latter one, there has been a tendency to dismiss elections because they appeared to be won rather overwhelmingly by the victors, were thought by observers to be obviously rigged and thus spurious, and sometimes data about them did not exist.

Africa gives us many different examples of the importance of elections, or their absence, in the politics of a country. There have been states where one-party systems were *de jure*: the FLN in Algeria, TANU in Tanzania, the CPP in Ghana, the *Mouvement National de la Révolution* in Congo-Brazzaville. There are some where no party organization exists to compete with the ruling party (Guinea and Mali, Ivory Coast, Niger, Liberia), and others where the one party dominates and has all seats in the legislature (Mauritania, Chad); there are still others where one-party dominance is almost complete in the parliament but where some opposition party seats exist (Malagasy Republic, Kenya, Uganda). There are various degrees of one-party dominance elec-torally, in terms of both final outcomes and percentage of votes. There have been multi-party systems where there is real bargaining in the legislature among parties (Uganda before mid-1965, Sierra Leone, and Somali Republic, for example). These lists are not exhaustive either as to category or membership within categories. I do not call attention to these as a set of party systems to be differentiated according to degree of one-party dominance. The Kenya African National Union (KANU) may dominate the legislature in Kenya, but it faces organized opposition that can turn out a vote against it. Even more to the point is the irrelevance or absence of legislative opposition in certain countries. A number of one-party systems are what Finer calls ". . . hastily cobbled-up "package" parties made up of the original competing factions"[49] as in Congo-Brazzaville up to 1963, Dahomey from time to time, Gabon, Togo on occasion, and some he does not mention—KANU at one point in Kenya, the Uganda Peoples' Congress (UPC) increasingly. If one pushes back into the pre-independence period some of the mass movements have a similar history.

Rather than point out the above for purposes of classification, I do so to suggest that the electoral process has been somewhat overlooked in the study of African politics. Once independence was achieved and a dominant party appeared to be ensconced, there was still much to be learned about the variety of one-party dominant regimes by examining electoral processes and not merely looking at the outcomes of elections as expressed in legislative majorities.[50] Although the presence or absence of minority parties may well be an important factor, we should not jump to the conclusion that systems can best be defined by this distinction.

We should be comparing political organizations with an open mind as to the importance of "one-partyness" for such things as electoral competition, amount and nature of coercion, kinds of rewards offered by parties, size and composition of the inner core of the organization, relationships between internal party hierarchies, formal structure, and ideology. Lest we fall into a new formalism, we should be careful not to make the initial assumption that the fact that only one political organization calls itself a party in a given country means a great deal for all the questions we can ask about the operation of that organization. It does mean, of course, that there is no challenging political party; but whether the ruling party can control village political organizations from some central power center, or implement economic plans made at the center, remain open questions.

Does this mean we are reduced to asking a set of ad hoc questions about political parties as they operate in society and thus must operate at a so-called low level of generality? I would not think so; we can frame propositions about the *operation* of political parties that would purport to hold true in all systems, or all African countries, or, for example, all countries with a certain ratio of subsistence to monetary sectors in their economies. I would focus on what I call subsystem variables that pertain to political parties. It might be asked, why choose electoral competition rather than size of administrative core at the party's headquarters? It has been precisely the difficulties posed by such questions that have thrown analysts back on very general formulations in the creation of typologies. But we are only going to be able to find out which particular factors are crucial for distinguishing among political parties by testing propositions relevant to the questions we ask. Our questions determine the kinds of propositions we should formulate. I am suggesting that, at this point, the most useful queries are those involving the operation of political organizations in and for the political system.

Political Machines

I have argued that the application of Soviet-derived models to African parties has not been very fruitful. This is not to say that all comparisons with communist systems are useless. In fact, the wide variety of communist one-party systems that could be subgrouped into various types—East European and Asian; large scale and small scale; indigenous and imposed; and around other possible unifying themes—have not been taken into account.[51] There are also American one-party systems that can be classified according to area: southern, New England, and Midwest; degrees of one-party dominance; rural or urban, and so forth.

There has been a wide-ranging literature on American political machines. Machines have been defined as parties that rely characteristically upon the attraction of material rewards rather than enthusiasm for political principles.[52] A great deal flows from this understanding of a particular type of political organization. The party machine's central function is not to frame or to discipline its members in the framing of the policies of government. Elections are important but this is so because they are elections for jobs, and winning them gives access to more jobs; internal division over policy questions is supposed to play little part in elections. To say that a party is not policy oriented does not mean that policy issues never arise, but rather that cleavages within the party are not over policy issues.[53] In analyses that stress material rewards as a goal of a political organization and its members, patronage and corruption are also emphasized. At the top of the hierarchy of the organization, "glory," "power" and being on the "inside" can be put forth as motivations for political activity; "honest graft" is a factor too. At lower levels, corruption is required until precinct captains can be induced to work from motives other than personal gain.[54] Such is Banfield's well-known description of the machine in its Chicago form.

None of the above, nor the emphasis on localism and self-interest in studies of machine politics, says anything about how democratic, representative, or noncoercive machines are. In fact, many descriptions of American political machines stress their toughness, their willingness to use coercion and to restrict popular participation at times.[55] Although I do not know the etymology of the word machine as applied to political organization, the term connotes a control mechanism: gears mesh; political units are cogs. In the American context, political machines are sometimes seen as maintaining an ongoing economic system by receiving economic benefits and distributing goods and services. Because the work on machines analyzes them as control mechanisms, they are often seen as status quo-oriented organizations. Studies that do mention the innovating functions that machines perform treat these as latent functions.[56] We need to show, not assume, what kinds of parties will be innovative and/or coercive under different circumstances.

The justification for bringing the notion of political machine to bear on the study of African politics must be found in the attempt to come to grips with intraparty relationships and not because "machine" implies an American model as a "good thing." For that matter, the inner cores of parties, including Leninist ones, are machines in that the permanent party bureaucracy operates in terms of material rewards. But since parties in the real world are concerned with both rewards and political principles, the need is to determine who is committed to what principles, and especially to find out what principles various levels of and groups within parties hold. Furthermore, we can compare parties to see what kinds of recompense they give to members for services rendered, and we can see what kinds of inner cores various parties have in terms of size and patterns of recruitment for paid officials. We could then call some political organizations "party-machines" if they met established criteria for size of cadres as a per cent of total membership and types of payment for various services. The point of this, however, is not to provide another label for political organizations but to focus on and understand the variety of organizations and organizational techniques manifest in African politics.

What we get from the literature on American machines is, above all, an understanding of the wide variety of organizations and organizational techniques, and a sense of the hereogeneity of groups that can find common interest.[57]

A few more points about political machines made in the American context are relevant here. Leadership has been a prominent topic in the discussion of American political machines, but analyses have been made which feature the boss, not the charismatic leader. Mayor Daley and bosses Hague, Crump, and Pendergast have received a great deal of ink and attention. But their personalities have not been emphasized in attributions of success. No one has suggested a non-secular basis for that success. Consider some nicknames. "Hinky Dink" Kenna, "Bathhouse" John Coughlin, "Big" Bill Thompson, "Good Jelly" Jones have names that are chummy not by accident. These nicknames express the bosses' accessibility, their personal contact with constituents—at least to begin with.[58] The names "The Redeemer" Nkrumah, "Mzee" Kenyatta (*the* Old Man), "Mwalimu" Nyerere (*the* Teacher) do not express service for a price, which was the essence of bossism.[59] The machine, as personalized and typified by the boss, fulfilled, in Merton's words, "the important social function of humanizing and personalizing all manner of assistance to those in need."[60] The machine played this role through its agents because the official government machinery was often remote and bound down by legalistic restraints. In other words, the machine was closer to the people than the bureaucracy. This was particularly true for immigrant groups, newly come to the big cities. In America, operating in a decentralized system, the boss was involved in the various levels of politics—city, county, state, and national—but his main concern was to maintain control over his own organization, his base of power, and to stay beyond the authority of higher echelons of power.[61] In Banfield's discussion of Chicago he says that "... a single actor—say the mayor of Chicago—can pursue a course of action only insofar as the formal decentralization is somehow overcome by informal centralization." The most important mechanism through which this is done is the political party or machine.[62] In their study *City Politics,* Banfield and Wilson see the machine as functioning to overcome a constitutional dispersion of authority typical of the separation of power.[63]

The machine was many things to ethnic communities. Bosses were often the most prominent members of minority groups. The largest payoffs to voters in American cities were symbolic and material; party tickets were ethnically balanced.[64] The machine was a channel for upward social mobility through politics as a vocation for those of the immigrant groups who had political aptitude. When the new ethnic groups carried traditions from their home country, they were often the traditions of personalized government action; influence was a direct personal relationship.[65] Another point emerges in the literature on ethnic politics in America. Robert Dahl shows how ethnic characteristics serve as a kind of comprehensive symbol for class and other criteria. Analysts have argued over how important ethnic considerations really are or ought to be but few have quarreled with Dahl's observation on New Haven, that politicians devised strategies on the assumption that whatever happened in elections could be adequately explained by shifts in ethnic voting blocks.[66] This kind of calculus has been evident in Africa too.

So far I have taken a number of points made about political machines in America out of a historical and social context in order to suggest that in thinking about leadership and ethnicity in Africa we might benefit from the work done on American politics. For reflection on politics to be useful in a comparative way, the things to be compared need not be held similar in time and place, although obviously we must be aware of what is indeed different about our situations. Thus, although nineteenth century America and mid-twentieth century Africa are very unlike with regard to social, economic, and demographic characteristics, because of a contemporary African concern with the relationship of political centers to peripheries, we might consider the matter of the locus of one-party systems and political machines in America.[67] In other words, we might ask questions about one-party systems that are not really statewide (in the South) or nationwide (in some African countries) to see what we might learn about the operation of factionalized and localized organizations under very different conditions. The aim would be to try to find out if intraparty relationships are independent variables.

But even on a descriptive level, accounts of American political machines bear many more resemblances to politics in Africa than descriptions of one-party systems made in terms of what I have called the mass-party-derived terminologies and typologies. On the descriptive level, students concerned with adaptation of governing African single parties to the problems of rule in their societies and those who have described the internal dynamics of individual parties in fact have been telling us a story about bosses, corruption, honest graft, local satraps, the politics of ethnicity, decentralization of authority, and rural- as well as urban-based machines.

In my own study of Tanzania, I argued that "TANU itself is a congeries of regional, district, and subdistrict organizations which communicate with each other and with Dar es Salaam only intermittently."[68] René Lemarchand says that the outstanding characteristic of all Congolese parties, whether mass or elite, was decentralization of the organization[69]—and this in what were often one-party provinces.

Zolberg has written a revisionist history of national movements and political parties on West Africa, arguing that the parties of Ghana, Guinea, Senegal, Mali, and the Ivory Coast did not need to be highly centralized and monolithic to achieve national independence under their banner and that, on the contrary, they reflected the pluralisms and lack of integration of their societies both before and after independence.[70] While African leaders have been described as charismatic leaders, we have also had implicit, or in some cases explicit, pictures of political bosses. Such was Zolberg's portrait of Houphouet-Boigny.[71] Henry Bretton's not very flattering account of Nkrumah as a political man also stressed his boss-like characteristics.[72] Concerning ethnic politics, we need hardly mention books; few studies of African politics do not treat political struggle and social change in terms of the movement of ethnic groups, the formation of ethnic associations in new urban areas, and ethnic conflict. Students of corruption in Africa have been many. Some have moralized about corruption,[73] while others have put forward a cost-benefit framework for analysis[74] and have broadly examined the function of corruption, especially having in mind the political machine as an interest group.[75] We also have overviews of political machines in Africa that look at the rural and urban components. Some of these explicitly use the words "political machine" to describe what they are dealing with. But others who have used a different language have nonetheless provided a picture of the machine in action.[76]

Bretton titles two chapters in his recent book on Nkrumah, "Building the Political Machine,." He says Nkrumah established himself as a political boss through a process of coercion, intimidation, and cooptation. He downplays the CPP itself ("The party possessed no independent power") and argues that Nkrumah had a personal political machine.[77] While the personal machine was entrenched, the CPP was still being extolled as the vanguard of the people, but the party *qua* party ". . . had been stripped of all power, potentialities, and initiative as thoroughly as the rest of the state aparatus."[78] Apter, too, has stressed the personal role of Nkrumah, but he has seen a charismatic leader who tried, and failed, to change the basis of public behavior by creating a new system of motivation. Apter has recently reaffirmed his view that the term charisma can be applied to Nkrumah, particularly during the years 1949–1954 and that charismatic leadership was important during a period of institutional transfer.[79] Apter also agrees that the CPP became an empty shell and that Nkrumah failed to create the new society he promised. But for Apter, the promise was important—in that it was an attempt to change the pattern of normative life and individual behavior. Nkrumah failed to restructure roles. He could not mobilize effectively. According to Apter, his failure was a structural one—that is, he could not build a political organization. But Apter, properly I think, stresses that the CPP, although never effective as such, kept changing, in both its role and its structure. "It lacked effective middle leadership, but its consequences, if only in negative terms, were for the people immense." Apter now emphasizes the orientational consequences of creating the first populist national body, rather than the organizational context of the CPP *per se*. It remains to be demonstrated that the CPP has had this effect on Ghanaian society, but it is possible for it to have had such an effect without being well organized. We might note that American political machines, through their socializing activities, also changed patterns of behavior without necessarily being self-conscious or ideologically elaborate about this, and without operating as a strongly centralized national political organization or having charismatic leaders.

Bretton describes Nkrumah's rule as the acquisition of personal wealth. He does not stress the functionality of this for political organization building nor does he make Greenstone's argument that corruption can offset a decline in political capacity that sets in after independence in African states, although Bretton sees the political machine as a principal beneficiary of "private regarding interest." Bretton's notion of the political machine is very close to that of critics of American machines, in that in both cases the machine is seen as being against, not for, mass mobilization, since mass mobilization is construed as inevitably leading to rival centers of power. Thus machines restrict suffrage and social participation in general, except insofar as those phenomena are conducive to the machines' maintenance in power. It is generally understood that the machine exists to maintain itself, although it may perform action leading to other ends (the public good, economic development, and so forth) in the process. Bretton's descriptions of the use of the instruments of coercion also bear strong resemblances to descriptions of American machine coercion, although Bretton's comparisons are to Hitler's SS rather than to Boss Hague's thugs.[80]

A somewhat ambiguous portrayal of a political machine in Uganda has been made by Colin Leys. He describes the Uganda People's Congress as ". . . a coalition of local organizations, or rather local political systems, each with its own political elite, including a small number of leaders operating at the national level." This party, which became increasingly dominant between 1962 and 1965 is seen by Leys as being not ineffective, although the UPC was stronger generally at the local level than it was at the center.[81] Many of the national leaders, including the Prime Minister-become-President Obote, remained heavily dependent on their local political bases. Leys looks at politics in one Uganda district, Acholi, where the UPC dominated and ran a closed spoils system. He shows how UPC leaders, both at the center and in Acholi, felt that *party* interest operated as a hidden hand that would facilitate good national outcomes—growth, development, unity. "The test to be applied to a parochial demand was where it fitted into the politics of securing party unity and party dominance. In other words, the significant moral boundary during these years (1962–1965) was between parties, rather than between the localities and the center."[82] Leys is not certain how many top UPC leaders had a clear objective of establishing a single-party regime, as opposed to reducing their political opponents to impotence. In any case, he says, the politics of party advantage were pursued so keenly that the rules of the game were rewritten in the process. Policy issues were systematically exploited for party purposes, "and party considerations were allowed to permeate into the fabric of rural life at almost every point.[83] The outcome of this spoils system was crisis at national and local levels as the opponents could not continue to play by the rules of the game.

Whether this kind of system is functional for economic growth and/or national integration is an important question, of course. Leys himself is ambivalent and sees pluses and minuses. People are brought into contact with "modern" patterns of life via spoils systems improvements, that is, pork barrel projects. The party hierarchy establishes a novel and influential channel of communication between district and national elites. Yet the UPC remains a coalition of local interests, rather than a unitary structure, "and the vitality of national party organization. . . . The skills demanded of politicians in operating such a system were, moreover, integrative in a sense calculated to create a nation of competing sub-systems rather than an integrated national system."[84]

Zolberg, too, has been ambivalent about the machine, a term he applied to the *Parti Démocratique de la Côte d'Ivoire*. While this political organization was shown to be successful in getting control of the government and bringing the country to independence its contribution to modernization was said to be more ambiguous.[85] "For the time being, the party remains essentially a political machine, capable of neutralizing many threats to its maintenance, capable of absorbing change, but not yet capable of constructing a new society."[86] Specifically, Zolberg shows how the PDCI reinforced ethnic cleavages as it tried to maintain itself. Zolberg was more positive about political machines in his later study of party-states in West Africa. He contends that the successes achieved by party-states stem from the retention of characteristics that can be described as those of a political machine—along with the persistence of bureaucratic institutions inherited from the colonial period.[87] His party-state emerges as a system where bureaucratic and patrimonial features coexist.[88] "The machine is particularly suited to govern small political communities in transition, and provides both flexibility and stability. . . . While retaining a great deal of flexibility, the machine can sustain a powerful central authority which will cope with certain community-wide problems if the boss is an enlightened one . . . a machine can coexist with a variety of economic arrangements. . . . Although it tends to redistribute income to the benefit of its own members, this membership basis tends to be broader than it would be in more hierarchical systems."[89]

Yet we must confront real questions that can be raised in a discussion of the utility of political machines, even if we agree that the one-party systems in

Africa contain party-machines at their political core and can be defined in terms of the characteristics of these machines as they operate in society. One problem has to do with the decentralized nature of the political organizations. Among students of American parties, E. E. Schattschneider took the view that the parties were loose confederations of state and local machines organized for limited purposes. Since the state and local parties' bosses want patronage, and that is nearly all they want, they accentuate decentralization.[90]

Decentralization has usually been anathema in literature on political development in Africa, which has stressed the need for the centralization of authority for national integration. More recently, counterarguments have been made. W. Arthur Lewis has attacked claims that the single party is the appropriate vehicle for resolving regional differences by arguing that the one-party system cannot deal with the pluralisms inherent in African societies. He has stated that both strong centers and strong provincial governments are required and that federalism, broadly conceived as a reasonable degree of provincial devolution, is necessary in Africa.[91] Lewis has said that increases in taxes collected in Nigeria stemmed from decentralization, and this is an answer to the people who claim that only highly centralized authoritarian governments can collect taxes.[92] Herbert Werlin has applied to the analyses of administration in Africa a federalist model (garnered from Sayre and Kaufman)[93] in which "elasticity of control" operates. Werlin's model is one in which governmental units at different levels work in harmony; he stresses informal arrangements and lack of coercion. The central government's full authority is brought to bear only when absolutely needed. Power should be "persuasive rather than coercive." But in Africa power is inelastic, and political control does not increase or decrease in reaction to need.[94]

I have argued that highly localized determination of political life need not be synonymous with disorder, anarchy and chaos. In fact, it may be the only way to avoid these conditions in African circumstances. This localized determination may go hand in hand with the vigorous self-interest of elites and even with corruption.[95] Werlin is right when he says that the proper question in Africa is: How can there be more centralization as well as decentralization at the same time? Power here should not be conceived as existing in a zero sum game. The only way to build strong central institutions in Africa is to create local building blocks. (We should also note that local and central do not have an absolute meaning and that in general many national political units in Africa bear functional resemblances in terms of size, of politically involved population, budgets, government personnel, and governmental capacity to counties or groups of counties in America.)[96] But local, as I suggested earlier, might not mean villages, but rather districts, or groupings of villages, or regions in different contexts.

> Because the resources in the hands of central elites are few, the elites have a hard time centralizing authority over their own local party organizations. This holds true whether African leaders opt for the American machine model for their parties or for the model of the Communist party of the Soviet Union. So far, they

have often equated modernity and political development with the construction of disciplined central organizations, first the ruling single-party and now the military. But the gap between image and reality cannot be closed by façades. And in African conditions there is no way of forcing central authority on the countryside.[97]

However, the low level of political capacity at the center must be offset by a modified and politicized version of the invisible hand working at the local level. The nation can be built in Africa through a congeries of regional, district, and subdistrict organizations that communicate with each other and the center. Each knows the others are there, but the organizations exist with full lives of their own. Political competition and decentralization are not, *per se,* inimical to development. In fact, if political development in Africa means creating effective political institutions, these are going to be political machines that are competitive and decentralized, whether within a one-party or multi-party framework.[98]

Conclusions

I have argued that typologies and definitions of African one-party systems derived from a literature that originally dealt with communist parties have been misleading. Research done on individual African one-party systems as well as multi-party systems shows us political organizations operating in terms familiar to students of American machine politics. I have suggested further that the machine may well be necessary in Africa. In passing, I have argued that where parties do exist the no-party state appellation cannot be applied, although there may be much wearing of two hats, government and party, by politicians, and the civil service may carry out important functions. The party still can be the most popular institution and the most concrete expression of the nation.[99] It may be the only expression of government's authority in certain rural areas.[100] The party may be functionally diffuse and still struggling to identify its own mission, but at the same time its search for purpose and definition is linked to a national search for identity and definition. Even where a party may disappear it may have crucially affected the normative life of the nation; perhaps this is the case in Ghana now.

African single parties have had an organizational autonomy which has been derived more from parties' identification with a set of values, a group of leaders, a national history than on any administrative insulation of the party from state agencies or any isolation of the party from the encroachment of functionally linked organizations such as trade unions and youth groups. Moreover, single parties have been distinctive channels for recruitment in Africa, even where some traditional leaders and some civil servants have been selected for posts precisely because of traditional status and administrative expertise. The point here is that party leaders have a choice among the civil servants and traditional leaders that they pick, rather than having some chiefly or administrative hierarchy make choices for them. Nor should we forget that it is still a party organ that makes recruitment choices, although these choices may be taking place at a local level for both local posts and for national ones.[101]

If it is true that African one-party systems are decentralized political machines, it is also true that the machines may become so loose and decentralized as to no longer constitute a single party. The political organizations are not bound to become more centralized. A question arises that can be raised for all African one-party systems: How do you maintain cohesiveness where there is no party competition around which to enforce consensus and where central elites cannot enforce consensus by coercive means? One answer is that national elites must bargain with middle-level and local ones, using what patronage and moral suasion they have, and applying coercion selectively. This can all go on through a network of informal political arrangements. Another answer is that if it is difficult to maintain cohesion where there are no electoral challenges unless coercion is used internally in the party and by the party vis-à-vis other political groups, elections may have a crucial place within one-party systems. Competition for posts within the party might fragment the organization. On the other hand, such elections give the party a chance to define itself within the society and to assert party criteria in the recruitment process. Moreover, internal elections can provide a chance to discuss issues and to stress what Schattschneider has called the public personality of the party. This presupposes a party sufficiently disciplined to hold a certain line around issues during the election. In the presence or absence of meaningful elections, one-party dominance will depend on certain other features, which have not received enough attention: size of constituency in numbers and land area, structure of the economy, level of the economy and economic growth rates, rate of social mobility into various levels of party leadership. Thus, although I have attempted to explore the meaning of one-party systems in Africa by focusing on what I called subsystem variables that pertain to parties, and have tried to use the concept of political machine toward this end, I am aware that an understanding of the meaning of one-party systems depends on delineating factors for social systems as a whole also.

Notes

I am grateful to the Center of International Studies, Princeton University, for research support and aid in preparation of this essay and to Professor Clement Moore who made helpful criticisms of this essay.

1. See David E. Apter, *The Politics of Modernization* (Chicago: University of Chicago Press, 1966) and *The Political Kingdom in Uganda* (Princeton: Princeton University Press, 1961), pp. 22–24.

2. James S. Coleman and Carl Rosberg, Jr., *Political Parties and National Integration in Tropical Africa* (Berkeley: University of California Press, 1966), p. 5.

3. Ruth Schachter Morgenthau, "Single-Party Systems in West Africa," *American Political Science Reciew* 55 (June 1961): 244–307; and *Political Parties in French Speaking West Africa* (Oxford: Clarendon Press, 1964), esp. pp. 330–358.

4. See Apter, *The Political Kingdom in Uganda,* and Philip Selznick, *The Organizational Weapon: A Study of Bolshevik Strategy and Tactics* (New York: The Free Press, 1960).

5. Robert C. Tucker, "On Revolutionary Mass-Movement Regimes," in Robert C. Tucker, *The Soviet Political Mind* (New York: Frederick A. Praeger, 1963), pp. 3–19.

6. Henry Bretton, "Current Political Thought and Practice in Ghana," *American Political Science Review* 52 (March 1958): 49–50, 57.

7. There have been no attempts I know of to take a close look at the lessons of Soviet political history, say from 1917–1933, in terms of the interactions of party with economy and the transformation of the CPSU as it undertook economic tasks in order to formulate propositions applicable to a wider universe.

8. Even before a recent revisionist literature on the Soviet Union, some authors had insisted that factions had persisted in Soviet politics even after Stalin's ascendancy. See especially, Franz Borkenau, "Getting at the Facts Behind the Soviet Facade," *Commentary* 17, No. 4 (April 1954): 393–400, where Borkenau describes a political patronage system or *sheftsvo.* Boris Nicolaevsky was another analyst who stressed that Soviet elite politics was a continuous struggle. In the 1960s, a "conflict" school has developed in the study of Soviet politics, as analysts now describe not only struggles at the top of the hierarchy but the clash of interest groups. Cf. Robert C. Tucker, "The Conflict Mode," *Problems of Communism* 12 (November–December 1963): 49–51; Sidney Ploss, *Conflict and Decision-Making in Soviet Russia* (Princeton: Princeton University Press, 1965); Carl A. Linden, *Khrushchev and the Soviet Leadership, 1957–1964* (Baltimore: Johns Hopkins Press, 1966).

9. Aristide Zolberg, *Creating Political Order: The Party States of West Africa* (Chicago: University of Chicago Press, 1966), p. 35.

10. Zolberg, *op. cit.,* and Zolberg's *One-Party Government in the Ivory Coast* (Princeton: Princeton University Press, 1964); Dennis Austin, *Politics in Ghana* (London: Oxford University Press, 1964).

11. Morgenthau, "Single-Party Systems in West Africa," pp. 295–296.

12. Morgenthau, *Political Parties in French Speaking West Africa,* p. 333.

13. *Ibid.,* pp. 351, 354.

14. Henry Bienen, *Tanzania: Party Transformation and Economic Development* (Princeton: Princeton University Press, 1970), pp. 3–19; Bienen, "What Does Political Development Mean in Africa," *World Politics* 20 (October 1967): 128–141; and see Chapter 2 of this book.

15. Coleman and Rosberg, *op. cit.,* p. 5.

16. *Ibid.,* pp. 5–6.

17. See Apter, *The Political Kingdom in Uganda.*

18. See Bienen, *Tanzania,* pp. 3–4.

19. David Apter, "Nkrumah, Charisma, and the Coup," *Daedalus* (Summer 1968), pp. 757–792.

20. Morgenthau, *Political Parties in French Speaking West Africa,* pp. 341–48. Zolberg, both in *One Party Government in the Ivory Coast* and *Creating Political Order* stressed that ethnic tensions were often exacerbated as political awareness rose. Crawford Young saw this too in *Politics in the Congo* (Princeton: Princeton University Press, 1965).

21. There are vivid illustrations of this in Young's work with regard to the MNC, Lumumba and Zolberg's work on the *Union Soudanaise* in Mali and the *Parti Démocratique de la Côte d'Ivoire* in the Ivory Coast.

22. Morgenthau, *Political Parties in French Speaking West Africa.*

23. Apter, *The Politics of Modernization,* p. 40.

24. David Apter, *Ghana In Transition* (New York: Atheneum, 1963).

25. It is true that Morgenthau saw some, but not all, mass-party top-level leaders—Sekou Touré in Guinea and Mamadou Konate in Mali (then the Soudan)—as enjoying a type of charisma, one limited by constitutional procedure and the power exercised by groups and

individuals within their parties. She also said that certain leaders of patron parties—Fily Dabo Sissoko in the Soudan and Sourou Migan Apithy in Dahomey—had a charisma comparatively unchecked by procedure though limited by the power of other patrons. Few other applied the concept of charisma to leaders of patron parties, and what the term means in Morgenthau aside from extraordinary qualities ascribed to a leader is unclear to me. See Morgenthau, *Political Parties in French Speaking West Africa*, pp. 339–340. Patron parties and parties of personality were terms employed by Thomas Hodgkin, in *Nationalism in Colonial Africa* (New York: New York University Press, 1957), and *African Political Parties* (London: Penguin, 1961), as Morgenthau points out, *Political Parties in French Speaking West Africa*, p. 336ff. Hodgkin also used the term "elite" parties for patron parties in *African Political Parties*, pp. 68–69.

26.   Both Hodgkin and Morgenthau acknowledged their debts to Maurice Duverger's *Political Parties* (London: Methuen, 1954).

27.   Morgenthau, *Political Parties in French Speaking West Africa*, p. 339.

28.   John A. Ballard, "Four Equatorial States," in Gwendolen Carter, ed. *National Unity and Regionalism in Eight African States* (Ithaca: Cornell University Press, 1966), pp. 261–279. Ballard says at one point that "MESAN was an entirely personal organization with each of its local agents responsible directly to Boganda (the leader until his death in 1959) himself" (p. 263). He also describes MESAN as a popular mass movement with direct ties between leader and members.

29.   Of course, the looser the definition of charisma, the easier to apply it anywhere and everywhere. But since one component of charisma was that the leader had wide popularity, patron party leaders were probably excluded on the grounds of limited appeal. Morgenthau allowed Lamine Kaba of the Kankan region of Guinea to be called charismatic although he "enjoyed charisma only within a locality considerably smaller than a territory" (*Political Parties in French Speaking West Africa*, p. 340).

30.   Zolberg points out in *Creating Political Order*, p. 138, that Houphouet-Boigny, who does not possess this style, is believed by many of his countrymen to be among the elect, specially designated to rule over them.

31.   There was a conference on leadership sponsored by *Daedalus* and the Institute of War and Peace Studies, Columbia University, held at the Sterling Forest Conference Center, Tuxedo, New York, October 19–21, 1967. The concept of charisma was discussed in a number of papers. Ann Ruth Willner has an interesting monograph, *Charismatic Political Leadership* (Princeton: Princeton University Center of International Studies, 1968).

32.   For a discussion of coups in Africa see Aristide Zolberg, "Military Intervention in the New States of Tropical Africa: Elements of Comparative Analysis," in Henry Bienen, ed., *The Military Intervenes: Case Studies in Political Change* (New York: Russel Sage Foundation, 1968).

33.   See Chapter 7 of this book.

34.   Morgenthau, *Political Parties in French Speaking West Africa*, p. 320.

35.   Richard L. Sklar and C. S. Whitaker, Jr., "Nigeria" in Coleman and Rosberg, *op. cit.*, p. 654.

36.   C. S. Whitaker, Jr., "A Dysrhythmic Process of Political Change," *World Politics*, XIX (January 1967), p. 209.

37.   *Ibid.*, pp. 9–20.

38.   Sklar and Whitaker, *op. cit.*, p. 622. Only people of northern Nigeria origin may be members of the NPC.

39.   *Ibid.*

40.   *Ibid.*, p. 625.

41.   *Ibid.*, p. 601.

42.   Audrey R. Chapman, "Ethnic Unions and the NCNC in Mbaise, Eastern Nigeria" (Paper delivered to the African Studies Association, Tenth Annual Meeting, November 1–4, 1967, New York City).

43. Work such as carried out by Nicholas S. Hopkins on Mali. See his *Popular Government in an African Town* (Chicago: University of Chicago Press, 1972). Also see Colin Leys, *Politicians and Policies* (Nairobi: East African Publishing House, 1967).

44. Wallerstein, *op. cit.,* p. 214.

45. *Ibid.* The *Union Soudanaise* had its political bureau, dissolved in August, 1967, and President Keita of Mali assigned full powers over the party and government to the *Comite National de Défense de la Révolution.* Subsequently the military took over.

46. *Ibid.,* p. 206.

47. *Ibid.,* citing Crawford Young, "The Congo Provinces Become Twenty-One," *Africa Report* (October 1963).

48. S. E. Finer, "The One-Party Regimes in Africa," *Government and Opposition,* II (July–October 1967), pp. 491–492.

49. *Ibid.,* p. 495.

50. The 1965 Tanzanian election has been a rather obviously fertile field for ploughing as Lionel Cliffe has shown in his edited work, *One Party Democracy* (Nairobi: East African Publishing House, 1967). There are interesting uses of election data in Zolberg, *Creating Political Order;* Austin, *op. cit.;* Herbert Weiss, *Political Protest in the Congo* (Princeton: Princeton University Press, 1967); and Sklar and Whitaker, *op. cit.*

51. I have already said the political history of the CPSU could be of great interest if applied in comparative studies. The revisionist studies of communist parties which are calling into question the totalitarian model should be useful too.

52. Edward C. Banfield, *Political Influence* (New York: The Free Press, 1961), p. 237.

53. Bienen, *Tanzania,* p. 88.

54. Banfield, *op. cit.,* p. 257.

55. See Dayton McKean's *The Boss: The Hague Machine in Action* (Boston: Houghton Mifflin, 1940).

56. Robert K. Merton, "The Latent Function of the Machine," from *Social Theory and Social Structure* (New York: The Free Press, 1957), pp. 71–81.

57. See V. O. Key, *Southern Politics* (New York: Alfred A. Knopf, 1949). Key has said of Boss Crump's Tennessee organization that ". . . his state organization was held together largely by prerequisities for office, the desires for office, the disciplinary tools inherent in the control of government and party machinery, and the capacity to trade with East Tennessee Democrats— and Republicans" (pp. 67–68). Key points to the internal controls the machine wields and its bargaining abilities, that is, organizational power and tactical flexibility. The bludgeoning and rewarding of local leaders is emphasized. In his discussion of the Byrd machine in Virginia, Key describes the machine as a system for recruitment and advancement of political leaders. It is not merely skilled management that produced a well-disciplined oligarchy, but selections through a process of cooptation and indoctrination (pp. 25–26). Through this process, the Byrd machine monopolized political talent, allowing loyal organization men to compete for the support of local leaders for state wide office (p. 23). In his description of Texas machines, Key notes how small-time bosses or *jefes* relied on traditional techniques in dealing with immigrant groups: counsel in solving personal problems; aid in economic distress; patronage; assistance before governing authorities. Key wrote that in Arkansas there were men of prominence who controlled votes and swung them not for money but for the "best man" (p. 196). Huey Long used outright thuggery sometimes, along with the means noted above, and had the loyalty of the masses, whom he reached via new channels of communication (p. 162).

58. As noted by Duane Lockard, *The Politics of State and Local Government* (New York: Macmillan, 1963), p. 219.

59. *Ibid.,* p. 200.

60. Merton, *op. cit.*

61. Lockard, *op. cit.,* pp. 223–224.

62.   Banfield, *op. cit.*, p. 237.

63.   Edward Banfield and James Q. Wilson, *City Politics* (Cambridge: Harvard University Press, 1963), p. 126.

64.   J. David Greenstone, "Corruption and Self-Interest in Kampala and Nairobi," *Comparative Studies in Society and History,* VII (January 1966), p. 207.

65.   Nathan Glazer and Daniel Patrick Moynihan, *Beyond the Melting Pot* (Cambridge: MIT Press, 1963), p. 224.

66.   Robert A. Dahl, *Who Governs?* (New Haven: Yale University Press, 1966), p. 53.

67.   Similarly, we might compare the interactions of party and economy in the USSR with patterns or interaction in very different contexts in Africa.

68.   Bienen, *Tanzania,* p. 413.

69.   Rene Lemarchand, "Congo (Leopoldville)," in Coleman and Rosberg, *op. cit.,* p. 588.

70.   Zolberg, *Creating Political Order.*

71.   Zolberg, *One Party Government in the Ivory Coast.*

72.   Henry Bretton, *The Rise and Fall of Kwame Nkrumah* (New York: Frederick A. Praeger, 1966).

73.   Ronald Wraith and Edgar Simpkins, *Corruption in Developing Countries* (London: Allen and Unwin, 1963).

74.   J. S. Nye, "Corruption and Political Development: A Cost-Benefit Analysis," *American Political Science Review*, 66 (June 1967), pp. 417–427.

75.   Colin Leys, "What is the Problem About Corruption," *The Journal of Modern African Studies* 3 (1965), pp. 215–230; Greenstone, *op. cit.*

76.   David Apter made interesting fusions of terminology and analysis when he referred to the CPP as ". . . a Tammany-type machine with a neutralist ideology." Yet organizationally, Apter saw the CPP as a composite of the British Labour Party and a communist party as Zolberg points out in *Creating Political Order,* p. 22. See Apter's *Gold Coast in Transition,* p. 202.

77.   Bretton, *The Rise and Fall of Kwame Nkrumah,* p. 46.

78.   *Ibid.,* p. 61.

79.   Apter's early ideas on Ghana were published in *The Gold Coast in Transition*; he then updated his study in *Ghana in Transition.*

80.   Bretton, *The Rise and Fall of Kwame Nkrumah.*

81.   Leys, *Politicians and Policies,* pp. 10–11.

82.   *Ibid.,* p. 101.

83.   *Ibid.*

84.   *Ibid.,* p. 104.

85.   Zolberg, *One Party Government in the Ivory Coast,* p. 319.

86.   *Ibid.,* p. 320.

87.   Zolberg, *Creating Political Order,* p. 159.

88.   *Ibid.,* p. 141.

89.   *Ibid.,* pp. 160–161.

90.   E. E. Schattschneider, *Party Government* (New York: Rinehart, 1958), pp. 129–169.

91.   W. Arthur Lewis, *Political In West Africa* (New York: Oxford University Press, 1965).

92.   W. Arthur Lewis, "Random Reflections on Local Development in Africa with Special Reference to West Africa," in *Local Development in Africa* (Summary Report of a Conference Jointly Sponsored by The Foreign Service Institute of the Department of State, The African Subcommittee of the Foreign Area Research Coordination Group, and the Agency for International Development, Washington, 1967), pp. 30–35.

93.   See Wallace S. Sayre and Herbert Kaufnan, *Governing New York City* (New York: Russell Sage Foundation, 1965), p. 584.

94.   Herbert Werlin, "Elasticity of Control: An Analysis of Decentralization" (Conference on African Local Institutions and Rural Transformation, Institute of African Government, Department of Political Science, Lincoln University, 1967). See also Werlin's "The Nairobi City Council: A Study in Comparative Local Government," *Comparative Studies in Society and History,* VIII (January 1966), pp. 183–186.

95.   Bienen, "What Does Political Development Mean in Africa," p. 140.

96.   Aristide Zolberg, "Political Development in Tropical Africa: Center and Peripheries," in *Local Development in Africa,* pp. 14–15.

97.   Bienen, "What Does Political Development Mean in Africa?" p. 140.

98.   *Ibid.,* p. 141.

99.   As Zolberg has argued for West African party-states, pp. 123, 126, and I have argued in *Tanzania.*

100.   Bienen, *Tanzania.*

101.   As, for example, when members of parliament are selected in district polls in Tanzania or regional TANU conferences select members of the National Executive Committee.

Chapter 4

Political Parties and
Political Machines in Africa

I have suggested that our thinking about one-party systems in Africa could benefit from analyses of American party machines, and especially those that have existed in one-party states.[1] My argument was not that American political machines constitute a model for African one-party systems. Rather, I said simply that politics as described in accounts of American party machines bears many more resemblances to politics in Africa than do descriptions of African one-party systems made within frameworks which single out ideology, formal party structure, and charismatic leadership as crucial variables. These frameworks or typologies which have proliferated in the study of new states, and African ones in particular, have meant to distinguish between parties which are concerned with national integration and far-reaching social change on the one hand and those which are status quo and based on a narrow class or ethnic grouping on the other. They are meant to distinguish between elite and mass political organizations; revolutionary and evolutionary ones; ideological and pragmatic ones.[2] While parties have been the defining political organizations for the typological characterizations, military and/or civil service regimes could be, in principle, similarly differentiated.

One reason that descriptions of American machine politics—which emphasize secular leadership, patronage, struggle of groups within the party and within society, self-interest, and localized politics—may sound familiar to students of African parties once they are studied on the ground is that politics shows these features when political organizations are examined at a certain level of analysis. With this in mind, the concept of political machines as it defines parties which rely characteristically upon the attraction of material rewards, rather than enthusiasm for political principles,[3] is a very limited one. To say this is not to say that there is any excuse for describing politics, whether it be the politics of "totalitarian systems" or African one-party states, or military regimes, as if patronage and struggle of self-interested groups did not exist. Soviet studies, for example, have long suffered from a relative neglect of these aspects of politics, in part because many of the characterizations of the system by its rulers were accepted, in part because it was not possible to have the close access to politics through firsthand research which would reveal otherwise. Above all, the idea was influential that a particular political elite in a totalitarian system was powerful enough to abolish personal and group struggle over parochial interests, through the wielding of organizational weapons and by terror, propaganda, and agitation. Recent studies have begun to disabuse us of this idea and, in the process, to make us refine, perhaps abandon, our past understandings and definitions of totalitarian systems.

Students of African one-party systems have rarely claimed that the parties they were looking at were so powerful that they could abrogate interest group politics; nor did they argue that the ruling parties were internally centralized because the inner party cores were so powerful that they could brook no dissension. Nonetheless, typologies were elaborated which did pose organizational weapons, mobilizational parties, and mass movement regimes which were engaged in a process of directed social change made possible by certain structural characteristics of the party, that is, centralized, hierarchical arrangements and institutionalized leaderships. Perhaps most important of all, the parties that defined the systems as mobilizational or revolutionary-centralizing were said to monopolize legitimacy, and within the party a single leader was seen to concentrate legitimacy in his own hands. This concern that analysts had for legitimacy is not surprising given that the states were newly independent, often not thought to be nations, that is, socially and ethnically unintegrated and with an elite that had emerged in a very short time-span and assumed power.

The focus on legitimacy led to seeing the ideology of parties and leaders as a distinguishing variable of systems. And the ideologies elaborated by leaders postulated a harmony of interest, an absence of class struggle in the social realm. While African leaders could not say that the nation was ethnically or tribally homogeneous, some denied that heterogeneity of their countries had, or should have, political import. The political community could remain monolithic as the single party gathered all under its wing. Opposition was seen in highly personal terms as, for example, when Sékou Touré asked his opponents to surmount their "self-love, complexes, rancor, selfishness and jealousy."[4] The individualism of Nyerere was the collective individualism of a certain strain of Rousseau and the French Revolution where individuals ought not to disagree about the essentials *of* a good society *in* a good society. Thus the diversity of individuals that Nyerere accepted could have no organized political expression. Not only an antiparty ethic exists in Nyerere's writings but an antipolitical ethic as well. His *Democracy and Party System* expresses a desire to abolish politics from society insofar as politics means conflict.[5]

Observers of the African scene did not jump to the conclusion that there was no conflict, anymore than the leaders who postulated conflict-free societies were unaware of dissension and disagreement, although both observers and leaders were engaged in a certain amount of wishful thinking and incantation. They hoped by invoking unity to create it. My point here is that the attention of students of African one-party states was on the formula for unity, ideology, and one-party structure rather than on political conflict. Where this conflict was overt, and particularly violent and ethnic, it was indeed considered. In fact, the tendency in such cases was to ignore party structures and ideology and presume they were not important, in, for example, Congo or Rwanda.[6] Conflict was seen as being tribal or regional and the more mundane struggles centering around internal party competition, electoral battles for office, and group economic self-interest were neglected. But where public order did not break down, there was an assumed connection between one-party rule and the maintenance of that order.

Similarly, it was believed that military coups tended not to displace the single mass-party authoritarian regimes.[7] However, as Samuel Finer has pointed out, between 1960 and 1966 in Africa (including Africa north of the Sahara) military interventions took place in eight of fifteen multiparty states and nine of twenty single-party states. Six single-party states had their governments overturned by violence between 1960 and 1967.[8] There were, of course, plots and civil disturbances that occurred while states were in a single-party condition. The problem is that, insofar as "single mass-party authoritarian regime" implied a monolithic party whose control extended out into all areas of the countryside enabling it to mobilize political and economic resources from a central core, such regimes did not exist.[9]

It has been said elsewhere that we might have known this deductively—that is, by inferring political consequences from economic or, more broadly, ecological conditions.[10] But the reasons these deductions were not made are of some interest, the more so because the failure to carry out certain kinds of research in the rural areas is related to this failure of deduction.

The salient political structures were national ones in independent Africa. The shift from observing colonial ruling institutions was natural enough. Furthermore, individual national leaders often personified their countries to observers. The parties which led the national independence struggle were perceived and heard, literally, through discussions with leaders. The impact of the parties was felt through the parties' presence in the capital cities and major towns and through the forcefulness of leaders. And there seemed to be few competing institutions or groups at the national level. The exception was the civil service as a potential counterweight to parties. But civil services were still not completely Africanized immediately after independence; civil servants were indispensable but they were in the shadows. It was party leaders who dominated independence celebrations, made speeches, and published articles establishing the party's ideology. Militaries were small, had little firepower, and usually remained officered by expatriates for some years after independence. Perhaps most importantly, at the national level indigenous economic interest groups were not manifest. Industry was in the hands of government or expatriates or minority "Asian" groups. The African interest groups that existed were not those of big businessmen or merchants or organized artisan associations, but rather trade unions and cooperatives. And these were seen as being linked to parties—transmission belts for them or integral parts of the party.

This was not entirely wrong, but neither was it very accurate. The few histories of trade unions and cooperative movements showed a sometimes uneasy relationship between them and parties or national movements prior to independence and it might have been expected that when independence was won, the new governments would be exacerbating relations through demands on economic organizations linked to the ruling party. Some countries did, indeed, have important farming groups. The cotton and coffee farmers of Uganda and the cocoa farmers of Ghana and Nigeria had played a role in the independence struggle. But insofar as these groups became visible to political scientists it was often through their identification with a particular tribe, Baganda, Ashanti, Yoruba. It was not that political scientists were unaware that tribal and economic grievances might reinforce each other, and thus that a particular ruling party could be very unpopular in Ashanti or Buganda. But the tendency was to see the national impact of unhappy cash crop farmers in tribal terms, because at this level immediate threats were posed to national unity through tribal separatism. Where cash crop farming was not being done by one or two major tribes, the questions were less frequently asked concerning the operation of the ruling party in these areas. Where there were subsistence farmers whom government was not reaching through tax mechanisms, government's popularity or unpopularity could not be posed in the same terms. But precisely how the party operated in these areas was never an irrelevant question either.

I am suggesting that the focus was on national structures or tribal/regional separatism rather than on bread-and-butter local issues of economic self-interest and patronage for groups and individuals, because analysts were concerned with national integration, and for obvious reasons the national institutions were more visible.[11] It also happened that research was easier to do in the capitals and that neither political scientists nor economists usually had the skills to work in the countryside in one or two places for long periods of time. Hence, a mutually reinforcing pattern of lack of empirical work, poor deductions, and a failure to perceive the need for different kinds of empirical research. This pattern has now been broken. Political scientists, economists, and sociologists are concerned with "micropolitics," and with rural change. As more historical work is done on the preindependence period, awareness is heightened of the role of farmers and of protest against enforced agricultural change.[12] As more research is done in the localities, the importance of "parochial" but non-tribal factors and issues becomes increasingly evident.[13] We are being brought into greater contact with politics in an everyday sense of the word. But as emphasis shifts from the macro to the micro, it becomes incumbent to make sense of the larger pattern—hopefully in a more realistic way. This requires that academicians from the various disciplines make their results known in terms of an explicit set of problems examined and couched in a shared language.[14] It requires, above all, the refining of new concepts which take account of the work now going on.

I think the notion of the political machine is worth exploring as an organizing concept, but not because the idea of a political machine constitutes a full-blown typology into which African political systems can be put. Moreover, in looking at the idea of political machines as described in the literature on American politics, it seems to me that the concept has not been an entirely successful one. That is, it remains a limited concept which is both too broad and too narrow at the same time. Perhaps the study of African politics can lead us to refine the concept so that it becomes more useful for the study of politics in general.

The concept of the political machine is too broad in that the characterization of parties that are concerned with material rewards, that is, with the perquisites of office—direct economic benefits—would apply to most parties for at least part of their history. No simple distinction can be made between parties that are concerned with rewards rather than political principle. Aside from the problems that arise in defining "political principle," and even the seemingly less vague term "issues," in the real world, parties are concerned with both. Ideological parties too are concerned with taking office and distributing offices even if they want to change the system after achieving power or during the process of so doing. Parties that have no interest in attaining office but simply exist to affect values or policies in society are rare birds; in any case, such parties are by definition not ruling parties. True, some parties appear more concerned with issues, change, and principles than others. Lenin did not forge the Bolshevik Party to create jobs for the boys. Quite the contrary, he looked forward to the breaking up of the administrative machine which was a major provider of these jobs. Nonetheless, the Communist Party of the Soviet Union did in fact put its personnel into jobs in government, factories, and farms; it abolished the distinction between governmental and nongovernmental jobs over wide functional areas in the economy and administration. Furthermore, the Communist Party itself became a major employer in the system, creating its own security apparatus and supervisory posts. The appeals of the Communist Party of the Soviet Union to the community at large were not and are not in patronage terms. Rarely do parties appeal exclusively in such terms, at least when the relevant political community is large and heterogeneous and there is competition electorally. In this sense, parties, as V. O. Key points out, are different from pressure groups. "Yet in one respect the inner core of the party—the machine or party organization—may be considered in the same category as a pressure group."[15]

Here Key is distinguishing between the party organization, that is, the permanent bureaucracy, and the party members at large, as did Robert Michels before him. Michels called attention to what he called the "echeloned aspect" of party.[16] African leaders have distinguished between party militants and those who were not militants, but to be a militant one did not have to be a permanent paid official. Rather, militancy is a state of mind and is expressed through national-building activities. For Michels and Key, the echeloned aspect is expressed organizationally and in terms of benefits received from membership. Michels says that the German practice was to pay for all services to the party:

> Whilst this deprives the party to a large extent of the spirit of heroism and enthusiasm, and of work done by voluntary and spontaneous collaboration, it gives to the organization a remarkable cohesion, and an authority over the personnel, which, though doubtless detracting from its elasticity and its spirit of initiative, and in essence tending to impair the very socialist mentality, constitutes nonetheless one of the most important and indispensable bases of the party life.[17]

In studies of African parties the tendency has been to treat the views of one man as if they were the belief system of an entire party. Without asking how an ideology elaborated at the top might be communicated, even disseminated, throughout the party (not to say the society as a whole), it has been assumed that TANU or the PDG or the Union Soudanaise held certain ideologies. This is not to deny that large segments of a given party's membership may be concerned with certain issues that have nothing to do with their economic self-interest, or their advancement, or their power and status. It is crucial to differentiate the kinds of issues, for examples, foreign/domestic, ethnic/economic, and the various combinations thereof that parties and elements of parties concern themselves with, and it is crucial to distinguish between styles of rule and commitments to policies. But in so doing we must be aware of the possibility of varying commitments of the different layers of party officials, of the distinctions between elected and appointed officials, and between officials and members at large.[18] Such distinctions are made all the time in analysis of American parties but they are much more rarely made in studies in African parties.

Concern with interparty relationships must be related to significant variables that distinguish polities. Obvious variables to be considered are size, heterogeneity, communication systems, levels and structure of economy, and nature of colonial administration. These variables can be related to propositions about party machines. For example, I have just asserted that parties rarely appeal in patronage terms to a large and heterogeneous political community. But where they are appealing to a particular ethnic group, and striving for either local power or a place in the national arena on the basis of being the spokesman for a given tribe or clan or religious group, then "ethnic" appeals are usually mixed with patronage ones. Where groups are fearful of their relative status and economic well-being, they are keen on having their own spokesman fill critical offices. Moreover, upward mobility for the group as a whole may be perceived, symbolically, in having one member rise high. Ethnically-based spoils systems exist in both one-party or multi-party systems in Africa. There is nothing new about this and since spoils systems are as old as human government and since the spoils of power are used to gain support for individuals and groups in all regimes, the simple identification of a spoils system with a party machine does not tell us enough. In other words, spoils system as part of the concept of party machine is not discriminating enough and its inclusion as a basic feature of a machine-type party is another example of the broadness of the concept of machines.

But we can raise questions about the functions of a spoils system and ask questions about structure too. On the functional side, spoils are means in the aid of financing party activities. The entire spoils system works to maintain discipline within a political organization, or, as Key notes, more precisely within segments of it.[19] Banfield, Wilson, and Merton have stressed the function of the boss in the American machines to overcome a constitutional dispersion of authority typical of the separation of powers,[20] and to organize, centralize, and maintain in good working condition the scattered fragments of power in American political organization.[21] The personalizing and human-izing of assistance and power has been noted.[22] Those who seek "irregular" assistance are not only the poor who do not know the rules of the legal game or don't want to play by them and those groups who come new to a given system, such as immigrants, migrants, upwardly mobile social groups, but also the large economic interests who want to have greater economic security and privacy.[23] The machine provides goods and services, albeit sometimes illicit ones.

In Africa machines function not to overcome a constitutional dispersion of power but to overcome a low level of political capacity at the center. Since the economic pie is small and usually not rapidly growing, it is difficult to distribute patronage as a means of centralizing authority. It is no accident that one of the most effective party machines has been the Parti Démocratique de Côte d'Ivoire operating in a country which has had one of the highest growth rates in Africa. But even where the economy is not expanding, the leverage even small amounts of patronage give may be great. In Africa, where large business interests are often foreign ones, the protection of privacy and the granting of ease of access involve foreign policy decisions. Some ethnic groups may be more concerned with defending their positions than advancing them. Martin Kilson has suggested that in African politics people are more often concerned with conserving rather than advancing interests because, given the general conditions of backwardness, people are less capable of regrouping political losses through alternate outlets.[24]

In other words, machines may be fulfilling functions comparable to those performed in America, but not precisely the same ones or not performing functions in the same way. Moreover, the relative importance of the functions, as well as the dysfunctional spoils activities, would have to be spelled out.[25] A number of analysts in developing countries have pointed to the obligations of extended families and loyalty to tribe or clan as generating pressures on bureaucrats to bring them to personal considerations instead of public duties. Social and economic gaps between high and low level civil servants, as well as high and low level party officials, also may increase propensities for corrup-tion. Civil service as well as party organizations may be geared more to integrative functions that economic performance, and thus nepotism and other irregularities appear.[26] To get at the functions of a party machine involves asking questions about the entire society, so that activities of the party organs become explicable. But at the same time, structural questions must be addressed, not only in terms of the specific arrangements of party, but also by relating party organizations to constituencies.

A rather old-fashioned concern for the uses (and misuses) of patronage may lead further than elaborations about "aggregating interest" activities of parties, particularly where organized interest groups, apart from organs within the ruling party itself, may not be evident. For the party itself, we can ask: Who becomes brokers rather than organizers or managers within the party? That is, who is in charge of distributing spoils; how centralized are decisions about patronage; how specialized are the party institutions for dealing with these matters? Do brokers and expediters appear from any special group in society?[27] More generally, we want to know how institutionalized are the roles for handling complaints within the party and in society; and are disputes settled largely by recourse to distribution of goods and services, coercion, or appeals on the basis of personality, and/or moral rectitude? Machines have been very much associated with the carrot and the stick rather than appeals to principles. This is only another way of saying that machines try to persuade with appeals to material rather than ideal interests; at least, this has been our definition of them in the past. Would examination of African parties lead us to revise this notion of machinelike characteristics since party organizations exist below the normative appeals that individual leaders make in Tanzania and Guinea, and in the past, in Ghana and Mali?

If a spoils system, manipulated by a party machine, exists underneath and even alongside a leadership at least rhetorically committed to social change and constantly making normative appeals to the party and society as a whole, how are we to understand it? It is possible to argue that the elite simply appropriates power and wealth to itself and sloganizes to justify its activities. Frantz Fanon has accused African elites of doing just this and Odinga has seen the Kenya African National Union's politicians clinging to position and abandoning principles because they have developed an appetite for power and property.[28] It could be said that normative injunctions are simply a style of rule. Whereas it may be acceptable to say that "someone is stealing in Beaumont, Texas today" in America, in Africa a moral reprobation attaches to regarding private interest as primary and thus "honest graft," theft, spoils, and patronage must be obscured by rhetorical appeals. No fundamental revision of an understanding of party machines is required here because the African machine would differ only in style rather than substance from the generic organization. This would not be the most fruitful approach, I think, and it can be traced to a conception of machines which is too narrow rather than too broad. Whereas a characterization of machines as parties concerned with material rewards rather than principles applies to most parties at least some of the time, an emphasis on spoils may obscure some important relationships between ruler and ruled even when the "latent functions" of machine operations are taken into account.

Oginga Odinga has said that "Political intrigue, caucus decisions and ambitions for office cannot thrive side by side with a vigorous popularly-based party machine, or democratic decisionmaking of any kind."[29] Pluralist theorists of democracy would disagree. It is interesting, however, that Odinga associates the term party machine with "popularly based" in opposition to political intrigue and caucus decisions. The political machine is not undemocratic per se for Odinga, because he envisions an inner core of the party which animates the party as a whole and is connected to the people, leading them as it at the same time identifies with them. His understanding of the party machine is of an organizing, vanguard machine. In pre-Soviet Rusia, Lenin's treatment of the vanguard was of a revolutionary inner core. After the seizure of power, his emphasis was on an organizing, controlling inner core.[30] The function of the party changed obviously although the leading role of the party did not. The tasks of the party were to undergo further changes as Stalin stressed the extractive roles and managerial roles of the CPSU. In the Leninist tradition, "party machine" refers not to spoils but to organizing capabilities. In Africa a number of ruling single parties have adopted Leninist organizational forms, often a Leninist rhetoric which stipulates leading roles, discipline, and militancy, although they have usually dispensed with the class struggle in favor of a more populistic mode. At the same time, African ruling single parties share many characteristics of decentralized political machines in that the organization is held together in good part by the perquisites of and desire for office, and internal cleavages within the parties are often not over policy issues.

My characterization of African parties as machines in the American sense which refers to spoils, bossism, and local autonomy would be readily accepted by most observers insofar as it was applied to the Parti Progressiste du Chad or the Uganda People's Congress, at least prior to 1965, and to the host of parties that have been dubbed patron parties or parties of notables. And use of "party machine" in the Leninist sense would be accepted for the so-called mass mobilization parties, the PDG in Guinea, the *Union Soudanaise* in Mali, TANU in Tanzania, and the Convention People's Party at an earlier time in Ghana. Yet the mass parties are machines in the American sense also and in the Leninist sense rather by aspiration of some of their leaders than reality of organizational strength. Moreover, some leaders who use the language of social revolution in a spurious and cynical way and who have no desire to encompass the entire population within their party or to be mass leaders may nonetheless want a tight and tough political machine around them, even if they rule by tolerating pluralism in the country as a whole—and making alliances with traditional groups.

At this point, I want to address myself to those situations where elites would like to construct parties that reach out for all members of the body politic and bring them under party control. Some party elites have aspired to forge an organizational weapon and to change the normative and social structure of their societies. Yet they have operated in an environment where it has not been possible to forge such an instrument and thus to accomplish these changes through central political direction. This same environment, and here I refer to that complex of features—low levels of economic development, poor communication systems, lack of urbanization, etc.—that we call under-development, has thrown parties back on playing integrative and distributive roles and periodically coercive ones, rather than extractive and systematically organized ones. In other words, the parties have tended to do what they could do. However, the process of economic development has required the ruling single parties to transform themselves into organizations different from what they were in the national movement phase and in the early independence period. But the circle has tended to be a vicious one for them; they could not expropriate the human and material resources necessary to rapidly build an organization that could extract economic resources and implement economic decisions. Thus the Leninist rhetoric and organizational forms have appeared ironic given the actuality of machine performance of distributive and integra-tive roles. Elites have appeared to the Fanons as parasites living off the people: a new bourgeoisie. Visions of the end to group struggles and group interests are seen as being self-serving. Appeals to nonpolitical motivations made at the top are posed against the activities of party leaders in the villages, districts, and regions, not to say those operating at the centers. At issue is not necessarily the matter of corruption versus honesty but politics versus anti-political ethics. Leaders who do not like the politics of politics appear as either knaves or fools in the light of both their own actions and those in their organi-zations who behave as politicians.[31] Their desire for rapid economic develop-ment leads them to organizational models and "administrative concepts" instead of "political concepts" based on a vision of interests in conflict, and awareness of the problem of reconciling diverse interests, as James Heaphey puts it.[32] But the conditions they operate within make them dependent on political machines, not organizational weapons.

Thus within the remaining "mass" ruling parties of tropical Africa two conceptions of political participation coexist with each other and in uneasy relationship with yet another type of political participation which has not been surrounded by any public conception at all but which exists in the world. The Leninist political machine mode calls for a widening of political participation, because, from an administrative point of view and from the viewpoint of increasing the scope of control, the more people that are brought into political action through participation, the better. But this is an envisioned participation in which all move toward the same goals in the same way. The American political machine mode, which is a reality in Africa but which has no rhetoric attached to it,[33] comprehends a different notion of political participation in which interests of various forms and types associate, conflict, and change alliances.[34] But there is, of course, yet another public conception of political participation in Africa in which decision-making is meant to be direct, centered in "the people."

Neither Leninist nor plebiscitary conceptions of political participation have been institutionalized in operating political structures. But because the aspirations of elites in African parties have been more than mere wishes—that is, elites have had political influence within their parties—African ruling single parties have been mixtures of different types of political participation, different styles or political modes, and different kinds of political functioning. At the center, decisions may well be made in accordance with democratic centralism, that is, in a highly centralized way. But decisions are rarely implemented throughout the country by commands flowing smoothly down through the hierarchy and radiating out to all branches without deflection and distortion. Moreover, while total political capacity may be very low at the center so that government and party seem ineffective when we raise questions about central control and efficiency in the economic and administrative realms, in certain political spheres the center may be effective. For example, top party elites may be able to veto party candidates down the line and appoint men they want. Furthermore, party leaders so far have monopolized ideology formulation. While we cannot conclude that the party elites are all-powerful, these constitute important powers which affect decision making in national plan formulation, foreign policy, and recruitment of party and governmental personnel.

Still, the discrepancies are real between the aspirations of elites in African one-party states and the possibilities for centralizing and extending political power. I have argued elsewhere with specific reference to Tanzania that the structure of the economy (agricultural/industrial balance, subsistence/monetary sector proportions), the level of resources (physical output in gross domestic product and per capita income), and productivity (of labor, capital/output ratios) have worked against the formation of a disciplined and centralized party, and have precluded the possibility of a totalitarian or "revolutionary-centralizing" system.[35]

If mobilizing mass parties are not extant in tropical Africa and are not going to come about in the foreseeable future, there are numerous other alternatives possible: military takeover, the persistence of ruling single parties that do not mobilize resources, machine politics American-style, competitive party situations, rule by administrative elites, breakdown of central rule, and various combinations of all these alternatives, some more likely than others. Here I do not want to discuss what may be the best institutional source for political development nor try to come to grips with the meaning of political development in Africa.[36] I take it for granted that, whether or not the only organization in Africa that can become a source of authority and can be effectively institutionalized is the political party,[37] political parties are not exempt from tendencies toward obsolescence, and that they may lose the loyalty of important constituents. Moreover, as Carey McWilliams has pointed out, an institutional system presumes that certain patterns of organization and behavior become so deeply identified with goals and values as to acquire a moral value themselves, and that institutionalized ends require a history of successful action before identification is achieved.[38] Precisely how success may be defined and by whom are important questions.

The discrepancy between postulated styles of rule, organizational forms, ideological symbols, modes of political participation, all on the one hand, and the operation of political machines working as patronage and spoils systems in decentralized fashion on the other, may be suggestive for looking into a number of problems. Specifically, internal party tensions between various levels of elites, and political competition between party elites and other elites—civil service, military—ought to be related to this situation. Similarly, elite/nonelite relationships and rural and urban protest ought to be viewed with these discrepancies in mind.

It may be no accident that Robert Michels, in analyzing the deradicalization of European Marxist parties in the late nineteenth and twentieth centuries, treated the patronage and spoils process in these parties, in the German Social Democratic Party (SPD) in particular. Michels, as is well known, also examined the process of rule by oligarchies in parties. More recently, Robert C. Tucker, treating both the SPD and the Communist Party of the Soviet Union, has written: "Not the end of ideology but rather the growth of a stable discrepancy between ideological symbols and political deeds is the true mark of deradicalizing change in once-radical movements"[39] For Tucker, it appears to be the fate of radical movements that survive and flourish for long *without* remaking the world that they undergo eventually a process of deradicalization. This process Tucker describes as having to do with the action pattern of the movement, its relation to its ideological goals, the development of its strategy and tactics, and, finally, its inner conflicts. The movement settles down and becomes reformist, although not necessarily conservative, that is, opposed to social change; rather it accepts the system it officially desires to overthrow and transform, and becomes absorbed in everyday party work.[40] The SPD that Tucker deals with remained an out-of-power party undergoing deradicalization. But the Communist Party of the Soviet Union had a worldly success by taking power, and Tucker is able to point to changes in party composition and adjustment to new realities at home and abroad in arguing his thesis. Although Tucker examined movements that existed over at least four decades, I find his analysis suggestive for studying African ruling parties once it is attached to a concern with explaining political machines.

We have been aware that elites who promised much before independence and when they took power have been vulnerable to attacks from counterelites as well as from mass protest once they confronted the stark realities of their environments. Arguments to the effect that Africa faces endemic instability are based on a postulation of intractable problems and rising expectations, a combination with presumably leads to frustration.[41] I am suggesting a narrower focus on the disparity between conceptions and realities of political participation and kinds of party organization. What we may be witnessing in Africa is a speeded up, highly telescoped process of deradicalization. The process is accelerated in Africa because of the perception on the part of elites at all levels in society of the difficulties involved in bringing about social transformation and economic growth. One possible reaction to these difficulties is to give up on trying to get economic growth and to try for national integration and a place in the sun for one's country by reiterating ideological commitments and stressing racial or ethnic solidarity where possible (that is, where a dominant ethnic core may exist as in Mali). But this reaction, be it conscious or unconscious, is fraught with danger for rulers. Party leaders become highly vulnerable to ostensibly efficiency-oriented elites—the military, police, and civil service. Thus the very perception of difficulties has required from ruling parties a new emphasis on governmental efficiency, on everyday work in economic affairs. While the connection can be made between the need to strengthen the party's organization and achieving economic development by arguing that the party will bring about development through its activities, party work more and more comes to mean collecting economic statistics, planning and supervising local agricultural projects hand-in-hand with technical specialists (where they are available), and having party members and officials themselves act as "economic" men.[42]

In his examination of communist and social democratic movements and parties, Tucker saw an inverse relation between a radical movement's organizational strength and the preservation of its radicalism.[43] This proposition seems well substantiated also in the histories of millennial movements. In Africa, while worldly success has come to nationalist movements, and they have acquired a bigger organizational structure along with a ruling place in society, these nationalist movements become ruling parties are still organizationally weak in terms of the tasks of rule and development. But organizational weakness does not seem to have fed the fires of radicalism in the sense of refusing to accept the established system and its institutionalized procedures as the framework for further efforts in the direction of social change. Rather, the rulers' perception of their organizational weakness seems to have accentuated movement toward accommodation with a numer of former targets: colonial powers, traditional groups, civil service personnel, private economic interest groups. Tanzania is an important exception. The Arusha Declaration and subsequent formulations and policies in the course of 1967 to 1969 do reassert Tanzania's independence and insist on government's hostility to the development of private economic interest groups. The Arusha formulations, however, return in many of their specifics to policies of the colonial period, albeit in a vastly different political and social context. The Arusha Declaration is both a reaction to and a recognition of the TANU government's inability to control change in Tanzania through central direction.[44]

Perhaps the explanation of the tendency toward accommodation and deradicalization lies in the fact that staying in power is of overriding importance, and, while African ruling parties are not becoming stronger in the sense of becoming organizational juggernauts, they nonetheless are ruling groups and thus have a stake in the maintenance of stability.[45] It matters whether a party is a weak organization out of power or a weak organization in power: deradicalization is probable in the latter case.

As for stability of the political system, the process of deradicalization does not guarantee it. Africa has already shown us cases of limited instability, as well as major instability associated with violence, for example, Nigeria and the Congo. There has been the military coup sequence which has changed the form of government but does not seem to have worked profound changes between rulers and ruled. This has occurred in a country ruled by a party which was Leninist in aspiration although it had American machine characteristics—Ghana and the CPP. It has occurred also, of course, in other one-party states.

It is not clear at this point whether or not stability can be maintained either by deradicalized party machines or by the military. The outcome will be influenced by factors involved in rural and urban protest that I have not dealt with here. There are factors internal to the parties which will be of importance too. For example, the place of the electoral process in both one-party states and multiparty systems remain in doubt. Yet the presence or absence of elections alters the nature of alliances and bargaining in machine politics. If political machines must settle disputes without recourse to an open electoral process, they may have to develop their own mechanisms of coercion and control, or manipulate state agencies that are specialists in coercion and control. This has been true of the American political machine as well as those in a Leninist mold. In Africa, where it is not possible to exert systematic coercion throughout entire societies, free elections may be a necessity for maintaining machine rule. Tanzania suggests that competition within a ruling single party for party and parliamentary offices does work to lessen dependence on coercion in a one-party state. And Tanzania is a case where the present leadership self-consciously seeks to strike ground between oligarchic authoritarianism and a fragmenting of the party which it is feared would multiply competing political organizations.

The development of oligarchic authoritarianism at the top of political parties while centrifugal forces are growing at other levels of the party and in society is a possible outcome in Africa. Ghana already gives us such a case. We should examine non-African party systems to come to grips with prospective outcomes. Thinking about political machines, be they the Congress Party in India, the SPD in pre-World War I Germany, the Communist Party of the Soviet Union, or state parties in America, will help us to clarify the problems of party development in Africa.

Notes

1. See Chapter 3.
2. See Chapter 2.
3. Edward Banfield, *Political Influence* (Glencoe: Free Press, 1961), p. 237.
4. Sekou Touré, *Expérience Guinéenne et Unité Africaine* (Paris, 1962), p. 32.
5. I have discussed Nyerere's ideology in *Tanzania: Party Transformation and Economic Development* (Princeton: Princeton University Press, 1967), pp 203–257.
6. It was not that students of the Congo ignored ideology and party structure, as Crawford Young's *Politics in the Congo* (Princeton: Princeton University Press, 1965) and René Lemarchand's *Political Awakening in the Congo: The Politics of Fragmentation* (Berkeley: University of California Press, 1964) show. But the Congo was rarely fitted into schemes that distinguished African parties along mass-elite lines or pragmatic/pluralistic versus revolutionary/centralizing. Aristide Zolberg in 1966 said, "Although the Congo crisis has attracted much attention as an

issue in international politics, it has little impact on the academic study of new states"; in "A View From the Congo," *World Politics* 19 (October, 1966): 137–149.

7. Morris Janowitz, *The Military in the Political Development of New Nations* (Chicago: University of Chicago Press, 1964), p. 29.

8. Samuel Finer, "The One-Party Regime in Africa: Reconsiderations," *Government and Opposition,* vol. 2 (July—October 1967): 505–506.

9. For a critique of this view with specific reference to military takeovers, see "Introduction," in Henry Bienen, ed., *The Military Intervenes: Case Studies in Political Change* (New York: Russell Sage Foundation, 1968). For analysis of the weaknesses in mass-party regimes, see Aristide Zolberg, *Creating Political Order* (Chicago: University of Chicago Press, 1966).

10. Zolberg, *op. cit.;* Bienen, "What Does Political Development Mean in Africa?" *World Politics* 20 (October, 1967): 127–141.

11. Richard Sklar criticizes the view that tribalism is supposed to be the most formidable barrier to national unity in Africa when he says that "it is less frequently recognized that tribal movements may be created and instigated to action by the new men of power in futherance of their own special interests which are, time and again, the constitutive interests of emerging social classes. Tribalism then becomes a mask for class privilege." See his "Political Science and National Integration—A Radical Approach," *The Journal of Modern African Studies* 5 no. 1 (1967): 6. Whereas Sklar prefers to stress class formation and class interests, I am referring to a clash of interests which may or may not be class or tribal but which do not have to be either. As Sklar himself points out, competition between groups for economic and political goods can be thought of within frameworks other than those of class struggle or ethnic heterogeneity. There are the conflict-model theorists who owe a great deal to Simmel and the theorists of pluralist competition who are so much in evidence in treatments of American politics and democratic theory.

12. See, for example, Lionel Cliffe,"Nationalism and the Reaction to Agricultural Improvement in Tanganyika during the Colonial Period," East African Institute of Social Research Paper, Kampala, 1964; John Kesby, "Warangi Reaction to Agricultural Change," EIASR, Kampala, 1964.

13. See, for example, Martin Kilson's political history, *Political Change in a West African State* (Cambridge, Mass.: Harvard University Press, 1966): Colin Leys's *Politicians and Policies: An Essay on Politics in Acholi* (Nairobi: East African Publishing House, 1967); Lionel Cliffe's electoral study, *One Party Democracy: The 1965 Tanzania General Elections* (Nairobi: East African Publishing House, 1967).

14. See Henry Bienen, "Political Factors in Agricultural Change," *Rural Africa* 3 (fall 1967): 13–14.

15. V. O. Key, *Politics, Parties and Pressure Groups* (New York: Thomas Y. Crowell, 1958), p. 381.

16. Robert Michels, *Political Parties* (New York: Dover Publishing Inc., 1959), p. 52.

17. *Ibid.,* pp. 115–116.

18. See Bienen, *Tanzania.*

19. Key, *op. cit.,* p. 402.

20. Edward Banfield and James Q. Wilson, *City Politics* (Cambridge, Mass.: Harvard University Press, 1963), p. 237.

21. Robert Merton, "The Function of the Political Machine," in Charles G. Mayo and Beryl L. Crowed, eds.,*American Political Parties* (New York: Harper and Row, 1967), pp. 425–427.

22. *Ibid.,* p. 428.

23. *Ibid.,* pp. 430–432; Key, *op. cit.,* p. 404.

24. Kilson, *op. cit.,* and Bienen, *op. cit.*

25. See the attempts of J. S. Nye, "Corruption and Political Development: A Cost Benefit

Analysis," *American Political Science Review* 61 (June 1967): 417–427; Colin Leys, "What is the Problem about Corruption?" *The Journal of Modern African Studies* 3, no. 2 (1956): 215–230.

26. See in particular, Bert F. Hoselitz, "Levels of Economic Performance and Bureaucratic Structures," in Joseph LaPalombara, ed., *Bureaucracy and Political Development* (Princeton: Princeton University Press, 1963), pp. 168–198, and Fred Riggs, *Administration in Developing Countries: The Theory of Prismatic Society* (Boston: Houghton and Mifflin, 1964).

27. Myron Weiner has described the Congress Party's creating a class of expediters within Congress who serve as a link between administration and citizens. Yet expediting was an old function in India and expediters *joined* Congress after it took power. Weiner points to traditional patterns of social life that may be important determinants of the kind of party organization which develops and its capacity to be effectual. See his *Party Building in A New Nation* (Chicago: University of Chicago Press, 1967), pp. 465–467.

28. Frantz Fanon, *The Wretched of the Earth* (New York: Grove Press, 1963); Oginga Odinga, *Not Yet Uhuru* (New York: Hill and Wang, 1967).

29. *Ibid.,* p. 286.

30. Compare Lenin's *What Is To Be Done* (1902) and his *"Left Wing" Communism: An Infantile Disorder* (1920). Both documents are "Leninist" in that they stress discipline and vanguard relation of party to masses. It was the tasks of the party that had changed between 1902 and 1920.

31. For a discussion of the antipolitical ethos of leaders of new states and a defense of politics, see Bernard Crick, *In Defense of Politics* (Chicago: University of Chicago Press, 1972), and James Heaphey, "The Organization of Egypt: Inadequacies of a Nonpolitical Model for Nation Building," *World Politics* 18 (January, 1966): 177–193.

32. Heaphey, *op. cit.,* p. 177.

33. This is not to say that politicians in Africa have no conception of the kind of politics they are in fact engaged in. Private expressions are not the same thing, however, as publicly articulated conceptions.

34. I have taken some of Heaphey's ideas on political participation and used them here for purposes different from his own.

35. Bienen, *Tanzania,* p. 261.

36. I have tried to do this in "What Does Political Development Mean in Africa?" *op. cit.*

37. For arguments about the efficacy of political parties as the best possible source for political development in new states, see Samuel P. Huntington, "Political Development and Political Decay," *World Politics* 17 (April, 1965), pp. 386–430, and Manfred Halpern, *The Politics of Social Change in the Middle East and North Africa* (Princeton: Princeton University Press, 1963), pp. 281–317.

38. Cary McWilliams, "Political Development and Foreign Policy," in Richard Butwell, ed., *Foreign Policy and the Developing Nation* (Lexington: University of Kentucky Press, 1969), pp. 11–40.

39. Robert C. Tucker, "The Deradicalization of Marxist Movements," *The American Political Science Review* 61, no. 2 (June 1967): 358.

40. *Ibid.,* pp. 348–349.

41. For only one example among very many, see James O'Connell "The Inevitability of Instability," *Journal of Modern African Studies,* no. 2 (1967): 181–92.

42. See Bienen, *Tanzania,* pp. 307–360.

43. Tucker, *op. cit.,* p. 348.

44. For a discussion of the Arusha Declaration, see Henry Bienen "An Ideology for Africa," *Foreign Affairs* (April 1969): 545–559. Also see Henry Bienen, *Tanzania* (expanded edition), chapter on "The Arusha Formulations."

45. I am not saying that stability is *per se* a valued thing.

Chapter 5

Party Politics in Kenya

Party Competition

Just as commentators on the Kenya scene have stressed the strength of the civil service and the provincial administration in particular, they have invariably noted the weakness of party and the fragmentation of the Kenya African National Union (KANU) in Kenyan political life. Discussions of KANU have stressed its inability to frame policy or to function as a channel of demands upward or orders downward. Indeed, politicians, civil servants, social scientists have gone so far as to deny KANU any meaningful role in Kenya, or even to attribute to it an existence beyond a nominal one.

If KANU has no political meaning, we must ask: why do some individuals invest time and money and energy competing for its posts at national and local levels? Moreover, we must also try to assess the consequences of party politics for the ways that demands are structured and political competition takes place. I argue below that KANU does provide an arena of competition in Kenya. It does provide a vehicle for participation for at least some people. And even if we should determine that KANU itself is moribund in many respects, we must see how this matters for participation.

The first thing to note is that Kenya is still nominally ruled by a party. This is not the case in a host of African countries where militaries have carried out successful coups and ended party rule once or more than once.[1] Moreover, KANU remains a dominant party. That is, party opposition has been consistently driven out of existence in Kenya, although not always by electoral competition alone. Administrative means have been wielded against the opposition parties. Government has at times refused to let opposition candidates contest seats, banned the Kenya People's Union (KPU), and jailed opposition leaders. Yet Kenya has not become a *de jure* one-party state as has Tanzania. And KANU has shown a capacity to be absorptive. That is, opposition has been coopted or intimidated back into KANU. Various leaders of all opposition parties have one time or another come back into KANU.

Originally, party competition was between KANU and the Kenya African

Democratic Union (KADU). Kenya's first general election in February 1961 was contested between the two parties. KADU polled only 16.4 percent of the votes, yet some of its candidates won over 90 percent of the votes in the Nandi and Kipsigis districts in the Rift Valley and in some coastal districts.[2] In a 1963 election, KADU was able to retain its hold on the minority tribes' allegiance through its own loose alliance system of factional leaders. Thus Kalenjin, some Luhya, Masai, and Coastal (Mijikenda) tribes continued to vote for KADU. When KADU leaders crossed the floor in 1964 to join KANU, prominent oppositionists became KANU Government Cabinet leaders. Thus Daniel Arap Moi, a KADU leader, is now Kenya's Vice President. The late Ronald Ngala, a Coastal leader, had been a Cabinet member.

The 1963 election saw the creation of another tribally based party, the African People Party. APP was a vehicle for the Kamba leader Paul Ngei. Because he did not receive the national power and status he wanted from KANU leaders, and because other KANU leaders were to form factional groups with Kamba leaders who opposed Ngei in his own home area, Ngei broke away and formed his own party. In the May 1963 general elections, Ngei's APP polled over 104,548 votes in six Lower House seats in the Machakos Districts of Ukambani to 6,935 for KANU and 12,090 for four independents.[3] Ngei, too was absorbed into KANU and became first the head of an important statutory board and then a Minister.

There were two strong impetuses to this early pattern of ingestion into KANU. Opposition was tribally based and thus not easily removed. A dominant alliance of tribes could prevail, but it could not obliterate opposition. Consequently, attempts were made to bring dissident leaders into KANU. This was possible since oppositions were not fundamentally rooted in policy differences nor in deep social cleavages but in ethnic competition for spoils. A group could be "brought in" by bringing in its leaders.

The other impetus for bringing blocs into KANU was the internal competition within that party itself. As KANU leaders fought with each other at the center, they sought to make alliances with groups in each other's district territory and also with those outside of KANU. Opponents of Odinga in KANU hoped to strengthen themselves by bringing in KADU leaders. When the former leaders of KADU came into KANU, the Odinga wing of KANU became increasingly isolated. At a critical KANU conference held in Limuru in 1966, it became clear that opponents of the ruling KANU group could be defeated with the aid of former KADU opponents.

One consequence of this pattern of fusion and bringing in contending groups was the concomitant development in patterns of fission. Groups who becme isolated in KANU split off. The fission-fusion pattern can be seen with the emergence, and then elimination, of the major opposition party to KANU, the Kenya Peoples' Union (KPU).

Oginga Odinga resigned his KANU Vice Presidency after he was clearly out-maneuvered at the Limuru conference and soon became KPU leader. The KPU was less of a congeries of district and tribal alliances than KADU had been. The KPU had a solid Luo base in the Nyanza Districts of Kenya and received support from Luo in Nairobi and in the other major towns where they worked, especially Mombasa. Splits within KANU itself and factionalism within Kikuyu areas gave the KPU some wedge in non-Luo areas. The KPU tried to extend itself beyond its Luo constituency by appealing to urban and agricultural workers and to landless elements. The Kikuyu leader Kaggia became deputy head of the KPU and his appeal was explicitly to poorer Kikuyu; moreover, he represented a pan-tribal appeal and personified the KPU's attempt to create a class party.

There were and are great difficulties in creating a class-based organization which would reach out to student elites and to marginals—landless, unemployed—and at the same time reach out to workers. In Kenya, unionized workers are already a labor aristocracy and have not been ready allies for recent migrants to cities and the rural and urban unemployed or student elites. Also, the KPU itself depended heavily on the personal positions of Kaggia and Odinga and this boded ill for creating a nonpersonalistic, class-based party.

Still, the KPU could not be defeated by KANU in its own Luo strongholds. Odinga and thirty other MPS resigned in April 1966, and constitutional changes were made immediately following the resignations, forcing them to stand again in by-elections. This resulted in the so-called Little General Election of 1966.[5] The KPU contested 28 of the 29 seats which were fought. KANU won 21 Lower House seats to the KPU's 7 and KANU won 8 Senate seats to the KPU's 2. But in the Nyanza or Luo areas where the KPU did win, the majorities were massive. This pattern was reproduced again in 1969 when a by-election was fought in a Nyanza constituency called Gem, where a KPU candidate again overwhelmingly defeated the KANU candidate.[6] Similarly, in a number of rural areas where KANU was strong, it won overwhelmingly. There were elections, however, which were more competitive. These were either in mixed ethnic areas or in swing areas, that is, areas where the ethnic groups were not clearly committed to the dominant KANU coalition based on massive Kikuyu support. Kamba, Teso, and Luhya areas were such and they continued to have internal factionalism which the competing parties tried to exploit.

The Government refused to allow contested municipal elections to take place in 1968 when the KPU would have challenged KANU in many towns. It also had banned the KPU by the time the first general election since 1963 was held in December 1969. At that time, some KPU leaders were in detention. But the pattern of taking opposition into or back into KANU prevailed. Kaggia, the deputy leader of the KPU, had come back into KANU before the December election and was allowed to stand in the general election even though it was a primary election where KANU membership was required.[7] Prior to his detention, Odinga was frequently asked to rejoin KANU and he did so in September 1971, some time after his release from detention. A former KPU leader, Dennis Akumu, became for a time head of the central trade union organization. Thus, the rise and end of the KPU did not represent deviance from the basic Kenya pattern. Indeed, that pattern depended more on KANU's own organization and social base, which in turn reflected many of the facts of Kenyan life that gave rise to opposition parties.

KANU itself had various ethnic bases and was vulnerable to ethnic-based appeals. KANU was not a mass-based party that could mobilize large numbers of voters to the polls and in which power and authority were concentrated in the party's central executive institution. Early writings on KANU stressed that KANU's objective was the organization of a mass movement and that it could be distinguished from the opposition KADU by its dynamism and by KADU's reliance on tribal and regional associations.[8] Yet Rosberg and Bennett, who made this comparison between KANU and KADU, noted that "from the moment of its establishment KANU was unable to achieve its aspirations and intentions of building an all-embracing centralized and unitary type of mass party."[9] And they focused their analysis on two important reasons why KANU never advanced beyond a confederal type of political organization: the leadership problem and the district base of power in KANU politics.

Leadership in Kenya

Many African countries came to independence with a party that had once been a national movement which had led the anti-colonial struggle. This national movement-become-party was often identified with a strong leader whose activities were frequently analyzed in terms of the concept of charisma. David Apter started this when he saw Nkrumah's role in Ghana as an attempt to transfer traditional loyalties into personal allegiances to him preparatory to transferring them to a new set of institutions.[10] Others used the notion of charisma more loosely than Apter and applied it to any strong leader who dominated his party or who cast a large shadow. More recently, African leaders have been portrayed more as bosses than as charismatic figures.[11]

The importance of personal leadership in Africa, whether that leadership be understood as charismatic, or more properly understood, I think, as leadership of a personal, political-machine type or patrimonial-traditional type, or combinations of the two types,[12] has been the other side of the coin of institutional weakness and decentralization. Personal machines can be centralized and they certainly can be tough and coercive as a number of American machines were. In the African context, however, personal leadership has been usually a substitute for effective institutions, and not a very good substitute even from the point of view of leaders themselves. And personal leadership has proved to be rather fragile with some few exceptions. Haile Selassie got high marks for durability in a patrimonial system; Julius Nyerere has tried to institutionalize a party with some success. Felix Houphuet-Boigny has ruled through a political party in eminently good "boss" style. Jomo Kenyatta has ruled above party, by manipulating factions, working through a relatively strong civil service, operating in a rather narrow sphere of concerns, utilizing his ethnic base but at the same time appealing to all Kenyans with the force of his historical position as "He who suffered for the Kenyan Nation," as the spokesman for Kenyan nationalism, as the Mzee or Elder of the nation.

Kenyatta has been accused of neglecting the construction of KANU. But the option of control through KANU was not open to him. Kenyatta was imprisoned after the famous Kapenguria trial. He remained in prison, often under conditions of extreme hardship when he was already at an advanced age, from 1953 until 1961. It was the period of imprisonment which solidified Kenyatta's hold on Kenya Africans, but it also removed him from operative control of any political organization in the criticial formative period of parties in Kenya.[13]

It was, of course, to Kenyatta's advantage not to become openly enmeshed in factional fighting in KANU if he could avoid it. Leaders would come away from meetings with him thinking he had accepted their position only to find out to the contrary. Kenyatta did take sides in KANU politics and he would throw the weight of the civil service to one side or another by allowing a particular faction to be registered as *the* KANU branch for a district or town. But he tried to cast himself in the role of arbitrator above the fray.

It has been Kenyatta's genius to perceive that he could maintain his position in Kenya only by avoiding KANU as an institution of rule. He would exhort the party and try to destroy contending parties. But Kenyatta never appears to have taken seriously the prospect of ruling through the party rather than through his governmental apparatus, despite injunctions to KANU to be better organized and disciplined.[14] To get involved in KANU politics would mean vying with individuals in their own bailiwicks and possibly losing at the district levels. Kenyatta intervened in extreme circumstances and on some of these occasions there had already been violence in internal KANU fighting. This occurred in Mombasa and Machakos. Then Kenyatta suspended party activity in the district involved. Usually, Kenyatta let factional politics take its course in the districts or he let his lieutenants at the center line up with various factions.

By not involving himself openly in factional politics, Kenyatta could be seen as *the* Kenyan leader. If other leaders tried to use Kenyatta for their own purposes in internal struggles, it is clear that Kenyatta used them and that he played this game best of all. Kenyatta grew into his own myth. That is, he became untouchable in Kenyan politics by being elevated by his lieutenants and by fulfilling their need for a unifier within KANU and in Kenya more generally. If, as Njonjo states, the cult of Kenyatta arose out of the need of other leaders to invent a neutral unifying symbol for a faction-ridden movement, Kenyatta used these needs himself.[15]

Kenyatta's major use of KANU has been as an arena in which to let others struggle for control of subsidiary resources. He has had no clear commitment to it and he has rarely invested his personal prestige in its doings.[16] He has certainly never devolved power to it.

To have done so would have been tantamount to giving up central rule to the district and subdistrict KANU organizations. For unlike TANU in Tanzania which had local roots and also a national center, KANU was weak at the center and frequently did not have grassroots organization. It has been a party of the middle, of notables, and district, municipal, town elites who have contended with each other in the many arenas Kenya provided: county councils, regional assemblies until they were abolished, KANU district and town branches, cooperatives, Harambee school committees, ethnic and religious associations.

KANU of the Districts

KANU has been characterized by the absence of strong central institutions, by the district and constituency base of its politics, and by its open internal factionalism. Because KANU's central institutions are weak and the party fails to operate in accord with its own constitutional provisions for elections of party officials and convening of party conferences and councils,[17] there has been a tendency to dismiss the party in Kenya. It is true that the Cabinet, Parliament, and the civil service were all dominated by an inner governmental executive while KANU's Governing Council and National Executive atrophied. It is also true that KANU was and is faction ridden and that the central KANU institutions have not functioned to make policy. National personnel changes are made without reference to party bodies. However, it would not be accurate to call Kenya a no-party state. Just as by deduction we should have earlier known that the so-called mass-mobilization parties could not penetrate the rural African countryside in ways alleged by commentators in the early 1960s, we should stop and pause to consider that the very vigorous factionalism within KANU, and the struggle over party posts mean that, for at least some people, KANU is an arena worth contending in. In various districts, KANU is an important resource for middle-level leaders as they contend for power. One should not jump to the conclusion that because a civil service is relatively strong and policy making is tightly controlled by a small group around the President that a party has no meaning.[18] We have to establish what meanings KANU has for various groups and what the consequences of specific factional patterns are.

We can say, however, that the KANU Constitution's assertion that "K.A.N.U. will govern the country through the established structure of the civil service . . . and administration" and that "K.A.N.U.'s policies will be reflected and implemented in the actions, administrations, and policies of the country through the decision of the Cabinet, Parliament, and the establishment of the necessary machinery for consultation and cooperation between the party, the public and he government" is true only in the formal sense that KANU forms the government with its parliamentary majority. Yet the majority within Parliament, even when the KADU and KPU were operating, was kept together by virtue of President Kenyatta's own authority and the operation of a reward system for Ministers, Assistant Ministers, and backbenchers alike. These rewards were channeled through the President's Office or through ministries which gave individuals appointments to statutory boards. In a study of the Kenya Parliament, Jay Hakes argues that the KANU Parliamentary Party behaves, by and large, in a cohesive way, but that neither national or district party organizations were determinant in leading to co-hesive action.[19] Indeed, Hakes maintains that party mechanisms operate in a haphazard manner. "The Chief Whip does not link the Government and the backbenchers because his access to the former is too limited." And party caucuses meet infrequently.[20] Hakes argues that after Kenyatta became President he ceased active participation in the day-to-day affairs of Parliament although he retained the prerogatives of Prime Minister. Subsequent leaders of Government business had little impact on the cohesion of Parliament.[21] KANU's organization in Parliament, as elsewhere in Kenya, was exceedingly loose.[22] However, if Government was opposed on issues important to it by significant numbers of KANU MPs, President Kenyatta would personally intervene in meetings of the Parliamentary Group of KANU (all KANU MPs).

Part of the very lack of discipline within KANU in Parliament can be attributed to the fact that opposition parties never threatened KANU's majority and thus backbenchers felt free to criticize in speeches and even to vote against Government. The question as to whether or not lack of discipline was a matter of MPs' performing representative functions for their constituents remains. If national party organizations were weak, did MPs feel compelled to act in accordance with constituency interests, or at least free to do so if they chose? Before trying to answer this question, it is necessary to understand the organizational basis of KANU in Kenya and KANU's relations with categorical groups, so that we can begin to come to grips with the pattern of factionalism which has obtained and try to assess its consequences.

The decentralization of KANU has largely been explained as a legacy of a colonial policy which tried to prevent the construction of a united national party which would encompass all ethnic associations in Kenya. While the policies of the colonial regime certainly weighed heavily on Kenyan politics as it evolved in the 1960s, the colonial inheritance was not the only factor which made for the maintenance of a district base in Kenya politics.

Participation, Elections, and Control

Kenya, like many African countries, had a marked increase in political participation in the terminal colonial and immediate independence period. The rise in activity has been treated as mass-type politics. But while the numbers of people voting increased and the number of work stoppages increased, this activity was led by elites: trade union organizers, party officials, better-off farmers were pressing their demands through organizational means. We can agree that there has been an independence style of participation centered around electoral activity and a post-independence style centered around individual petitioning for favors through direct dealing with the bureaucracy and other institutions with resources.[23] The critical point, however, is that the people who led the activities of a mass nature were those who would subsequently be well placed to engage in direct bargaining to further their own interests even when mass political participation was limited and at times curtailed. In other words, district politics in Kenya first fed on and was organized around mass activities.[24] Later the district competition continued between persons well-placed to compete as elites contended with each other. However, mass politics was reined in.

The increase in numbers of politically ambitious people who entered new political arenas opened up in the decolonization process gave further impetus to the subnational nature of competitive politics. It also provoked a counter-reaction as attempts were made to control this participation. One of the major consequences of intense factionalism was the proliferation of controls designed to lessen the costs of factionalism. But these controls did not eliminate competition among elites in trade unions, cooperatives, KANU branches. What they did do was to divorce elites from their own constituencies and in a sense give them more freedom to contend with each other in irresponsible ways.

In many districts, Mombasa for example, the pattern of national-district ties overlay local ethnic, clan, religious, and occupational conflict. Neither the fact that KANU had relatively little to offer in the way of material rewards nor that elections for offices were curtailed ended factionalism, which continued as a struggle over KANU position and within trade unions and ethnic associations. Kenyan leaders feared all along that elections would lead to an increase in tension, as political elites or would-be-entrants into the political elite competed. Elaborate security measures were taken at election meetings where supporters could be stirred up against each other.

In 1963–64 the response to increased demands for elite entrance into the political system had been to proliferate the posts available for competition—House and Senate seats, regional assemblies, municipalities. In the late 1960s and early 1970s, both the high-level civil servants and the top leaders were unhappy with the large number of politicians they had to take account of. The demands the top elite feared most were not those of the masses for more schools or clinics or even jobs but those of the political elite for more posts.[25] The top leaders felt that an increase in the number of politicians would lead to costs in terms of payrolls and patronage deals. More importantly, it was feared that power would become so fragmented that the society would become ungovernable. Moreover, while political competition increased and arenas proliferated—at the same time resources for competition were not highly centralized and thus competition could not be easily controlled—all organizations and associations were "pressed into the role of supplementary structures for the attainment of status, power, and high salaries."[26] Ethnic associations, trade unions, cooperatives all became steppingstones or bases for political competition, rather than institutions primarily designed to carry out their stipulated functions. The constitutional changes after 1964 were designed to let leaders restrict elite competition and participation through administrative means. Preventive detention measures, abolition of regional assemblies, ending of independent candidacies, not allowing the KPU to compete—all were measures designed for the same end.

Participation was restricted from below, but elite competition was not effectively restricted. In fact, the number of contested seats went from 84 in 1963 to 96 in 1969.[27] In the 1969 election, only about 47 percent of the registered voters, estimated at around 3½ million, actually went to the polls. Turnout was low in the 1969 elections, but well-placed persons flocked to compete. Five lecturers at the university resigned to fight the 1969 election.[28] Three mayors resigned; all subsequently lost. Many city councillors contested too. Education officers, labor union leaders, teachers, chairmen of Government boards and corporations, and civil servants were prominent aspirants.[29] There was an average of nearly four candidates for each of the 158 seats with as many as 10 candidates in some contests.[30]

Urban seats tended to attract large numbers of candidates.[31] Since the urban areas are multitribal, individuals could assume that their opponents would split votes on ethnic grounds.[32] It had been clear even before the 1969 election that the towns had ceased to provide a forum for nontribal appeals. Indeed, aside from Nairobi, where Tom Mboya, a Luo, had won in a tribally mixed constituency in 1963 and where early voting patterns had shown some tribal crosscutting, the towns after independence did not provide a context for nontribal politics. The politics of Mombasa was the politics of an array of ethnic and racial coalitions. In Nakuru, tribe was the main distinction.

What had happened in Kenya was that in the years since independence no national party organization had appeared which could slate candidates without reference to tribal affiliation. Leaders wanted to run in their own home areas. Moreover, while in the pre-independence elections of 1957 and 1960 constituencies cut across tribal lines, by 1969 constituences were tribal, with the exception of the towns. But in the towns, competition for jobs and spoils on a tribal basis had become dominant. It was in the towns that intense competition took place for licenses and loans for African traders and businessmen who were now replacing Asians. Even in municipal and civil service jobs, it was felt that competition was taking place on tribal lines. The towns, rather than being melting pots, were becoming the major locus of friction because tribal feelings had increasingly been polarized, and the towns were the place where people of different tribal origin were in the closest contact with each other. Tribal feeling was often expressed as anti-Kikuyu feeling because it was Kikuyus who were perceived to be controlling Government, new jobs, and loans. And it was Kikuyu who had probably spread over the widest area of settled Kenya and into many towns.[33] But as unemployment continued to be a growing problem in Kenya and arable land became increasingly scarce, by no means were all tribal tensions Kikuyu versus non-Kikuyu.[34]

It has been important for the development of factionalism and elite competition in Kenya that elections take place and these elections do help make Kenya a representative system, as I shall argue below, but it is also clear, as we have seen, that Government has imposed strong constraints over the electoral system, which have worked to narrow mass participation. The restrictions on participation in party politics from below have worked to emphasize the personalistic aspects of Kenya politics which were already strong, since they rested on an ethnic base. There has been little investment in party building at the top and the leaders have made it difficult to build a national party system. KANU remained a congeries of district and sub-district, personal and ethnic machines. Insofar as a national party system has existed in Kenya politics it is one of patron-client ties built around individuals who cross into each other's districts and/or organizations.

The perception of KANU's weakness as an institution has hindered the possibilities of strengthening it since politicians have not believed that central KANU institutions could carry their careers. Therefore few efforts were made to get beyond some critical point where KANU institutions could be used to strengthen the center and be the vehicle for political power for individuals. The one exception in political careers was that of Tom Mboya whose original base of power was Nairobi, where he organized the trade union movement and subsequently founded the Peoples Convention Party which did not have a tribal base. It was Mboya, who, as Secretary General of KANU, did try, intermittently, to build a base within KANU for his own power. In part, Mboya did not have a natural Luo base since he was not from the Luo heartland and since Oginga Odinga preempted Luo political loyalties. Toward the end of his life, which was cut short by assassination in 1969, Mboya was trying to build a district base in South Nyanza. But he was one major politician who relied at times heavily on KANU at the center. Mboya was also frustrated by other contenders in Kenya who chipped away at his own trade union base and who had district bases of power which could not easily be attacked from the center because central resources were weak and because ethnic loyalties were strong.

KANU has been made up of district and subdistrict associations which have their own bosses. At times, a dominant figure emerged, like Odinga in Central Nyanza, where his hold on Luo loyalties was very strong. Elsewhere, as on the Coast, a prominent leader like Ronald Ngala did not have a secure ethnic base and his enemies at the center were able to maneuver among his enemies locally. Moreover, the town of Mombasa provided the jobs and posts and trade union organizations for Ngala's opponents to wield against him. Yet a different factional pattern existed among the Kamba where Paul Ngei purported to be a tribal spokesman and was often successful in promoting this role for himself but had to contend with a part of his land being organized against him on clan lines. Sometimes, a subgroup of a tribe supported an important leader, as when Martin Shikuku was "the voice of Butere," an area of Luhya settlement. In all of these cases, leaders saw themselves as bosses of an area and rather explicitly recognized that they were operating local political machines.[35] That is, the main concern of the bosses' party organizations was to distribute rewards to supporters and to mobilize support for leaders. This support included getting votes in parliamentary elections and local elections, and KANU district and branch elections.

It must be emphasized that elections counted in Kenya despite the fact that they were often highly constrained by administrative procedures and despite the fact that neither KADU nor the KPU came close to parliamentary parity with KANU. It makes a difference for political competition and participation whether a one-party system comes into being through electoral majorities and subsequently overwhelming electoral dominance or whether the single party is legislated into existence or uses purely administrative-coercive means to achieve dominance.

That national leaders had to fight elections meant that they had to go to their constituents to renew support. The necessity to mobilize support, however, was not confined to periodic, if relatively frequent, elections. National leaders had to be able to demonstrate to each other and to Kenyatta that their constituencies were solid. This meant dominating in local factional struggles, which frequently took place in the arena of KANU branch and district elections.[36] In these arenas, it was necessary to line up support of those who would vote in the elections for branch or district chairman or committee members. There were also elections for other officers, e.g., secretaries and treasurers. No matter what the constitutional provisions, elections were held under various arrangements. This is one reason why it was important for leaders to mobilize as much support as they could. It was not always clear, even in an oligarchical setting, just who would count.[37] Moreover, leaders wanted control of district councils or municipal councils, where a chairman-ship could provide the base for opposition to a KANU district or branch leader. The constituencies might overlap but not be precisely the same. Leaders had to demonstrate strength in a number of arenas, including trade union organizations, if they operated in an area of rural workers or in urban settings. Leaders wanted to be perceived as the spokesmen for ethnic groups. This meant that they had to try to accumulate power first in the ethnic/district setting. But the many arenas and the relatively few resources of most leaders have meant that it is difficult to do this, and many national leaders have been vulnerable in their home areas. Other national leaders infringe on their territories.

It has been argued elsewhere that the very process of contending elections accentuates the importance of ethnicity in Africa since parties often have an ethnic base, and opinion leaders emphasize ethnic identification as a primary criterion for choosing a party. The dependence of village voters on ethnic labels to determine which party to support heightens their own sense of ethnicity.[38] In Kenya, too, the fact that there were many elections meant that factions were often tied to ethnic groups for purposes of organizing votes. These ethnic groups were sometimes clans in the rural areas or ethnic associations in the towns. In Mombasa, race and religion provided loyalties to organize around.

Tribe has not usually been the major unit in the factional pattern of Kenya politics. Kenyans refer to tribes like Kikuyu or Luo or Masai. But, while individuals may identify themselves as part of one of these groups and may see others as belonging to other tribes, factional groups are usually subtribal. Factional alliances also can cut across tribes when high-level political leaders create their coalitions in order to compete at the center. They put together a group which may contain individuals from different tribes and subtribes. Certain groups which are described as tribes have great difficulty in acting as a solidary group at any time. This is true for the Luhya, a large tribe as listed in the census, but a group without cohesion and with many local splits and internal distinctions.

In a politics of factional alliances as fluid as Kenya's, subgroups move in and out of dominant alliances. Tribal solidarity can be invoked against others when the tribe is internally divided. This happens among Kikuyu. Mboya and Odinga tried to center Luo allegiances around themselves and each had his own political machine. After Mboya's assassination, great emphasis was placed on Luo unity among Luo. At the same time, oathing took place among Kikuyu in order to bind Kikuyu together. In times of crisis, leaders try to create tribal unity. But the more common pattern is that of fragmented ethnic groups which are called tribes but in which subgroups compete with one another and can often be detached from the main group and brought into a new factional grouping. Individual leaders claim to speak for subgroups and to "bring them into" a factional alliance through their attachment to some national network.

Factionalism and Regime Support

The Kenya setting is one in which the politics of patron-client networks cuts across both occupational and ethnic groups. The type of political participation that attaches to the patron-client and machine modes of politics is one in which interests of various forms and types associate, conflict, and change alliances, and in which Government responds to relatively strong interest groups on an *ad hoc* basis. The rhetoric of plebiscitary decision making in which "the people" are publicly said to be at center stage cannot obscure this reality in Kenya any more than Leninist forms of party organization should necessarily be taken seriously elsewhere in Africa. It would be less accurate to conceive of party in Kenya as a linking mechanism between center and periphery or even as filling the gap between the parochial and national spheres than to see it simply as an institution which provides numerous arenas for political competition and also which, in given places and times, transmits demands upward and sometimes provides support for Government.

Kenyatta's own leadership style can be viewed in the Kenya context as an adaptation to the realities of a non-egalitarian society, yet one which is still basically not stratified by class. This is the leadership style of the patron or "big man," or what in Kenya is called the *samaki kubwa* or "big fish."

No one to my knowledge has described local politics in Kenya the way that one observer has described local politics in Kita, a Mali town where extensive political participation by all segments of the community was one of the cornerstones of the political system.[39] However, some of the characteristics of a participant system do apply in Kenya. Retention of individuals in major political roles reflects their success in obtaining more support from the public than their rivals are able to get.[40] True, some of the inner core around Kenyatta have no clear political base of their own and some have been propped up with administrative support, but by and large political leaders must demonstrate their local base of strength. While Kenya does not share with Kita the characteristic that political pressure from the bottom is far more important than Government initiative from the center, people and institutions in Kenya are responsive to popular pressure. A regime can be responsive to popular pressure by being representative, even though there is no norm that all people will participate in the making of decisions that affect them. That is, the regime can deliver goods and services which are highly valued and it can provide for turnover in the individuals who represent without actually altering the relationship between elites and non-elites. Kenya's factional system does both these things.

It would be a mistake to dismiss the many elections Kenya has had because participation has narrowed and the elections have not been completely open and unrestricted by Government. Elections have been important although they led to a renewal of the *kind* of elite that remained in power. Turnover of individuals gives people the feeling that there is a response possible to poor, that is, ineffectual, representation.[41]

Elections have served as the battleground for intra-elite competition and as the connecting link between elite and mass. Indeed, one of the consequences of a system of controlled elections was to provide for some representation by elites of mass demands, and to provide channels for political participation without altering the basic relations of elites and masses.

In Kenya, cleavages inside KANU have rarely been over policy issues, with the exception of the split which led eventually to the KPU's formation where land issues and socioeconomic issues in general were articulated. The muting of issues has been one consequence of factionalism in Kenya. The unwillingness of the regime to let competitive party politics flourish as viable opposition politics hinders the development of issue politics, too. We have also noted the penetration of all institutions with factional politics, and thus the politicization of functional and associational groups that then had to be controlled with the same *raison d'être* which had operated to limit party politics. As KANU itself often ceased to be the significant arena for factional encounters, the press became full of reports of trade union conflict at the center; and, in rural areas, school committees and cooperatives often became the forum for factional struggle.[42]

Nongovernmental institutions have become politicized and faction-ridden, and power is fragmented in Kenya, as elsewhere in Africa. And while in Kenya both civil service and military have been strongly institutionalized, as compared to other African countries, they are unable nonetheless to exert authority over the whole territorial entity they rule. That is, a great deal of political life still goes on outside the reach of central rulers. Nor can a ruling personal clique extend its client system in such a way that power flows from the top to all the nooks and crannies. But despite the rhetoric of need for social mobilization and economic development, there is no evidence that Kenya's rulers think they can wield total power. They have limited goals, and the institutions and resources at their disposal are often sufficient unto their ends.

Notes

1.   For a discussion of military intervention in Africa, see among others: Claude Welch, ed., *Soldier and State in Africa* (Evanston: Northwestern University Press, 1970); Henry Bienen, ed., *The Military Intervenes: Case Studies in Political Development* (New York: Russell Sage Foundation, 1968); Ruth First, *Power in Africa* (New York: Pantheon, 1970); Ernest W. Lefever, *Spear and Scepter* (Washington: The Brookings Institute, 1970).

2.   George Bennett and Carl Rosberg, *The Kenyatta Election: Kenya 1960–61* (London: Oxford University Press, 1961), p. 185 and passim.

3.   For a discussion of the APP and the 1963 election in general see Clyde Sanger and John Nottingham, "The Kenya General Election of 1963," *The Journal of Modern African Studies* 2, no. 1 (1964): 1–40. After a system of National Members bonus seats was applied, KANU had 83 seats, KADU had 33, and the APP had 8 in the Lower House. In the Senate it was 20, 16, and 2 respectively as KADU was better able to translate its support with minority tribes into Senate than House seats.

4.   A valuable study of the KPU is Susanne Mueller, "Political Parties in Kenya: The Politics of Opposition and Dissent 1919–1969" (Ph.D. thesis submitted to the Department of Politics, Princeton University, 1972).

5.   When the KANU majority passed retroactive legislation making MPs who changed parties contest new by-elections, MPs who had announced that they would join the KPU were told that they could remain in KANU if they renounced their switch to the KPU. A number did so but were made to contest the by-elections anyway. The Kenya pattern of reincorporation into KANU has never been based on good will toward opponents. It was not a live-and-let-live attitude which governed, but a necessity of politics stemming from the recognition of internal KANU divisions and ethnic-district fragmentation in Kenya. For a discussion of the Little General Election of 1966 see Gertzel, *The Politics of Independent Kenya,* pp. 73–124; John Harbeson, "The Kenya Little General Election: A Study in Problems of Urban Political Integration," IDS Discussion Paper No. 52, Nairobi, June 1967; David Koff, "Kenya's Little General Election," *Africa Report* 11, no. 7 (October 1966): 57–60; George Bennett, "Kenya's Little General Election," *World Today* 22, no. 8 (August 1966): 336–343.

6.   See John Okumu, "The By-Election in Gem," *East Africa Journal* 6, no. 8 (June 1969): 9–17.

7.   The legislation establishing the 1969 primary required KANU membership for six months before a candidate could stand. Exceptions were made for some civil servants and for Grace Onyango, an important Luo leader and KPU leader and for Kaggia, former Deputy Chairman of the KPU.

8.   Rosberg and Bennett, *op. cit.,* p. 27.

9.   *Ibid.,* pp. 41–42. Implicitly, KANU was being compared to what, in the early 1960s, were thought of as strong mass mobilization parties, e.g., TANU in Tanganyika, the Convention Peoples Party in Ghana. For a "revisionist" analysis of African one-party systems see Aristide Zolberg, *Creating Political Order* (Chicago: Rand McNally, 1966).

10.   David Apter, *Ghana in Transition* (New York: Atheneum, 1963).

11.   For a discussion of Nkrumah as a political boss see Henry Bretton, *The Rise and Fall of Kwame Nkrumah* (New York: Praeger, 1966). For a general discussion see Zolberg, *op. cit.*

12.   Guenther Roth, "Personal Rulership, Patrimonialism and Empire-building in the New States," *World Politics* 20, no. 2 (January 1968): 194–206, has elaborated on the concept of

patrimonialism as applied to new states. He distinguishes two kinds of patrimonialism: the historical survival of traditional patrimonial regimes and personal rulership linked to material rewards and incentives. I call the latter type machine politics and reserve the use of patrimonial for Roth's first type.

13.   It is an irony of history that Kenyatta was to be offered chairmanship of three parties he showed relatively little interest in. In detention, the detainees Kaggia, Fred Kubai, Paul Ngei, and Kunga Karumba had formed a party, the National Democratic Party, replete with symbols, flag, and constitution. Kenyatta was made its head, although he seemed to have little interest in it. He was offered the chairmanship of KADU, which he refused, and he then accepted KANU's chairmanship.

14.   See Jomo Kenyatta, "The Party Dynamic," in *Suffering Without Bitterness* (Nairobi: East African Publishing House, 1968), pp. 298–301.

15.   A. Njonjo, "The Succession Crisis in Kenya" (unpublished paper, Princeton, 1971).

16.   Kenneth Good, "Kenyatta and the Organization of KANU," *Canadian Journal of African Studies* 2, no. 2 (1968): 132.

17.   The KANU Constitution called for an annual delegates' conference every year, but until a conference was called at Limuru in March 1966 there had been none since 1962. There are various versions of the KANU Constitution. The ones I have seen are mimeographed; it is interesting that KANU has never widely circulated printed versions of its own Constitution. Nor do versions exist in every major tribal language. The earliest version of the KANU Constitution called for the All-Union Executive Committee having the power to convene conferences at quarterly intervals as directed or recommended by the Supreme Council of the Union. The later ones referred to the National Executive Committee convening an August conference every year. These Constitutions are not dated. For a discussion of KANU's failure to comply with Constitutional Provisions on finances, meetings, suspension of members, and nominations, see Taita Towet, "KANU: The Neglected Constitution," *Kenya Weekly News* (Nakuru), April 18, 1969, p. 8.

18.   For a discussion of the no-party state argument, see Immanual Wallerstein, "The Decline of the Party in Single Party States," in Weiner and LaPalombara, *Political Parties and Political Development,* pp. 201–216; and Robert Rotberg, "Modern African Studies: Problems and Prospects," *World Politics* 18, no. 3 (April 1966): pp. 365–78. My own discussion of the subject can be found in Chapters 2 and 3.

19.   For a discussion of patronage as distributed to MPs see Jay E. Hakes, "Patronage and Politics in Kenya: A Study of Backbencher Membership on Statutory Boards" (unpublished paper).

20.   *Ibid.,* p. 1.

21.   Jay E. Hakes, "The Parliamentary Party in Kenya," a paper presented at the International Studies Association South-Southwest Regional Meeting, October 14–7, 1970, p. 5.

22.   *Ibid.,* Hakes notes that Whips sometimes voted against the Government.

23.   Marc Howard Ross, "Grassroots in the City: Political Participation and Alienation in Nairobi after Independence," unpublished paper, Bryn Mawr, 1971.

24.   I am now using the word "district" very loosely. Not only the administrative district party organizations but also the county councils, municipal councils, and KANU branches, subbranches, can all be considered part of district, as opposed to national politics. So can struggle within regional assemblies during the *Majimbo* Constitution period of regionalism. Struggle for control of KANU provincial Vice Presidencies has an immediate national aspect. Sometimes the line is blurred when national figures meddle in district factionalism or trade union branch struggles.

25.   An increase in the numbers of people who contended for power has been discussed for the terminal colonial periods and the first phase of independence in Africa. It is clear that the very fact of elections in the context of weak institutions led to instability. See Crawford Young, *Politics in the Congo* (Princeton: Princeton University Press, 1965); Herbert Weiss, *Political*

Protest in the Congo (Princeton: Princeton University Press, 1967); Richard Sklar, *Nigerian Political Parties* (Princeton: Princeton University Press, 1963).

26. Richard Sandbrook, "Patrons, Clients and Factions: New Dimensions of Conflict Analyses in Africa," *Canadian Journal of Political Science* 5, no. 1 (March 1972): 113.

27. Jay E. Hakes, "The Weakness of Parliamentary Institutions as a Prelude to Military Coups in Africa," paper presented at 43rd Annual Meeting of the Southern Political Science Association, Gatlinburg, Tennessee, November 11–13, 1971.

28. Their resignation was ruled by the Registrar of University College, Nairobi; it was not directly compelled by Government.

29. There were complaints in the letters to the editors of the press that highly trained technical personnel like lecturers and doctors were trying to become MPs and as a consequence their scarce skills would be lost to the nation.

30. Goran Hyden and Colin Leys, "Elections and Politics in Single Party Systems: The Case of Kenya and Tanzania," *British Journal of Political Science* 2, no. 4 (1974): 261–292.

31. *Ibid.* Nairobi had an average of 5.6 candidates for each of its 8 seats. In the local government elections which were first held in February 1970 but then postponed, more than 150 people announced that they would contest 10 seats. *East African Standard,* January 23, 1970.

32. Candidates stood as clan candidates in rural areas. In some cases, the tribal base of rural politics was made clear also.

33. By 1948, one-third of the Kikuyu population lived outside their home districts of Kiambu, Nyeri, and Muran'ga. There were over 330,000 Kikuyu migrants, and Kikuyu were already the first or second most populous group in 14 of Kenya's 36 districts at that time. Despite the forced repatriation of Kikuyu to their homeland during Mau Mau, by 1962 more than 715,000 Kikuyu were outside their home areas; this was 44 percent of Kenya's Kikuyus. The 1948 census showed that about 42 percent of Kiambu Kikuyu, 32 percent of Nyeri Kikuyu, and 22 percent of Muran'ga Kikuyu lived outside their home district. Edward Soja, the *Geography of Modernization in Kenya* (Syracuse: Syracuse University Press, 1968), pp. –54–55.

The second largest group of migrants are Luhya who have moved in a more concentrated way to areas near traditional placed of settlement. Luo have migrated outside Kenya to Uganda and Tanzania and have been concentrated in their migration to Nairobi, Mombasa, and to certain areas of occupational specialty in Kenya. *Ibid.,* p. 55.

34. For a stress on Luo-Kikuyu tensions, see Stanley Meisler, "Tribal Politics Harass Kenya," *Foreign Affairs* 49, no. 1 (October 1970): 111–121.

35. See George Bennett, "Opposition in Kenya," in *Opposition in the New African States,* University of London, Institute of Commonwealth Studies, No. 4 (October 1967–March 1968), pp. 55–64.

Hyden and Leys described different kinds of machines in the 1969 elections: (1) The personal clientele of a rich, professional incumbent or a newcomer with political experience. These displayed organizational strength and financial clout. (2) A second type often closely linked with the first was the machine of the party elite. Candidates who were close to Kenyatta invoked him and their ties to him. (3) The long-standing factional machines of individuals outside the President's inner core. These are essentially the organizations of the wealthier and more educated members of particular tribes. Hyden and Leys, *op. cit.* Their machine types are loose descriptions rather than systematic typologies of kinds of machines.

36. After 1966, KANU was organized with a Vice President as head of each of Kenya's seven provinces. These were Central Province, made up almost exclusively of Kikuyu areas; Nyanza, which was largely, although not completely, Luo; the Rift Valley, which had increasing numbers of Kikuyu migrants into Kalenjin areas where a number of small tribes, e.g., Masai, Kipsigis, Nandi, live and where there are also numbers of Luhya and Luo on tea estates, in the towns, and in some rural areas; Eastern Province, with large numbers of Kamba but also Embu and Meru who are related to Kikuyu; Western Province where there are many different tribes with especially significant numbers of Luyha who are themselves broken into many subgroups; Coast

Province with Mijikenda people and the inhabitants of Mombasa; the sparsely settled Northern Province; and Nairobi, which has its own Vice President and which is close to half Kikuyu. Below the Provincial level are Kenya's districts. Excluding Nairobi, Kenya has 40 districts. The districts vary widely in population. The three northern districts are all under 100,000 each, while large districts in Nyanza Province are all over 650,000. These districts are usually fairly ethnically homogenous, at least insofar as tribal groups are concerned. But often, the designation "tribe" includes different subgroups who may be inhabiting the same district. At times, a district will include elements of major tribes. This is true where there are urban centers. Soja, *op. cit.*, p. 54, gives figures for the two largest ethnic groups as a percentage of total size in districts.

37.   G. Lamb confirms this point. He noted that in Muran'ga district it was hard to count the opposition or to mobilize support. The locational KANU organizations were fragmented, and factions did not possess good enough information to predict with accuracy support that they were likely to get. Since annual delegates' conferences were not being held, nor were party conferences, anyone could claim chairmanships. See G. Lamb, *Peasant Politics* (London: St. Martins Press, 1974).

38.   Observers of Nigerian politics have frequently linked elections to a rise in ethnic conflict. See Paul Anber, "Nigeria and the Ibos," *Journal of Modern African Studies* 5, no. 2 (September 1967): 163–180 and James O'Connell, "The Inevitability of Instability," in *ibid.*, pp. 181–192. Also see Young, *op. cit.*, and Weiss, *op. cit.* for analysis of elections and ethnicity in the Congo.

39.   Nicholas S. Hopkins, *Popular Government in an African Town* (Chicago: University of Chicago Press, 1972).

40.   *Ibid.*, p. 218.

41.   The 1969 general election resulted in 93 new faces in a Parliament of 158 elected constituencies. Among the casualties were 5 Ministers and 13 Assistant Ministers. Half of the former MPs who actually contested seats lost. There was an infusion of trade union leaders into the new Parliament, but it is not at all clear that this represented any alteration of the political elite, since trade unionists had used their organizations to move into the regime before.

42.   Lamb, *op. cit.*, suggests that in one district even when factional encounters fell off in KANU after 1966, party standing was still an important qualification for competition elsewhere.

PART II
Armed Forces and Society

Chapter 6

Foreign Policy, The Military, and Development: Military Assistance and Political Change in Africa

Politics and economics in the developing countries can be studied as part of international affairs.[1] There has, in fact, been a large literature on colonialism and its inheritances. And those who focus on imperialism or neocolonialism have analyzed the impact of external forces on the societies of Asia, Africa, and Latin America. More recently, studies of modernization have argued that there are important connections between national political systems and the international system, and the idea of a transnational politics has emerged. Some studies argue that nonindustrialized or traditional societies are changing under the impact of modern, industrial systems; their concern is to show a world transformation which manifests itself as a generalized Westernizing process.[2] But there has been more interest in analyzing a worldwide process than in examining the specific impact the foreign policies of great powers are having on new or developing states. The imbalance should be rectified because twentieth-century foreign aid may be as significant for domestic political change in recipient countries as nineteenth-century colonialism was. Insofar as this is currently admitted, it is maintained by analysts who see the CIA or the KGB subverting domestic polities, or by those who see the capture of elites via technical assistance and have a cosmic view that the expansion of American, Soviet, or Chinese "influence" somehow changes the patterns of politics in the receiving country so that they emulate the patterns in the donor state.

We can account for the paucity of studies on the impact foreign policies have on political and economic development in the third world. We have had a hard enough time describing the aims and scope of foreign policies; it has been even more difficult to analyze political development in given countries, not to say regions.[3] We have not been able to say with confidence what political development is in the most simple sense of political happenings. We have been hard put to determine priorities of various factors in the development of a polity.

But perhaps we are now able to define more clearly what political develop-ment means, as we get better monographs on national politics and as concepts are tested for a generality of application sufficient to permit comparative analysis of their precision and relevance. Thus, we begin to understand better the conditions for development. But, as Robert Packenham points out, it is important to distinguish between knowledge of the conditions for development and knowledge of the ways to bring development about, especially by the instruments of foreign policy.[4] The reluctance to assess the impact of foreign policies on development may be traced, in part, to a belief that very many variables are at work and that policies can cut very many ways, producing intended and unintended effects and long-run and short-run consequences.[5] Furthermore, the belief that foreign aid, and even direct intervention via occu-pation, has been and will be marginal to an indigenous development process[6] may well be operating among American academics, as well as foreign policy makers and implementors. Our own claims to nonintervention in domestic affairs of other states, along with the futility that has been felt over our inability to intervene effectively to change domestic patterns of certain states, strengthens this belief in the marginality of impact.

My own view is that the United States is the most heavily engaged, or implicated, of all the great powers in the process of development, or non-development, in the *tiers monde*. This is because the United States has the largest economic and military assistance programs, exports the most per-sonnel, governmental and nongovernmental, and is the great power with the most significant trading relations for the Latin American states and for some of the African and Asian states. Furthermore, it intervened directly and massively in Vietnam.

Here I focus primarily on United States policy in one sphere: military assistance. And I examine some connections between military assistance and political development in tropical Africa. Of all the conventionally delimited areas of the world, Africa has been the least studied in terms of the link between national and international[7] systems and, more specifically, in terms of the connection between foreign aid and political development. Some atten-tion has been given to foreign aid and economic development in Africa because it has been impossible for anyone who wanted to write about five-year plans or growth rates to neglect the large foreign component in government or private domestic investment.[8] Similarly, it should be required—for anyone who wants to explore the military coups that took place in Africa in the 1960s and to assess the prospects for political change that the military poses in Africa—to examine patterns and influences of military assistance. For not only have the nature and scope of postwar military aid programs had significant consequences for the level of armament and tension in Africa and for the balance of power regionally and on the continent as a whole, but within African states military assistance programs have affected the domestic politi-cal configuration.[9]

It is particularly hard to assess the impact of various military assistance programs. Along with problems of evaluation in multifactor situations and the lack of rigorous schemes available for assessing the role of military assistance, we are in a realm where the basic data are especially hard to come by. Much of it is classified. The United States and Britain publish more of their military assistance facts than France, the Soviet Union, or China, and in the absence of hard data on the scope of French military assistance, one could not hope to carry out the kinds of correlations between military assistance and coups that Charles Wolfe, Robert Putnam, and Charles Wheatley have done—the last two using Latin American data.[10] Furthermore, with a sample restricted to African countries who have had coups, we would be on thinner statistical ice than the universe of countries with military coups puts us. (The African militaries are providing us with more samples every few months, however.) Even if we had good enough statistical analyses to give us correlations between military assistance and certain political phenomena, like coups, and even if we could make some statistically backed statements about the direction of relationships, e.g., a coup occurs after military assistance rises, we would surely not be satisfied with extensive statistical analysis. We need intensive studies of the impact of specific military assistance programs on political development in single countries.[11] Since I have not utilized the data I have here to make the kinds of correlations Wheatley and Wolfe and others have made, and since I do not examine any one country's political development in terms of military assistance, I do not claim this to be a study of the impact of military assistance on political development in Africa. Rather, I point to certain aspects of political development in Africa and describe the evolving military assistance programs, with emphasis on American military aid, in the hope of noting implications of aid programs and drawing some connections.

We shall see that the United States military assistance programs are small both in absolute terms and relative to American military assistance in other regions. We shall also see that the number of armed forces, but not police forces, the United States is aiding is declining. But the fact that the programs are small in United States terms does not mean they are unimportant for African political development. And the fact that at present there are dominant voices in Congress and in the Departments of State and Defense for limiting American military assistance in Africa does not mean this will always be the case. We can be certain the pressure for assistance from Africa will become more intense. For example, in July 1967, both Congo (Kinshasa) and Nigeria asked for American assistance in domestic crises.

Furthermore, military assistance in Africa is very interesting in its own right. The arguments for and against military assistance in Africa revolve around the role of the military as modernizer rather than as a bulwark against foreign aggression or subversion from internal communist parties. Issues of international politics arise where there are African arms races— northern Africa, the Horn—or where great powers are involved in domestic strife, e.g., Nigeria and the Congo. The confrontation of white minority regimes in southern Africa with independent black states raises a host of important questions in the military assistance realm. Still, it is the role of the military as a ruling group which already confronts policymakers who must frame assistance programs. Military regimes in 1966 ruled in six of fourteen western African states, and three of eight central African states (see Table 1); the Sudan has had military rule; the military is a powerful and coalition partner in Uganda and the Somali Republic. The prospects for military rule are good in these and other countries, notably Ethiopia. The scope and nature of assistance becomes both a matter between donor states and recipient ruling military regimes, and a question of the further evolution of military regimes.

The discussion of the impact of military assistance on developing countries has been concerned largely with the incidence of coups and the scope of assistance;[12] the literature on military intervention has been concerned with exploring the correlations between intervention and political development and the role of the military as modernizer.[13] I suggest here exploring the relationship directly between military assistance and political development.[14] In this context, assistance to ruling military elites is not my entire concern. The way civilian rulers use the military is certainly another. This use can be for development purposes or civic action. It can be for counterinsurgency purposes. And it can be for maintaining or changing the domestic political balance through employing the military directly against one's opponents. For, as one author has suggested, "Although *coups* which result in change of government attract the most attention, the most frequent *coups* in Africa are probably those initiated by an incumbent government against threatening individuals or groups (real or alleged), and those launched by a ruler or dominant faction against their associates."[15] Obviously, in this regard, the police and paramilitary forces and thus assistance programs run by the Agency for International Development (AID) will interest us also.

African armies are for the most part small and lightly equipped.[16] The largest tropical African armed force was under 50,000 (Ethiopia) until the expansion of the Nigerian army during the civil war; and on a scale for inhabitants per serviceman and serviceman per square mile of territory, African armies rank low in world area comparisons.[17] In mid-1966, the ratio of total men in the armed forces to the combined populations of the thirty-five countries listed in Table 1 is 1:1900; France is 1:780.; China 1:260; and the United States is 1:65. Somali Republic has the highest ratio of 1:242 and Liberia the lowest of 1:4,956. These thirty-five countries south of the Sahara have armed forces totaling around 300,000 and low reserves forces of about 126,000. There are around another 250,000 men in *gendarmeries* and national police. Thus, the security forces for Africa amount to approximately the same number as those of South Korea.[18]

The African armies are almost exclusively infantry batallions; some have light artillery. With the exception of the north African countries and Ethiopia, air forces are small. Few African countries have anything in the way of a navy. Military manpower usually comprises less than 1 percent of the population. The police forces and *gendarmeries,* which have been neglected in the study of armed forces in Africa, are often larger than the armies proper and often do not have significantly less fire-power.

In many French-speaking African states, the *gendarmerie* functions as a national constabulary, although it is sometimes integrated into the armed forces. There are both fixed and mobile units with responsibilities for public order and internal security. Internal security is usually the *de facto* mission of the armed forces as well since few African armies can as yet carry out foreign operations. African armies have, however, served with United Nations forces in the Congo and do man the borders of their countries. Thus, their function is not purely internal. And in the future they will probably be involved in local or regional conflicts. Since many police forces are on a par with or outnumber the armed forces, and since their missions are overlapping, it is to be expected that the police as well as the army would be involved in politics. And, in fact, ruling military regimes have been coalitions of police, army, and civil servants in Ghana and Nigeria. Until 1962 the *gendarmerie* of Senegal was under the Ministry of the Interior, but after M. Diá's coup against President Leopold Sédar Senghor failed, the *gendarmerie* was put directly under the Minister of the Armed Forces. The *Sûreté* and the Republican Guard of Senegal remained under the Minister of the Interior; this was an example of balancing the police forces themselves rather than concentrating them within one ministry.[19]

When the costs of defense forces as a share of GNP or of total government budgets are calculated, the cost of police expenses are not included. But given the comparability of internal security function for both police and armed forces, and given the nature of the *gendarmerie* and mobile police forces as paramilitary units, this may not be the most useful way of calculating defense costs. Because the population in Africa is so predominantly rural and because it is typically scattered, internal security would be a problem whatever the political problems. Since Africa is marked by a host of forms of violence (revolutions, coups, rejection movements; organized group violence for both political ends and robbery; and individual murder and assault as well as guerrilla fighting and border wars), the costs of internal security come very high.[20] (We leave aside for a moment the question of whether the first political leaders of the newly independent states have themselves raised the cost of internal security and whether the military has raised these costs.) In Uganda, for example, about 14 percent of recurrent revenue is devoted to police and prisons.[21] Much of the expenditure of African armies can be counted as internal security expenses.

We see from Table 3 that Africa ranks low for defense expenditures as a percentage of GNP as compared to other world areas. In fact, sub-Saharan Africa would rank even lower because the north African countries pull up the figure for defense spending as a share of GNP.[22] However, the defense costs defrayed through military assistance are not included. These are a very significant share of defense expenditures—and for those countries having defense treaties with France, not only equipment and training but perhaps also deferment of recurrent costs have been taking place. African countries, moreover, are not carrying out research and development programs.

We also see from the figures in Table 1 that a number of African countries have defense expenditures that are comparatively high as a share of GNP for developing countries. Kenya, Congo (Brazzaville), Senegal, and Upper Volta are all above 6 percent. In the figures of the Arms Control and Disarmament Agency (ACDA) for 1964, Congo (then Leopoldville, now Kinshasa) was the only country in all of Africa, excluding the United Arab Republic (U.A.R.), that had more than 6 percent of its GNP accounted for by defense expenditures.[23] That defense expenditures are rising in Africa is certainly true. In countries with major armed forces by sub-Saharan African standards we can see the substantial increases. Calculating the impact of defense costs on the economic growth of developing countries has been a major concern for both ACDA and AID. But, generally, arguments have cut both ways, as they have in discussions of political effects. When military assistance becomes massive, there is a fear that inflation will occur in the recipient country and that domestic budgets will not be able to bear the strain of absorbing the attendant costs of expanding the military. And there has been a recognition within all branches of the aid-giving establishment that the political and social contexts are sometimes such that military assistance will either not be possible by itself or will perhaps be counterproductive unless it is accompanied by economic assistance. Thus, a large component of American aid since World War II has been in the realm of defense support or supporting assistance; 17 percent of the total fiscal year 1966 request to Congress for AID programs were in this category. Supporting assistance is used: ". . . to enable countries to make a contribution to the common defense, or to internal security, greater than their economies can support unaided; . . . to maintain economic stability in countries where the absence or drastic reduction of current support would probably involve disastrous economic and political disintegration; . . . to provide, along with other aid sources, an alternative to Sino-Soviet bloc aid where such aid threatens a country's independence or otherwise conflicts with vital U.S. interests."[24]

Supporting assistance is supposed to go to those countries where "essential growth prerequisites of stability and security must be established." It has largely, but not exclusively, been used in "forward defense" countries that are located on the Chinese or Soviet periphery. As a share of AID programs to Africa, supporting assistance has been declining since 1961, with the exception of 1964 when the Congo received a large dose of it. For individual sub-Saharan countries, supporting assistance was large only in Guinea and the Congo. The latter had major security problems, but for Guinea supporting assistance was a way of getting economic aid into the country under a quasi-defense guise as it has been for many non-African countries. We shall see that military assistance too has been used as a way of getting extra economic aid to Africa.

Indeed, an argument has been made that military assistance can be a spur to economic development. The provision of military equipment on a grant basis avoids the use of foreign exchange. The assumption here is that military expenditures would occur whether aid was given or not and that they would thus come out of development budgets. Many recipients of military assistance are countries where troops are recruited from those who live at subsistence level. If forces were cut back, the economies could not easily absorb the manpower. Furthermore, local demand is said to rise as an effect of assistance programs. Above all, the military can directly increase economic growth via its own programs of social and economic development and through its own internal activities which provide nation-builders, such as literacy programs. Thus, the argument here is for the military as modernizer and for militarily sponsored civic-action programs. On the negative side, along with inflationary pressures mentioned previously, assistance programs are seen as merely whetting the appetites of the military for hardware which is not economically productive, and the military is seen as a consumer of scarce resources and services and a utilizer of scarce trained manpower.[25]

It is clear that military assistance has in certain placed led to inflation, and domestic unrest has been accentuated by economic dislocations. Military assistance has had positive economic benefits, too. Nothing can be gained from such generalizations and "on the one hand this" kinds of analyses. Similarly, highly generalized discussion of the military as nation-builder or modernizer in developing countries is difficult to sustain because military forces differ in terms of skills, social composition, fire-power, relations with civilian society and political groups, and they differ with regard to their own organizational formats. Above all, the societies in which they operate constrain or allow their activities to develop in various ways. Thus, if we want to be able to deal with these arguments for the economic and the even more obscure political effects of assistance, we must focus on the scope and nature of military assistance to Africa and the role of the African military in political development.[26]

Tropical African countries receive military assistance from the great powers: the United States, the Soviet Union, France, Britain, China, and from many western European countries including West Germany, Belgium, Sweden, Norway, from eastern European countries who both sell arms and supply equipment, from Canada and Israel, and from other developing countries, particularly the United Arab Republic and India.[27] Some African states have received their assistance from one source, for example, Liberia; others have begun to lessen their dependency on a single source. Thus, some of the French-speaking countries who have preserved good relations with France have nonetheless requested American assistance—Senegal for one. Other French-speaking countries have received both American and Soviet assistance—Guinea and Mali being cases in point. Ethiopia, too, has non-American sources now. Even where a country has been linked to France by a bilateral defense agreement and regional defense agreements, the United States has given some token assistance, e.g., Dahomey.[28]

The main advantage of widening sources is obvious: the lessening of dependence on a single donor. However, there are real disadvantages, also. Too much diversification leads to lack of standardization of equipment and training. The militaries themselves object to this; moreover, they fear splits within their ranks on the basis of cliques formed during overseas experience in various training programs. They do not want an officer corps that is perhaps already split along regional, ethnic, generational, and career experience lines further fragmented in terms of military assistance sources. And this is not necessarily a matter of receptivity to different ideologies or political influences. Rather, it is a fear that solidarity groups may form simply on the basis of shared experiences in different settings.[29] The civilian rulers may feel ambivalent about diversification, too. Although it may be tempting to try and split the military by tying one segment to one donor and playing it off against another, this is a dangerous game. Disunity is a double-edged sword. Lack of cohesion among military elites may promote coups. Syria and Korea are notable examples. In Ethiopia, splits in the military allowed the emperor to survive the Imperial Bodyguard revolt of 1960, and Nkrumah was building his own professional counterforce to the army when he was overthrown.[30] Moreover, diversification of assistance sources brings its own pressures on the civilian rulers. Consider the following case: after the Tanganyikan army mutinied in January 1964, first British and then Nigerian troops came to provide for public order. By the time the army was in the process of reconstruction, Tanganyika was Tanzania; military assistance was being received from West Germany, East Germany, the Soviet Union, China, Britain, Israel, and Canada. Zanzibar's army was trained and equipped from communist sources. And the United States gave police assistance. The Congo is another example. After the uprisings there, the Armée Nationale Congolaise was receiving assistance from Belgium, the United States, Italy, and Israel. Dissidents, meanwhile, were receiving arms and assistance from the U.A.R., the Soviet Union, and China.

I do not intend to sketch the various assistance programs.[31] We can mention that in certain places the Soviet Union has been the major donor. Its current North African programs are very large. It is attempting to transform the U.A.R. and Algerian armies and is becoming increasingly involved with the Nigerian military. In tropical Africa, it became involved with government-to-government aid to the Congo for a brief time and then its aid was given in clandestine fashion to dissident groups. Currently, its major program is in the Somali Republic where its aid through 1966 was reported to be above $30 million.[32] Close to one hundred Somali officers are supposed to have been trained in the U.S.S.R. The Soviet Union was also involved in aiding the Ghanaian army at one point and in building a special Ghanaian military force outside regular army channels. Guinea, too, received Soviet credits following its break with France. All told, by 1964 total military assistance from communist states was put at over $60 million.[33] Whether all this money was expended is another matter, since Soviet aid is in the form of credits which are not always drawn upon.

Soviet military aid to Africa has not been confined to those states that are either carrying out "radical" domestic policies or even those that have lined up with the U.S.S.R. on many foreign policy issues. Somalia could not be put in either category. Rather, Soviet military assistance to Africa, as its foreign aid in general, seems to be a flexible instrument for trying to further rather short-term Soviet political aims.[34] Although Soviet commentators have maintained that a number of countries south of the Sahara—Dahomey, Nigeria, Upper Volta, and others—in which military governments have come to power have received big amounts of American weapons along with related ideological and political concepts, they have not stated any explicit cause and effect between American assistance and military rule.[35] Nor have Soviet analysts of the African military been categorically negative about their subjects. They have maintained that the view that military coups are merely reactionary and militaristic is unsound; similarly, the view that the army is the only all-national force capable of heading a national liberation movement is also unsound. Rather, armies should be seen as playing the role of weapon of the state where insufficient class differentiation and immaturity of social relations brings about a situation wherein one class cannot direct the revolutionary process singlehandedly. Furthermore, the army did not stand apart from the struggle for national liberation. Algeria's army is cited here and its composition—poor peasants, workers, and petty bourgeoisie—is stressed. The role of parties in former colonies is important in this respect in Soviet eyes. National-front-type parties united diverse forces and were not prepared to solve post-independence problems. But the army cannot take the place of a party as the guiding force for society, as the army has no clear political or ideological platform and no experience in leading the class struggle. Moreover, the army is not unified socially and ideologically, and it splits over the issue of which paths to development should be followed. The army can turn into a tool of reactionary forces, the more so because "the army is a societal institution in which democratic ideas can live rather placidly alongside reactionary views."[36] This analysis is worth citing at some length because it shows greater awareness of the role of the army and the pitfalls of army rule—albeit pitfalls from Soviet points of view—than many American writers concerned with the role of the military in developing countries have shown.

We move on to United States assistance and will not treat British and French aid in any detail—but not because the latter are unimportant programs. In fact, both have been more important than U.S. military aid in Africa in terms of men trained and impact on internal politics. British officers seconded to African countries commanded armies even after independence and still do for certain states (Malawi, Zambia). And where there are African commanders in chief, Britons may command air forces or navies (Kenya). Some 300 uniformed British still work with Kenya's 5,000-man army.[37] And British troops intervened in Uganda, Kenya, and Tanganyika in 1964 to restore order and to shore up heads of state in the three countries.[38]

French troops, too, have intervened to restore a head of state in Gabon, and they continue to be stationed on African soil, although in declining numbers. France has defense and military assistance treaties with some states, and assistance agreements only with others. Although French cadres do not take command posts, they do fill staff and technical posts in African armies.[39] Between 1960 and 1964, over two thousand African officers and noncommissioned officers were trained by France. And there have been annual quotas for Africans in French officer schools running into the hundreds.[40]

One reason for not dealing with French and British programs is that their published figures for the nature and scope of their assistance are highly inadequate.[41] More important is the fact that their programs seem relatively stable and decided on, whereas American military assistance to Africa seems more an open question (despite the congressional limits imposed on the program). The reason for this is that Britain and France as retrenching in Africa, whereas demands will be made for America to play a steadily growing role. However, present American policy to "supplement" the ex-colonial powers' military and economic aid to Africa and to keep the lead in military assistance may not be maintained.

The distinctions between military assistance and economic aid can be drawn by definition, but since the collateral effects of each impinge on military and economic factors, the interrelatedness of the two is ever-present. We could differentiate between military and economic aid on the basis of the form of the aid: if the item is a howitzer there is little problem; if it is an earth-mover, the use could be economic or military and we would have to consider actual use as well. The basis of distinction could be the objectives of the donor: are we primarily concerned with immediate military effects of assistance? We can also distinguish military and economic assistance in terms of the administering agency of the aid program.[42] Supporting assistance has been considered economic aid in part because it is administered by AID, but, when the aid program is defended before Congress, the military aspects are stressed in order to get congressional support. (Some congressmen have argued for a clear distinction between the military and economic aspects of the foreign assistance program for a long time, with all military assistance separated from the foreign aid bill and put on the budget of the Department of Defense. This has already been done for military assistance to Laos and Thailand, and aid to Vietnam is in a special category, too.)

Arms sales can be considered assistance, too, if the credit provisions are for soft loans. Certainly the political implications of sales have been seen by critics and supporters of our arms sales programs.[43] The share of American arms sales to developing countries has been under 10 percent of total sales. Since 1963, the credit transactions to Africa have been classified. Perhaps the hardest thing to measure is the flow of small arms via private manufacturers and clandestine channels. Biafra has received its small arms in this way, as have a number of African governments and rebel movements. United States sales programs have received less oversight fron Congress and less publicity than our military assistance programs.[44] For Africa, United States arms sales have been insignificant, at least south of the Sahara, so we are not concerned with American arms sales at this point.[45]

Military assistance itself can be divided into three categories: (a) military assistance, which provides military equipment, training, and related services; (b) supporting assistance, which is at various times described in military terms rather than economic; (c) contingency funds used for the same purpose generally as supporting assistance in those emergency situations which cannot be anticipated.[46]

Until 1963, United States military assistance in tropical Africa was administered by the Department of the Army, with the Deputy Chief of Staff for Operations (DCSOPS) having primary responsibilities for these military assistance programs (MAP) normally assigned now to unified commands. (Prior to 1963, the Ethiopian MAP was supervised by the Commander in Chief European Command.) At the end of 1963, the United States Strike Command was assigned additional responsibilities as Commander in Chief (CINC) Middle East, Southern Asia, and Africa South of the Sahara (CINCMEAFSA). In this capacity, CINCMEAFSA has unified command responsibilities for planning and administering military assistance programs as well as commanding all military assistance advisory groups (MAAGS) and military missions.[47] The unified command, in this case CINCMEAFSA, reports to the office of the Director of Military Assistance in the Joint Chiefs of Staff and the unified command gets policy objectives and order-of-magnitude dollar guidelines from the director. The director of military assistance receives directives and overall guidelines from both the Joint Chiefs and from the Office of the Assistant Secretary of Defense for International Security Affairs (ISA). The Assistant Secretary of Defense, ISA, is charged with the responsibility of directing and administering the military assistance programs, subject to the direction and authority of the Secretary of Defense. At the same time, the MAP personnel in the field are subject to the authority of the Department of Defense hierarchy; they also work under the authority of the ambassadors and work with members of the country team. The Director of Military Assistance also sends program recommendations to the State Department, AID, and the Bureau of the Budget.

One would expect difficulties in coordination with the various overlapping organizational hierarchies within the civilian and military wings of the Defense Department and between Defense and other agencies. One might also expect that, whatever the provisions of the Foreign Assistance Act of 1961, which gives the Secretary of State authority over foreign assistance, which he in turn has delegated to the Administrator of AID, the Department of Defense which exercises primary responsibility in the field of military assistance would dominate the formulation of assistance policy. In the small African programs, both the civilian wing of Defense (ISA) concerned with assistance and State and AID have more impact on the contours of assistance policy than they have where there are big programs. In CINCMEAFSA at the end of 1964 there were thirty-six military personnel and fourteen civilian personnel in military assistance work. Most of them were not concerned with Africa south of the Sahara.[48] Military personnel in the assistance program for Africa feel that AID and State have considerable say in the administration of military assistance for Africa.[49] The AID personnel, in turn, feel that military assistance is particularly inappropriate for Africa in the light of its stark development needs and its distance from the Sino-Soviet periphery. The AID personnel concerned with Africa have more antipathy for the African military as a ruling group than have the military personnel. Yet, many officers involved in assistance programs, both in the field and in Washington, and military personnel seconded to ISA or to political-military affairs desks within the State Department do not have exaggerated ideas about the capacity of African militaries for either maintaining political order or achieving political development.

It is probably true that AID's voice has been heard in interdepartmental meetings on military assistance to Africa more than elsewhere. For one thing, there are no large ongoing programs in tropical Africa. For another, Congress has established a $25-million limit on provision of direct military grant equipment to all of Africa,[50] although this can be avoided via interest-free loans. And sub-Saharan Africa has been the area of least American involvement politically and economically as well as militarily. Thus, in the context of a relative lack of interest, AID has comparatively more influence on military assistance policy in Africa than in other areas. (The emphasis on military civic action in Africa, however, has been at least as much, and probably more, of an interest of ISA than AID.) Finally, the police assistance programs are operated by the Office of Public Safety, which is located within AID.

The official statement of AID on police assistance notes that the Public Safety Program seeks: "1. To strengthen the capabilities of civil police and paramilitary forces to enforce the law and maintain public order with a minimum of physical force, and to counter Communist inspired or exploited subversion and insurgency. 2. To encourage the development of responsible and humane police administration and judicial procedure and to improve the effectiveness of civil police and paramilitary forces, and to enable them to become more closely integrated into the community."[51]

In Africa where civil police and *gendarmerie* perform security and paramilitary functions, and where policemen have been partners in military regimes, AID's public safety programs are important and enhance the role of AID (although the Office of Public Safety has its own separate identity within AID). The public safety funds come out of country budgets. Also, AID provides training for civil police and for field forces. The requests of police for aid tend to be "lighter" (that is, weaponry does not include artillery); it is less expensive. An American presence can be obtained, a concentration on internal subversion is possible, and arms races are not furthered. This is not to say that there is no danger for political development in aiding police forces. Janowitz raises the possibility that mobile police forces are instruments of potential political intervention. While police forces are less costly, they can be even more disruptive to the internal political balance because they are more likely to rely on local coercive pressure and have less of a sense of national goals.[52] "In fact, it might be argued that, in the absence of the army as a counterforce, the police would tend to expand their political power in new nations with weak political institutions, and their intervention might be highly unstable and fragmentary."[53] Since there are armies in Africa, with the few exceptions of Gambia, Botswana, and Lesotho, there is also the possibility of army-police struggle. Posing hypothetical questions will not be nearly as useful as examining specific police recruitment patterns and analyzing actual police-civilian and police-military relations. The kind of weaponry and training the police receive will affect these relations.

The public safety programs of AID came to $2,541,000 for fiscal year 1966 and $3,550,000 for fiscal year 1967. This was one of the smallest categories of the functional fields into which AID broke its assistance, and it came out of a total project commitment for Africa in 1966 of $141,488,000.[54] During this same fiscal year, 1966, AID provided development loans of close to $100 million and supporting assistance of $26 million. Military assistance for fiscal year 1966 was $24 million. The country breakdown on 1967 can be seen on Table 7.

The United States gives military assistance to Africa for a number of reasons, all of which have been noted in congressional hearings. The official line, as expressed by the men from the military and civilian wings of the Department of Defense, from the State Department, and from AID, who appear before the hearings of the Senate and House Appropriations and Foreign Relations committees, is a true telling. With specific reference to Africa, Secretary of Defense Robert McNamara gave three reasons for military assistance, one of which was deleted from the record of the hearings: (a) American interest in the independence of Africa. Military assistance helps counteract communist influence and control; (b) Military assistance helps maintain friendly regimes that are capable of maintaining stability, which is a precondition for orderly social and economic development.[55] Secretary McNamara's third and deleted reason, we may speculate, had to do with maintaining American base and overflight rights on African soil.

When General Paul D. Adams, then CINCMEAFSA, appeared before a congressional committee, he neglected to mention base rights and communications facilities but he did cite the following as objectives of United States military assistance to Africa south of the Sahara; first, to foster an anti-communist, free-world oriented community; second, to assist in the development of an internal security capability and political stability essential to economic growth; third, to contribute to the existence of viable and friendly governments; fourth, to provide recognition of new countries and to assist them in assuming the responsibilities of their independence and sovereignty; and, fifth, to prevent an African arms race.[56] General Adams also noted the importance of creating a United States presence—to give "an alternative to the Chinese and Russians who are competing to take over the countries in time."

A specific program, Ethiopian MAP, was described as "maintaining satisfactory relations with the Ethiopian Government, which continues to make important communications facilities available to us. Concurrently our program prevents Soviet encroachment into the military field in this strategically located country. Our assistance provides an internal security capability for the Ethiopian armed forces and provides the capability for these forces to contribute to U.N. operations such as those in Korea and the Congo."[57]

There have been other public allusions to bases in North Africa and to tracking stations, need for worldwide communications net maintenance, and overflight rights.[58] Here, military assistance essentially is used to purchase needed facilities. A communications base in Asmara, Ethiopia, an all-weather air base in Libya (Wheelus), port facilities in Liberia (Roberts), overflight rights and landing privileges in the Sudan, all are related to military assistance programs. This is perhaps the most straightforward exchange. Political influence deriving from military assistance and aid programs as development tools are much less clearly achieved. And whether a country's internal security is furthered by military aid is also a question to be explored empirically. Spokesmen for the aid program do not even suggest that African militaries can directly add to American national security by providing forces that can substitute for American forces. In fact, Congress insisted in 1963 that any aid not strictly needed for purposes of internal security in Africa was prohibited unless the President determined otherwise.

In the 1960's American military assistance has largely been geared to short-term political objectives. Military aid has been provided in small quantities to a number of countries in order to maintain political ties both with African ruling civilian groups and with the potential or actual military ruling elites. The United States has been the primary source of assistance for Liberia and Ethiopia and has been a major donor to the Congo. There have also been military assistance programs in twelve other sub-Saharan states (including the Sudan).

Although these programs are small by comparison with American military assistance programs elsewhere (see Table 8), they grew in size after commencement of assistance to Ethiopia in 1953.[59] By 1967 the proposed military assistance to Africa was $31.8 million (See Table 9). This was 3.1 percent of total United States military aid.

The present level of military assistance at $31 million represents a concentration of programs in fewer countries. The Clay Committee had argued, "We believe that the problems created by military assistance programs in the African countries would be greater than those they would resolve."[60] It argued for an end to small, scattered programs. At the same time, AID was moving toward a concentration of economic aid in fewer African countries.[61] The congressional limit of $25 million on equipment (twelve modern jets amount to about $25 million) militated for phasing out the small programs. Moreover, there was another congressional limitation on the number of countries that could receive American assistance of any kind— forty. Thus, small programs in Senegal, Guinea, and Mali were speeded up and phased out.[62] In tropical Africa, only Ethiopia, Liberia, and the Congo now have MAP, along with Libya, Morocco, and Tunisia in northern Africa. Only Libya could afford to purchase weapons. America has already refused a number of requests for assistance and sales. Assistance to Ghana was terminated in 1964, when relations with Ghana deteriorated. When the late Prime Minister Balewa of Nigeria asked for a jet squadron in 1961, Secretary of State Dean Rusk stressed its unsuitability, and the cost of annual maintenance was pointed out as equaling the cost of educating five million

Nigerians.[63] There has been a resistance to meeting such requests for heavy weapons, and those responsible for military assistance in ISA and the Joint Chiefs have maintained that aid to Africa in their realm has been for training and for logistical support, communications equipment, small arms, and the establishing of civic action battalions. A functional breakdown of assistance is given for 1962 in Table 10.

Here training does not emerge as a primary component of military aid. Through 1965, 2,721 Africans (including North Africans) were trained in the United States and another 199 were trained at overseas areas. This does not include, of course, training on the ground via mobile teams and MAP people in formal and informal ways. The costs of training through 1965 were $13.9 million of a total cost of over $1 billion for all American military training programs.[64] This was less than 10 percent of American military assistance in dollar terms. For the relatively large Congo program, which has been justified on the grounds that training is the major need of the Congo's army, through 1966, $830,000 of the $18.8 million the Congo received was for training.[65] Of the $31.2 million proposed for assistance to tropical Africa in 1968, $.5 million will go for training. Furthermore, the average MAP personnel strengths have been very small. In 1967, 17 military and no civilians were in Liberian MAP administrative and mission training. The Congo had 29 military personnel, Guinea 16, Mali 4 (there had been as many as 24 in 1965), Nigeria and Senegal 2 each. Only Ethiopia had a large number of personnel with 187 military and 3 civilians.[66] Ethiopia had the largest number of men training in police programs at the International Police Academy.

It is important to note the limited scope of training in the American military assistance programs, even when we have taken account of the overall limited scope of the military assistance program in Africa, because it was implicitly through training programs that the objectives stated by Secretary McNamara and General Adams for military assistance to Africa were to be achieved. Short-term political influence via ties with the military can be had, perhaps, by provision of equipment. But inculcation of values is presumably achieved through the training process.

Colonal Quintus C. Atkinson has stated: "The United States perhaps recognizing this danger of military coups as a part of the objective of 'Free World Orientation' has engaged wherever possible in the training of selected African military personnel in U.S. service schools and in the education and training of other potential leaders in U.S. civilian college programs. These programs not only supply much needed training and education but also offer the opportunity to develop leaders in the democratic tradition. To many United States officials these leadership programs offer more chance of long range success than the more transitory popularity gained from furnishing hardware."[67]

There has been a debate within the military and civilian agencies concerned with military assistance over the nature of training programs. Many individuals doubt whether democratic values can be inculcated via training programs and whether it is the place of the instructors at the various service schools to do so. Furthermore, there is a belief on the part of civilian and military people alike that coups are going to take place in Africa whatever the nature of American training programs and, for that matter, whatever the nature of military assistance programs. To counter these objections, the argument is made that programs should be geared to exploiting leadership qualities, both in the selection of personnel to be trained and in the latter training.[68] Nation-building qualities and nonmilitary aspects should be stressed. General training in administration, encouragement of precepts of public and social responsibility, and personal ethics should be given.[69] It has been explicitly stated that if the military are going to play political roles, they should be trained to do so.[70]

But how do you train an individual or a group for political roles? The principles of administration can be set forth rather clearly, at least for administering bureaucratic, rationalized organizations. Yet these principles, applied to institutions of state in new nations, do not guarantee success. In Africa, if a civil servant is going to be effective in putting across a local program, he may have to be part community-development officer and part politician. There are no models of bureaucratic behavior that can be transferred simply. Political roles are even harder to define. To be able to teach someone how to be effective politically requires a great deal of knowledge about the indigenous society. Is such knowledge about African societies readily available? If so, it has not been evident in the academic community.[71] Do those who train the trainees have this knowledge? Can you teach military assistance personnel who are going to MAP programs in Africa about their countries in a month at the Military Assistance Institute?[72] Is this knowledge going to be gained at Fort Bragg's Army Special Warfare Center and School or Fort Gordon's Army Civil Affairs School or the United States National Interdepartmental Seminar on Problems of Internal Affairs?[73] I think we can be very skeptical. When Africans come to the United States will they be receptive to such teaching? Will courses in civics be anything more than banal affairs, and, where they are, how happy will be the governments and militaries who send their people? This is not to suggest that nothing can be taught concerning development to military personnel, both American and foreign. It is to suggest that we are on strange ground ourselves in this endeavor.

Furthermore, the view that we can teach principles of modernization to foreign military personnel without getting into specific problems of local politics is fatuous. Indeed, the views that the military is the elite best suited to carry out modernization in new states and that "how to modernize" can be taught by stressing good "nation-building" principles—the civic responsibility of the citizen to the state, the role and importance of national symbols, and the identity of views between the people and their government[74]—are both rooted in an apolitical image of development. The idea that United States military assistance should stress training in nation-building so that military assistance will not just have collateral benefits for economic and social development but direct benefits through military nation-building activity gained its impetus from a view of the military as modernizer in the new states.[75] This conception in turn gave rise to military assistance for civic action.

We are by now familiar with the argument that the military is a relatively modernized institution in developing countries and that it is oriented toward industry and professionalism; it is available to outside contact, operates on rational norms with a receptivity to technological change, and is socialized to a wider national set of values. It is argued that an "informed soldiery drawn from all elements of the population is not only well-placed to transmit national values to the populace" but also that "properly employed the army can become an internal motor for economic growth and socio-political transformation."[76] The rub here is "properly employed." For by now we are also aware that the analyses which considered that discipline and organization were the key qualities necessary for institutions to act with political effect, and that because the military could intervene successfully against other groups, it could be a dynamic force for modernization and bring order out of chaos have not everywhere been correct.[77] It is one thing to prevail against other political groups through possession of weapons, organization, and discipline. It is another thing to create political order, or even to bring about stability. The proposition is well supported that it is easier for the military in developing countries to accumulate power than to govern as a ruling group.[78] We have learned that the coups that bring the military to power often carry the seeds of factionalism within the military, if it is not split already.[79] Furthermore, if the military is to rule, it must be a political actor and cannot stand above politics. Thus, a major claim made for the military—that it represents the entire nation and is perceived to be above political strife—ceases to be viable, once the military gains power (if it had any merit to begin with).

There is another problem. Militaries in many countries are not disciplined and well-organized; they are not melting pots or well-assimilated groups that have been forged into a cohesive entity. In Africa, small militaries of a few thousand men have been able to bring down civilian regimes. But these new rulers make up neither in legitimacy nor coercive ability what they lack in political talent. There is no evidence that African militaries have the political talents requisite for rule in Africa. They are not reaching down to the grass roots. There have been attempts to make African armies nation-builders by changing patterns of recruitment and having the army carry out civic-action programs—building roads, irrigation works, etc.,—and by changing names. Thus the Tanganyika Rifles became the Tanzanian Peoples' Defense Force: youth-wingers and party people were enlisted and the army began economic projects. (The French-speaking armies have carried out economic projects for a long time.)[80] But not all militaries want to carry out civic-action projects, not all do it efficiently. The reliability of a politicized army, both for ruling militaries and for civilian regimes, is doubtful. In Africa, of course, the reliability of the essentially mercenary armies constructed by colonial rules proved to be tenuous, too.

When armies come to power in Africa, their leaders, be they ex-noncommissioned officers from the colonial forces or new graduates from Sandhurst, St. Cyr, and Fort Gordon, do not show particular skill in manipulating political groups via persuasion, flexible policies, and bargaining abilities. Both the Nigerian and Congolese military elites seem to be lacking in these skills—

to name only two glaring examples. Are "political" sentiments expressed, for example, when Colonel Lamizana of Upper Volta, commenting on rumors that the former chief of state, M. Yameogu, would remain in office after military intervention, declared, "This is to know how poorly the military man I am, because my honor as a soldier and my dignity prohibit me from such compromises"?[81]

As different military factions begin to make alliances with various civilian groups, a pattern that has become typical in Latin America and the Middle East may occur: institutionalized intervention of the military does not promote political development and bring about political stability; furthermore, the military does not give up aspirations to rule and in fact cannot disengage from the politics of rule.

When we begin to make concrete what we mean by political development in Africa we should be talking about creating effective political instruments.[82] Public order means domestic tranquility. Political order means institution-building. It is not a terminal state once reached, forever achieved. There are, as yet, no nationwide political structures in Africa that can enforce the will of ruling national elites, no matter whether these elites are of traditional lineage groups, civilian bureaucracies, the military, or the ruling single-party—where it still exists.

For tropical Africa we can agree with Huntington's general point for developing countries that the only organization which can become a source of authority and which can become effectively institutionalized is the political party.[83] This does not commit one to the view that attempts at centralized one-party systems will work. Political competition and nondirectiveness are not necessarily inimical to development. They are required for it in Africa. Indeed, political machines that are competitive and decentralized may well be a useful model for Africa. If this is so, the military will hardly be the group most appropriate for manning the machine.

If we should be highly skeptical about the military as the bearer of modernity and the creator of political development in Africa, then we must look carefully into the consequences of military assistance for the balance of political power in African countries. This argument has particular weight because the many reasons given for military assistance elsewhere are recognized as being inappropriate in Africa. We do not look to African military forces as being useful against external aggression from outside Africa, and we are not interested in strengthening the defense forces of the free world by adding African military units, nor do we think that military assistance should be used to stabilize given areas through balance-of-power politics. The places where this might apply, the Horn of Africa and the Maghreb, worry us as they become involved in arms races. Thus, the arguments for military assistance to Africa hinge on: (a) developing the military as modernizer; (b) creating strong military and paramilitary forces to assure the independence of a country against internal subversion; (c) enhancing American political influence through connections with the military and by getting leverage with governments who request assistance. If, however, the present phase of military rule and initial military interventions turns out to be short-lived or highly unstable in Africa, then American political influence might be lessened if relationships with new civilian elites are affected by past military assistance programs. It is also possible that military assistance does not add to internal security in Africa but rather lessens it. And it is at least conceivable that the only way militaries in Africa will successfully contribute to development is by restricting their own growth and the importation of hardware.

We have no hard conclusions to offer, but in order to take account of these questions we must now try to assess certain effects of military assistance in Africa.

It is perhaps easier to see the absence of effects of assistance programs than to specify negative or positive effects. For example, the evidence is as scanty in Africa as elsewhere that former Secretary McNamara was correct when he said, "The experience we have indicates that the exposure of the military officers to our schools acquaints them with democratic philosophies and the democratic ways of thinking which they in turn take back to their countries."[84] We do not have good "before" and "after" gauges of the attitudes of foreign personnel who come to train in the United States. The impression of some of those who train foreign and military personnel is that the trainees are hardware oriented. (The impression of observers, too, is that the trainers are hardware oriented.) We know the military elites are political actors on home ground, but we have as yet little knowledge of how they are influenced by either training programs or a general socialization process.[85] It may be that interpersonal relations at United States training programs neither supply a basis for communications about United States policy and strategic intentions nor effectively communicate values about the role of the military. This does not mean that career and educational experiences are not important. Janowitz suggests that they may be more important than the traditional categories of social background in explaining political attitudes. But so far, we do not know the impact of our training program on these attitudes.

What we do know is that American-trained officers have participated in coups and that men trained for civic action in Latin America and having career experiences with civic-action activities turn their attention to what may be called coup politics. There is also evidence that personal relations are struck between American military personnel and foreign officers. But we can be wary, as Henry Bryoade was not when he said that "military leaders play an important and in some cases controlling role in most of the states of the area and these leaders are on the whole progressive, friendly to the West, and distrustful of the Soviets."[86] Bryoade was referring to the Middle East.

Insofar as militaries directly carry out nation-building tasks, they do so, in American terms, through civic-action programs. "Civic action" has sometimes been used synonymously with "counterinsurgency" because both involve militaries with civilian populations. Civic action, however, stresses the nonviolent use of the military. "Civic action is the use of indigenous and foreign military and paramilitary forces on projects useful to local populations in fields such as education, public works, agricultural, transportation and other projects which contribute to economic and social improvement."[87] MAP-supported civic action is designed to encourage and support the use of local forces in activities that contribute to economic and social development, and to assist in the prevention and elimination of insurgencies inimical to free-world interest by improving the relations between army and population. Congress amended the Mutual Security Act in 1959 to provide specific legislative endorsement for civic action, and President Kennedy directed the Departments of State and Defense to undertake expanded support of civic action in developing countries in 1961. The increased number of African countries that were receiving American military assistance in 1963 was in part a reflection of interest in civic-action programs in Africa. Civic action also served as a way of getting more economic aid into Africa.

There was support for civic-action programs in Africa by AID personnel because they considered such programs as the least evil among the military assistance alternatives. Within the State and Defense departments interest quickened in the military as a force for development, and civic-action programs were seen as direct contributions to economic development and as useful components of counterinsurgency programs. The economic aspects of development were stressed. "The purpose of the non-military operations, such as civic action, is to help eliminate the economic cause of discontent that provides the breeding ground for insurgency."[88] Although there was no interest within the Defense Department in turning African armed forces into civic-action forces, civic action was seen as an appropriate mission for army contingents. For one thing, there was no danger that civic-action activities would unduly detract from what would be primary military purposes elsewhere, namely, defense. The United States had no interest in bulding large defense forces in Africa and feared an African arms race. Furthermore, it was felt that civic action would not be contrary to the long-term development of private enterprise and a sound civilian economy since there was so little private enterprise in any case. Military officers, seeing that civic action was "in" at high levels in the government, began to see a new army mission in its sponsorship. And for Africa, it was clear that civic action represented a way to get military assistance established. In fact, the Foreign Assistance Act of 1966 stipulated that military assistance to Africa must be for civic action or internal defense.

The civic-action programs now started in Africa are considered to be in early stages with a large potential for expansion. The civic-action programs in tropical Africa usually take the form of assistance for engineering projects. Engineering battalions are rehabilitating schools, constructing roads, and providing sanitation. The United States has provided the equipment, materials, and training for these projects. Since individual items are not detailed, it is not known here precisely what equipment is called civic-action equipment. The claim is that only light equipment is provided. This has meant, in Latin America at least, patrol boats, training for airborne units, and transport and communication material.[89] Some essentially new battalions are being supported by American civic-action assistance. Military spokesmen have claimed for Liberia that civic-action projects have enhanced the government's program of rural and tribal integration into national life.[90] We have as yet no studies corroborating this or denying it. Skepticism has been evident over the positive results of civic action in Latin America and limitations on civic-action programs have been stated elsewhere.[91] And the warning has been sounded that, as the military gets involved with civilians and perhaps some of the least-satisfied elements—the youth or the rural populace in particularly under-developed areas—and as it gets more control over resources, it might activate those resources against the regime.[92] "However, much depends on how this [civic action] is done, for deep involvement by an army in such non-military matters can also lead to corruption and inefficiency. Foreign advisors who stress the importance of the military's role in nation-bulding may inadvertently be encouraging the army to judge its record—and its hopes—against that of a lack-luster regime"[93]

However, there has been little calculation in the past of the impact of civic-action programs on politics in countries receiving military assistance. This is undoubtedly related to Packenham's finding that among aid administrators the sociological and psychological dimensions of political change are not perceived or are not salient factors in their implicit models of political change, and that the American experience has produced an attitude of disdain toward the idea of a possible technology of political development.[94] Perhaps this lack of calculation also reflected the small concern within the American government over the prospects for military rule in Africa. The "marginality of impact" view,[95] plus the notion of modernizing militaries operating on army corps of engineer principles, have, in the context of the relative absence of American interests in Africa, led to a posture where small military assistance programs were supported to gain short-term political goals without a hard look at the consequences of these programs. Even where there was uneasiness over the wisdom of military assistance, if African leaders wanted token programs, the United States gave them these prior to 1965. If there were stronger political interest, larger programs were undertaken.[96]

The desire for an American presence and for ties between donor and recipients has led to a concern with the impact of American assistance in one important political area: the propensity for coups. Moreover, congressmen are always raising the possibility of a connection between assistance and coups. In the past, Latin American military coups occupied congressional attention; more recently, African military interventions have been prominent.

We have already said that we do not know precisely what values are transmitted by military training programs. But, whatever the struggle of conscience, whatever the reluctance (or keenness), African officers have intervened in politics. And they have intervened in former British colonies as well as former French ones. There is no reason to suspect that American-trained officers have been any less inclined to intervene than their colleagues trained at Sandhurst or St. Cyr.[97] Although there have been American military assistance programs in Liberia, Guinea, Mali, Senegal, Nigeria, Sudan, Ghana, the Congo, and Ethiopia, only in Ethiopia and the Congo was assistance going on at the time of an attempted coup. Since all African armies receive foreign military assistance from somewhere, we can find a perfect correlation between coups and assistance at the grossest level of analysis. Some of the smallest armies have revolted—e.g., Togo, Gabon—and so have the largest (Ghana, Nigeria, and Ethiopia). The claim is probably true that some African armies would intervene even if they were armed with bows and arrows, and that they would be strong enough to overthrow civilian regimes even with that kind of weaponry. This argument has been made in support of the null-effect hypothesis of military assistance. In the absence of data on the French and British assistance policies, we cannot thoroughly investigate the proposition that the conduct of armed forces in domestic struggles may be conditioned by institutional and national ties with the outside. But even for small armies receiving small amounts of assistance, it would be very useful to examine the impact on military responsiveness to government control that institutional dependence on foreign military assistance may represent.

Wheatley has done this for 54 countries over the period 1950–1964. (Liberia, Guinea, and Ethiopia were the only sub-Saharan African states included.) He sets up a simple "exchange of services" model where the military provides a responsive means for the use of force in the pursuit of government goals while the government reciprocates by providing human and material resources for the military.[98] He elaborates four hypotheses worth listing: "1) The smaller the proportion of total material resources consumed by the military which derive from domestic sources, the less responsive the military to the domestic regime; 2) The higher the absolute levels of military resource consumption, the stronger the association between the proportion of total resources derived from domestic sources and the degree of military responsiveness to the domestic regime; 3) The greater the proportion of domestic material resources consumed by the military and the smaller the proportion of total military consumption they provide, the less responsive the military to the domestic regime; 4) The greater the number of external sources and the larger the proportion of total military resources these provide, the less responsive the military to the domestic regime."[99] Unresponsiveness, in Wheatley's use, includes failure to resist—or assistance to—insurgents or the calculated attempt to remove government incumbents or to alter the structure of governme We would also want to know the likelihood that the military would take independent positions on foreign and domestic issues. This is harder to establish because infighting may be less well-known. But it is especially important in the context of military assistance because the donor may have it in mind to encourage military dissidence in foreign or domestic policy.

Wheatley was concerned with relating the onset of coups to military assistance compared to domestic resource levels.[100] We cannot find out with public figures for enough countries in Africa whether military assistance was rising as a share of defense expenditure before coups.[101] In East Africa, mutinies took place for higher pay, and then defense costs went up as salaries were raised. Subsequently, military assistance increased in Tanzania and the numbers of donors proliferated. But what the ratio of assistance to new costs was is not known to me. Similarly, defense costs have gone up both in western African states which had coups, some of which were also pay strikes, notably Togo, and in states that have not had coups. It may be that military assistance has no causative correlation and that factors completely internal to African politics are more important.

But we should note here that many of the factors mentioned by students of African coups can perhaps be gotten at by looking at military assistance. Changes in size of the military, composition, technology, image of self, all are related to military assistance because African militaries are dependent on aid for carrying out structural changes and increasing the size of the armed forces. The argument made by some proponents of military assistance, that armies would get money earmarked for capital development if assistance is not forthcoming, can be true only up to a point. Furthermore, internal politics in a given country as well as regional struggles for influence can be related to military assistance because outside powers have an interest in the complexion of regimes and in African external relations. After the coup, the United States determined to furnish Ghana aid to stabilize the nation's economy, to service debts, and to modernize the Ghanaian security forces.[102] Great powers also may intervene in crises of internal security—the Congo and Nigeria being cases in point. Thus, military assistance and coups may be related, but not merely in terms of the resource-mediation/modern-responsiveness that Wheatley posits.[103]

Our concern with development leads us to ask: what happens when the military does take over? Do defense budgets rise and, if so, are they financed out of greater foreign assistance or domestic resources? We are interested in the reasons defense budgets rise, too. Zambia has the fastest rising defense budget in tropical Africa. But Zambia borders on the Congo and on Rhodesia. Yet, the civilian government may be responding to internal political pressure as well as felt security needs. A military regime in power may spend money on the army in order to make payoffs to its major constituent. Or it may make such a botch of rule that it begins to rely more and more on the coercive apparatus and thus incur high costs for maintaining itself.[104]

It has been argued that African politics already manifest a major transformation: the shift away from political power as a technique of rule to a reliance on force.[105] Rulers resort to force when power and legitimacy fail. If African ruling militaries fail to legitimize themselves they will have to rely on instruments of force rather than the manipulation of political power.[106] Do we then meet spiraling demands for assistance? The Congo already shows this pattern, revealing how hard it is for the United States to extricate itself from military assistance in a continuing crisis. There is evidence that the United States would like to end its Congo military assistance programs, or at least curtail them. Nor does the Congo appear to be a country listed for country development-support emphasis under new AID concentration policy. Yet at a time when Congress is particularly uneasy about American interventions and military assistance, air transport and troop support are sent to the Congo (during July 1967) after strong requests from the Congo government for help against a mercenary insurrection. Such a request can be refused. In this case it was felt that political ties required the sending of assistance. Moreover, it was argued, and proved to be true, that even such limited assistance could be crucial for the short-run military situation. In this context, with a history of past military and political support, it is hard to get out.

In other words, military assistance in Africa is not merely the provision of material and services to another state but often means giving aid that can tip domestic political balances precipitously. The Congo is simply the most dramatic example of this because its politics have been violent and military forces have frequently been in struggles with other military and quasi-military groups. The recipient state is willy-nilly in a client relationship in Africa to the donor, who willy-nilly finds himself up to his ears in domestic politics without really seeing how he can direct those politics.

If it turns out to be true, as argued here, that African militaries do not have the political resources to run African politics nor are they modernizers, then assistance which makes the military an ever "heavier" institution in society but that is not able or designed to change the fundamental nature of the militaries will not be conducive to an orderly process of political development.

So far American military assistance has reconstructed certain military forces through massive aid and direct military intervention. Korea and Vietnam are cases in point, although the latter may be more significant for the questions it raises about the limits of American military assistance and intervention. In Africa, it cannot be said that MAP has been used as "one of the most useful available instruments for American foreign policy for meeting the challenges of the systematic revolution in the underdeveloped areas."[107] Nor has MAP been looked on as not only a military program but also a broadly-gauged sociological and organizational undertaking.[108] Aid has been used for direct rather than indirect influence.[109] The biggest programs have been where the United States has had bases, and assistance has been in the nature of *quid pro quo.* I have largely ignored the foreign policy aspects of assistance here to concentrate on the domestic consequences of these small programs. It is possible for big powers with many huge programs to overlook the impact of small programs on small states with porous and fragile political structures and to concentrate on short-term political influence rather than long-term political development.

Table 1

Armed Forces of Sub-Saharan Africa as of 1966
(excluding gendarmeries and police)

Nation	Armed forces	Inhabitants per serviceman	Annual defense budget (million) dollars)	Percentage of total budget	Percentage of GNP	Active reserves (not police)
Eastern Africa						
Ethiopia	35,000	634	31.2	17.0	2.3	8,000
Sudan	18,500	789	40.0	17.7	4.4	
Somali Republic	9,500	242	6.7	18.1	4.8	
Tanzania	3,000	3,440	7.2	3.8	0.3	4,000
Kenya	4,775	1,906	10.2	6.9	9.8	
Uganda	5,960	1,235	17.0	10.2	1.5	
Southern Africa						
South Africa	23,000	829	322.0	19.9	3.5	53,000
Rhodesia	4,345	963	16.9	6.6	1.9	38,300
Zambia	3,000	1,200	13.5	5.7	2.5	2,000
Malagasy Republic	2,800	2,143	9.1	8.8	1.0	
Malawi	850	4,350	1.5	3.3	1.1	?
Botswana						
Lesotho						
Central Africa						
Congo*	32,000	478	22.5	14.5	1.7	
Cameroon	3,000	1,366	15.8	19.5	4.2	
Burundi*	950	2,737	.97	6.9	.7	
Congo (Brazzaville)	1,300	615	3.8	8.9	10.9	
Rwanda	1,500	2,007	1.3	9.7	.7	
Chad	700	3,857	5.8	13.5	1.8	
Central African Republic*	500	2,400	2.3	7.9	.6	700
Gabon	300	2,000	2.5	7.6	5.1	
Western Africa						
Nigeria*	11,500	4,956	54.0	9.9	.9	
Ghana*	9,000	844	42.0	7.4	2.5	
Guinea	3,000	685	5.9	8.1	3.1	
Senegal	4,700	659	21.1	11.6	7.6	
Ivory Coast	3,600	972	8.8	6.9	2.4	
Liberia	3,580	698	3.1	6.7	1.8	
Mali	3,500	1,280	8.8	21.2	3.2	
Sierra Leone*	1,360	1,618	2.6	4.9	1.3	
Upper Volta*	1,700	2,470	2.8	14.1	6.1	1,000
Niger	1,500	2,000	3.7	10.8	1.2	
Dahomey*	1,400	1,429	4.1	12.0	2.0	
Mauritania	1,100	909	4.1	17.9	5.1	
Togo	600	2,500	2.8	13.5	4.1	
Gambia*						

*Ruled by military regimes as of June 1967.

Source: Charles Stevenson, "African Armed Forces," *Military Review* 47 (March 1967): 18–24.

Table 2

Comparison of Armed Forces and Civil Police Gendarmerie

Nation	Armed forces	Civil police or gendarmerie
Eastern Africa		
Ethiopia	35,000	28,000 plus 1,200 in frontier guard
Sudan	18,500	10,000
Somali Republic	9,500	5,000
Tanzania	3,000	1,350 *(including a parachute company)*
Kenya	4,775	11,500 *(including a light plane wing)*
Uganda	5,960	5,500 *(including General Service Units and air wing with light transport and copters)*
Southern Africa		
South Africa	23,000	28,000 police, plus 15,000 reservists, 51,500 Kommandos *(part-time rural militia)*
Rhodesia	4,345	6,400 active, 28,500 reservists
Zambia	3,000	6,000 *(including 6 platoons of Mobile Police with light aircraft)*
Malagasy Republic	2,800	1,000 gendarmerie & 600 civil police
Malawi	850	3,000
Botswana		
Lesotho		
Central Africa		
Congo	32,000	21,000 civil police, 5 gendarmerie battalions
Cameroon	3,000	3,000 gendarmerie, 5,900 civil police, 1,800 mobile police
Burundi	950	1,000 gendarmerie, 850 civil police
Congo (Brazzaville)	1,300	
Rwanda	1,500	750
Chad	700	550 gendarmerie, 1,950 civil police
Central African Republic	500	500 gendarmerie, 700 Republican Guard 22,000 and 330 civil police
Gabon	300	600 gendarmerie, 900 civil police
Western Africa		
Nigeria	11,500	24,000
Ghana	,9000	9,000
Guinea	5,000	1,000 civil police, 900 gendarmerie
Senegal	4,700	1,500 gendarmerie, 3,000 civil police
Ivory Coast	3,600	1,500 gendarmerie, 800 civil police
Liberia	3,580	700 police, 5,000 militia
Mali	3,500	1,000 gendarmerie, 600 civil police
Sierra Leone	1,360	2,050
Upper Volta	1,700	1,500 gendarmerie, 300 civil police
Niger	1,500	1,300 gendarmerie, 400 civil police
Dahomey	1,400	1,200 gendarmerie, 1,000 civil police
Mauritania	11,000	800 civil police
Togo	600	1,000 gendarmerie, 300 civil police
Gambia	None	150 paramilitary field force

Source: For armed forces I have used Stevenson, *Military Review* 47 (March 1967): 18–24; for police or *gendarmerie* I have used Wood, *The Armed Forces of African States.* Wood and Stevenson have many comparable figures for armed forces, but they disagree in various places, too. Although the publication date for Stevenson is later than for Wood, some of Wood's figures seem more up to date; others do not.

Table 3

Defense Expenditures and Selected Economic Data
for Less-Developed Countries,[a] by Region, 1964

Region	Midyear Population	GNP[b]	Defense		Public Education Expenditures[d]	Public Health Expenditures[d]
			Expenditures[c]	Percentage of GNP		
	(in millions)		*(in billions of U.S. dollar equivalents)*			
Europe	109.0	53.0	$ 2.5	4.7	$ 3.2	$ 1.3
Latin America	229.2	74.0	1.7	2.3	2.2	0.9
Far East	1,036.1	105.4	6.8– 9.8	6.5–9.3	3.9	0.9
Near East	82.1	19.2	1.4	7.2	0.9	0.3
South Asia	611.1	55.7	2.1	3.9	1.3	0.4
Africa	222.1	24.2	0.5	2.1	1.0	0.4
Total	2,289.6	331.5	15.0–18.0	4.5–5.4	$12.5	$ 4.2
Percentage of world total	(71.2)	(17.3)	(12.1–13.0)		(14.3)	(11.1)

[a] For this table, less developed countries include Albania, Bulgaria, Greece, Portugal, Spain, Turkey, Yugoslavia; all of the Near East and Far East except Japan; all of Latin America; and all of Africa except the Republic of South Africa.

[b] For most free-world, less-developed countries, GNP statistics are based on U.N. data for prior years. For less-developed countries where official national accounts data are not available or are considered to be inadequate, estimates were prepared from available information.

[c] Data have been generally adjusted to concepts used by NATO.

[d] The quality and comprehensiveness of these data vary significantly from country to country. Data generally relate only to central government expenditures. In many countries, provincial and local governments have a major role in education and health.

Source: United States Arms Control and Disarmament Agency, *World Wide Defense Expenditures and Selected Economic Data, Calendar Year 1964,* Research Report 66-1 (Washington, D.C., Jan. 1966), Table III, p. 17.

Table 4

Defense Expenditures and Gross National Product
for Selected African Countries, 1960, 1962, and 1964
(*in millions of U.S. dollar equivalents*)

	1960		*1962*		*1964*	
Country	GNP	*Defense Expenditures*	GNP	*Defense Expenditures*	GNP	*Defense Expenditures*
Ethiopia	812	15	900	19	982	22
Ghana	1,324	14	1,518	33	1,675	39
Nigeria	3,300	16	3,715	24	4,120	48

Note: Gross national product and defense expenditures are in current market prices generally
converted at official exchange rates. Defense expenditures have been adjusted generally to the
concepts and definitions used by NATO.
Source: *World Wide Defense Expenditures,* p. 19

Table 5

AID Expenditures—Appropriation Category by Region
and Country—Fiscal Year 1966
(*thousands of dollars*)

Country	Total	Develop-ment loans	Technical coopera-tion/ Develop-ment grants	Supporting assistance	Contin-gency funds	Contribu-tions to Interna-tional Organi-zations
AFRICA	212,140	90,160	76,730	42,953	1,271	1,024
Algeria	834		678	156		
Burundi	292		292			
Cameroon	3,453	2,005	1,135	313		
Central African Republic	1,468		1,468			
Chad	1,164		1,164			
Congo (Brazzaville)	38		38			
Congo Kinshasa) [a]	22,285		1,423	20,004		858
Dahomey	460		460			
Ethiopia	7,830	741	5,803	1,276	10	
Gabon	557		557			
Gambia	102		102			
Ghana	29,545	28,642	903			
Guinea	7,214	141	2,876	4,215	−18	

Table 5 (*continued*)

Table 5

AID Expenditures—Appropriation Category by Region and Country—Fiscal Year 1966
(*thousands of dollars*)

Country	Total	Develop-ment loans	Technical coopera-tion/ Develop-ment grants	Supporting assistance	Contin-gency funds	Contribu-tions to Interna-tional Organi-zations
Ivory Coast	2,340	1,694	646			
Kenya	3,777	448	3,329			
Liberia	21,241	14,565	6,676			
Libya	454	−4	458			
Malagasy	602		602			
Malawi	1,695		1,695			
Mali	1,782	42	951	654	135	
Mauritania	185		185			
Morocco	20,240	6,280	854	12,972	134	
Niger	1,117	339	778			
Nigeria	20,530	4,579	15,951			
Rhodesia and Nyasaland	1		1			
Rwanda	410		410			
Senegal	165		148	17		
Sierra Leone	1,549		1,539			10
Somali Republic	5,654	1,294	4,360			
S. Rhodesia	7		7			
Sudan	3,493	67	3,426			
Tanzania	3,920	2,062	1,858			
Togo	1,088		1,088			
Tunisia	27,047	24,496	2,551			
Uganda	3,443	1,654	1,789			
Upper Volta	367		367			
Zambia	808		808			
East Africa Regional	3,268	1,116	2,152			
Africa Regional	11,509		6,998	3,346	1,000	165
Regional USAID Africa	205		205			

[a]Now Zaire.

Table 6

French Military Assistance, 1964

(*in millions of dollars, excluding gifts of equipment*)

Cameroon	1.84
Central African Republic	1.40
Chad	1.36
Dahomey	—[a]
Gabon	.88
Ivory Coast	2.00[b]
Malagasy Republic	11.66
Mauritania	1.30
Niger	1.00
Senegal	1.40
Upper Volta	—[c]

[a]A French gift of military vehicles was worth $2 million.

[b]There was a 340-man mission in 1963.

[c]No monetary breakdown available from the source.

Source: M. J. V. Bell, *Military Assistance to Africa* ("Adelphi Papers," No. 15, Dec. 1964, ISS). Addenda and Errata Pt. I, March 24, 1965, pp. 1–4. Bell put French military assistance to Africa at $46.6 million in 1963 and $48.4 in 1964.

Table 7

AID's Public Safety Assistance to Africa

(*in thousands of dollars obligated*)

	1966	1967	Total through fiscal year 1967
Central African Republic	77	334*	214*
Chad	141	39*	312*
Congo (Kinshasa)[a]	526	2,437	4,207
Dahomey	34		
Ethiopia	408	199	2,378
Kenya	77		553
Liberia	211	323	2,526
Malagasy	42	34*	408*
Niger	40	18*	560*
Rwanda	208	191	661
Somalia	647	320	3,804
Tanzania	64	*	182*
Tunisia	30	9	150*
Upper Volta	36		
Total	2,541	3,550	15,955

*As of March 31, 1967.   [a]Now Zaire.

Sources: Figures for 1966 from the Statistics and Reports Division, Office of Program Coordination, AID, as published in AID, *Report for July 1, 1965–June 30, 1966* (Washington, D.C., 1967), 31. Figures for 1967 and total figures from Office of Development and Planning, Bureau for Africa, AID.

Table 8

Military Grant Aid Programs—Chargeable to
Appropriations Deliveries by Fiscal Years

Africa	1950-1955	1956	1957	1958	1959	1960	1961	1962	1963	1964	1965	1950-1965
Cameroon								0.2				0.2
Congo (Kinshasha)[a]									0.1	5.0	2.3	7.4
Dahomey							0.1	*				0.1
Ethiopia	4.8	4.0	4.7	8.8	5.2	7.0	6.0	10.9	10.9	10.3	8.3	80.9
Ghana								*	*	*		*
Guinea											*	*
Ivory Coast							0.1	*				*
Liberia			0.1		*		0.3	0.4	1.2	0.7	0.5	3.1
Libya				1.1	0.3	0.9	0.3	1.3	0.4	1.5	2.2	8.1
Mali							0.1	0.7	0.1	0.2	0.5	1.6
Morocco						0.3	2.1	1.5	6.1	6.0	2.3	18.4
Niger							0.1	*				0.1
Nigeria								*	*	0.3	0.2	0.5
Senegal							0.1	1.6	0.5	0.1		2.3
Sudan						*	*	*	*	*		0.1
Tunisia							2.7	2.3	5.7	3.5	0.9	15.1
Upper Volta							0.1	*			*	0.1
Total	4.8	4.0	4.8	9.9	5.5	8.2	11.5	17.8	26.1	28.0	17.4	138.0

*Less than 50,000.   [a]Now Zaire.

Source: Department of Defense, *Military Assistance Facts* (Washington, D.C., May, 1966), p. 14. McArdle gives higher figures for U.S. military equipment and training assistance to African states, 1950–1964, putting Ethiopian assistance, for example, at $11.3 million for 1963 and Liberian at $2.0 for the same year. Her sources are cited as U.S. Department of State, *Report to the Congress on the Mutual Security Program for FY 1961,* p. 22, and International Development Agency, *Proposed Mutual Defense and Assistance Program for FY 1964,* p. 177. McArdle's figure may be higher because all training costs are included. See Catherine McArdle, *The Role of Military Assistance in the Problem of Arms Control* (Center for International Studies, MIT, Aug. 1964), p. 69, Table a.

Table 9

Fiscal Year 1967 Proposed Military Aid

	Amount	*Percent*
Europe	36,129	3.5
Near East and South Asia	240,125	23.4
Africa	31,816	3.1
Far East	387,340	37.7
Latin America	71,999	7.0
Regional costs	68,991	6.7
Worldwide costs	190,600	18.6
Total	1,027,000*	100.0

*This is total obligational authority and includes both $917 million in new obligational authority requested for fiscal year 1967 and $110 million in estimated recoupments and reappropriations from prior year programs.

Source: *Military Assistance Facts,* p. 2.

Table 10

Functional Breakdown of U.S. Military Assistance
to Africa, Fiscal Year 1962
(*in millions of dollars*)

Supply operations and nutritional surveys	2.3
Training	2.8
Total fixed charges	5.1
Spare parts	2.4
Attrition	1.0
Other consumables	0.4
Total force maintenance	3.8
Aircraft	0.9
Ships	0.6
Tanks, vehicles, and weapons	5.4
Missiles	
Electronic and communications equipment	1.3
Special programs	11.2
Other	2.0
Total force improvement	21.5
Total	30.4

Source: U.S. House of Representatives, Appropriations Committee, Subcommittee on Foreign Operations Appropriations, *Hearings for FY 1963,* p. 543, cited in McArdle, p. 68.

Table 11

Number of African Participants in Public Safety
Programs in the U.S.A.

	1965	*1966*
AFRICA	79	101
Chad	2	
Congo (Kinshasa)		6
Ethiopia	29	25
Kenya		3
Liberia	10	5
Sierra Leone		1
Somalia	17	23
Tanzania	13	17
Tunisia	4	17
Uganda	4	
Upper Volta		2

Note: There were no Africans in public safety programs being trained by the U.S. in third countries.

Source: AID, *Operations Report, FY 1966*, p. 108

Table 12

Number of U.S. Government Technicians in Public Safety
Programs in Africa as of June 30, 1966

Central African Republic*	1
Chad	1
Congo	6
Ethiopia	7
Kenya	7
Morocco	1
Rwanda	2
Somalia	2

*Listed as East African Republic in AID document.

Table 13

U.S. Military Assistance Funds for Civic-Action Programs
in Africa—Fiscal years 1962–1966*
(*in thousands of dollars*)

	1962	1963	1964	1965	1966
Congo (Kinshasa)				**	
Ethiopia			167	6	5
Guinea				783	152
Liberia		463	66	88	9
Libya			6		
Mali			5	230	162
Senegal		183	66	276	306
Sudan			**		
Tunisia			2		
Upper Volta				8	8
Total		646	312	1,391	642

*Fiscal year 1962 was the first year that civic-action assistance was so identified in MAP.
**Less than $500.

Source: U.S. House of Representatives, Committee on Foreign Affairs, *Hearings, Foreign Assistance Act of 1966,* 89th Cong., 2d Sess., 1966, p. 1040.

Notes

1. This present work grows directly out of a concern with American policy that was foreshadowed in Henry Bienen, ed., *The Military Intervenes: Case Studies in Political Change* (New York: Russel Sage Foundation, 1968). The Inter-University Seminar on Armed Forces and Society, under the chairmanship of Professor Morris Janowitz, has generously provided financial assistance for the continuous research. Furthermore, discussions with colleagues at formal and informal gatherings of the Inter-University Seminar have been invaluable. As a member of the seminar, I happily acknowledge the debt owed to the Russell Sage Foundation in support of our work. Equally valuable to me has been the support of the Center of International Studies at Princeton. This work could not have been possible without the help I received from many individuals in the Department of State, Agency for International Security Affairs, and the Office of the Special Assistance for Military Affairs in the Joint Chiefs of Staff. My acknowledgement of thanks to the various organizations and agencies cited in no way is meant to distribute the responsibility for the results here produced.

2. For a review of some of these works and a critical analysis of what he calls eurhythmic change (further change toward the characteristics of the society from which the original change derived), see C. S. Whitaker, Jr., "A Dysrhythmic Process of Process of Political Change," *World Politics* 19 (January 1967): 190–217.

3. See my "What Does Political Development Mean in Africa?" *World Politics* 19 (October 1967): 128–41.

4. Robert A. Packenham, "Political Development Doctrines in the American Foreign Aid Program," *World Politics* 18 (January 1966): 230.

5. Among the few studies that have tried to come to grips with the impact of foreign aid on development in recipient countries are Amos Jordan, *Foreign Aid and the Defense of Southeast Asia* (New York: Frederick A. Praeger, 1962); Charles Wolf, *Foreign Aid: Theory and Practice*

in Southeast Asia (Princeton: Princeton University Press, 1960). These are more cost-effectiveness studies of various combinations of United States deployments than analyses of impacts. Wolf's *United States Policy and the Third World* (Boston: Little Brown, 1966) does the latter.

6. Packenham's study of Agency for International Development middle-level personnel established that one important segment of the government at least views foreign economic aid as having marginal effects on internal development, *World Politics* 18 (January 1966): 228.

7. There have been studies of Africa as a subsystem in the international system, e.g., I. William Zartmann, "Africa as a Subordinate State System in International Relations," unpublished paper, and I. William Zartmann, *International Relations in the New Africa* (Englewood Cliffs, N.J.: Prentice-Hall, 1966).

8. See Andrew M. Kamarck, *The Economics of African Development* (New York: Frederick A. Praeger, 1967).

9. Catherine McArdle, in *The Role of Military Assistance in the Problem of Arms Control* ("Center for International Studies," MIT, August 1964) has addressed herself more to the consequences of military assistance for the balance of power between states because she believed the nature of the difficulties precluded the possibility of assessing impacts of military assistance programs (pp. 8–10). Another study with an arms control focus is Lincoln P. Bloomfield and Amelia C. Leiss, "Arms Control and the Developing Countries," *World Politics* 18 (October 1965): 1–19.

10. Charles Wolf, "The Political Effects of Military Programs: Some Indications From Latin America," *Orbis* 8 (1965): 871–93: Charles Wheatley, "Some Inter-National Dimensions of the Role of National Military Forces in Internal Political Conflict," paper prepared for the 1965 meetings of the American Sociological Association, Session on the Sociology of War and Peace: Robert Putnam, "Toward Explaining Military Intervention in Latin American Politics," *World Politics* 20 (October 1967): 83–110.

11. We are only now getting studies of the genesis of particular coups in depth. See, for example, Bienen, ed., *The Military Intervenes.*

12. Among those who argue that American military assistance does not create coups are Wolf in both of the studies alluded to and Captain David Zook, Jr., "United States Military Assistance to Latin America," *Air University Review* 14 (September–October 1963): 82–85. Among those who argue that there are positive correlations between coups and American military aid are Herbert Mathews, "When Generals Take Over in Latin America," *New York Times Magazine,* September 9, 1962, and many congressmen as well as academics. See, for example, U.S. Senate, Committee on Foreign Relations, *Hearings, International Development and Security,* 87th Cong., 1st sess., pt. II, May 1961, pp. 610–12, 681, 669.

13. On military intervention and political development, see Martin Needler, "Political Development and Military Intervention in Latin America," *American Political Science Review* 9 (September 1966): 616–22; Edwin Lieuwen, *Arms and Politics in Latin America* (New York: Frederick A. Praeger, 1965); Morris Janowitz, *The Military in the Political Development of New Nations* (Chicago: University of Chicago Press, 1964). Many books have been concerned with the role of the military as modernizer, including those just cited. Also see the following bibliographies: Peter B. Riddleberger, "Military Roles in Developing Countries: An Inventory of Past Research and Analysis" (Special Operations Research Office, March 1965); and Moshe Lissak, "Selected Literature on Revolutions and Coups d'Etat in the Developing Nations," in *The New Military: Changing Patterns of Organization,* ed. Morris Janowitz (New York: W. W. Norton, Inc., 1965).

14. To some extent Wolf has dealt with this subject, and others have written of fundamental changes in the balance of power which military assistance brings about. There has been less analysis of the effect of military assistance on ruling elites. A recent study which takes this up is Willard F. Barber and C. Neale Ronning, *Internal Security and Military Power: Counter-insurgency and Civic Action in Latin America* (Columbus: Ohio State University Press, 1966). Also see Annex D, *Report of the President's Committee to Study the United States Military Assistance Program* (the Draper Report), Washington, D.C. 1959, vol. II, by the Foreign Policy

Research Institute of the University of Pennsylvania. I have not seen a report by W.P. Davison, "Political Side Effects of Military Assistance Programs" (RAND Corporation, 1960).

15. Aristide Zolberg, "The Structure of Political Conflict in the New States of Tropical Africa," paper prepared for delivery at the 1966 Annual Meeting of the American Political Science Association, New York, September 6–19, 1966, p. 13.

16. For material on African armies, the source I have found most useful is the publications of the Institute for Strategic Studies (ISS) in London, particularly, David Wood, *The Armed Forces of African States* ("Adelphi papers," no. 27, April 1966): M. J. V. Bell, *Army and Nation in Sub-Saharan Africa* (Adelphi Papers," no. 21, August 1965); M. J. V. Bell, *Military Assistance to the African States* ("Adelphi Papers," no. 15, December 1964): also M. J. V. Bell, "The Military in the New States of Africa," paper given to the working session, "The Professional Military and Militarism," Sixth World Congress of Sociology, September 1966; James S. Coleman and Belmont Bryce, Jr., "The Role of the Military in Sub-Saharan Africa," in *The Role of the Military in Underdeveloped Countries,* ed. John J. Johnson (Princeton: Princeton University Press, 1962), pp. 359–405; William Foltz, "Military Influences," in *African Diplomacy,* ed. Vernon McKay (New York: Frederick A. Praeger, 1966), pp. 69–70; George Weeks, "The Armies of Africa," in *A Handbook of African Affairs,* ed. Helen Kitchen (New York: Frederick A. Praeger, 1964), pp. 188–236.

17. For armies of other areas, see ISS, *The Military Balance,* 1965–66 through 1975.

18. Charles Stevenson, "African Armed Forces," *Military Review* 47 (March 1967): 18–24.

19. For a good description of a police force in Africa see Foreign Areas Studies Division of the Special Operations Research Office, *United States Army Handbook for Senegal* (Washington, D.C.: American University, August 1963), pp. 443–54.

20. Colin Leys has given us a most useful typology of violence in Africa in his "Violence in Africa," *Transition* 4 (1965): 17–20. War subsystems refer to the feuding of tribes and clans as a way of life.

21. *Ibid.,* 19.

22. Algeria, with an armed force of 48,000 men, was spending 3.2 percent of GNP in 1964. For the same year Morocco, with an army of close to 45,000, was spending 4.8 percent; Tunisia, with an army of 16,000 was spending 3.1 percent, and Libya, with an army of 6,000 was spending 3.6 percent. See United States Arms Control and Disarmament Agency, *World Wide Defense Expenditures and Selected Economic Data, Calendar Year 1964,* Research Report 66–1 (Washington, D.C., January 1966), 11–12.

23. Stevenson's figures for defense budget as a share of GNP were published in 1967. The Arms Control and Disarmament Agency's were published in 1966 using 1964 calendar year. There are many discrepancies between them which perhaps may be accounted for by the rapid shifts in government spending. The governments' figures upon which they are based are variable also. For some countries the same data are used.

24. AID, Principles of Foreign Economic Assistance (Washington, D.C., 1965), p. 20.

25. Those arguments are summarized, among other places, in Harold Hovey, *United States Military Assistance* (New York, 1965), pp. 219–24.

26. See Janowitz, *The Military in Political Development,* for a comparative study on the military in new nations.

27. Stevenson, "African Armed Forces," Stevenson, p. 22, notes that 23 nations give military assistance to African countries.

28. For French defense agreements see *West Africa* (London) August 24, 1963, reprinted in Kitchen, *Handbook of African Affairs,* pp. 233–235. For the texts of certain published agreements see *Collective Defense Treaties* (Washington, D.C. 1967), pp. 165–166. Also see Wood, *Armed Forces of African States,* for a brief resume of aid for individual African states.

29. See Philip B. Springer, "Disunity and Disorder, Factional Politics in the Argentine Military," in *The Military Intervenes,* pp. 145–168.

30. See Colonel A. A. Afrifa, *The Ghana Coup* (New York: Humanities Press, 1966).

31. This can be found in Bell, *Military Assistance to the African States*; McArdle, *Role of Military Assistance in Arms Control*; and in the ISS publication by John Sutton and Geoffrey Kemp, *Arms to Developing Countries* ("Adelphi Papers," no. 28, October 1966).

32. Marshall Goldman, *Soviet Foreign Aid* (New York: Frederick A. Praeger, 1967), p. 180.

33. McArdle, *Role of Military Assistance in Arms Control,* p. 78.

34. For a discussion of Soviet military aid programs and their motives see *The Soviet Military Aid Program as a Reflection of Soviet Objectives* ("Georgetown Research Project," Atlantic Research Corporation, June 1965).

35. V. Sibirsky, "Washington's New Frontiers in Africa," *International Affairs* (Moscow) 2 (February 1967): 73–77.

36. A. Iskendrov, "The Army, Politics and the People," *Izvestia,* January 17, 1967, p. 2.

37. *The Economist,* May 27, 1967, p. 900.

38. See Chapter 7, this volume.

39. Lt. Col. Bernard L. Pujo, "South of the Sahara: Defense Problems in French Speaking Africa," *Military Review* (February 1966): 33.

40. *Ibid.,* p. 34.

41. Press and periodical reports can be assembled. Sutton and Kemp have done this and they provide material on origin of aircraft, tanks, etc. House of Commons, Papers, *Civil Appropriations Accounts and Civil Estimates* reported military aid to Africa where there were small programs: Libya, Sudan, Somalia, Mali. Nigeria was not reported after 1960; Ghana and Kenya were not reported. Data on Tanganyika and Uganda were incomplete; Sierra Leone was not reported.

42. John H. Ohly, "A Study of Certain Aspects of Foreign Aid," Annex G of the *Draper Report,* pp. 282–283.

43. Henry Kuss, Deputy Assistant Secretary of State for International Security Affairs and the man in charge of arms sales, has argued that from the military point of view we stand to lose all the major international relationships paid for with grant aid money unless we can establish professional military relationships through the sales media. U.S. Senate, Committee on Foreign Relations, Subcommittee on Disarmament, *Hearings, United States Armament and Disarmament Problems,* 90th Cong., 1st Sess., 197, p. 147.

44. A staff study prepared for the use of the Committee on Foreign Relations, *Arms Sales and Foreign Policy* (Washington, D.C., 1967), argues that at a time of increasing congressional oversight of military grant assistance, emphasis has shifted from these programs to a concentration on military sales. In fiscal year 1961 sales were 43.4 percent of grant aid; in 1966 sales stood at 235.1 of aid (p. 2).

45. Reported sales for Africa south of the Sahara were $1.3 million for Liberia between 1956 and 1965 and $0.3 million for Nigeria in 1965. Ethiopia acquired some naval vessels and some jets with interest-free loans. McArdle, *Role of Military Assistance in Arms Control,* p. 74. Total receipts from military sales for all Africa from 1961 to 1965 were $11.2 million. They were estimated at $1. million for 1966 and 1967. Total sales 1961–1965 were $4.6 billion. From Department of Defense, *Military Assistance Facts* (Washington, D.C., May 1966), p. 19.

46. AID and Department of Defense, *Proposed Mutual Defense and Development Programs FY 1965* (Washington, D.C., April 1964), p. 30.

47. Detailed descriptions of the administration of military assistance can be found in Hovey, *U.S. Military Assistance,* pp. 139–140, and *Information and Guidance on Military Assistance* prepared by the Evaluation Division of Military Assistance, Deputy Chief of Staff, S and L Headquarters, United States Air Force, 10th ed. (Washington, D.C., 1966), pp. 15–22. A very valuable commentary on administration of MAP in Africa is provided by Colonel Quintus C. Atkinson, "Military Assistance in Sub-Saharan Africa" unpublished M.B.A. thesis, George Washington University, 1966). I am grateful for Colonel Atkinson's making this work available.

48. Hovey, *U.S. Military Assistance,* p. 144. The unified command for the Pacific had 80 military personnel; for Europe it was 60 military and 29 civilians. For Latin America it was 24 military and 7 civilian personnel.

49. Atkinson, "Military Assistance in Sub-Saharan Africa," notes that AID is both a referee in economic and military assistance plans and competes with Department of Defense for funds, p. 23.

50. AID can fund equipment which normally would be furnished under military aid. It can pay part of the costs of training military personnel. Economic funds can be used to build local production facilities for the military. On the other hand, military aid can pay for paramilitary unit buildup, and military aid can be used for provision of consumable items which are needed for strengthening the military.

51. AID, *Information on the Office of Public Safety and the International Police Academy* (Washington, D.C., 1966).

52. Janowitz, *The Military in Political Development,* p. 101.

53. *Ibid.,*

54. Figures for 1966 are from the Statistics and Report Division, Office of Program Coordination, AID, as published in AID's *Report for July 1, 1965–July 20, 1966.* (Washington, D.C., 1967), p. 31; 1967 figures are from AID's Office of Development Planning, Bureau for Africa.

55. Statement of Secretary of Defense Robert McNamara, in U.S. House of Representatives, Subcommittee on Appropriations, *Hearings, Foreign Assistance and Related Agencies Appropriations for 1967,* 19th Cong., 2nd Sess., 1967, pt. I, p. 513.

56. Hovey, *U.S. Military Assistance,* pp. 107–108, citing General Adam's testimony before the House Foreign Affairs Committee in 1964.

57., U.S. House of Representatives, Committee on Appropriations, *Hearings, Foreign Operations Appropriations,* 1964, 88th Cong., 1st Sess., 1963, p. 296, cited by Atkinson, p. 57.

58. G. Mennen Williams, "U.S. Policy in Africa," *For Commanders* 5 (July 1965): 1.

59. McArdle claimed that the United States was the largest single donor of military assistance in Africa through 1964. McArdle, *Role of Military Assistance in Arms Control,* p. 67. This may not have been true for Africa south of the Sahara as compared to French assistance, although the Ethiopian program was undoubtedly the largest effort by far until the Soviet program in the Somali Republic. France gave $81 million worth of equipment to African countries as "independence gifts." Bell, *Military Assistance to Africa.*

60. Department of State, *Report to the President from the Committee to Strengthen the Security of the Free World* (Clay Report) (Washington, D.C., 1963), p. 10.

61. As Ambassador to Ethiopia, E. Korry, in an unpublished report, argued that this should be done. Also see President Johnson's Special Message to Congress on Aid to Foreign Lands in *The New York Times,* February 10, 1967, p. 16. And Anthony Astrachan, "AID Reslices the Pie," *Africa Report* 12 (June 1967): 8–15.

62. There actually was a time lag between the Clay Committee's recommendations and the weeding out of countries in MAP because programs negotiated in 1963 had to be completed and because the idea of civic action and counterinsurgency took hold in Africa.

63. Vernon McKay, ed., *Africa in World Politics* (Chicago: 1963), p. 40, cited in McArdle, *Role of Military Assistance in Arms Control,* p. 77.

64. *Military Assistance Facts,* p. 31.

65. *Foreign Assistance and Related Agencies,* 1967, p. 731.

66. *Military Assistance Facts,* p. 24. In the small programs with two or four MAP people, individuals will plan programs, be involved with selection of indigenous personnel for training, and be watchdogs in program implementation.

67. Atkinson, "Military Assistance in Sub-Saharan Africa," p. 72, citing United States Department of Air Force, *Information and Guidance on Military Assistance,* 9th ed. (Washington, D.C., 1965), p. 15.

68.   One interesting example is the selection of African students to attend college in the U.S. and then go on to military training here. Socialization and training theoretically are combined. What this will mean for the careers of those who do it remains to be seen, both with respect to their values and the vulnerability of their political position.

69.   Annex E of *Draper Report,* "Training and Education under the Assistance Programs," by the staff of the committee, pp. 137–160.

70.   See also C. Windle and T. Vallance, "Optimizing Military Assistance Training," *World Politics* 15 (October 1962): 91–107.

71.   See Henry Bienen, "What Does Political Development Mean in Africa?"

72.   Hovey, *U.S. Military Assistance,* p. 146, gives some material on Military Assistance Institute (MAI) courses. American military assistance personnel are now passing through MAI, which has its own staff and also has guests from agencies of the government and the academic community for lectures. Military attachés do not pass through MAI but go to other institutes for training. There is great sensitivity within both AID and the Defense Department to the need for getting military and police assistance personnel who can train men in the intricacies of modern weapons or criminalistics, police or military administration, and the development tasks. As Byron Engle, the director of the Office of Public Safety, has said, "The Man we are looking for doesn't really exist. He must have executive police experience or he won't go very far as an advisor. He must also know something of military affairs, intelligence, language, and international politics." *Information on the Office of Public Safety and the International Police Academy.*

73.   For a brief sketch of curriculum at training centers, see Barber and Ronning, *International Security and Military Power,* pp. 148–156, and Lt. Doyle C. Ruff, "Win Friends . . . Defeat Communism," *Instructors Journal* 2 (July 1964): 25–34. Also see *Military Assistance and Training Programs of the U.S. Government* (New York, 1964).

74.   *Draper Report,* Annex E, p. 154.

75.   Windle and Vallance, "Optimizing Military Assistance Training" pp. 91–107.

76.   *Draper Report,* Annex E, p. 151.

77.   See Lucien Pye, "Armies in the Process of Political Modernization," in *The Role of the Military in Underdeveloped Countries,* ed. John J. Johnson (Princeton: Princeton University Press, 1962), pp. 69–90, and Guy Pauker, "Southeast Asia as a Problem Area in the Next Decade," *World Politics* 11 (April 1959): esp. 339–344.

78.   Morris Janowitz, "Organizing Multiple Goals: War Making and Arms Control," in *The New Military: Changing Patterns of Organization,* ed. Morris Janowitz (New York: Frederick A. Praeger, 1965), p. 29.

79.   Bienen, *The Military Intervenes.*

80.   The Ivory Coast Army's insignia is a badge and a hoe.

81.   Quoted by Walter A. E. Skurnik, "Political Instability and Military Intervention in Dahomey and Upper Volta," paper presented at the annual meeting of the African Studies Association, Bloomington, Ind., October 1966, p. 15.

82.   See Bienen, "What does Political Development Mean in Africa?" and Aristide Zolberg, *Creating Political Order: The Party States of West Africa* (Chicago: Rand McNally, 1966), p. 93.

83.   Samuel Huntington, "Political Development and Political Decay," *World Politics* 17 (April 1965): 429. Huntington argues that military juntas may spur modernization, that is, industrialization, urbanization, increased literacy, rise in income, but that they cannot bring about political development, which he defines as the institutionalization of political organizations and procedures (p. 393). African militaries are not likely to bring modernization, in Huntington's terms, either. And in certain cases, rather than bringing about public order, they accentuate tendencies toward chaos (Nigeria) or create disorder (East Africa in 1964).

84.   U.S. Senate, Committee on Foreign Relations, *Hearings, Foreign Assistance Act of 1962,* 87th Cong., 2d Sess., 1962, p. 76, cited in Barber and Ronning, *Internal Security and Military Power,* p. 218.

85. There is the aphorism attributed to F. Houphouet-Boigny: if you want a man to be a good bourgeois, send him to Lumumba University in Moscow, but if you want to radicalize him, send him to the Sorbonne.

86. U.S. Senate, Committee on Appropriations, *Hearings, Mutual Security Appropriations Act for 1954*, 83rd Cong., 2d Sess., 1954, pp. 921–922, cited by Edgar Furniss, *Some Perspectives on American Military Assistance* (Center of International Studies, Princeton University, June 1957), p. 17.

87. *Information and Guidance on Military Assistance,* 10th ed., p. 12.

88. Gen. Curtis Lemay, "Strategic Advantage is Key to All Tasks" (Air Force Information Policy Letter: Supplement for Commanders, no. 125 Internal Information Division, SAF), p. 11, Pentagon, cited by Barber and Ronning, *International Security and Military Power*, p. 162. Barber and Ronning noted that economic aspects of development were stressed by military officers in personal conversations. Packenham concluded the same thing for AID officials. Some officials that I met in the Office of Public Safety and the International Police Academy were very sensitive to what an AID pamphlet calls "the social climate of stability and security." (See AID, *Information on the Office of Public Safety and the International Police Academy,* p. 2.)

89. Barber and Ronning, *Internal Security and Military Power,* p. 240.

90. U.S. House of Representatives, Committee on Foreign Affairs, *Hearings, Foreign Assistance Act of 1966,* 89th Cong., 2d Sess., 1966, p. 1045.

91. See Davis B. Bobrow, "Limitations on Civic Action," in *Arms Controls in the Developing Areas,* ed. Edward W. Gude, Davis B. Bobrow, Clark C. Abt ("A Unicorn Study," Phase II report, for the Directorate for Arms Control, Office of the Assistant Secretary of Defense for International Security Affairs, Contract Number SD-125, prepared by the Strategic Studies Department, Missile and Space Division, Raytheon Company, Bedford, Mass.), pp. 131–41.

92. William Foltz, *"Military Influences,"* p. 88.

93. Fred Greene, "Toward Understanding Military Coups," *Africa Report* (February 1966): 11.

94. Packenham, "Political Development Doctrines in American Foreign Aid," pp. 232–233. Aid administrators now feel that they are beginning systematically to look at the impact of U.S. AID programs. It may well have been the instructions of Congress, more than the urgings of academics or individuals within AID, that has led to this concern. For Title IX of the Foreign Assistance Act of 1961, as amended now states (from 1966): "In carrying out programs authorized in this chapter, emphasis shall be placed on assuring maximum participation in the task of economic development on the part of the people of the developing countries, through encouragement of democratic private and local government institutions." The House Committee on Foreign Affairs asked AID to develop new criteria by which the agency could evaluate its success in implementing Title IX. AID's *Report to the Congress of the Implementation of Title IX* (Washington, D.C., May 10, 1967) shows a broader approach to the development process than heretofore.

95. The new policy of concentrating aid in target countries in Africa will lead to an erosion of the "marginality of impact" view.

96. We must distinguish between token programs—for example, sending eight trucks to Dahomey in 1962 and 1963–and those like the assistance programs to Liberia which, though small by American standards, would have impact on internal developments.

97. Whatever the legitimacy of intervention in the eyes of British, French, and American trainers, it is probable that barracks talk about politicians is not too respectful, although Peter Calvocoressi assures us that in Britain "it would be repugnant to the military mind to become involved in the dissemination of political ideas." *World Order and the New States* (London: Frederick A. Praeger, 1962), p. 55.

98. Wheatley, "Role of National Military Forces in Internal Political Conflict," pp. 1–2.

99. *Ibid.,* p. 3–6.

100.   Wolf had a similar concern in "Political Effects of Military Programs." He concluded that large military aid programs do not seem to be associated with more restrictive and authoritarian institutions. Aside from problems of talking about political development in these terms [derived from Russell H. Fitzgibbon and Kenneth F. Johnson's "Measurement of Latin American Political Change," *American Political Science Review* 55 (September 1961): 515–526], coups are not dealt with *per se*. Needler has related military overthrows of governments to deteriorating economic conditions but not at all to military assistance. He concludes that because of internal military factionalism, U.S. positions can influence "swing men" among the Latin American militaries. But his discussion here is of recognition and nonrecognition, not of assistance policies. Needler, "Political Development and Military Intervention in Latin America," pp. 624–625. Wheatley found that Latin American states diverged from the correlations he found elsewhere with regard to the connection between military responsiveness and indicators of the salience and effectiveness of government mediation of resource flow. Janowitz in *The Military in Political Development* has suggested that fundamental differences in the history of militarism in South America make this area atypical of developing areas. It may be that when American spokesmen have denied the connection between military assistance and military takeovers, the Latin American experience has been uppermost in their minds.

101.   To my knowledge, none of those who have dealt with coups in Africa have even attempted to relate assistance to their onset.

102.   *The New York Times,* May 16. 1967.

103.   As Wheatley himself notes, "Role of National Military Forces in Internal Political Conflict," p. 27.

104.   David Apter has posited a situation where there is an inverse relationship between information and coercion in a system. *The Politics of Modernization* (Chicago: University of Chicago Press, 1966), p. 40.

105.   Aristide Zolberg, "Military Intervention in the New States of Tropical Africa," in *The Military Intervenes,* pp. 71–102.

106.   The distinction between power and force is made by Zolberg, who utilizes Talcott Parson's analysis, "Some Reflections on the Place of Force in Social Process," in *Internal War,* ed. Harry Eckstein (New York: 1964, p. 59.

107.   *Draper Report,* Annex C, "A Study of United States Military Assistance Programs in Underdeveloped Areas," p. 51.

108.   As the Draper Report suggested should be done; *ibid.*

109.   Edward C. Banfield, *American Foreign Aid Doctrine* (Washington, D.C.: American Enterprise Institute for Public Policy Research, 1967) has noted that aid can bring some desired condition through a transformation of society. That is, via indirect means a political culture might be altered; in direct influence, culture is taken as a given and direct political results are the goal.

Chapter 7

Public Order and the Military in Africa:
Mutinies in Kenya, Uganda, and Tanganyika

The overriding problems for most African countries are the maintenance of public order and the creation of political order.[1] The two terms are not identical. "Public order" refers to a stable situation in which the security of individuals or groups is not threatened and in which disputes are settled without resort to violence. 'Political order" refers to a process of institution-building and the creation of stable patterns of politics. It is not some terminal state that exists forever, once attained. Groups vie for authority and struggle for shares of valued things, but they do so in a context of effective operation of political instruments, through which both rulers and ruled act.[2] A crisis of political order raises the specter of public disorder.

Problems of public disorder came most dramatically into focus as violence broke out in the Congo after independence was granted in 1960. The Congo seemed to be an example of disorder that stemmed from a failure of national integration in a country of great ethnic and geographical diversities and in a context of precipitate withdrawal of the colonial power.[3] Africa provides other examples of large-scale turmoil which may have taken a greater toll of life and which were marked by tribal or ethnic-religious violence—for example, the Sudan, Nigeria, and Rwanda. The postcolonial history of most African countries, however, has not been marked by this kind of overt public disorder.

Perhaps because Africa has not been pervaded by violent public disorder, the study of new African states has been organized in terms of problems of development and integration. African elites have also discussed their problems in these terms. However, a concrete definition of problems of political development or national integration in Africa must account for a situation in which central or national authorities are unable to exert authority over the territorial entity they "rule." This phenomenon is not unique to Africa. The claims of any central government to rule must be measured against the realities of local autonomy, de jure or de facto. Many areas of life in which centralized determination is taken for granted in western polities which call themselves "decentralized," "loose," or "democratic" are outside the scope or even the reach of national authorities in Africa. In the power realm, nationwide political structures are either nonexistent or too weak to enforce the will of ruling national elites, no matter whether they are of traditional lineage groups, civilian bureaucracy, or the military. There is a failure of centralized authority in the realm of legitimacy. Although many African one-party states claim that only disciplined parties can mobilize for development, it is often in these very states that values are not authoritatively allocated for the society as a whole by central authorities.[4]

Highly localized determination of political life need not be synonymous with disorder, anarchy, and chaos. In fact, it may be the only way to avoid these conditions in certain circumstances. A problem of political order arises when some national or central body tries to bring its rule over subnational entities. Whether a problem of public order develops depends on the nature of the resistance to this effort. Similarly, subnational groups, political organizations, or governments may struggle with each other for control of the center or for other reasons. The form and substance of the struggle determine whether a crisis of political order exists. Thus, to make a judgment about the kind of order problem that exists when some local unit cannot enforce compliance within its own boundaries, we should know what kind of effort is being resisted, how the resistance is being manifested, and what the governing body is doing to secure compliance. Usually, it is not difficult to make such a determination. For African countries, public disorder is a constant threat because political order is fragile or has not even been achieved.

Africa has many political, economic, and social incongruities because certain patterns of actions are national in scope, while others, parallel or intersecting, are not. For example, many African countries have communication systems which now provide rather easy dissemination of ideas and mobility within national boundaries. A monetary sector of the economy may co-exist spatially with a subsistence sector in every region, tribal area, and natural geographic unit; but individuals who live near each other in terms of miles can live worlds apart, if one grows cash crops and another does not. National institutions—armies, parliaments, heads of states, political parties—have a presence and a real meaning, but they may not be able to enforce their orders throughout most of the country and may be ignored in various degrees by the majority of the people. One of the most striking incongruities is the existence of elites who strive to rule their countries from capitals or regional centers but who cannot impose their wishes on local elites and who reach nonelites little, if at all. We may feel that anarchy exists because national elites are in fact trying to make their will felt. We then speak of a collapse or breakdown of order when we really mean the failure of central rule.[5]

The problem of public order has been posed in another connection in Africa. In 1965–1966 civilian authority failed dramatically as the military seized power in Congo-Kinshasa, Dahomey, Central African Republic, Upper Volta, Nigeria, and Ghana. Army leaders who took power did so in the name of averting disorder. In Nigeria, Congo, and Upper Volta, disorder actually existed, but there were no indications that this situation was about to occur in Ghana. In Nigeria, the Army was itself responsible for furthering breakdowns of public order, as in East Africa in 1964 when the Armies of Kenya, Uganda, and Tanganyika had themselves disrupted public order.

In Africa the claim has also been made that military elites are suited for short-term clean-up of corruption, for starting or revitalizing economic development, and for preserving or establishing national integration because the military speaks for the entire nation, without regard to religious or parochial tribal distinctions. Almost everywhere the short-term aspects of military rule are stressed. The norms of a civilian-ruled polity seem to be accepted, so far, by the military in Africa. At least army leaders speak of a return to civilian rule.[6]

The reasons military elites are able successfully to intervene and are motivated to do so are obvious. In a situation in which all institutions operate from weakness, if the military exists at all, it is an important political organization. No matter the degree of professionalization within the officer corps, the level of technology, the organizational format of a particular military force, an army/police in Africa is always a potential political factor because it can exert some strength in what is essentially a domestic power vacuum. Moreover, the military *claims* to be a national group rather than a parochial one; and if the claim is widely accepted, the military then constitutes a reservoir of legitimate authority. We cannot take for granted this reservoir of authority.[7] Not every military elite thinks of itself as reflecting and incorporating national aspirations, although this may be an area where "demonstration effects" are at work and the military in one country begins to conceive of itself in this way after contact with other militaries or after seeing military take-overs made in these terms. Even when the military considers itself the embodiment of national ideals, the population at large may not accept this claim. When the military enters the political arena as a ruling group, the reservoir, if one has existed, has a tendency to run dry quite quickly. Nonetheless, when civilian governments are discredited, the military may be able to intervene without force because it does retain legitimacy untainted by civilian failures.

Of course, the technology of the military in new states is relevant for intervention in domestic politics. "The military" usually means infantry batallions which can be deployed in urban centers. These battalions are sometimes supplemented by airborne troops and a special forces police which may have some motorized weaponry. Army and police are often both national forces and constitute a kind of superpolice.[8] (As armies grow and the military comes to include artillery and airborne units, greater distinction between police and army is likely.)

We cannot generalize easily about the ideology of military leaders, because both the social origins of officers and their career lines differ within and between African countries. We can, however, say that military leaders are peculiarly indisposed to tolerate public disorder—even if their actions sometimes lead to such a state. There are less certain grounds to argue that they are also indisposed to tolerate corruption, lack of economic development, tribalism, or parochialism of any kind. Military leaders have been accused of and implicated in corrupt activities.[9] They have been deeply involved in the very systems they overthrew in Ghana and Nigeria. And the military itself is often driven by ethnic cleavages, and it acts as an interest group at times not even pretending to be acting in the national interest but rather making overt interest group demands. The East African mutinies of 1964 were a case in point. While the military may be indisposed to disorder, it may be the prime mover for disorder. The instruments of violence are not always used in the interest of stability. The Force Publique's mutiny in the Congo was, after all, not only a response to a breakdown of authority but also a cause of chaos. The mutinous armies in Tanganyika, Uganda, and Kenya tried to take advantage of governmental weakness to put forward their demands and in so doing created disorder. In Tanganyika this led to riots by elements of the population of Dar es Salaam. President Olympio was assassinated by soldiers in Togo in circumstances that remain as yet unclear.

It remains to be seen whether the military leaders who took power in 1965–1966 will be able to solve economic and political problems. Already it is being maintained that the military can be more effective than a political party and that this is one of the most significant factors in the changed African scene since 1964.[10] But there is some doubt already that the army and police are stable and powerful factors in otherwise fluid and powerless societies.[11] Stable they are not. Their societies are fluid and often no groups are able to impose some central rule over the whole society. But this does not mean that African societies have no power groups or that the military will be able to remake societies in their own image, provided they have one.

Since the military has intervened so widely in Africa, and probably will continue to do so, it is essential to detail the nature of the interaction of the military with its environment. To determine the situation in a specific country, it is important to know the composition of the military elite and the structure and size of the total military force. More generally, it is important to consider how the military fits into the political system and what social and economic constraints, as well as political ones, are imposed on the form and substance of military intervention.

I have chosen to examine the East African mutinies of January, 1964, in order to approach the questions of public order and the nature of military intervention in Africa. The mutinies of the two infantry batallions of the Tanganyika Rifles and elements of the Uganda Rifles and Kenya Rifles demonstrated clearly the relationship between the military and civilian authorities in Africa and the problem of creating authoritative structures, although the armies were not trying to and never seized power. In fact, the very parochialness of the armies' demands and the vulnerability of ostensibly popular civilian governments were illustrated. Moreover, the nature of the military force itself was revealed, with regard to its internal composition, organization, and leadership, as well as its relationship to the police and to interest groups.[12]

The three East African armies never did assume power. In East Africa it would not have been difficult to topple governments. To constitute a military government would be another matter. This situation never occurred because British troops intervened to uphold constituted rule in Kenya, Uganda, and Tanganyika. The British intervention is important because non-African states have influenced the nature of the military in Africa (although not always its role), through their provision of equipment, training, organization, and an ethos for African military forces. And great powers overtly have been the final arbiters of military intervention in the Congos (Brazzaville and Leopoldville), the three East African cases, and Gabon.

The Military in East Africa

A great deal of the literature about the military in new states has dealt with elites. Edward Shils, for example, discussed the military, stressing officer classes, the intelligentsia, gaps between towns and countryside, and disparities in education and socialization among segments of a population. Shils' category of modernizing military oligarchies described a system where a military elite constitutes itself as a ruling group. However, he noted that most African countries have no indigenous military elite.[13] This is less true today than it was at the start of the 1960's; Africanization of officer corps has taken place. Still, African armies are small in terms of absolute size and as a percentage of the total population. Many officers are either recently graduated from a short course in military affairs abroad or, more rarely, from military institutes where they matriculated. Some are former noncommissioned officers from World War II promoted during the current Africanization program.[14] With this in mind, we must immediately consider the term "military rule" itself. Generals or colonels may seize power and claim to be ruling a nation in the name of the army, but no "modern" military elite exists in any Sub-Saharan African country because the number of officers is so small and African officers with western officer training are so recent.[15]

At the time of the mutinies in January, 1964, the East African military forces were examples of African armies which were essentially battalions officered by expatriates.[16] Kenya's officer corps was more Africanized at the time of independence (December, 1963) than either the Tanganyika Army at the time of independence (December, 1961) or the Uganda Army at independence (October, 1962).[17] But the three armies were very similar because they were all formed from the British-trained and-commanded King's African Rifles; in addition, they all had little firepower and no tanks or artillery. The Kenya Army had more mobility and firepower than the others, since it possessed scout cars, more troop carriers, and light mortars. Kenya's advantage in weaponry and transport stemmed from its need in its northern territories, where it was and still is confronted with Somalia's territorial demands and the hostile activities of Somali *shiftas* or guerrillas. Furthermore, Kenya was a main British base in Africa, and the British had put more hardware into

Kenya than into Uganda and Tanganyika. And finally, the Kenya police force was by far the largest and best equipped in East Africa, since it had been developed during the Mau Mau crisis of the 1950's. At the end of 1963, Kenya had three army battalions of 2,500 men and a 11,500-man police force. Uganda had one battalion until 1963, when another was added, bringing the army near to 2,000 men. The Uganda police force was 5,500, not including the separate police force of the kingdom of Buganda, which totaled around 600, although there were close to 200 Buganda in the Uganda police.[18] Tanganyika's army and police force were slightly smaller than Uganda's, although even before the January 1964 mutiny the government was thinking about increasing the size of the army and establishing an air force.

The United Kingdom and Israel were providing Tanganyika and Uganda with miltary assistance, and Britain was both assisting Kenya's military force and defraying items in the defense budget. The stated annual defense budgets were under $1.75 million each for all three countries, and none of them wanted to increase defense expenditures. Africanization of the officer corps had proceeded slowly, precisely because East African political leaders were trying to keep costs down. Officers were paid very well by local standards. Any expansion in number of officers or replacement of British was bound to push up defense costs. Enlisted men were perhaps less realistically treated. They were not paid particularly well compared to semiskilled wage labor in the civilian economy. Furthermore, enlisted men and noncommissioned officers did exist in larger numbers than officers and could act as a pressure group. After independence, their grievances over wages were at the root of the mutinies. Political leaders had not appreciated the depth of discontent in the armies.

It is often argued that African countries cannot afford and do not need armies because their security problems are internal. In any case, no African country could withstand aggression from a major non-African power. Furthermore, it is claimed that African resolution to settle disputes without force, pan-Africanism, and the Organization of African Unity (OAU) are going to obviate the necessity of armies. African political leaders have sometimes sounded these very themes. Many have been sorrowful about the creation and expansion of their armies. When he was Prime Minister, President Nyerere of Tanganyika said, "We'd rather spend our money on bread [than on an army.]."[19] Yet many African countries do have external security problems, which are particularly severe in East africa.

Kenya continues to face demands made on its northern territories by Somalia, and the Kenya police and army have been engaged in countering Somali raiders who live within and without Kenya. The border between Tanganyika and Kenya has not always been quiet as tribes move across it in their migratory patterns.[20] Tanganyika has had disturbances on almost all its borders. Its long Lake Tanganyika border with the Congo was the pathway for various Congolese factions to cross into Tanganyika. And Tanganyika played an important role in supplying eastern Congolese opponents of the Congo Central Government through Kigoma, the major Tanganyika town on the lake. Rwanda has been unstable since its own independence in 1962. Rwandan refugees came into northwestern Tanganyika during 1962–1963 and the border has been highly unstable. Tanganyika has had hostile relations with Malawi on one part of its southern border. And even its border with Zambia was disturbed during the Lumpa uprising in Zambia. Above all, Tantanyika has been a major base for liberation movements in southern Africa and has been a sanctuary and staging ground for Mozambique freedom fighters. Tanganyika army units have faced on Mozambique. The movement of refugees and guerrillas into Tanganyika has created internal as well as external security problems, as men with arms and families without means of sustenance move into the territory.[21]

Uganda, too, has had extremely tense border situations and very pronounced internal security problems. It shares a long land border with the Congo and faces on the area which saw the most intense fighting in the Congo during 1963–1965. Sudanese refugees coming down from the north and Rwandans coming up from the south have created problems. Nomadic tribes have raided Uganda territory from Kenya—an example of what has been called "war subsystems,"[22] that is, the feuding of pastoral tribes and clans. This feuding is pronounced among the northeastern Uganda nomadic tribes, the Karamojong and the Turkana. Uganda also has its "rejection movements," that is, movements which either want complete separatism from Uganda, some form of autonomy, or separation from some particular Kingdom or district administrator. The Ruwenzururu movement of western Uganda, the struggle between Sebei and Bagisu around Mt. Elgon, the lost countries issue between Buganda and Bunyoro, and the place of Buganda within Uganda are all examples. Uganda, which has by far the highest murder rate in East Africa (one murder for about every 10,000 people) also suffers from organized gang violence, called *kondoism*.[23] In a country which has one policemen for every 1,000 people, of whom only one in ten lives in a town, relatively wealthy cash crop farmers who live rather far apart provide a target for organized gangs. Thus, about 14 percent of recurrent expenditures is devoted to police and prisons alone. Part of the army expenditure is devoted to internal security as well, since the army has policed, albeit ineffectively, the western Kingdom of Toro where the Ruwenzururu movement is located.

The small armies of East Africa might be thought to have enough to do policing the borders and carrying out internal security functions; but in these countries, as elsewhere in Africa, there has been a feeling that armies ought to perform constructive social and economic work.

The French made nonmilitary use of armies before they granted independence, and some independent French-speaking states continued to use the army for compulsory agricultural work and for road building. The role of the army as a modernizing and integrating force in society has sometimes been stressed. The Israeli model is cited by African politicians, who claim that men from all areas and tribes will "melt" in the army and that they will bridge gaps between the state and society. The army will, they say, stand as a symbol of the nation while it performs real nation-building tasks.

Within East Africa, such ideas were most explicitly stated in Tanganyika. When Oscar Kambona was Minister for External Affairs and Defense, his speeches stressed the importance of the army for economic development and national integration. President Nyerere has always talked about the army as an instrument for nation-building. In Kenya and Uganda, political leaders spoke publicly in a similar vein, but little was done to employ the military in economic or social service projects. Army personnel did clear land on training assignments, but they were much more likely to appear for ceremonial occasions than as part of a systematic program for development. Furthermore, despite pressure from the youth wings of ruling political parties, particularly the Tanganyika Youth League of the Tanganyika African National Union (TANU)[24] and the Uganda People's Congress (UPC) youth group, and despite the inclinations of some political leaders to use the youth wings as a military or paramilitary force, recruitment procedures for the army remained the same as the preindependent selection process. In Uganda, the recruitment bias for northerners was retained since the political leadership of the UPC was itself northern-based. But the men recruited were not necessarily political followers or even politically aware. Rather, they were picked for the martial virtues: physical fitness, combativeness, and so on. In Tanganyika, recruiting teams traveled about, signing up men with the same characteristics. The choices often were made by noncommissioned officers who had themselves been professional soldiers in the King's African Rifles. In 1963, the two tribes that had traditionally supplied many army recruits—the Hehe of central Tanganyika and the Kuria of the Lake Victoria littoral—were reported to be still supplying 25 percent each of new recruits.[25] Training courses remained British-oriented and lacked educational content.[26] And although the government announced its intention to have universal male registration for military and nation-building purposes, no universal training or conscription program was implemented.

In Kenya, the army mutiny broke out less than a month after independence. The internal self-government of the ruling Kenya African National Union (KANU) regime itself was only seven months old.[27] Yet the KANU government had begun to inject a new note into recruitment and organization of army and police forces. In Kenya, the opposition Kenya African Democratic Union (KADU), which drew its strength from tribal groups outside Kikuyu, Luo, and Kamba (the three largest in Kenya), had argued for localization of police power in line with its determination to maintain strong regional and subregional political and administrative entities. When the *Majimbo* Constitution, which had defined a Kenya of strong regions, was abolished after the KANU victory, police powers became increasingly centralized in fact as well as in theory. But at the same time, within the ruling KANU party, individual leaders struggled to see Kamba, Luo, or Kikuyu in responsible police and army positions and the Luo-Kikuyu leadership of KANU began to try to end the dominance of Kamba within the Army.[28] At the same time, Luo-Kikuyu rivalry for patronage posts in the military and positions of influence proceeded and remains still. This, however, was not a result of the infusion of military and police into the politics of nation-building or modernization, but of a struggle for power defined in tribal-political terms long familiar in Kenya.

Because of this struggle, Kenya's political leadership more self-consciously attempted to master its own military force. This attempt was obscured because Kenya came to independence later than Uganda and Tanganyika and because the British retained a much greater military presence in Kenya through bases and training programs. In Tanganyika, the government believed itself popular—and with real justification. TANU had won overwhelming electoral victories, and Nyerere was liked throughout the country. Government and TANU leaders took for granted army loyalty and treated the army as another institution they had inherited from the British colonial regime. There had never been a struggle between civil servants and political leaders in Tanganyika. The idea of nation-building, as expressed by Nyerere and top TANU leaders (but not all middle-level leaders in TANU), conceived of a unity by amalgamation; there was no feeling that the civil service or military had to be radically remodeled right away or purged. The aim was to create a synthesis of state and party institutions over time.[29] And for the immediate future, the TANU government saw advantages to preserving civil service and army as political institutions.

In Uganda, the UPC leadership, and particularly the inside group around Prime Minister Obote, had close ties with the few Uganda officers who were also northerners. The main political problems for the UPC were the place of Buganda and politically organized Catholicism, which was the base for the Democratic Party. UPC leaders felt secure about the army of northerners on both these issues.

Specific political issues were largely irrelevant to the causes and outcomes of the East African mutinies. All three governments were fragile in terms of the overriding internal problems they faced. But the decisive factor was the fragility of ruling institutions in East Africa per se. Although one could argue that by the end of 1963 Uganda, Tanganyika, and Kenya were in different phases in their respective political dynamics and that their internal problems had important differences, it was the striking similarities of the inability of the government to deal with essentially parochial demands of enlisted men and noncommissioned officers which revealed the crisis of order in East Africa, and which is illustrative for Africa as a whole.[30] The time factor was of importance, not as much in comparing the three East African situations but in comparing East Africa and West Africa. The absence of an East African officer corps distinguished the East African armies from Ghanaian and Nigerian armies which had been Africanizing their officers over a ten-year period, or from the former French territories, which underwent a crash Africanization program in their armies from 1956–1960.[31] Thus, there were no East African officers who could, by virtue of rank and authority, control or head off mutinous enlisted men. On the other hand, the absence of a corporate officer group inhibited the transformation of a strike for more pay into an overt demand for military control of government or military participation in civilian regimes. The lack of indigenous officers was a mixed blessing.

The Mutinies

Late on Sunday night, January 19, 1964, troops of the first battalion in Dar es Salaam left the Colito Barracks located some eight miles from the center of the city. They came into Dar es Salaam and quickly took control of key points: radio station, police stations, airport, and State House—the home and office of President Nyerere.[32] During the early morning hours the mutinous troops, led by a sergeant, rounded up British officers who lived in a residential area between the barracks and the city. They had already seized the British officers at the barracks, although the Tanganyika Rifles' Commander, Brigadier Patrick Sholto Douglas, escaped. The leader of the mutiny, Sergeant Ilogi, offered the command of the Army to Lieutenant Elisha Kavona, the only university graduate among the Tanganyike officers. He had not been in on the plot but "thought it prudent to accept."[33]

At first, the mutineers made only two demands. They wanted to get rid of their thirty-five British officers and they wanted higher pay.[34] The mutineers negotiated with ministers, for both the President and Vice-President Kawawa were in hiding. Oscar Kambona, the Minister for External Affairs and Defense, who was also Secretary General of TANU, was the major government negotiator. He was unable to end the mutiny although he succeeded in limiting demands so that no overtly political ones were made.

During these first two days, the police remained on the sidelines.[35] The police force had lost its field force, that is, its best armed and most martial troops, because 300 of them had been shipped to Zanzibar after the Zanzibar Revolution. The Dar es Salaam Army battalion met no resistance of any kind. Apparently, the Minister for Home Internal Affairs requested Kenya troops but the Minister for External Affairs later countermanded this order, probably doubting their reliability.[36] The 800-man second battalion of Tanganyika Rifles at Tabora, which is about 400 miles northwest of Dar es Salaam, mutinied on January 21. They seized their British officers and their senior African officer, Captain M. S. H. Sarakikya, who is now the ranking Tanzanian officer and a brigadier.[37] The Tabora mutiny led to early and limited looting; but once Sarakikya gained control, the looting stopped.

In Dar es Salaam, however, looting was more severe. The breakdown in public order, the absence of Nyerere, the incapacity of his ministers to end the mutiny, the careful and quiet action or nonaction of the police, all created a situation in which mobs formed easily. Hostility to Asians and Arabs was expressed and interracial killing broke out in some quarters of the city. Initially some soldiers looted, but later the army moved to control looting.

President Nyerere emerged on January 21, and the leaders of the mutiny reiterated that they wanted no coup, only Africanization and higher wages. Neither the President nor Mr. Kambona was able to get the troops back to their barracks. The President tried to minimize what had occurred. He never defined "the trouble" as a mutiny, although he made it clear that he believed the whole affair was a disgrace and had done irreparable damage to Tanganyika. In his broadcasts to the people he seemed still under the constraint of the mutineers.[38] And in fact, it was not until British troops landed on January 25 from HMS Centaur, which had been lying off the Tanganyika coast, and took Colito Barracks, scattering the first battalion into the bush with some little loss of life, that the mutiny can be said to have come to an end.[39]

Between January 21 and 25, the mutiny began to take on more political tones. No revolt of military force could be without major political implications. But it was only after the mutiny had started that dissident trade-union leaders, political opponents of TANU, and a handful of dissidents within TANU emerged to take advantage of the situation and to make explicit political demands. Political demands were not expressed during the Kenya and Uganda mutinies simply because the mutinies did not last as long there and because government leaders, less caught by surprise, were able to take stronger stands.

Logistical factors rather than a disparate political context led to a different pattern in Kenya and Uganda from that of Tanganyika. Just as the mutiny spread from Dar es Salaam to Tabora, it spread from Tanganyika to Uganda and Kenya. The demands in the latter two countries were the same: Africanization of the army and higher pay for enlisted men and noncommissioned officers. The physical contiguity of the three countries, the basic similarity in internal army organization, and relationship of the army to British officers and training programs; and the analogous place of army to society in general and political leadership in particular made likely the rapid infection of mutiny from one country to the other. No *explicandum* of foreign subversion is necessary.[40] Nor were common East African military arrangements per se responsible for the contagion. There were no such arrangements by 1964.[41]

There was, however, a signal event in the political history of East Africa which formed the backdrop to the mutinies and helps to explain why the first link in the chain was Tanganyika. On January 12, 1964, the government of the Sultan of Zanzibar, which had only recently been installed, was overthrown.[42] Never before in East Africa had an independent government been confronted with force in the name of revolutionary government. Never since the British overthrew indigenous rulers and drove the Germans out of East Africa had force been successful in replacing one government with another. Of all the East African countries, Tanganyika had been characterized, prior to 1964, as the one where violence as a means of obtaining change had been virtually nonexistent. True, during the German colonial period, the Hehe of the southern highlands had fought against the colonial rulers in the 1890's; and again southern tribes fought against the Germans in the widespread Maji-Maji Revolt of 1905–1907. These were the most widespread and intense struggles against colonial rule in East Africa until the outbreak of Mau-Mau in Kenya. But since 1907, aside from the British fight against the Germans in World War I in Tanganyika, there had been neither revolt nor the large-scale tribal violence which characterized Uganda's separatist movements.

Thus, violence and the overthrow of constituted rule in Zanzibar made an immediate and deep impact in Tanganyika. This impact was even greater because the Sultan's rule was ended not only in the name of African nationalism against a minority Arab rule supported by foreign imperialists, but it was also made in the name of a class war of workers and peasants against exploiters. The shock waves from Zanzibar traveled rapidly across the narrow sea to Tanganyika. Legitimacy had been called into question. Dissident groups were more willing to use illegitimate means in the three East African countries than they had been before the Zanzibar Revolution. Tanganyika, the closest to Zanzibar geographically, and with the most intimate political connections, felt the first and deepest impact.

Another event triggered the Dar es Salaam mutiny. Two weeks before its outbreak, President Nyerere made a major policy speech. On January 7, he asserted that preference would no longer be given to Africans over other citizens of Tanganyika. Formerly, the policy had been one of localization but with an emphasis on redressing the imbalance in the number of Africans who held responsible posts. Now Nyerere linked a policy of no discrimination against Tanganyika citizens to the needs of a new Five Year Plan which would require utilizing all the trained personnel available. This speech alarmed trade-union officials, including the assistant general secretary of the Kenya Federation of Labour, who feared that Tanganyika had dropped its policy of Africanization.[43] The army was disturbed too, although the speech did not affect the army because all officers were British expatriates and not non-African Tanganyika citizens.[44] Nor were there non-African noncommissioned officers or enlisted men. In fact, according to one reporter, senior British officers and the Ministry of Defense "were already working out, on the initiative of British officers, a plan for the complete Africanization of the officer corps by the end of 1964."[45]

At the very start of the Tanganyika mutiny, the Ugandan government showed its sensitivity to the question of Africanization when the Minister of the Interior, Felix Onama, expressed confidence in British officers but announced plans to bring companies under African command by the end of 1964 and battalions by the end of 1965.[46] Despite Mr. Onama's remarks of January 22, elements of the Uganda battalion stationed at Jinja mutinied on January 23. Jinja is about 50 miles east of Kampala, Uganda's major town and capital and a little farther yet from Entebbe, the administrative headquarters. Jinja was the main army base, although many troops were at several points on the Rwanda, Congo, and Sudan borders. Others were in the Kingdom of Toro, trying without effect to end the Ruwenzururu rebellion; troops were also at Moroto in the far north of Uganda near Kenya. Prime Minister Obote justified his appeal for British troops on the grounds that security forces were stretched thin across Uganda and "unruly elements," which existed in all countries, might try to take advantage of this situation. No doubt he had the riots in Dar es Salaam very much in mind in the context of Uganda's own explosive town population and tribal, regional, and religious difficulties. At the same time that he called on British troops (they came from Kenya and from British ships off the East African coast), Mr. Obote promised an upward revision of pay, said British troops would not be needed long, and called the mutiny a "sit-down strike," denying a mutiny had occurred and affirming the loyalty of the troops. Indeed, the mutinous troops had held Mr. Onama prisoner for a while but they never left Jinja to head toward Kampala. The difference between being eight miles away and more than fifty miles away proved important. The troops could not have had the element of surprise they achieved in Dar es Salaam. A small number of police might have held them up on the Kampala-Jinja road. And because of the dispersion of the Uganda army throughout the country, there was no large concentration of troops in any one spot. Political leaders might find a number of morals here based on geography and the advantages of stationing armies away from capitals.

Kenya's political leaders received these blessings, too. Furthermore, British troops were already on Kenya soil and could be called on immediately. On January 24, Prime Minister Kenyatta moved to head off a Kenya mutiny. He announced a plan to increase the size of the Kenya Rifles by 1,000; he admitted that there were certain "anomalies" in the pay of African soldiers. And at the same time, British troops were on the move in Kenya and coming into Kenya from Aden. Nonetheless, two barracks mutinies occurred that night. One was at Langata Barracks a few miles outside Nairobi, Kenya's capital, and the other was at Lanet Barracks near Nakuru about one hundred miles northwest of Nairobi along the main Uganda-Kenya road. In Nairobi the British quickly seized control of key points and in Nakuru they took the armory. At Nakuru African officers and sergeants as well as at least 150 soldiers remained loyal. By January 25, the Kenya mutiny had ended. On this same day the British moved to end Tanganyika's unsettled situation by disarming the troops there. And in Uganda, British soldiers surrounded the camp at Jinja, seized the armory, and induced the mutineers to surrender.

The repercussions for the three countries seemed to vary in severity in accordance with the degree of length and disruptiveness of the mutiny. President Nyerere had the worst situation. He had called in the British after losing control. Furthermore, the Tanganyika Army was in ruins. Many mutinous troops were put in detention and tried. Others were sent back to their homes. The two battalions of the Tanganyika Rifles were disbanded, and it was determined to build an entirely new army. Meanwhile, Nigerian troops were requested to provide security after the British left and until new battalions could be formed. Demonstrations were held in support of the President in Dar es Salaam and district and regional centers. It was reported that when Nyerere said he was sorry to have called in British troops, there were chants of "We forgive you."[47]

The Mutinies Reconsidered

The collapse of government authority in Tanganyika and the reliance on British troops in Uganda and Kenya made it abundantly clear that whatever the popularity of the governments involved and the personal position of individual leaders, the East African governments could neither prevent mutinies nor counter them once they occurred. However, although the mutineers could have brought down the government in Dar es Salaam had they wished, and but for the presence of British troops they could have done it in Uganda and Kenya, too, the armies could not necessarily have replaced the civilian governments.

In Tanganyika, it would be one thing to occupy the capital and another to impose rule over the whole country—to command the regional and district political and administrative hierarchies. The army had neither the personnel nor the will to do so. Nor could the army take for granted even the support that TANU gets as the party which brought the country to independence. One does not have to argue that TANU "mobilizes" the population through a network of functioning party organizations in order to affirm that the party does legitimate the orders that civil servants give, and does provide self-legitimation and authority for political leaders who form the government. The army had no place in the popular consciousness throughout the country, so that it could compete with TANU as a legitimizing force. It provided no symbol of the nation as a whole; it was not seen as an organization which stood above politics and self-interest.

Even where political opposition to the ruling party was overt and organized as in Kenya and Uganda, the armies did not provide any possible alternative to civilian rule. In Uganda, the army would have been seen as even more "northern" and non-Bantu than the ruling UPC. Because of its ethnic composition, the army would have faced even more severe integrative problems than the UPC. In Kenya the army with its Kamba dominance would have faced similar Kikuyu and Luo opposition. Armies in new states are particularly vulnerable to problems stemming from ethnic and religious heterogeneity, because the army is itself often associated with specific ethnic groups and because the norms of the military may lead to an insensitivity to ethnic-religious values. And these are not mutually exclusive possibilities.

Army personnel sent to administer or politically to oversee districts in any of the East African countries would have been even more cut off from the local population than the political leaders and civil servants on the spot. We have seen how necessary is the collaboration of civil servants to new military rulers in Ghana, Nigeria, the Sudan, and elsewhere. In East Africa, there had been some hostility between civil servants and political leaders. The civil servants considered the political leaders less educated and less knowledgeable, and the politicians sometimes resented civil service lack of support for the national movement before independence, and condescending attitudes after it. But in Tanganyika, in particular, where Africanization of the civil service came late, where there are many contacts between civil servants and politicians, and where Nyerere always emphasized a community between them, political antagonisms were never very far-reaching. And this was true in East Africa as a whole compared to states in West Africa—Nigeria, Ivory Coast, and Ghana in particular (where there were more developed and entrenched civil services), or compared to Mali and Guinea (where civil servants may feel themselves under political pressure). In some African countries civil servants may feel themselves more radical than the political leaders; in others, a more radically sounding political leadership stands out. In East Africa, civil servants have had no poiltical stance per se. But they undoubtedly would have found one in an army-run regime which came into existence through a coup. For the civil servants would have felt freer to make interest group demands; they would have felt their compliance essential to maintenance of the regime; and they would have felt themselves vastly better educated than privates and noncommissioned officers, who had little formal education.

Furthermore, whether civil servants in East Africa are technical specialists or administrative generalists, they rely on district and regional party officials to put their programs into effect. Where bureaucratic norms are not widely understood or accepted, and where outsiders have a difficult time exerting their influence, it is hard to see how army men posted to a district could in fact get compliance, given the small coercionary apparatus at their disposal.

It would be tempting to conclude that at least at the center government must have been indeed fragile in Tanganyika, since a battalion of a thousand men could control the command points without opposition from either the body politic or any organized group. But would this be an accurate assessment? The mutineers had an advantage, because Dar es Salaam is cut off from the rest of Tanganyika's population centers. It would have been difficult to mobilize people from outside the capital to move against the army (just as the army could not easily have forayed out into the countryside). During the mutinies the regional and district headquarters, with the exception of Tabora and Nachingwea, continued to be run by the TANU and civil service hierarchies. There was apprehension in places but no looting in the towns or countryside. In some districts, instability at the center led to attempts to settle old scores, but only rarely did people try to get rid of local TANU leader. When it was clear that order was reestablished in Dar es Salaam, some local TANU leaders did try to imprison those who had openly opposed them. But on the whole, the regions and districts stayed calm, probably because of their removal from the center, the difficulty in communications, and the diffuseness of local politics. These conditions themselves have made it difficult, if not impossible, for the army to impose itself over the sixty districts which comprise the seventeen regions of Tanganyika.

The army would have faced all the problems that the present TANU leaders face, many of which confront most African leaders: a sparsely settled country with its population in major clusters along the peripheries; an economy which does not provide the material requisites for exerting central control; regional, district, and village organizations which operate with a great deal of autonomy; severe personnel shortages; the persistence of traditional patterns of social, political, and economic behaviors. Furthermore, the mutineers would be dislodging the figure with the greatest popularity and authority in Tanganyika—Julius Nyerere. An army without trained administrators would have had to rule without the center that did exist—those few national leaders who have the consent of their party and civil service hierarchies to rule, even if they cannot exert close control over those hierarchies.

Since the army did not claim to be ruling, a wait-and-see attitude prevailed even among TANU activists within Dar es Salaam. Naturally, there was a disinclination for unarmed men to oppose armed soldiers. What is striking in restrospect is that so few people took advantage of a chaotic situation to push their own ambitions. At the top, the President and at least one of the ministers[48] called attention to the loyalty of the Minister for Defense, Oscar Kambona, who negotiated with the rebels when the President went underground. Kambona had been accused within Tanganyika and in the West of being ambitious and radical. When the President praised Kambona's courage in reducing the effects of the troops' mutiny, he was doing more than voicing his appreciation; he was asserting that TANU had stayed united.[49]

Since the TANU Annual Conference and National Executive Committee meetings were due to convene just as the mutiny broke out, there was ample opportunity for TANU regional and district leaders to take part in any revolt, along with middle-level leaders or dissident top leaders who resided in Dar es Salaam. Of the more than 200 regional and district leaders who came into Dar es Salaam, only one—a TANU district secretary and head of government in the district (area commissioner)—was implicated. No parliamentary secretary (junior minister) was involved. Certain chiefs and Muslim leaders (sometimes the same people) who had opposed TANU, or as in the case of the leading dissident, Chief Fundikira, a former TANU Minister who had broken with the party, were not connected with the mutiny.[50] No civil servants were involved.

There were very good reasons for the solid loyalty from civil servants and from middle-level TANU leaders. Aside from Nyerere's personal popularity and the cohesiveness of his ministers and their personal loyalty to him, the dangers of trying to make common cause with the mutineers should have been apparent to any would-be leader of a coup. The soldiers did not distinguish between shades of political opinion within the cabinet or within TANU. When they were in the streets they were as likely to attack a parliamentary secretary who had taken a radical position on economic policy or even on Africanization as one who had not. Any government official was an "in"; the mutineers saw themselves as "outs." They wanted a bigger slice of the pie. Only some disaffected trade-union leaders, whose demands for higher pay and Africanization were the same as the soldiers' demands, and who knew the trade unions would be governmentalized in any case, joined in. Most of the leadership of the Tanganyika Federation of Labour did not—for trade union leaders were "ins," too. And all those who were privileged perceived that if the soldiers saw themselves as being "outs," then what of the urban unemployed and those primary school dropouts who would have been glad for the salary of a lowly private? These are truly the "outs." Once the dam burst, once the legitimacy of government was entirely pushed aside and Nyerere's person removed, where would the demands of the "outs" end? And who could draw the line again between "ins" and "outs"? Thus, even if there was middle-level leaders who had grievances, this was not the base of support they wished, and the demands of the mutineers were not the issues they wanted to exploit. In January, 1964, there were no revolutionaries in Dar es Salaam willing to use a mutinous army to call forth the urban unemployed and the rural underemployed.[51] Rank-and-file trade union members were themselves privileged, since a fraction of the Tanganyika population are wage-earners. While they wanted higher pay and more rapid advancement, they were also not unaware of the existence and dangers of an unemployed mob.

The Kenya and Uganda mutinies probably were nipped in the bud too quickly for any overt support to have developed for the soldiers among dissidents (and both countries had an ample share of oppositionists). Kenya, the most urbanized and industralized of the East African countries, had (and still has) the most severe unemployment problem. Its own trade union federation was factionalized. Moreover, there was land hunger in Kenya; the area around Lanet Barracks was a sensitive one in this respect because it was an area of European settlement. There was no indication that grievances became more intense on these issues after the mutiny, which would have been the case if the soldiers had been identified with, or if political groups had been willing to exploit, the soldiers' demands for their own purposes. Uganda had its share of profound social cleavage, which had been aggravated by the desire of the UPC government to move toward a one-party system.[52] But the opposition Democratic Party and Kabaka Yekka were not inclined to try to make cause with or capital out of the mutiny. Rather, they saw a weakening of an arm of the government. This arm could not be harnessed to their own ends, but it could not so easily be used against them either.

Because the armies of East Africa were not highly visible in the capitals, much less in the country as a whole, and because they were seen to be British-organized armies—mercenary armies, as it were—they were not thought of as national bodies. Thus, there was little or no identification with them before or during the mutinies. When British troops came into East Africa, the situation changed. Independent African governments had called in the former colonial ruler. These governments were alrady sensitive to their vulnerability on the issue of economic progress. Immediately after the mutiny a Tanganyika government statement insisted that, "Neither the people nor the Government have ever failed to stress the need for economic and social advance as a corollary to independence, and the whole people are mobilized for this purpose."[53] Later on the Minister for Finance said that the legitimate grievances of our soldiers were "part of the grievances of all our people which is poverty."[54] Now they faced attacks on their own independence and on racial grounds. It was not inconceivable that in the future the armies would be seen as the carriers of nationalism who had been struck down by the British.[55] Thus, the nature of military force reconstruction became a most immediate and sensitive political problem, especially in Tanganyika.

In Uganda and Kenya, the entire army had not been so thoroughly implicated. In Uganda mutineers were dismissed and transported home. In Kenya, about 170 soldiers were eventually dismissed and another 100 court-martialed. (In Tanganyika, the death penalty was sought by the government for a number of men, but the harshest penalties were fifteen years for Sergeant Ilogi and ten years for some others.) It was only in Tanganyika that the army had to be thoroughly reconstructed, since neither battalion could be relied on. The reconstruction of the Tanganyika army and the aftermath of the mutinies in all three countries provide almost as much insight about the political systems of East Africa and the place of the military forces in them as the mutinies themselves.

The Aftermath of the Mutinies

When they occurred, the mutinies seemed to be events of major importance. Although Prime Ministers Obote and Kenyatta de-emphasized them, Mr. Nyerere spoke openly of the catastrophic consequences of the Tanganyika revolt. He feared that Tanganyika's image of stability had been shattered. However, as attention shifted inside Tanganyika to the union with Zanzibar and the Five Year Plan and then to a new constitution for party and state, the events of January seemed less significant. Similarly, in Kenya and Uganda, new events and crises came to the fore. But the significance of the army mutinies did not diminish.

The attempt to build and rebuild military forces in East Africa has become entangled in cold war politics and to some extent in a growing rivalry among the East African countries. This development is only partially a result of the mutinies themselves. Internal rivalries in Kenya have centered around the army as political leaders have sponsored their supporters for training abroad and have tried to gain control of the military force; these leaders have, in turn, been associated with and aided by various external powers. In Uganda, the intervention of the army in the Congo fighting brought the army into greater prominence, and the subsequent use of the army to end the power of the Kabaka of Uganda and President of Uganda, Sir Edward Mutesa, made it clear that the present UPC government's power rests on the army's support. So far, the army does not seem to have a clear political complexion in terms of international alignments or domestic policies in Uganda or Kenya. But in both, the training and equipment of the armies have become issues between domestic political factions. The importance of the mutinies in this regard is that they highlighted the power of the armies and their unreliability, as well as the need to reconstruct them. Thus, the strengthening of the armies and their entanglement in both domestic and international imbroglios takes place against the background of the past mutinies, not to mention the coups elsewhere in Africa.

Tanganyika provides us once again with the greatest insight, for there the attempt to build a new security force has become most entangled in different and rival foreign programs in Zanzibar and Tanganyika. It is in Tanganyika also that the most striking attempt is being made to politicize and nationalize the army while tying it to the ruling party.

Immediately after the landing of British troops on January 25, Nyerere called for a new army to be built around the TANU Youth League (TYL) but by February 12, Vice-President Kawawa was saying that the Youth League was "another nation-building group" but that it lacked leadership. A new category—National Servicemen—would provide leadership. TYL members would be recruited into special village centers and the National Servicemen would be leaders of such centers.[56] Youth League members flocked to be recruited into the National Service. Local TANU secretaries used the promise of an army job to get people to take out TANU cards or to pay back dues. (Some of the people who were promised by local secretaries that they would enter the army were patently physically unfit.) Recruitment was carried out by traveling teams, which would view men gathered by the regional police officers and the regional commissioners. John Nzunda, simultaneously Deputy Secretary General of TANU and Parliamentary Secretary, and other parliamentary secretaries also recruited. Non-commissioned officers who had been loyal took part too.

After the mutiny, many TANU Youth League members eventually were recruited into the army. Political loyalty was a definite factor in recruitment, but the idea of enrolling TANU Youth League members at TANU offices to form a new army was not sustained. It was found necessary to put forward the more encompassing concept of the National Service. These criteria emerged: new recruits for military forces must be citizens aged eighteen to twenty-five and unaccompanied by family. They must be able to read and write Swahili. Infantry officers must have completed Standard XII (the equivalent of high school).

In a change of portfolios in May, 1964, defense became the responsibility of the Vice-President, Mr. Kawawa. Both the National Service and Youth sections and the headquarters of the Tanzanian People's Defense forces are part of his portfolio.[57] A regular army of four battalions and an air wing are being formed.[58] Individuals join the National Service. After three months of National Service training which includes taking part in nation-building activities, such as bush clearing or road construction, recruits are given the opportunity for selection by the army or police.[59] Or they may choose to enter a specialist unit for paramilitary training in the last six months of their two year's training. Those who do not enter the armed forces are to establish new village settlements and stay on as settlers if they wish. They may be recalled for military duty. Initially, it was stated that all young men would be liable for National Service duty. But limited funds restrict the numbers of National Servicemen to about 3,300 during the Five Year Plan period of 1964–1969.

The government has adopted a number of measures aimed at ensuring political loyalty of the armed forces and integrating the army with TANU. All members of the military and the police can now join TANU. On June 24, 1964, Vice-President Kawawa told recruits that they were citizens of the country and could participate fully in the politics of the United Republic. Mr. Kawawa told the recruits that the practice of refusing soldiers the right to participate in the politics of their countries was introduced by the colonialists.[60] (However, the independent Tanganyika government took three years to change this rule.)

Police and soldiers have enrolled en masse in response to the opening of TANU. In fact, they enroll as whole units. Company commanders are heads of the TANU committee established in the company. Officers are expected to do party liaison work and to explain to the troops their role in Tanzania's development.

An Honorary Commission in the People's Defense Forces with a rank of colonel was granted by President Nyerere to S. J. Kitundu, the Coast Regional Commissioner and a resident of Dar es Salaam. Mr. Kitundu was also appointed by the President as Political Commissar of the Tanzania Defense Forces, effective November 6, 1964. This post is not a listed position of the Ministry of Defense. It is designed to give a TANU official a high army position. But so far Mr. Kitundu has had no operational direction of the armed forces.

Before the mutiny, TANU Youth Leaguers were often required to police meetings, to set up formal roadblocks to prevent smuggling, and even to collect taxes. In certain places, TANU personnel did constabulary work. These informal and irregular procedures have now been formalized.[61] To prepare them to "defend Tanganyika in the event of the country being attacked," members of the nation's Police Force, Prisons Service, National Service, and TANU Youth League are to undergo full military training with modern weapons. A reserve force for national defense is to be created.[62] A field force of militarized police will exist in each region. Also, special village police consisting of volunteers working under two regular policemen will be posted to villages, particularly those where there was occasional trouble, such as border areas.[63] People are told that their obligation is to help these police and act as citizen police-helpers. It remains to be seen whether such a national reserve will come into being as an effective foce. Villages that are in fact sparsely settled areas, spread out for miles, are hard to police. And Tanganyika has had one of the smallest salaried police forces in the world in relation to the population and the size of the country. To rectify this situation, there has been established a Special Constabulary of volunteers who undergo training for police work. Special Constables have been recruited from the TANU Youth League. Most regions have such a force, but it is best organized in Dar es Salaam where there are almost 250 uniformed Special Constables and over sixty Women Constables.

None of these measures guarantees a loyal and pliable security force. An army with a large element of politically aware youth from the TANU Youth League may be difficult for the leadership to control. The TANU Youth League has been troublesome in the past and there have been sporadic attempts at governmental control by incorporating the Youth League into a Ministry of Culture and Youth. However, the Youth League has retained its identity. There already have been difficulties in the army since the mutiny, although these have not been related to the new recruits. The government decided to accept some of the disgraced mutineers back into the army as a stopgap measure when the Congo border situation became very tense. Shortly thereafter, there was trouble in the army which has not been explained.[64] There were also rumors that a Zanzibar unit which was shipped to the southern region near Mozambique was undisciplined and had to be shipped back.

Aside from the difficulties in building a loyal and stable force, the Tanzanian government has problems in financing and training its security forces. The training of this force has created international incidents. President Nyerere's decision to accept a Chinese training team for his army provoked warnings and outrage in the West. The President replied that the maximum risk was that the army would revolt, which had already occurred with an army that was not Chinese-trained. Other countries had refused his requests. Nyerere's reply was understandable, but in the meantime his military helpers could hardly be more varied. Israel now helps with the National Service; and West Germany was training an air wing before a crisis in West German-Tanzanian relations, after which Canada took over this training. Meanwhile, the Zanzibar units received Chinese, East German, and Soviet training and equipment. Not only do these arrangements pose technical difficulties for training, but Tanzanian security is related to international politics in a very marked way.

Nonetheless, it is clear that Tanzania intends to have a security establishment closely tied to TANU. The different militarized forces are designed to guard against any one branch repeating the January mutiny. But the government is not primarily worried about overt force being directed against it from within; it is worried about its own inability to exert force internally.

In other words, the central problem of the TANU government is: How can it assert itself in Tanganyika in the countryside? The National Service, the TANU Youth League, the Field Force of Military Police, and the special village police are all attempts to make the central will felt through creating new organizational forms. Another characteristic response has been the merging of TANU organizations and the defense forces. This tendency can be considered as politicizing the security forces. But perhaps it is more useful to see the enrolling of army and police in TANU, and the creating of defense TANU units as an attempt to strengthen TANU. A parallel with the entrance of civil service into TANU is clear. By incorporating these functional units, TANU does not so much extend its control—for the TANU center is limited in its ability to do this with its own territorial organizations—as give itself more concrete meanings and manifestations. TANU's functions are diffuse. They became specific by incorporating functionally specific organizations. TANU lacks executive and administrative personnel, so it recruits civil servants, policemen, and soldiers.

All groups and individuals must be within TANU so that no group or individual can threaten it from outside. TANU leaders feel that separatisms can be contained inside the party's embrace. They believe that the major difficulty with the army that mutinied was that the army was outside TANU. It was not informed about TANU goals and did not have contact with TANU leaders.[65] It remains to be seen whether the new army proves a more reliable instrument.

Conclusions

The stark facts of life in Tanganyika were driven home by the mutiny. The center was basically cut off from the rest of the country geographically and politically. Fewer than a thousand armed men could bring the government down, but the TANU organizations outside Dar es Salaam could keep "ruling." The army mutiny illustrated the discontinuities between the center and the districts. It also illuminated a paradox in Tanganyika: The very absence of central political control has permitted a relatively stable situation in the countryside. The turmoil in Dar es Salaam during the mutiny, the subsequent concerns of East African federation and planning, and the strains of international politics did not much touch the countryside.

And here is the major lesson of the mutinies in Kenya and Uganda, as well as Tanganyika: It is easy to end civilian governments in Africa. They can be disbanded in capitals with little trouble, given the concerted effort of a single battalion. But so far no army has ruled a tropical African country for even a few years and has exerted as much central authority, keeping the degree of public order that governments led by party leaders did prior to their removal. Perhaps army administrations will be more successful with the problems of economic development and national integration than their civilian predecessors. But there is little concrete evidence on which to base this sanguine prediction. In fact, there is reason to believe that army leaders who have little power at their disposal in terms of equipment and personnel will not be able to make up in force what they lack in legitimacy.

In East Africa, the mutinies were not military take-overs in conventional terms. They could not become so in the absence of military alliances with civilian groups and particularly with elements of the ruling parties. The armies of Kenya, Tanganyika, and Uganda lacked one of the most important properties of a bona fide army; they were without an indigenous officer corps. Their small size and relative lack of firepower and mobility would not have prevented their "taking over" in the sense of occupying the capital city. But they could not hope to rule even to the extent that civilian governments had ruled. Thus, there was no hope of attaining legitimacy through effectiveness. The mutinies themselves weakened the legitimacy of the military, although esteem was partially restored for them by British intervention.

Whether or not the East African militaries try to engage in either take-overs or coalitions with the parties now ruling or with some other political group depends on many factors. These factors pertain to developments within the military, within civilian elites, the relationship between them, and the way problems arise and are solved or not solved in society. In Tanganyika, TANU hopes to tie the military to the ruling party by suffusing it with TANU goals, by close supervision of the army by political leaders, and by division of power among military and quasi-military branches. In Uganda, a community of interests is being assumed between a segment of the UPC leadership and the army leadership based on common ethnic groupings, and a mutual hostility to

Buganda separatism. In Kenya, a change in recruitment in favor of the two largest tribes, Luo and Kikuyu, and military involvement in the north against Somalis is expected to maintain civilian leaderships.

None of these attempts guarantees civilian supremacy in the future. Now that the East African armies are officered by Africans they present a different, and somewhat unknown, quantity. The past mutinies can influence in different ways. They showed how easy it is to stage a coup; and since 1964, the numerous coups elsewhere in Africa have reinforced this example. But the mutinies also cast armies into disrespect, and East African officers may be at pains to show that their armies are disciplined and reliable. This resolve may weaken, should civilian regimes be unable to handle particular crises or have to call on the army, as did the Uganda government when it ended the Presidency of the Kabaka of Buganda. Our views here are speculative. What we do know is that the East African armies could intervene to bring down their governments, should they be so motivated. But we also know that they will run into all the difficulties of power and legitimacy already described. The mutinies revealed the real limits on military intervention in East Africa.

Notes

1. The countries referred to are those in Tropical or Black Africa.

2. It seems to me that Aristide Zolberg means by "political order" the creation of an institutional order which is defined by effective political instruments. See Aristide Zolberg, *Creating Political Order: The Party-States of West Africa* (Chicago: Rand McNally and Co., 1965), chap. 4, pp. 93–127.

3. The Congo has seemed to observers to be a unique or vastly exaggerated example of disorder and disunity in Africa. Recently the argument has been advanced that the Congo is not unique, but that African political systems are characterized by unintegrated sets of elites and that the type of disorder associated with the Congo is likely to emerge elsewhere. See Crawford Young, "The Congo and Uganda: A Comparative Assessment," paper presented at the Ninth Annual Meeting of the African Studies Association, Bloomington, Indiana, October 26–29, 1966. See also Aristide Zolberg, "A View from the Congo," *World Politics* 19, No. 1 (Oct. 1966): 137–149.

4. For a discussion of authoritative allocation of values, see David Easton, *The Political System* (New York: Alfred A. Knopf, Inc., 1953); and his *A Framework for Political Analysis,* (Englewood Cliffs, N.J.: Prentice-Hall, 1965).

5. It is interesting that the feudal periods in Europe are not generally characterized as anarchic but as the restoration of order after a period of breakdown of all order—the Dark Ages. Present American policy makers support the continuation of African political units in their present territorial form. The thread of the United States Congo policy is the commitment to the maintenance of central government. There is a mistrust of "overcentralization," where it cannot work, as in the Congo, Nigeria, and even in more seemingly homogeneous entities. But a breakup of these entities would be seen as a regression from the model of the national state toward a less civilized type which existed in some former period.

6. This may be more than lip service. A commitment to civilian rule on the part of the military can also stem from a perception of the difficulties of ruling. General Ankrah of Ghana has wondered out loud about the personal benefits of being a ruler.

7. Morris Janowitz in *The Military in the Political Development of New Nations* (Chicago: University of Chicago Press, 1964, p. 44) uses the phrase "reservoir of legitimate authority" in

his discussion of characteristics and potentialities of the military in new states. Undoubtedly, the legitimacy of the military as a ruling group is affected by the nature of the military's intervention. As Janowitz points out, it is important to distinguish military interventions as to whether they are "designed" or "reactive." That is, do the military intervene with positive and premeditated intent, or do they react to civilian weakness and even civilian pressure on them to intervene? *Ibid.,* pp. 16, 85, 113.

8. *Ibid.,* p. 33.

9. Nigeria's cases of corruption in the military have been on a grand scale. Three officers of the Nigerian Navy embezzled nearly 10 per cent of the 1964 naval budget. M. J. V. Bell, *Army and Nation in Sub-Saharan Africa,* Adelphi Paper No. 21. Institute of Strategic Studies, London, August, 1965, p. 2.

Ranking Ugandan officers have been involved in lurid stories of smuggling ivory and gold and using Uganda's involvement in the Congo for their own benefit.

10. W. F. Gutteridge's "Introduction" to David Wood, *The Armed Forces of African States,* Adelphi Paper No. 27, Institute of Strategic Studies, London, April, 1966, p. 2.

11. J. Kirk Sale in "The Generals and the Future of Africa," argues that this is true for Ghana and other African countries. *The Nation,* March 21, 1966, pp. 317–318.

12. In other words, the East African examples give us a chance to test the propositions about the military in new states that Janowitz puts forward in *The Military in the Political Development of New Nations* as he singles out the critical variables: organizational format, skill structure and career lines, social recruitment and education, professional and political ideology, social cohesion, and poltical intervention. *Op. cit.,* pp. 27–29.

13. Edward Shils, "The Military in the Political Development of New States," in John J. Johnson, editor, *The Role of the Military in Underdeveloped Countries* (Princeton, N.J.: Princeton University Press, 1962), pp. 53–54.

14. The present commander of the Ugandan Army, Colonel Amin, has been a soldier for twenty years. He served in Burma as a private and was promoted to sergeant major after World War II. After Uganda's independence, he became a captain and subsequently received further promotions.

15. Officers in the Sudan are almost all from north of the Sahara but they have been on the scene longer than most African officers. Ethiopia, too, has some long-term officers. There are, of course, some traditional military elites, for example, in northern Nigeria and parts of Mali.

16. The following sketch of the size and composition of defense forces in Kenya, Uganda, and Tanganyika is drawn from a number of sources: *A Handbook of African Affairs,* edited by Helen Kitchen (New York: Praeger, 1964), pp. 205–206, 225–226, 228–229), reproduces data published in *Africa Report,* January, 1964. Harvey Glickman's "Impressions of Military Policy in Tanganyika" (RAND Corporation, November, 1963) and his *Some Observations on the Army and Political Unrest in Tanganyika* (Pittsburgh: Duquesne University Press, 1964) have been consulted for material on Tanganyika. I have also used East African press reports, government documents, and interviews carried out during 1963–1965 in East Africa. Data on the size and composition of the East African defense forces as of 1966 can be found in David Wood's *The Armed Forces of African States (op. cit.)* and in *Reference Handbook of the Armed Forces of the World,* edited by Lawrence L. Ewing and Robert C. Sellers (Washington: Robert C. Sellers and Associates, 1966).

17. Kenya also had more British officers than Tanganyika or Uganda. East Africans began to enter Mons Officer Training School and Sandhurst only after 1957. By 1963 there were Tanganyikan, Kenya, and Ugandan officers; but British officers still held top command positions. However, by then East africans were taking officer training courses in Israel as well as in Britain.

18. The size of the Bugandan forces was constitutionally set with a ceiling of 650 men of all ranks. Buganda could not unilaterally change the size. The governments of Buganda and Uganda never reached agreement on the proper strength of the former's force; nor was agreement reached over the precise powers of the Uganda Central Government's Inspector-General of Police over the Kabaka of Buganda's police. This issue, among others, was still outstanding in May, 1966,

when Uganda Army units shelled the Kabaka's palace and fought his police force, which defended it.

The tribal composition of the Uganda policy mirrored the tribal composition of the army in that recruitment was predominantly from northern Nilotic tribes rather than from southern Bantu tribes. The Acholi, Iteso, and Lango were represented in the army and police by more than their share of the Uganda population. See *Annual Report of the Uganda Police* (Entebbe: The Government Printer, 1961), p. 4.

19.   See Julius Nyerere's *The Second Scramble* (Tanganyika Standard Limited, Dar es Salaam, 1962) in which he downgraded the idea of a Tanganyikan army in favor of a UN or African army.

20.   Tanganyika has restricted labor inflows from Kenya. In 1965 a Uganda army convoy picked up military equipment in Tanganyika and crossed the Kenya border on the way back to Uganda without Kenyan permission, causing an imbroglio between Kenya and her East African neighbors.

21.   Tanganyika is hardly "a country with as few external and internal security problems as any in Africa," given these circumstances. M. J. V. Bell, *op. cit.,* p. 4.

22.   Colin Leys, "Violence in Africa," *Transition* 5, No. 21 (1965): 17–20.

23.   *Ibid.,* p. 19.

24.   TANU is the ruling party in the Tanganyika part of the United Republic of Tanzania. The Afro-Shirazi Party rules in Zanzibar.

25.   Glickman, Harvey, *Some Observations on the Army and Political Unrest in Tanganyika, op. cit.,* p. 5.

26.   *Ibid.*

27.   KANU won an electoral victory in May, 1963, after the KADU-KANU coalition was dissolved.

28.   The Kamba leader, Paul Ngei, has alternately been in and out of KANU governments.

29.   See my article, "The Party and the No-Party State: Tanganyika and the Soviet Union," *Transition* 3, No. 13 (1964): 25–33.

30.   Colin Leys, in "Recent Relations Between the States of East Africa" (*International Journal* 20, No. 4 (1965): 510–523), has argued that the time factor in East Africa was crucial by 1963. Tanganyika had been independent for more than two years. Uganda more than one; and Kenya was just becoming independent. Moreover, Tanganyika was a political and economic vacuum. Uganda had relatively strong social, economic, and political subsystems within the national political system. Kenya had problems of a white majority, the confrontation of large tribal groups, and urban unemployment.

31.   Bell (*op. cit.*) points out that it was not the forthcoming requirements of independence, which was not contemplated in 1955, that prompted the French to undertake this crash program to upgrade the manpower reserves of *Afrique Noire.*

32.   In the following account of the East African mutinies I have drawn on my own "National Security in Tanganyika after the Mutiny," *Transition* 5, No. 21 (1965): 39–46. I have also made use of a very comprehensive account compiled by Christopher Hobson of the University of Chicago Department of Political Science, based on newspapers and journals and on his own first-hand experience.

33.   Keith Kyle, "Mutinies and After," *The Spectator* No. 7075 (January 31, 1964): 139. Kavona was appointed second in command by the President after order was restored. Some months later he was put under preventive detention. No explanation was given then or since. His earlier actions may have been held against him, and it was rumored that he was involved with dissident troops later on.

34.   The request for more money involved a demand for a raise in base pay for privates from about $15 per month to more than $37 per month.

35.   Police in many African countries have taken this position during army coups or internal army struggles.

36. See "The Brushfire in East Africa, from January 1 to February 13, 1964," *Africa Report* 9, No. 2 (February 1964): 21.

37. One report said that Captain Sarakikya was being marched at bayonet point to a cell in Tabora when the signal appointed him commanding officer came through from Dar es Salaam. He ordered the mutineers to desist and took control; and he supervised the shipping out of British officers and noncommissioned officers. *Tanganyika Standard* (Dar es Salaam), January 30, 1964, p. 5.

38. When asked in a press conference on January 23 what action would be taken against the mutineers, he ended the meeting without answering.

39. On January 25, Sarakikya had withdrawn arms from his troops in Tabora. But British paratroopers landed there anyway and took control of the town. At Nachingwea, where a company had been facing the Mozambique border, army troops who had asserted themselves in the town surrendered to local police.

40. The fact that the army appeared well organized in Dar es Salaam and the chain effect of the Dar mutiny gave rise to rumors about foreign intervention. Chou En-lai was about to visit Tanganyika, and China was specifically mentioned as an instigator of the difficulties. There appears to have been no truth to these rumors. On January 27, the Tanganyika government issued a press statement that the revolt was not connected with outside subversion and noted that it was not in any way communist-inspired. Then on January 30, the government felt compelled to deny that the implication of the January 27 statement was that the mutiny was connected with any popular movement.

41. From 1957 to 1960 there had been an East African Land Force connected with the old East African High Commission. The East African Common Service Organization replaced the High Commission in 1960, but it did not take on defense coordination. And with independence each country became responsible for its defense, even in the area of administration where the high command had some responsibilities. There was a common East African navy, but within a week of Tanganyika's independence, it was announced that the East African navy would be disbanded. The East African Defense Committee was disbanded in October, 1963. See David Johns, "Defense and Police Organization in East Africa," paper presented to East Africa's Institute of Social Research Conference, December, 1963.

42. The organization of the Zanzibar Revolution, the role of particular individuals, the amount of outside support, and the part played by Tanganyikans remain very murky still.

43. Trade-union leaders took up the cry and said the President's policy was contrary to Africanization. One representative of the Local Government Workers Union said that Nyerere was taking Tanganyika back to colonial days. See *Tanganyika Standard,* January 9, 1964, p. 3. Toward the end of 1963, the Grand Council of the Tanganyika Federation of Labour had rejected the government's proposal to integrate the TFL with the government. When the British landed troops at the end of January, certain trade-union leaders were arrested and incarcerated under the Preventive Detention Act. Some trade-union leaders did go out to Colito Barracks during the mutiny to encourage the troops and politicize demands. However, the government arrested some on grounds of national security, although they did not support the mutiny but simply opposed the government's trade union policy.

44. Frene Ginwala, "The Tanganyika Mutiny," *World Today* 20, No. 3 (March, 1964): 93–97.

45. Kyle, *loc. cit.*

46. *Africa Report, loc. cit.*

47. This occurred at a meeting of the *Umoja Wa Wanawake,* or Women's League. See *Tanganyika Standard,* January 30, 1964, p. 1.

48. Austin Shaba, Minister for Local Government, who was in London during the mutiny. See *Tanganyika Standard,* January 30, 1964, p. 5.

49. See *Uganda Argus,* Kampala, February 13, 1964, for Mr. Nyerere's remarks.

50. Chief Fundikira even rejoined TANU and took his place once again in the Tanganyika Parliamentary Party to show his solidarity after the mutiny.

51. If any Zanzibar leaders were so inclined, they were either preoccupied in Zanzibar or judiciously quiet.

52. See *Tanganyika Standard,* January 8, 1964, p. 1.

53. *East African Standard,* Nairobi, January 31, 1964, p. 1.

54. *Sunday News,* Dar es Salaam, February 7, 1964, p. 7.

55. Hobson reports that in a straw poll he conducted among high school students largely living in Temeke, an outlying industrial section of the capital, 75 percent opposed the calling in of Britain and better than 50 percent thought the army's mutiny had been justified. It is very probable that the fact of British intervention affected subsequent views about the army mutiny, although I have no "before" and "after" data to support this theory.

56. *Tanganyika Standard,* February 12, 1964, p. 5.

57. Tanganyika's and Zanzibar's armies are now merged in the Tanzanian Defense Force. I do not know whether this is effective operationally.

58. Three battalions will be in Tanganyika and one in Zanzibar. Plans to form a navy have been announced.

59. Wood reports that half of army personnel is to consist of volunteers from National Service, *Op. cit.,* p. 18.

60. *Nationalist,* Dar es Salaam, June 25, 1964. p. 2.

61. The Reserve Forces Bill legalizes paramilitary training and functions of the TYL.

62. The reserve is to be made up of 4,000 volunteers. Wood, *loc. cit.*

63. *Reporter,* Nairobi, February 12, 1965; *Nationalist,* February 2, 1965, p. 1.

64. The September 12, 1964, headline of the *Nationalist* read: "U.R. (United Republic) Army Arrests." The text of a government announcement was printed: "In active pursuance of its duty to maintain the integrity and safety of the United Republic the Government yesterday found it necessary to arrest and detain a small number of servants of the Republic. This number included officers and other ranks of the United Republic Army, who were of doubtful loyalty and guilty of insubordination by default." It was on this occasion that Elisha Kavona was arrested.

65. Interviews.

Chapter 8

Military and Society in East Africa: Thinking Again about Praetorianism

The Problem

The army seized power in Uganda in January 1971.[1] It had revolted in 1964, along with the armies of Kenya and Tanzania, but civilian regimes were restored and maintained in all three East African countries until the Uganda coup.[2] In the latter country, however, there was considerably more friction between civilian leaders and armed forces and much more instability within the army from 1964–71 than in Kenya and Tanzania. This article will consider whether the concept of praetorianism, as developed in the works of Samuel Huntington, helps explain the differences in the evolution of relationship between armed forces and society in these three East african countries.

Huntington's fundamental proposition about military intervention states that "the most important causes of military intervention in politics are not military but political, and reflect not the social and organizational characteristics of the military establishment but the political and institutional structure of the society."[3] The author will argue here that variations in the social and organizational characteristics of armed forces *do* make a difference with regard to the propensity of the military to intervene. Moreover, while there is always *some* relationship between the social/organizational characteristics of the military and the political/institutional structure of the society, ways in which the evolution of the social and organizational characteristics of the military can to some extent be cut away from happenings in the wider society will be shown. In other words, at a certain level of generality changes within the military do not depend very closely upon changes within the larger society. Comparisons will be made of both the political/institutional structures and the armed forces of East Africa in order to defend this point of view.

It must be acknowledged in advance, however, that there is insufficient information about the various East African militaries. Indeed, until we have more detailed empirical studies of African militaries, we cannot deal with major questions concerned their modernity or how these military regimes make decisions, who makes them, and what political goals govern their decision making. So far, the argument that the military are the relatively modern groups in society rests solely on assertions. No one has shown how the military become rational, cohesive, universalistic, disciplined, and industry oriented.[4]

The point is not that all military regimes have failed to be modernizers. But there is a risk in inferring qualities about armed force organizations because they have chains of command, tables of organization, uniforms, and weapons. This warning should have particular force in respect to African armed forces, for many of these are still extremely small-scale organizations with only a few battalions and some thousands of men in large countries with populations in the millions. They are usually predominantly infantry battalions with little firepower or mechanization.

In addition, information is inadequate as to how officer corps are recruited, what norms govern officer behavior, how officers, noncommissioned officers, and enlisted men relate to one another, and how the latter categories operate.[5]

The Concept of Praetorianism

The idea of praetorian societies has made an impact on recent studies of the military in developing countries for two reasons: (1) because its proponents have often been critical of the idea that the military are best suited to mdoernize their societies; and (2) because the analysis moves away from a discussion of the actual organization of armed forces and focuses instead on society at large and, more specifically, on patterns of political participation and institutionalization.[6]

Huntington defines a praetorian society as one in which there is a general politicization of social forces and institutions. "Countries which have political armies also have political clergies, political universities, political bureaucracies . . . ,"[7] he declares. These institutions involve themselves in politics not only over issues that concern them but also over issues that affect society as a whole. The praetorian society has neither specialized political institutions to mediate conflict nor accepted rules of the game for resolving conflict.[8] Another important feature that Huntington attributes to such a society is the fragmented nature of political power: "It [power] comes in many forms and in small quantities. Authority over the system as a whole is transitory. . . ."[9]

Huntington distinguishes between types of praetorian society according to levels of participation. Societies with weak political institutionalization can be oligarchical praetorian, radical praetorian, and mass praetorian, depending on the breadth of the participation. Conflict becomes more intense as participation increases: "In a praetorian oligarchy politics is a struggle among personal and family cliques; in a radical praetorian society the struggle among institutional and occupational groups supplements that among cliques; in mass praetorianism, social classes and social movements dominate the scene."[10]

While Huntington does not deal with tropical African cases in much detail, he classifies the African pattern as one of radical praetorianism in which political participation is brought about first by a civilian nationalist intelligentsia. This is then dislodged by middle-class officers because the civilians lack the ability to mobilize political support continuously and because they cannot organize political strength "to fill the vacuum of authority and legitimacy left by the departing colonial rulers."[11] In radical praetorian systems, according to Huntington, military intervention is usually a response to political action by others, and especially to the escalation of social conflict by such groups as students or labor organizations. In this context, military intervention serves to halt the rapid mobilization of social forces into politics. It defuses the explosive situation and often marks the end of a sequence of violence in politics.[12]

Huntington has much more to say about praetorian societies in Latin America, the Middle East, and Asia than in Africa. He compares Africa in the 1960s to Latin America in the 1820s, finding a decay of political authority and institutions in both. He argues that African elites failed to impose mass institutions; and he cites the single parties as inappropriate for their societies, declaring that "The African one-party state became a no-party state."[13] Since Africa was less stratified than Latin America and the middle class broke into politics at a later historical period, radical rather than oligarchical praetorianism came about.[14] Presumably Huntington considers the African armies a progressive force, since he states that, "Thus, paradoxically but understandably, the more backward a society is, the more progressive the role of its military; the more advanced a society becomes, the more conservative and reactionary becomes the role of the military."[15]

The discussion of praetorian systems by Huntington is not an ideal-type analysis. While the different types of praetorian society are described in terms of clusters of characteristics having to do with levels of participation, the analysis is not really typological. Real societies in time and place are put into a particular category. Indeed, the discussion proceeds without reference to "pure forms" or caveats about classifying real systems in terms of typological constructs. Yet the concept of a praetorian society is broad and Huntington's own discussion proceeds with fairly large brush strokes, although much historical detail is provided in addition. While there are many insights and useful contributions in Huntington's treatment of military intervention, this author has many doubts about the applicability of the praetorian analysis to tropical Africa.

The military and society in Uganda, Tanzania, and Kenya will be examined here with a view to evaluating the usefulness and pointing out the limitations of the idea of praetorianism, and specifically to making comparisons of the roles of the military in East Africa.[16] The discussion will first focus on the societal context, as Huntington properly directs, and then examine military characteristics and interventions.

East Africa: Praetorian Societies?

In trying to assess the applicability of the praetorian concept to East African societies, a few basic points can be made.[17] First, Kenya, Uganda, and Tanzania have significant differences in degree of industrial development, scope and modernity of communications systems, and levels of urbanization. Kenya stands highest on the indices in all these areas. Second, there are major differences in ethnic composition; ethnic politics are less salient in Tanzania than in either Uganda or Kenya. Ethnic conflict has been extremely complex in Uganda, which has undergone north-south cleavages, Bantu–non-Bantu divisions, Baganda–non-Baganda axes, religious splits, clan and regional conflicts in the north, and separatist movements in various parts of the country.[18] Kenya has had major tribal and regional conflicts, too, and an increasing Luo-Kikuyu polarization. While all three countries have had one-party systems at various times, they have arrived at this state by quite different routes and the end condition has had different meanings in Uganda, Kenya, and Tanzania.

Despite the differences noted in the preceding paragraph, plus their many social, economic, political, constitutional, and cultural distinctions, all three East African countries share one feature common to tropical African polities: power is fragmented. Here Huntington's characterization holds, at least if it is roughly drawn. This author has argued elsewhere that central or national authorities in Africa are unable to exert authority over the whole territorial entity they rule because a great deal of political life goes on outside the reach of the central rulers. Values are not being allocated for society as a whole by central authorities, whatever the rhetoric of mobilization for development through centralized political structures. Nationwide political structures are too weak to enforce the will of ruling national elites, whether these elites are traditional lineage groups, a party elite, civilian bureaucracies, or the military.[19]

After admitting a fragmentation of power and a weakness of central institutions common to all three countries, however, it does not follow that the level of effectiveness of political institutions is the same in Kenya, Uganda, or Tanzania, or that the presence or absence of legitimate intermediaries does not vary significantly in East Africa. The fact that power is fragmented reveals a lot, but by no means everything, about the nature of power and authority in a system. Central institutions may be weak, but there can still be authority as well as accepted "rules of the game."

It is important not to overhomogenize our treatment of political societies in Africa. Indeed, much of the writing on African parties has done just this. After observing the weakness of parties in terms of the goals set by party leaders and the needs of society, and after comparing the rhetoric of rule with the performance of political structures, many observers have dismissed African parties out of hand. The fact remains, however, that not all African parties have become defunct; and not all one-party systems have become no-party systems.[20]

TANU (Tanganyika African National Union) cannot mobilize the population of Tanzania for economic development tasks in the way that the Communist party functioned in the Soviet Union in the 1930s.[21] TANU was unable to avoid a military revolt in 1964 or to mobilize the civilian population against the rebellious soldiers in Dar es Salaam or up-country towns. It was no more effective in obviating a revolt or ending it in 1964 than civilian institutions in Kenya and Uganda that same year.[22] Nonetheless, TANU provides legitimacy to leaders at low, middle, and high levels in a way that the Uganda People Congress and KANU (Kenya African National Union) do not. The Uganda People's Congress which incorporated elements of two former opposition groups—the Democratic party and the Kabaka Yekka party—had always been faction-ridden. President Jomo Kenyatta and the civil service invest KANU with authority. Only at very local levels do party leaders *qua* party leaders make decisions in Kenya, and even here civil servants play a major policy as well as executive role. In Kenya, too, the ruling party incorporated former members of opposition parties—the Kenya African Democratic Union, the African Peoples Party, and the Kenya Peoples Union. KANU has been essentially a party of fragmented district organizations.[23] But Kenyatta's role has been such that he could prevail in KANU and the Cabinet with less challenge than President Obote was subject to in Uganda. Furthermore, when the late Tom Mboya was secretary general of KANU, some attempt was made, albeit rather unsuccessfully, to create a national KANU headquarters staff and a meaningful KANU center.

The argument here is that all East African parties have been weak, but that there have been major differences in the role and functioning of TANU as compared to the UPC and KANU. And even as between the Kenyan and Ugandan parties, there were significant differences. While the KANU government was challenged by KANU back-benchers in 1965–66 and while the breakaway KPU had a bastion in the Luo areas of south and central Nyanza, KANU was never on the verge of coming apart as the UPC was in early 1966.[24]

The institutional differences can be pushed with regard to nonparty organizations, also. Tanzania has perhaps had the weakest civil service of the three countries, Kenya the strongest; but Tanzania has had TANU as compensation. In Uganda the civil service has been relatively competent for a tropical African country, but southerners, and particularly Bagandans, have dominated that service. Ethnic tensions in Uganda have given rise to more sustained and sharper outbreaks of violence than have taken place in Kenya since independence.[25] There has been less mobility of civil servants in this context and less consensus among civilian elites, with the result that creation of a national civil service has not proceeded in Uganda to the extent that it has in Kenya.

So far the argument has been that Uganda has the least effective civilian institutions and the most severe ethnic tensions in East Africa. Tanzania has the most institutionalized political system in that it has the strongest, best articulated party, with a set of professional political leaders who are legitimate intermediaries able to moderate group conflict. Civil servants in Kenya carry out many of the political functions that the TANU officials do in Tanzania. Current party strength in Tanzania and civil service strength in Kenya depend on the authority of Julius Nyerere and Jomo Kenyatta, respectively.

It is difficult to say with any certainty which of these two institutions will survive better the passing of the "Founding Father." Kenya's civilian institutions seem under greater pressure now because Kenyatta is an old man and the succession struggle is already underway. But the Kenya civil service delivers more goods efficiently than TANU does and it provides the Kenya government with a stronger grid for influencing behavior thrugh its administrative services. Kenya's civil service, acting in conjunction with police and armed forces, or threatening to invoke these actors, is probably a stronger coercive force than TANU. TANU, on the other hand, seems more effective in working for longer term value change and even short-term exhortation. Any judgment about institutionalization must therefore be made in terms of different kinds of functions performed. It would be rash to conclude, given the general situation of power fragmentation and transient authority, that either TANU or the Kenyan civil service will prove durable vehicles for rule in their present forms.

Before turning directly to the East African military, it may be useful briefly to examine Tanzania, Kenya, and Uganda in the light of some of Huntington's other characterizations of radical praetorian societies. One of the major facets of these societies in his view is that they provide a setting in which social forces confront each other nakedly.[26] What is striking about many African societies, however, is the low degree of politicization of social forces in national politics. First, social classes themselves are rather weakly formed. Although Tanzanian leaders may fear the formation of an urban and working-class aristocracy, ubanization in Tanzania is very low and the industrial labor force very small.[27] In Uganda there is a growing number of cash crop farmers with significant differences in income. There are, in addition, more stratified land relationships in Buganda than have existed elsewhere in most of East Africa.[28] But Uganda is not a country where one can see social forces organized in class terms (if by class we still mean economic-occupational divisions). There are, of course, elite-nonelite distinctions in Both Uganda and Tanzania, as well as levels of power, wealth, and status within the elites. The Tanzanians have moved, in the Arusha formulations, to try to minimize these distinctions.[29] But in both Uganda and Tanzania the African middle class consists almost entirely of government (both civil and party) servants, a very few military officers, some more prosperous farmers and traders, and a few professionals—mostly teachers.

The government elites participate in *national* issues and are located in the national arena much more than others in middle-class roles. In Uganda and Tanzania, however, the elite has been a narrow one and a "rules of the game" has operated, at least outside of the realm of overt ethnic conflict. In Kenya, on the other hand, much more social division has taken place in class terms: the industrial working force is bigger, and there are more gradations among

African urban and rural dwellers. Kenya has a landless proletariat and a more severe "land hunger" problem than Uganda or Tanzania. Moreover, class divisions have proceeded furthest among the government's own ethnic base—the Kikuyus. And since the commercial and industrial sector was more developed in Kenya than elsewhere in East Africa, and government has been rapidly Africanizing the commercial sector and pressuring for Africanization of small businesses and managerial position in larger enterprises, a Kenyan African business class is growing up. Individuals in this group have interlocking relationships with political elites. Yet, in Kenya, too, there is low participation in national politics by economically defined social forces.

Social forces face each other "nakedly" in East Africa, as elsewhere in Africa, in the realm of ethnic politics. In Uganda, ethnic groups have vied for control of the central institutions of authority and power; but many ethnic conflicts are fairly localized as, for example, the hostilities in western Uganda. These localized conflicts have national ramifications when the national balances of power are disturbed or when the local conflict is carried to the national level through central institutions—either party, civil service, or army. Since the army is recruited mostly from northerners in Uganda and since there are many ethnic conflicts in the north, the stability of the national political arena is called into question. Where class and ethnic relationships interesect as, for example, when cocoa farmers in Ghana are mainly Ashanti or when cotton and coffee farmers in Uganda are heavily Baganda, then the chances that social forces will confront each other at the national level increase. But even in Uganda and in Kenya, where class and ethnicity are heavily intertwined, it is difficult to see large-scale group involvement in national politics.

Nor has East Africa been characterized by urban instability up to now. Violence, which has been more pronounced since the end of colonial rule in Uganda and in northern Kenya than elsewhere in East Africa, has been essentially a rural phenomenon. Neither the city mob, nor the students in the national universities in capital cities, nor even the capital garrisons have been determining factors in politics or created much violence. If, as Huntington says, the distinctive character of radical praetorianism is urban instability, East Africa is notably free of this. Only in Kenya is there a sense that the government is looking to a rural middle class and trying to maintain Kikuyu peasant support as its major base of strength against other ethnic communities. The regime is aware also of the potential of the cities for future instability. In Tanzania, the TANU government has consistently tried to mobilize the rural areas. But this is less a reaction to challenge from urban elements than an attempt to create development in an overwhelmingly rural society and to build political support somewhere in the system so that rural goals can be carried out.

One of the major difficulties in judging the praetorian character of a society is the problem of measuring political participation. Elections alone do not give much indication of the involvement of people in politics. An analysis of the strength and direction of interest group demands would be essential. How does one weigh persistent demands against ad hoc participation on certain salient issues? Levels of interest in national politics rise in Kenya every time a rumor about President Kenyatta's health spreads. The army is not a day to day actor in Kenyan internal affairs but at times of crisis—when Tom Mboya was assassinated, when Oginga Odinga was arrested, when riots occurred in Kisumu in Central Nyanza, i.e., whenever tensions rise and the fear of increased mass participation in politics takes place—the armed forces become more salient. A massive increase in participation could trigger military intervention in Kenya. But this kind of participation would itself be a response to political crisis, not the result of long-term trends.

In both Kenya and Tanzania it is difficult to measure the ratio between institutionalization and participation. In part, the measures for each are not precise. Furthermore, scholars may not even be looking in the right places to understand participation. If the military were suddenly to intervene again in Tanzania or Kenya, one could not attribute the specific intervention to the society's becoming "more praetorian," unless it were possible to show an increase in participation or a weakening of institutionalization.

In Huntington's analysis, the condition of the society as one with weak institutions is of course important. Under these conditions, military intervention is a possibility and the focus is not on the specific timing of the intervention or the relationship of the intervention to an ad hoc set of poitical events. Still, one wants to know why a condition—in this case nonintervention by the military—may persist for some time and then suddenly change. If the importance of participation and institutionalization and the relationship that obtains between them are singled out as the critical variables, one could look for some change in those variables if intervention occurs. Thus, even if one avoids making ex post facto judgments about the nature of the praetorian society after a coup, it is still necessary to take into account factors specific to individual armed forces in order to have complete explanations about military interventions and military regime performance. Can anything be learned in this respect which can be applied to the Uganda coup?

East African Armed Forces

Huntington suggests that at one phase of a society's development, instability and coups are to be explained in terms of changes in the nature of the military. This is when instability and coups are associated with the emergence of the middle class. Instability and coups associated with the emergence of lower classes are, however, due to changes in the nature of society itself.[30] It is probably more profitable to look at relationships between the military and society as interacting processes. Even in societies where there is rapid expansion of lower-class participation, differences in the armed forces may well be significant for short-run outcomes in politics. Where the military is the carrier par excellence of middle-class interests and values, differences in the military's recruitment, organization, career experiences, size, and the like may also be crucial for politics. Indeed, it is necessary to distinguish between armed forces organizations in societies that may roughly look alike precisely because it is impossible to attribute to the military the qualities of modernity that Huntington ascribes to them in praetorian societies.

The levels of discipline and organization of armies vary enormously in tropical African countries. Many of these armed forces have been neither melting pots nor well-assimilated groups forged into a cohesive entity. Relative to other groups in a society, the military may or may not be a modern institution. It may or may not be honest and efficient compared to other national institutions such as ruling parties and civil services. It may or may not monopolize the individuals in a society who have technical skills or entrepreneurial talents. As more information about the recruitment and operations of the individual military becomes available, it will be possible to judge the accuracy of the general statements about armed forces both for the military itself and as compared to other groups in African societies. This author predicts that the new data on African armies will significantly modify the generalizations on armed forces organizations.

There are some notable differences among the armed forces of Uganda, Kenya, and Tanzania in their relationships with civilian institutions and with

Table 1

Armed Forces and National Statistics
in Three East African Countries, 1968–70*

Factor	Country		
	Uganda	*Tanzania*	*Kenya*
Population	9,675,000	13,000,000	11,075,000
Gross National Product**	$785 million	$900 million	$1,230 million
Total armed forces	6,700	7,900†	5,400
Estimated defense expenditures, 1968	$20,030,000	$10,900,000	$17,900,000
Total national budget, 1968–69	$183,050,000	$255,000,000	$248,000,000

*All figures are from Richard Booth, "The Armed Forces of African States, 1970," *Adelphi Papers,* No. 67 (May 1970); the Institute for Strategic Studies, London, pp. 18–19, 22.

**All monetary figures are quoted in U.S. dollars.

† Plus 4,000 voluntary reserves

each society as a whole. Variations in the politics of the three countries are apparently related to differences in the military as well as in the institutionalization of the political systems. Moreover, at least some major variations among the armed forces do not depend on the wider societal development. They are differences intrinsic to the evolution of the armed forces that can be explained by both indigenous and exogenous factors in the development of the respective militaries and their narrowly conceived experiences.[31] The differences in the East African armed forces thus become independent variables which must be evaluated.

The three East African armed forces differ little in terms of size or force components. Table 1 reproduces the vital statistics of the Ugandan, Kenyan, and Tanzanian armed forces in societal perspective.

The statistics for size of armed force and for defense expenditures usually vary from source to source. There is fairly close agreement, however, on the figures given in the table.[32] Kenya's army is put at a total strength of 4,700 by the Institute of Strategic Studies. It is comprised of one brigade of four infantry battalions and a support battalion, including a paratroop company. Uganda had two brigades in 1970, each consisting of two infantry battalions, and an independent infantry battalion. Tanzania has four infantry battalions, plus tanks and some artillery.

All three armies have grown in firepower in the last few years; the Tanzanian army has doubled in size and the other two have grown by almost 1,000 men each. The Tanzanian armed forces started from a smaller base in the mid-1960s; they were more thoroughly dismantled and reorganized after the mutinies of 1964. The Kenyan army had already been built up by 1964 to confront the Somali *shifta* in northern Kenya.[33] Uganda's defense budget was already over seventeen million dollars per year by 1967. Thus, it has risen less rapidly than Tanzania's, which was up more than 50 percent, and Kenya's, which had grown by almost 75 percent. Uganda's early high cost of defense probably represents a buildup of air force. Presently, Uganda has an air force of 450 men and 19 combat aircraft, including MIG 15s and 17s and 12 Magister armed trainers. Tanzania has an air force of 300 men and no planes; but it expects combat aircraft from the Soviet Union.[34] Kenya also has no combat aircraft, although it has 450 men in the air force. In addition, Kenya has 250 men in the naval forces and Tanzania has 100.

In discussing African armed forces it is impossible to ignore police and gendarmerie units, particularly because "military" regimes have more often than not consisted of coalitions of army and police. (This was clearly the case in Ghana.) African police forces have sometimes performed security and paramilitary functions and have been motorized and had significant firepower in comparison to the army proper.[35] In Kenya, in particular, the police force is large—11,500 men—and well-equipped. The civil police operate a light plane wing and include general service units (GSU). Each GSU is a paramilitary force for riot control. These units were used by the government to clear the University College of students in 1969.[36] Police units were used in the north (in addition to army units) to provide security against Somali *shifta* raiders. Tanzania has a police force of 7,500, which includes a marine unit. Uganda's police force of about 7,000 has an air wing and an 800-man general service unit. The Ugandan army, or at least elements within it, have feared at times that the GSU was becoming a personal arm of Obote under the direction of his security chief and cousin, Akena Adoko.

While there are surface similarities in terms of size, size as a percentage of total population, firepower and defense expenditures, the three East African armed forces are different in several important respects, such as discipline, professionalism, the nature of the officer corps, and military-civilian relationships.

Since 1964 the Ugandan army has been the most salient in the politics of East Africa. It has been relatively the least disciplined armed force; it has been called upon to play the most active internal role; and it seems the most riven by internal factionalism. There is of course an interaction between the weakness of the civilian institutions and the degree of discipline and factionalism inside the armed forces. But it can be shown that certain patterns within the armed forces and the specific tasks that the Ugandan army was called on to perform accentuated the prominence of the army in politics and at the same time weakened its internal cohesion.

At the beginning of 1964, all the East African armies were in the process of trying to build an African officer corps. (Africanization of the officer corps took place later in East Africa than in those West African states that became independent sooner.) Kenya was newly independent in 1964; Tanganyika had become independent only at the end of 1961, and Uganda in 1962. At the time they attained independence, Tanganyika, Uganda, and Kenya had six, fourteen, and eighty African commissioned officers respectively.[37] This represented 9.4 percent, 21.9 percent, and 48.5 percent of the commissioned officer corps of the three countries.[38] By the summer of 1963, 40 percent of Tanganyika's sixty-three commissioned officers above the rank of Warrant Officer were Tanganyikans (one was an Asian).[39] The figure was 58 percent if twenty-eight Warrant Officers are included.[40] As Harvey Glickman has pointed out, it was not until 1957 that East Africans were accepted at Sandhurst.[41]

In the rapid Africanization programs, roughly three streams of officers came into being: (1) former noncommissioned officers, often with World War II experience, who were promoted to officer rank; (2) British-trained officers who had attended overseas schools, some of whom could be broken into a subgroup of those who had had short-service training (For example, in 1963 Tanganyika had eight lieutenants on short-service commission who had trained at Mons Officer Training School in Britain.[42]); and (3) political protégés who went for military training to new military assistance donors—not to England. Michael Lee reports that a Ugandan Minister sent some of his protétés for military training to Israel, without informing or consulting commanding British officers.[43] Kenyans were sent to the Soviet Union under the sponsorship of Oginga Odinga. Tanzania proliferated the number of military aid donors so that at one time her armed forces were receiving assistance from Great Britain, Canada, Israel, China, and West Germany. Not all officers who went to non-British training programs were "politicals," however, and thus there could be movement from one category to another. Brigadier General Opolot, commander of the Ugandan army from 1964–66, was a long-time professional who had served as an noncommissioned officer (NCO) in the colonial army, but who also received Sandhurst training later in his career.[44]

The conflict between these officer streams was most pronounced in Uganda, which experienced the most rapid military growth in tropical Africa outside of Nigeria. The former expanded its army by over 40 percent a year without a large reserve of trained manpower to call back into service.[45] Uganda had good reason to expand its army, since civil war in the Congo spilled over, creating refugee problems and instability in western Uganda. Similar situations existed in the north as refugees from the southern Sudan moved in and out of Uganda,[46] and in the south, when Tutsi refugees from Rwanda came into the country. In addition, there has been a long-standing problem of intratribal cattle raids between Turkana and Karamojong in the north,[47] which has necessitated sending in the army from time to time to keep the peace in that huge and sparsely settled area.

In western Uganda, an even more serious problem confronted the army. Two tribes, the Bwamba and the Bakonjo, were trying to free themselves from domination by the Batoro in what came to be known as the Rwenzururu separatist movement. Because this movement was in the Ruwenzori Mountains area bordering on the Congo, it was difficult for the Ugandan army to operate there.[48] Indeed, the army itself was a disruptive force in the area, foraging and sometimes using roadblocks to extort money. Eventually, the army moved out to the plains area and essentially gave up the mountains to the movement.[49] On the Congo border also the army did not seem to function as a disciplined body. Arbitrary arrests of individuals took place,[50] and the then Deputy Commander of the Army and Army Chief of Staff, subsequently Commander of the Army, Idi Amin, was accused by opposition members of Parliament of looting from the Congolese.[51] In both the Congo area and the Ruwenzori region, the army failed in its mission to provide public order, experiences that were demoralizing for the army. In the Congo operations, in addition, factionalism developed within the army over differences in policy toward the Congo rebels.

The army was more successful when it confronted Buganda, parts of which rose in arms against the central government in May 1966. The army defeated the force of the Kabaka (King) of Buganda, consisting of Buganda police and exservicemen, in a battle at the Kabaka's palace.[52] It then had to occupy Buganda. Again, charges of brutality and arbitrary behavior were made, and the occupation was a continuing source of tension between civilians and military. Since the army was heavily northern or "Nilotic," its role in Buganda was perceived in ethnic terms. When the Kenyan army was involved against Somali *shifta* in northern Kenya, it could by contrast project an image in the country of a national unifier. But northern Kenya is a sparsely settled area, removed from major concentrations of people, and the Somalis were a small minority of Kenya's total population. Buganda, on the other hand, has been the heartland of Uganda. It is the wealthiest part of the country, its people are the best educated, and it is the geographic center. Destruction of the Buganda regime by a northern army raised fears among Bantu peoples at large. Thus, the Buganda occupation did not project the army as a national unifier, at least not in the short run.

The increase in the size of Uganda's army and the defense costs incurred could be explained by border problems and internal security needs. But the pressures for increase came also from the army itself, and these were weakly resisted by the civilian leadership. In the mutinies of 1964, Uganda's civilian leadership responded far more weakly than either Kenya's or Tanzania's. The Uganda civilian authorities did not deal harshly with the mutineers. While the Tanzanian army was totally reconstructed, the Ugandan army was granted its major demands: pay increases[53] and immediate Africanization of the officer corps. A new infantry battalion was formed with officers promoted from the ranks.[54]

The assertion has been made that Uganda's officer corps is strikingly different from Kenya's.[55] While no direct surveys of Kenyan or Ugandan officers' attitudes have been undertaken, it appears that Kenya's promotion of African officers came later than Uganda's. Thus, Uganda had a greater share of promoted NCO's compared to foreign-trained officers. As late as the end of 1966, Uganda had only twelve officers in training abroad, compared to four times that many Kenyans.[56] But at the senior levels, more than 60 percent of those holding the rank of major or above in Kenya had been *effendis,* a position in the colonial armies halfway between officers and enlisted men— i.e., a warrant officer position.[57]

The difficulties between younger and better educated officers and former NCO's who had been promoted was greater in Uganda than in Kenya. Lee states that by 1964 the Ugandan army had reached a delicate state, and he relates the mutiny to the return from Britain of cadets who had trained at Mons. The direct entry officers now outnumbered the former NCO's by twenty-one to sixteen.[58] General Opolot, who himself bridged the gap between the two categories, was replaced in October 1966 and arrested under emergency regulations operating in Buganda.[59] Indeed, Uganda's rapid expansion of the army was marked all along by a very high rate of officer dismissal.[60] A number of captains and junior officers were brought up for court-martial on charges related to an alleged aborted coup in 1965. When Obote purged his cabinet in 1966, a number of younger, better educated Bantu officers were implicated with the dismissed ministers in a plot against the prime minister.[61]

J. M. Lee has described the breakdown in discipline and the factionalism within African armies in general in terms Huntington might well have used:

> The conventions of colonial days which separated the army from the rest of the community were broken down, precisely because the officer corps tended to be subject to the same tensions as civilian elites. . . . the regime in power was not obliged to take measures which would give it control of the army; the political community recolonized it. The army became the battleground for warring factions if large sections of the community found it impossible to identify with the regime. In these conditions it is not surprising that the army's sense of professionalism is significantly lowered. . . .[62]

The fact remains that Kenya's army did not break down in the way that Uganda's did. Although Kenya had a mutiny, the army was stabilized once civilian authority was reasserted. This may be in part because Kenyatta had more personal authority than Obote. Furthermore, Kenya's ethnic splits had not reached the point that Uganda's had in 1964. Kenya was not without ethnic struggle, however, especially Luo-Kikuyu conflict, which became more intense later on.

Kenya had an advantage in that its army recruitment worked to insulate the army from the major ethnic conflict. The Kamba had provided a disproportionate number of recruits to the colonial King's African Rifles and they maintained this position. They were still the largest single tribe represented in the officer corps in 1966, with 28 percent of the total compared to their population share of 11 percent. The Kikuyu had 22.7 percent of the officers and 19.2 percent of the population, and the Luo officer component was 10.3 percent, although Luos made up 13.9 percent of the total population. The Luyha were the most underrepresented large tribe, with only .4 percent of the officers whereas they comprised 12.9 percent of the people.[63] Thus the Kamba, who were outside the main ethnic conflict, were the most important group in the army.[64]

Kenya was not without its own tribal competition for positions of authority in military and police forces, however. Indeed, Kenya's political leadership tried early on to master its own armed forces in a self-conscious way. But the importance of the Kamba in the Kenyan army may have insulated that army from Kikuyu-Luo tensions at a critical period. There has, however, been a progressive Kikuyuization of the officer corps in the last few years as there has of the civil service. The Kikuyu are the best educated Africans in Kenya, and political sponsorship of Kikuyus in the government service is a clear feature of Kenyan political life.

Lee reports that the Kikuyu had as many officers as the Kamba by 1967. He sees the growth of Kikuyu officers and the relative diminution of officers from small tribes such as Nandi and Kipsigis, who had played some role in the colonial army, as an attempt to make the army more broadly representative.[65] Yet the fact that the general service unit has increasing numbers of Kikuyu officers, and that the army proper has been commissioning more Kikuyus than any other tribe[66] has led many to feel that the Kikuyus are becoming over-represented.

The issue of Kikuyuization is a sensitive one in Kenya; the insulation of the army from ethnic struggle cannot be taken for granted in the future. But there are factors which may continue to make armed forces in Kenya more disciplined and freer of ethnic conflict than those in Uganda. Uganda and Tanzania moved in 1964 to end a British presence in their armed forces. But in Kenya, British training missions continued; British officers remained seconded to the Kenya armed forces; British units trained in Kenya, and had contact with the Kenya armed forces even when the British base system in Kenya was ended and facilities were turned over.[67] Kenya continues to send most of her naval cadets to the Royal Naval College at Dartmouth; her airmen and signalmen learn their duties in England, and army personnel train at Sandhurt, Mons, and the Imperial Defense College. The British impact remains great and works in the direction of making the Kenyan armed forces relatively well trained and effective.

The very factor of past success is important in the future evolution of the armed forces. It has been suggested earlier in this article that Uganda's army was not up to the military tasks it was given. Kenya's army, on the other hand, has acquitted itself well. This keeps rather narrowly defined professional norms viable, as action within the scope of the norms is perceived to be feasible. If the Kenyan army were called on continuously to put down overt ethnic strife, as appeared possible after Tom Mboya's assassination, it would be increasingly difficult to keep the army insulated from tribal conflict. The Kenyan army, like the Ugandan, might well be unsuccessful in such endeavors. Furthermore, it cannot be assumed that Kenya will avoid indefinitely the factional alliances between civilian and military groups that have occupied Uganda's army. Up to now, however, a balancing of battalion commands, and even an increasing Kikuyuization of the officer corps have not led Kenyan civilian politicians to use the army or parts of it as a political base for their own personal power.

Kenya does have nonmilitary bases for political power. The present Kikuyu ruling group can rely on its civil service, on a growing commercial and small business group, and on a more prosperous farming class. It can appeal at large to Kikuyu sentiment. Unlike President Obote in Uganda, the Kenyan political leadership is not forced to politicize the army. In Kenya, then, factors intrinsic to the armed forces have interacted with wider societal factors to create a military less engaged in politics in a day-to-day way, and not the sole arbiter of the regime. A particular crisis around the succession to Kenyatta could conceivably trigger military intervention; but it does not appear that the basic problems in Kenya attendant on phenomena of social change will, in the short run, lead to military intervention on the praetorian model. In other words, Kenya's class evolution, the conjunction of tribe and class, regionalism, and Kikuyuization do not seem to be leading to military intervention along the lines set forth in Huntington's concept of praetorian society.

The argument here has been that we can compare Uganda's and Kenya's societies, their armies, and the interaction of army and society. But there are fundamental differences between the Ugandan and Kenyan armies that are not entirely dependent on societal factors, but themselves operate as independent factors. It may be useful to look briefly at the way Tanzania as well went about reconstructing its army in order to see if any factors unique to the Tanzanian military can be isolated.

It was stated earlier that the then Prime Minister Obote in effect denied that a mutiny had taken place in Uganda in 1964. In Kenya, Kenyatta noted the gravity of the army action that year, but he did not condemn the entire armed forces as such. Kenya reconstructed its army by continuing with a process of professional training which utilized British officers.[68] In Tanzania, on the other hand, Nyerere condemned the army as a whole,[69] disbanded it, and set about creating new armed forces.[70] The aim was to construct an army that would be politically loyal. Of course, that was the aim in Kenya, too, but in

Tanzania the pool for recruitment of the army was to be TANU and TANU-affiliated organizations, and commitment to party norms was to be the basis for the initial formation of the new armed forces.[71]

In May 1964, defense became the responsibility of Second Vice-President Kawawa; both the National Service and youth sections and the headquarters of the Tanzanian People's Defense Forces are now part of his portfolio. A regular army composed of four infantry battalions, one artillery battalion, and one tank company was formed by 1970. An air wing was also created.

It has been estimated that about 2,000 of the 5,000 who had passed through national service by the end of 1967 were absorbed into the security forces as regular soldiers or policemen.[72] The national service provided a reserve which could be called up, as well as a sizable number of recruits to the regular army. It is important to note that the army's recruitment was selective, and it became standarized. Not all army recruits were from national service.[73] Moreover, those who entered the army became full-time soldiers.

Conclusions

Certain inferences may be drawn about the three countries under discussion. It does not appear that the Tanzanian Peoples Defense Force has been completely free of internal conflicts or that relations between the military and civilian leaders have been without any tension, although the army has posed no threat to the TANU government since 1964. Both the Kenyan and the Tanzanian governments seem to have insulated their respective armies from major political and ethnic issues during the last ten years. In both cases, the personal position of the leader was stronger than in Uganda. In addition, the Kenyan civil service and TANU provide institutional bases of support not available in Uganda. At the same time, the Kenyans were able to build on a military much less internally split and with better trained men than the Ugandan army. The Tanzanians started afresh in 1964 with a much more thorough housecleaning than the Ugandans undertook. In a more consensual society, the Tanzanians appear to have had some success in welding the army to the TANU government, although it is not clear that specific TANU institutions have played a major role in this process. The Tanzanian army is itself occupied with conflict on the southern border with Mozambique; and such a preoccupation with external rather than internal conflicts acts to keep an army out of constant intervention in domestic affairs. If the army handles the external conflict creditably, it works to increase the possibilities of building a disciplined force in the future.

It cannot be assumed that the Kenyan or Tanzanian armed forces will not become increasingly active in domestic politics or that their military will never make coups. But this article has tried to suggest that there is a much greater probability of military intervention in Uganda because of the nature of the society. Indeed, as General Amin was reported to have said after the 1964 coup, the Uganda army had been rather openly keeping the regime in power.

The Uganda coup may not have been well planned;[74] it may have been triggered by Amin's own perception that he would be removed soon and his awareness of the growing power of nonregular army forces.[75] But these were mere precipitants of the coup;[76] basically, it was caused by underlying conditions in Uganda that differed from those in Tanzania and Kenya in important respects.

We can perhaps draw some conclusions about the prospects for military rule from certain features shown by the intervention itself. The reason why a miltary intervenes is important. Armed forces can make coups for rather narrow professional and interest group reasons: they can claim that the army is not being paid enough, that its honor is being sullied, or that it is being destroyed by the politicians; or they can have personal fears of particular officers. Alternatively, the military may intervene for broad political goals.

In Uganda, the military seems to have reacted to personal fears of the officers, to growing discontent with the way the regular army was being treated, and to unhappiness about the political situation, especially its ethnic components. An important factor is that the military was internally split before and during the coup. In effect, one part of the military fought against another part that was more closely allied with Obote. Yet General Amin and his colleagues moved slowly and cautiously after the coup. They do not appear to have had clearly drawn political goals. The new cabinet that Amin announced was composed largely of civil service personnel—it had two soldiers, three politicians, and seventeen civil servants. Only three Baganda were in the cabinet although the coup was at first enthusiasticlaly received in Baganda. If the military remains internally split and if the officers in Uganda are not political animals, then the prospects for either successful or long-term military rule are diminished.

This article has tried to show that we should not overhomogenize African societies or their armed forces. We shall have to continue to explore the interrelationships between armed forces and societies and our comparisons are going to have to deal with interactions.

All three East African countries discussed in this article have problems of political participation and political order. However, the army's intervention in politics cannot be deduced from a ratio of participation to institutionalization. We must agree that military explanations do not explain military interventions and that the general politicization of social forces and institutions must be examined.[77] At the same time, knowing about rates of mobilization, degrees of social cohesion, and levels of political institutionalization will not tell us all we want to know about the potentialities of military intervention in a given society.

The discussion of East African armies and societies suggests that institutionalization and performance of the armed forces are critical factors.[78] But analysis of the armed forces—the special conditions which pertain to each individual military—must be linked to wider societal factors.[79] This means we should be studying the *connections* among variables.

We examine the recruitment procedures of armed forces within the context of analysis of class, ethnicity, and factional cleavages in society at large. We examine attitudes of soldiers not in isolation, but by looking at the various groups and social formations that espouse ideologies and programs. Thus we look at the nature of the participation of armed forces in politics by analyzing patterns of political participation throughout a society.

At the same time, in order to understand political participation in society at large, we must examine the internal workings of armed forces organizations.

Notes

1.   Reports of the Uganda coup may be found in *Foreign Broadcast Information Service,* Daily Report, Middle East and Africa, 25 January 1971–1 February 1971; *New York Times* 25 January–1 February 1971; *Economist,* 6 February 1971, p. 27, 30 January 1971 pp. 14–15; *East African Standard* (Nairobi), 25 January 1971 ff., and *Uganda Argus* (Kampala), 25 January 1971 ff.

A recent analysis of the 1971 Uganda coup is in Michael F. Lofchie, "The Uganda Coup: Class Action by the Military," *Journal of Modern African Studies* 10 (May 1972): 19–36. Two replies critical of Lofchie's arguments are John D. Chick, "Class Conflict and Military Intervention in Uganda," *Journal of Modern African Studies* (December 1972); 634–637; and Irving Gershenberg, "A Further Comment on the 1971 Uganda Coup," in *ibid.,* 638–640. Another major analysis of the Uganda coup is Michael Twaddle, "The Amin Coup," *Journal of Commonwealth Political Studies* 10 (July 1972): 112–128.

2.   See Chapter 7.

3.   Samuel Huntington, *Political Order in Changing Societies* (New Haven: Yale University Press, 1968), p. 194.

4.   For a discussion of the modernizing capabilities of the military in developing countries, see Henry Bienen, ed., *The Military and Modernization* (New York: Atherton/Aldine, 1971).

5.   Some interesting work has been done recently on compositions of officer corps in Africa. For a general study, see J. M. Lee, *African Armies and Civil Order* (London: Chatto and Windus, 1969). On Nigeria, see John Colas, "Social and Career Correlates of Military Intervention in Nigeria: A Background Study of the January 15th Coup Group" (Paper delivered at Annual Meeting, Inter-University Seminar on Armed Forces and Society, Chicago, October 9–11, 1969). Also on Nigeria, see Robin Luckham, "Authority and conflict in the Nigerian Army, 1966: A Case Study in the Transfer of Military Institutions" (Paper presented to Seventh World Congress of Sociology, Varna, Bulgaria, September 1970).

6.   The ideas of the praetorian state and praetorian society have been developed in Huntington's *Political Order* and in Amos Perlmutter, "The Praetorian State and the Praetorian Army," *Comparative Politics* (April 1969): 382–404, and Perlmutter, "The Arab Military Elite," *World Politics* 22 (January 1970): 269–300. Also see David Rapoport "A Comparative Theory of Military and Political Types," in Huntington, ed., *Changing Patterns of Military Politics* (New York: The Free Press, 1962), pp. 71–101, especially pp. 71–74. This essay was based on Rapoport's "Praetorianism: Government without Consensus" (Ph.D. dissertation, University of California, Berkeley, 1960). Huntington's arguments will be used for discussion here.

7.   Huntington, *Political Order,* p. 194.

8.   *Ibid.,* p. 196.

9.   *Ibid.,* pp. 196–197.

10.   *Ibid.,* pp. 197–198.

11.   *Ibid.,* p. 200.

12.   *Ibid.,* p. 212 and pp. 216–217.

13. *Ibid.,* p. 200.

14. *Ibid.*

15. *Ibid.,* p. 221.

16. In the discussion which follows, my aim is to consider Huntington's idea of praetorianism for the light it may throw on civil-military relations in East Africa. I am not here interested in reviewing *Political Order in Changing Societies.*

17. For political analyses of East African countries, the following may be consulted: Stanley Diamond and Fred. G. Burke, eds., *The Transformation of East Africa* (New York: Basic Books, 1966); Bienen, *Tanzania: Party Transformation and Economic Development* (Princeton: Princeton University Press, 1970); William Tordoff, *Government and Politics in Tanzania* (Nairobi: East African Publishing House, 1967); G. Andrew Maguire, *Toward "Uhuru" in Tanzania* (New York: Cambridge University Press, 1969); Goran Hyden, *Tanu Yajenga Nchi: Political Development in Rural Tanzania* (Lund: Uniskol, 1968); Burke, *Local Government and Politics in Uganda* (Syracuse: Syracuse University Press, 1964); David Apter, *The Political Kingdom in Uganda* (Princeton: Princeton University Press, 1962); Julius Nyerere, *Freedom and Socialism* (Dar es Salaam: Oxford University Press, 1968); Nyerere, *Freedom and Unity* (Dar es Salaam: Oxford University Press, 1967); John Nottingham and Carl Rosberg, Jr., *The Myth of Mau Mau* (New York: Frederick A. Praeger, 1966); Oginga Odinga, *Not Yet Uhuru* (New York: Hill and Wang, 1967); Cherry Gertzel, *The Politics of Independent Kenya* (Nairobi: East African Publishing House, 1969); Gertzel, Mauré Goldschmidt, and Don Rothchild, *Government and Politics in Kenya* (Nairobi: East African Publishing House, 1969).

18. See M. Crawford Young, "The Obote Revolution," *Africa Report* 11 (June 1966): 8–15.

19. These remarks are taken from Bienen, "What Does Political Development Mean in Africa?" *World Politics* 20 (October 1967): 128–141.

20. See Chapters 2 and 3.

21. Bienen, *Tanzania.*

22. See Chapter 7.

23. For the district base of KANU politics, see John Okumu, "Charisma and Politics in Kenya," *East Africa Journal* 5 (February 1968): 9–16.

24. There are certainly many "almost" parallels one could draw between KANU and UPC. Uganda cabinet ministers were arrested under Obote, while in Kenya Odinga and other Luo M.P.'s were incarcerated in late 1969 after they had left the government and were already in opposition. Bildad Kaggia, a former assistant minister, had earlier been put in detention after he also had left the government.

25. For a discussion of violence and ethnicity in Uganda, see Martin R. Doornbos, "Kumaryana and Rwenzururu: Two Responses to Ethnic Inequality," in Robert Rotberg and Ali A. Mazrui, eds., *Protest and Power in Black Africa* (New York: Oxford University Press, 1970), pp. 1088–1138. Also see G. S. Engholm and Mazrui, "Violent Constitutionalism in Uganda," *Government and Opposition* 2 (July-October 1967): 585–599; Colin Leys, "Violence in Africa," *Transition* 5 (March–April 1965): 17–20; "A Special Correspondent, "The Uganda Army: Nexus of Power," *Africa Report* 11 (December 1966): 37–39.

26. Huntington, *Political Order,* p. 196.

27. While Dar es Salaam has recently been growing by about 10 percent annually, the urban population as a whole grows at about 6 percent in Tanzania. In 1970, the urban population was around 5 percent of the total; there were 10 towns of 15,000 or more people. See *Tanzania Second Five-Year Plan for Economic and Social Development 1st July 1969–30th June 1974* 1 (Dar es Salaam, 1969): 176–182.

28. Tanzania's northwestern region has also had a stratified land system, called the *nyarubanja,* in the Eastern Buhaya area, which was not so different from Buganda. See Hyden, *Tanu Yajenga Nchi,* p. 79.

29. Bienen, "An Ideology for Africa," *Foreign Affairs* 47 (April 1969): 545–559.

30. Huntington, *Political Order,* p. 222.

31. I argued in Chapter 7 that the decisive factor in the army mutinies of 1964 was the fragility of East African institutions *per se.* I am now arguing that we must explain the role of the armed forces in East Africa since 1964 in terms of the interaction of specific armed forces with their environments. While the emphasis here is on domestic environments—that is, the societies of each East African state—a full consideration would include the interactions of the East African armies with the international environments. The 1964 mutinies, for example, must be related to the Zanzibar Revolution. See Bienen, "National Security in Tanzania after the Mutiny," *Transition* 5 (April 1965): 39–46. Explanations of subsequent civil-military relations must take into account the liberation movements in southern Africa and Tanzania's army, the Kenya-Somali conflict, the Congo upheavals, and the refugee problems in southern and northern Uganda and the reaction of the Uganda army to the refugees.

32. Colonel T. N. Dupey, ed., *The Almanac of World Military Power* (Harrisburg: Stackpole Books, 1970) gives armed forces figures very close to Richard Booth, "The Armed Forces of African States, 1970," (see Table 1) for Uganda, a smaller armed force number for Tanzania, and considerably larger figures for Kenya because internal security forces are included in the latter. See pp. 208–209, 246–247, 252–253.

33. In 1967, armed forces were put at 3,000 for Tanzania, 4,775 for Kenya, and 5,960 for Uganda. See Charles Stevenson, "African Armed Forces," *Military Review* 47 (March 1967): 18–24; and David Wood, "The Armed Forces of African States," *Adelphi Papers,* no. 27 (April 1966).

34. Dupey, p. 248, puts the size of the Tanzanian air force at 400 men.

35. For a discussion of African police forces, see Christian Potholm, "The Multiple Roles of the Police as Seen in the African Context," *Journal of Developing Areas* 3 (January 1969): 139–158.

36. See Bienen, "When Does Dissent Become Sedition?" *Africa Report* 14 (March/April 1969): 10–14. See also Chapter 6.

37. From Lee, *African Armies and Civil Order,* p. 44.

38. *Ibid.* At the time of independence, Kenya had 13.9 percent Africans in its gazetted police officers, Uganda had 42.9 percent, and Tanganyika 10.4 percent. Since police played a large internal security role in Kenya after Mau Mau, the relatively high percentage of Kenyan African officers in the army may have been the other side of the coin of low percentage of Kenyan Africans in the police officer corps.

39. Harvey Glickman, *Some Observations of the Army and Political Unrest in Tanganyika,* Duquesne University, Institute of African Affairs, Paper No. 16 (Pittsburgh, 1964), p. 4.

40. *Ibid.*

41. *Ibid.*

42. *Ibid.*

43. Lee, *African Armies and Civil Order,* pp. 75–76.

44. A Special Correspondent, "The Uganda Army," p. 38.

45. Lee, *African Armies and Civil Order,* p. 105.

46. From time to time the government of the Sudan threatened to pursue Sudanese rebels into Uganda.

47. Leys, "Violence in Africa," *Transition* 5 (April 1965): 18–10. Leys reports that in only nine months of 1961, 253 people were killed in Karamoja.

48. For a discussion of the separatist movements in western Uganda, see Doornbos, "Kumaryana and Rwenzururu," esp. pp. 188–1136.

49. A Special Correspondent, p. 39.

50. *Ibid.*

51. A motion by an opposition M.P. to suspend Colonel Amin was passed in the National Assembly with only one dissenting vote. See *Africa Report* 11 (March 1966): 22. Colonel Amin was later cleared by a commission of inquiry and became head of the army as Obote consolidated his power with Amin's support.

52. There were more than 18,000 Baganda exservicemen in the 1950s who were veterans of World War I and II. See Eugene Schleh, "Post-Service Careers of World War Two Veterans: The Cases of Gold Coast and Uganda" (Paper delivered at 1967 Annual Meeting, African Studies Association, New York City, November 1–4), p. 9.

53. As of 1967, the annual starting salaries of nonofficers were considerably higher in Uganda than in Kenya. A Kenyan sergeant received about $1,000 a year compared to a Ugandan's $1,500. A private received about $350 in Kenya, $600 in Uganda. Officers had more nearly comparable salaries from second lieutenant up. Lee, p. 94.

54. A Special Correspondent, "The Uganda Army." p. 38.

55. *Ibid.*

56. *Ibid.*

57. Lee, *African Armies and Civil Order,* pp. 42, 108–109.

58. *Ibid.,* p. 108.

59. A Special Correspondent, "The Uganda Army," p. 39.

60. Lee, p. 105, says that it may be the highest on the continent.

61. A Special Correspondent, "The Uganda Army."

62. Lee, *African Armies and Civil Order,* p. 106.

63. *Ibid.,* p. 110. The Luyha had 16.5 percent of the police, while the Kikuyu had 11.2 percent, Luo 8.5 percent, and Kamba 9.8 percent. Lee's figures for the officers are for 1966, but the population shares are based on the 1962 census. The police figures are also for 1962.

64. The Kamba areas also had given support to the Kamba leader's own party—the African People's Party, in the 1963 elections, rather than to either KANU or KADU, the major parties. In the 1966 Little General Election, Kamba areas gave some support also to the opposition Kenya Peoples Union. The Kamba, then, have been an important "swing" tribe in Kenya.

65. Lee, *African Armies and Civil Order.*

66. The social pages of the *East African Standard* frequently announce the marriage of young Kikuyu officers to daughters of prominent Kikuyus. A study of marriage and political/economic relationships would be most interesting in this area.

67. A 1968 issue of Majeshi Yetu (Armed Forces Journal) makes interesting reading. It is published with English and Swahili pages, is well written and professional. By-lined articles can be found by C. L. Galloway, Commander A. A. Pearse, and Major A. M. Tippett, among others.

68. See the statement by then Prime Minister Kenyatta of 25 January 1964, reprinted in Gertzel, Goldschmidt, and Rothchild, eds., *Government and Politics in Kenya,* p. 562.

69. Kenneth Grundy, *Conflicting Images of the Military in Africa* (Nairobi: East African Publishing House, 1968), p. 29.

70. The bulk of the two battalions in Tabora and Dar es Salaam were dismissed and mutineers were sent back to their home areas. They had to report periodically to area commissioners. Internal security was provided first by British and then by Nigerian troops.

71. The following discussion is taken from Bienen: *Tanzania,* pp. 374–380. I have also commented on the formation of new Tanzanian armed forces in the previously cited "National Security in Tanzania after the Mutiny," and in Chapter 7.

72. Lee, *African Armies and Civil Order,* p. 150. I estimate that somewhat fewer than 5,000 men actually passed through the national service by 1967.

73. *Ibid.*

74. *The Economist* made this assertion in its issue of 6 February 1971, p. 27.

75.   General Amin reportedly said that a secret meeting was held on January 11 at which a decision was taken to murder him and others. Amin was said to have claimed that the President, then in Singapore, was kept abreast of the plot throughout by communications with the Minister of Internal Affairs. *Foreign Broadcast Information Service,* Middle East and Africa, January 1971, p. U-6.

76.   Twaddle also uses the language of "precipitants" and "preconditions" following the terms in Harry Eckstein, "Introduction: Toward the Theoretical Study of Internal War," in Eckstein, ed., *Internal War* (Glencoe: The Free Press, 1964), pp. 1–32. Twaddle, "The Amin Coup," sees the Uganda coup not so much as an army mutiny as part of an internal war situation. Lofchie, "The Uganda Coup" (p. 19) argues that the Uganda army "can best be understood as a kind of economic class, an elite stratum with a set of economic interests to protect." Chick, "Class Conflict . . ." (p. 634) takes Lofchie to task over the notion of stratum and class as applied to the Ugandan army, and both he and Gershenberg, "A Further Comment . . ." doubt whether the Obote government threatened the military's interests.

77.   Huntington, *Political Order,* p. 194.

78.   I have greatly benefited from reading Abraham Lowenthal's "Armies and Politics in Latin America: A Review of the Recent Literature," *World Politics* 27 (October 1974): 107–130. Lowenthal emphasizes the need to examine institutionalization within armies and to analyze the comparative strength of civilian and military organizations in specific countries.

79.   Perlmutter, "The Arab Military Elite," p. 276.

Background to Chapters 9–11

From the time of military takeover in January 1966, Nigerian military governments on many occasions had asserted their commitment to a return to civilian
rule. These assertions were hardly atypical of military regimes in Africa.
However, the Nigerian military leaders were frequent in their announcements,
spelled out their plans for a return to civilian rule, and took important steps to
bring civilians into both state military governments and the federal military
government.

From 1967 to 1974, civilians functioned as civil commissioners in the
Nigerian federal military government and in state governments. The civilians
that were brought into both federal and state levels were a mixed group. Some
were individuals who had not been active in politics prior to the 1966 military
coup. Others were major politicians either at national or regional levels. For
example, Chief Awolowo, a dominant personality in contemporary Nigerian
nationalism who was at one time leader of the Western Region and who had
also been jailed for treason in 1962, entered the federal government in 1967 as
did Aminu Kano, one of the major opponents of the civilian Nigerian Peoples
Congress regime in the Northern Region.

What follows is a report on politicians and civil servants under a military
regime. It is a field report on deposed leaders, some of whom reentered politics
under military auspices, but who did so very much for their own purposes. It
was possible to carry out interviews with these politicians precisely because
Nigeria is not a police state. Individuals talked freely about their attitudes and
roles once guaranteed anonymity, and many people did not even care about
being identified.

From September 1972 to June 1973, we collected data on politicians
under a military regime in Nigeria. Our aim was to reveal the realities of
military rule in Nigeria from the perspectives of an elite partially cut off from
power. We interviewed two sets of politicians. One group consisted of former
members of the Western House of Assembly from the old Western Region.
We interviewed 54 of the surviving 128 members of the Western House who
had served in the turbulent years 1960–1966.

All interviews were carried out by me and my colleague at the University of
Ibadan, Martin Fitton. Interviews were typically from 2 to 4 hours long.

Sometimes we were both present; at other times only one of us was present during the interview. All interviews were carried out in English. Generally, the Yoruba politicians spoke English with a range of fluency. We had a structured questionnaire, but we often departed from the order of the questions. The interviews were in depth and sometimes an individual was reinterviewed. Interviews were carried out in homes, offices, and places for recreation. Our sample included a wide and representative range by party affiliation, age, occupation, and geographical location.

During the period 1960–1966, Nigerian politics was in almost constant crisis. The Western Region, with about ten million people, was the scene of intense factional and party struggle.[1] The ruling Action Group (AG), which had dominated nationalist politics in the West and which was led by Chief Awolowo, split in 1962. A rump faction, led by Chief Akintola, who subsequently became premier of the West and was assassinated in the first military coup of January 1966, took over the government of the Western Region after a period of administration by the federal government. Akintola formed a new party, the Nigerian National Democratic party (NNDP), by bringing new people into politics and by using the carrot and stick to bring into his party former AG politicians and politicians from the National Congress of Nigerian Citizens (NCNC), which more and more became a party of the Ibo-dominated Eastern Region.

Internal struggle among the Yoruba in the Western Region became inextricably tied to regional maneuvering in the Nigerian federation. The Northern-dominated federal government increasingly had to prop up its ally in the West, the Akintola regime. Personal and political animosities became very bitter. The Western election of 1965, like the 1964 federal election in the West, was marked by violence and chicanery. Violence in the West and breakdown of government there were the primary causes of military intervention in 1966.[2] In brief, this is the background to our interviews with members of the Western House of Assembly (MHAs), one source of politicians.

The other source of politicians that we interviewed consisted of those people who served as civilian commissioners in the military governor's cabinet. From 1967 to 1971, the then Brigadier Robert Adeyinka Adebayo, governor of the Western State which had been created when Nigeria was broken from a federation of four regions into a twelve-state system, ruled with a cabinet made up of civilians. Many of these civilians were former politicians who had served in either the Western House of Assembly, the National Assembly, or both.

These commissioners held various portfolios such as lands and housing, finance, local government and chieftaincy affairs, health, and so forth. Heading certain statutory boards at various times gave one commissioner rank and cabinet status. The police chief of the Western State, the general officer in command of the troops in the Western State, and the attorney general were members of the cabinet.

In the Western State, the military governor appointed twelve commissioners on June 30, 1967. However, some replacements were made between

1967–1971. Moreover, a number of positions not listed as cabinet posts in the original announcement came to be so considered by at least some of the incumbents and their commissioner colleagues. Certain statutory corporations listed as commissioner posts in 1967 subsequently ceased to be listed. Three permanent secretaries attended cabinet meetings regularly: the permanent secretaries for finance and for political and administrative affairs in the military governor's office, and the secretary to the military governor. If one takes the widest latitude in defining cabinet membership, the cabinet would include the twelve original commissioners plus later appointments, the *ex officio* appointees, and certain chairmen of commissions and boards, and the Governor. We met with thirteen of the twenty-two men who could be considered members of the cabinet during 1967–1971, including the then Governor Brigadier Adebayo.

Our aim in carrying out these interviews was to examine the interrelationships between military and civilian personnel. We rejected at the start the idea that dichotomizations of regimes as military or civilian would be very useful. We can define a regime to be a military one if certain conditions are met, but we should bear in mind that "civilian" is a rather large residual category; thus, we should be looking at the various group and institutional alliances that are made across the civilian-military boundary lines. Nigeria provided a good setting in looking at civilian-military relationships because we were able to interview politicians and because the military was relying on civilians to perform important political functions.

Politicians were a group whose support or opposition might be critical to the success of a military regime. If we could find out what they were doing politically, if we could find out how they viewed the regime and their own past, present, and future roles, we could better understand some of the possibilities of transition from military rule, or prospects for the maintenance of a military regime. We could better analyze the real-world situation of ongoing civilian-military relations.

Interviews with the MHAs allowed us to get at the attitudes and functioning of grass-roots politicians while the idea in examining cabinet government in the Western State was to look at decision-making under a military regime. Cabinet members were able to make comparisons between the way they operated as politicians in a civilian regime with their activities under a military head of government. This was possible since the cabinet in the Western State was not a cabinet of technicians or professionals. Although it had some doctors and a university professor, it was a highly political body. Most of the commissioners had been prominent politicians during the 1960s, or even much earlier, and were still major figures in Western State political life. If discussions with MHA's would hopefully allow us to say something about middle-level politics under a military regime, interviews with cabinet members would enable us to comment not only on the interaction of high-level civilian politicians and military men, but also on the relationship of civil servants to both military and civilian politicians.

Findings are presented in Chapters 9–11. These findings are cut away from the context of Nigeria as a federal republic. They are to some extent cut away from the recent political history of Western State Nigeria. What we can say about that history here is that Nigeria's military leadership needed civilians, both civil servants and politicians, in the running of the country. Prior to military rule in 1966 there had been a good deal of social mobilization and political participation. There were parties of long standing prior to 1966. Many regional and national elections had been held in the decade 1956–1966. As mentioned, the country had been in turmoil since 1962. While politicians had been discredited in the eyes of many people by 1966, political networks were still viable. These points have special force for the Western State.

The problems for military governors in the West were more intense than for those of other parts of Nigeria. The West had gone through a period of extended crises from 1962 to 1965. Elite factionalism was extremely bitter and was expressed in party struggle and by internal splitting within the parties. After the first coup in January 1966, the AG had a leadership, but its paramount leader, Chief Awolowo, was in jail. His strength in what was left of the AG was great enough that he could delegate nominal leadership. Without Awolowo, there would have been much more fragmentation of AG leadership.

In the Nigerian National Democratic Party, there was no clear-cut leadership left after the January coup. The former NNDP leader, Akintola, was dead. The deputy leader of the NNDP, Fani-Kayode, had been a leader of the National Congress of Nigerian Citizens prior to joining the NNDP. He himself had challenged Akintola's leadership before the coup and he was not widely accepted by NNDP people. Many NNDP leaders were in hiding or keeping a low profile. The NCNC had been shattered when most of it moved into the NNDP in 1964–1965.

There was certainly no clear-cut civilian leadership, apart from Chief Awolowo himself, that the military government in the West could turn to. Moreover, the splits in the West had by no means been confined to a leadership struggle over spoils of office. The elites of power in Western Nigeria had been able to mobilize nonelites for political struggle. And there is good evidence that conflict in the Western Region was not solely an elite phenomenon. Intra-Yoruba conflict took place over distributions of goods and services which affected large numbers of people. Farmers who wanted roads built in their areas, and people who wanted schools, hospitals, and so forth participated in a struggle for spoils. There were also felt differences over whether one was an Ijebu, Ibadan, Ijesha, Ekiti, Egba, or Ondo Yoruba. These differences permeated the masses. Yoruba were and are internally split by ethnic group distinction and religious differences inside the wider ethnic-language group. Local conflicts chiefly over lineages penetrate deeply too. Elites often encouraged such conflicts, using them to organize support. But this does not mean that the cleavages were somehow phony or that a false consciousness prevailed among the masses because nonclass distinctions were important politically.

Thus, a military government in the West faced a politically mobilized population. It operated in a context where the West was still relatively well-off, vis-à-vis the rest of Nigeria, by income and education, but the comparative advantage was diminishing. The West in 1966 was conscious of the odd-man-out role it had played in independent Nigeria and the pivotal role it could play in the future. Army officers themselves were conscious of past history and future possibilities. In fact, they were especially conscious of the weak Yoruba position in the then 10,000-man Nigerian army at both officer and enlisted men ranks. There were high-level Yoruba officers, but not enough middle-level ones. Thus, the three military governors between 1966 and 1974, Fajuyi,[3] Adebayo, and Rotimi,[4] stressed the need for the West to be unified as it faced the future. Said diplomatically, this meant the West should be a model of unity for the country as a whole. But bluntly said, the West had to be unified as it confronted other areas of Nigeria. And, between 1967–1970, the country had a civil war that was raging.

For the Yoruba military in the West then, there were overriding problems. One was political unity among civilians. The other was the weakness of the Yoruba position in the armed forces nationally and in the West itself, for troops from the North were stationed in the major political and strategic centers of the West. A major demand of Western civilian leaders was the removal of non-Western troops from the West and an increase in Yoruba in the armed forces. These demands were met between 1967–1969. But the timing of the demands and the way they were to be voiced were not always agreed on by civilian and military leaders. High-level officers felt that the Yorubaization of the army in the West had to be done, but that it was not in the best interests of political leaders to come out and say so since it was the Yoruba officers whose lives were at stake. This was but one example among many of the interaction of civilians and military on critical issues where there was agreement on goals, but not on process.

Notes

1. It seemed to make sense to concentrate analyses of civilian-military relations in the Western State rather than in Nigeria as a whole. For one thing, we were both based in Ibadan. This location gave us access to politicians in the Western State. In one year it would not have been possible to carry out the same kind of study all over the federation. Western State, with a population of anywhere between nine to twelve million, depending on whose figures one believes, is larger than most African countries. It has a capital city, Ibadan, with close to two million people and is heavily urbanized by African standards. It has one of the most advanced educational systems and one of the best developed administrative services in Africa.

2. For a discussion of the crises in the West see: B. J. Dudley, *Instability and Political Order: Politics and Crises in Nigeria* (Ibadan: University of Ibadan Press, 1973); John P. MacKintosh, *Nigerian Government and Politics* (Evanston: Northwestern University Press, 1966); S. K. Panter-Brick, *Nigerian Politics and Military Rule* (London: Athlone Press, 1970), especially Dudley's chapter on the West. For a discussion on the Nigerian coups see: Robin Luckham, *The Nigerian Military* (Cambridge University Press, 1971); Anthony Kirk-Green, *Crises and Conflict in Nigeria*, Volume I (London: Oxford University Press, 1971); S. K. Panter-Brick, *op. cit.*,; N. J. Miners, *The Nigerian Army, 1956–1966* (London: Methuen and Co. Ltd., 1971); Ruth First, *Power in Africa* (New York: Pantheon, 1970), esp. pp. 144–168 and pp. 278–362.

3.   Lieutenant Colonel Fajuyi was the first military governor of the West; he was appointed after the first coup in January 1966. He was killed in Ibadan along with General Ironsi, the first military head of state in Nigeria, in July 1966, during the second coup.

4.   General Adebayo was removed as governor of the Western State by General Gowon in 1971. He was replaced by then-Colonel Rotimi, the general officer in charge of the Western State.

Chapter 9

Military Rule and Political Process: Nigerian Examples

Presently, a consensus exists with regard to the way both scholars and policy makers think about the military in developing countries. Most commentators think that both academic work and policy analysis should emphasize the effect of the armed forces on society. In the case of military governments, we should look at the way in which they rule, at the political, social and economic changes military rule produces, rather than at the coming-to-power process itself. Gutteridge expresses this view with regard to Africa when he says, "The phenomenon of the violent seizure of power is now of less significance . . . than what is done with it once it has been seized."[1] This concern with the effects of military rule comes about in part because nearly half of independent Black African states are at present nominally ruled by armies. And in many countries the period of military rule has now lasted longer than the initial period of civilian rule after independence. But there are other reasons for directing attention to the effects of military rule. The many studies of miiltary coups did not, in the minds of a number of observers, establish strong generalizations relating the way a military government came to power and organizational variables. The type of coup was not linked to the size of the armed force, the level of professionalization of the army, the career experience of the officers taking power. Nor were military coups related to social characteristics such as level of urbanization, ethnic cleavage, or economic growth rates. Military coups in Africa were made by large and small armies. They were led by both junior and senior officers. They took place in singleparty and multiparty systems. Relatively cohesive armies carried out coups, as did fragmented armies. Motives for the initial decision to act varied, and motives often shifted during the coup process. Such factors were hard to understand, and, in the end, motives seemed not to be crucial to later development. Perhaps all commentators would not go as far as Zolberg when he argued that "the most salient characteristic of political life in Africa is that it constitutes an almost institutionless arena with conflict and disorder as its most prominent feature."[2]

Most, however, would agree that instability is endemic or inevitable in Africa; and given this, the military will participate in and often dominate political activity.

As "the military" was examined in individual studies the term itself was demystified. Armies were shown to be fragmented institutions: military groups were divided in terms of generation, ethnic cleavage, rank, educational background, and ideological commitment.[3] As military rule was examined empirically, it became clearer—and we should have known it a a priori, that the sharp distinction drawn between military and civilian regimes was an over-simplification. "Military" is a label pasted over many, very different governments. The "military" regimes differed in terms of mixtures of civilian-military authority, size of the armed forces, policy outlooks, degree of centralization of authority, and in their willingness to use coercion.

The view became widespread that military regimes in Africa were a type of mixed regimes. Military and civilian governments clearly faced the same economic constraints, the same social and ethnic cleavages. The argument then became: who rules, or the nature of civil-military relations, do not matter for the important outcomes of economic development, urbanization, and political stability. And these outcomes would not be determined in Africa either by specific institutional format or by a specific political constellation. The statistical analyses of cross-national, aggregate data seem to support this view. McKinlay and Cohan concluded that "while some military regimes are clearly distinct, as indeed are some civilian regimes, a sizeable proportion of military and civilian regimes are indistinguishable in terms of performance."[4] Jackman went further and argued that the impact of military regimes on social change did not vary with regard to societal development since military regimes have no singular effect on social change, irrespective of level of economic development.[5] This thesis was put forward in general for developing countries, and regional breakdowns did seem to alter the conclusion.

It is not surprising that empirical work should conclude that: (1) military regimes do not in aggregate form a distinctive regime type in terms of performance; (2) there is a degree of diversity within military regimes which is not dissimilar to the diversity found within civilian regimes; (3) the general degree of similarity or dissimilarity between military and civilian regimes varies from one variable, or one category of variables, to another.[6]

Are we ready, however, to abandon the idea that there are no important differences between civilian and military regimes? Does it not matter that it is military personnel who perform political and decision-making roles and who assume the important political positions by virtue of their place in the military hierarchy? Are we ready to say that military in power is *merely* another political actor?

It has been hypothesized that the special organizational and normative features of armed forces as institutions set them apart from other social and political groups. Of course, only empirical work can show whether or not there are distinctive norms attached to armed forces, or whether or not recruitment and socialization processes create institutions which have distinctively their "military" boundaries, personnel, and norms able to be differentiated from those of society as a whole. A significant body of work does argue that professional militaries retain their character as insular communities and that while "they have certain features associated with civilian bureaucracies . . . [they] differ from those organizations insofar as they are structurally adapted to fulfill a unique, primary function."[7] Observers have maintained that the military's orientation towards combat and its special socialization processes lead to a greater concern for corporate autonomy, a fear of factionalism, and an emphasis on hierarchy and chain of command.

African armies, however, are not oriented towards combat. At least, they rarely engage in external warfare. They have a hard time maintaining equipment. They import technology and often send their officers abroad for training, and in that sense they are not autonomous. Considerable doubt has been cast on the insulation of the African military from the rest of society and on the distinctiveness of the military socialization process in Africa. Recruitment has been shown to be influenced by ethnic and regional origin. Clique groups of officers usually share an ethnic or geographical background. If professionalism is measured neither by the statements of individual officers nor their commitment to civilian rule, but by independent criteria—such as demonstrated logistical ability, the maintenance of a chain of command, or skills developed in combat or engineering missions—then the level of professionalism in African armies cannot be said to be high.

Nonetheless, let us assume that armed forces as institutions do have some distinctive organizational characteristics, and let us assume recruitment, socialization, and functional requirements do set the military off from other institutions in society, at least in some ways. Even granted those assumptions, it might not follow that social change or economic growth can be traced to certain, identifiable, organizational features of the military government in power. Too many other variables may intervene between military decision-making and socio-economic outcomes. In fact, strategies for development or maintaining political control may be as varied among military governments as they are among civilian governments. Cross-national, aggregate data may show that military and civilian regimes cannot be differentiated by their effects on economic growth and social change, whether these effects are broadly conceived of as modernization and social mobilization, or even if more specifically seen as a change in the level of political activity as measured by the banning of legislatures and parties.

It may be that the level of investment as a share of gross national product or the relative political stability of a regime are not the most useful indicators of military and civilian regime differences. From what we know about organization of armed forces, I suggest it is more rewarding to look for regime differences in the process of politics itself. Let us look at the way political decisions are made by the military elite. Let us look at the kinds of links between elites with various organizational bases and nonelites. Let us look at the patterns of political participation that evolve. Granted, it is difficult to compare societies in the aggregate with regard to political participation or competition. Granted that certain concepts are difficult to operationalize because commentators do not agree about the relative importance of phenomena to be measured. We can, however, describe the ways in which various elites attempt to represent groups and individual interests. We can try to describe how different personnel are interested in having grass roots ties and how organizational structures influence patterns of representation and participation.

The ties between the institutional characteristics of a particular military organization and political processes might be closer than the ties between organizational characteristics and social change as a whole, or specific policy outcomes. Particularly, political processes should differentiate between military regimes or between some military regimes and some civilian regimes. The term "process of politics" is a loose, grab-bag notion; however, looking at process rather than outcome seems to make sense because, as Ames points out, "since all regimes face constraints, using policy outcomes as a test of true goals really asks whether the regime was powerful enough to realize its goals."[8] Moreover, policy outputs—conventionally understood as industrialization, rates of economic growth, the level of investment, etc.—while important, are by no means the only indicators of change. We cannot, in any event, relate these factors back to military rule, per se.

First, it may be useful to look at civilian-military relations in terms of decision-making patterns. This would entail looking at how information is gathered and processed within the military government. It would entail analyzing patterns of deliberation, representation, and pronouncement in military and civilian regimes, or between regimes with different combinations of civilian and military authority. Looking at the processes of politics would also involve looking at how decisions are implemented. How much discussion is there of implementation, and at what political and social levels is discussion carried on in the society? How is the political demand for civilian compliance made?

Research on decision-making in military regimes is not easy to carry out. Nor is it easy to know the military's role in the decision-making process in civilian regimes, although the military's particular stance on a specific policy question may be known. The research problems are more practical than analytical. Scholars do not usually have access to military personnel. Individual scholars have been able to contact officers, but systematic interviewing of armed forces' personnel to obtain data on social background, attitudes, and political connections with civilians has been rare. Moreover, soldiers' perceptions of their roles are not the only relevant perspectives. The civilians who interact and coexist with military personnel should be interviewed as well. Their perception of the military government is crucial.

The Nigerian Case

This case study attempted to examine political processes under military rule in Nigeria. The Nigerian military has been relatively widely studied.[9] Nigeria has a disadvantage from the point of view of studying a military regime in power. The individual state governments are headed by military and police personnel, as well as the national, federal government. Studying military-civilian relationships in Nigeria means accounting for variations between all the states of the Federal Republic of Nigeria. Consequently, instead of attempting an analysis of the Nigerian Federal Republic, I chose to concentrate on one state in the federation, the Western State.

The Western State was subdivided in 1976 when Nigeria became a nineteen-state instead of a twelve-state Federal Republic. I would not argue that the Western State was characteristic of Nigeria as a whole, nor that the Western State contained all patterns of Nigerian politics (any more than one African country could represent all African countries). One additional problem is raised. Since the Western State was a part of the Nigerian Federal Republic, civil-military relations in the Western State were directly affected by the politics of Nigeria and by civil-military relations in other states. In this sense, since work was not done in other states, the analysis of civilian-military relations in the Western State is incomplete. For example, it would have been extremely useful to have had information on civil-military decision-making in the Executive Council of the Federal Republic of Nigeria. Decisions taken in the Executive Council, in the Supreme Military Council of the Federal Republic, and in individual ministries of the Federal Republic importantly affected politics in the Western State. While some interviewing was focused on civilian-military relations at the center, in Lagos, our chief concern was not Nigeria as a whole but the Western State.

The Reentry of Civilians

The Nigerian army coup in January 1966 ended civilian rule. The military government initially put civilian politicians in cabinet positions in order to widen its base of support before and during the Nigerian Civil War. A civilian-military dyarchy existed from mid-1967 until towards the end of 1974 because the military government thought civilian help was necessary to mobilize civilian energies, to handle representative functions at both central and grass roots levels, and to unify disunified states in the federation. The military created institutions in which civilian politicians could participate, but where they would also be used and controlled. These institutions were in turn used by the civilian leaders to build a base of power independent of the military, to obtain some leverage in a political system they no longer controlled.

The military created or recreated civilian or mixed civilian-military institutions for the purpose of gathering, processing, and disseminating information and for the purpose of making decisions. These institutions were used to examine civil-military relations and the "process of politics" in a military regime.

In this chapter, I discuss cabinet government in a military regime. In Chapters 10 to 11, I discuss civilian consultative bodies, such as advisory councils and Leaders of Thought, and civil service-military relationships.

A discussion of cabinet government in a military regime in the Western State hardly encompasses all aspects of civilian-military political processes. This discussion will illustrate a fundamental problem for military regimes in Africa. The military for all its factionalism and fragmentation puts a high priority on corporate cohesion. The military's claim to power and legitimacy is based on the assertion that it is the corporate embodiment of the state. Characteristically, African armies have failed to deal with constituency problems. African military governments have been unwilling to be representative to avoid a threat to the armed forces' corporate cohesion and identity. Issues which might split armed forces internally are usually avoided. This discussion also illustrates the military's failure to establish grass-roots political support. The regime relied on civilian politicians to make contact for them in rural areas. I am reluctant to talk about the ways that officers made decisions because military officers, aside from the Governor, did not play prominent roles in cabinet discussions. Rather, they dealt with the military governor outside his cabinet. The critical mass of military personnel was present at the federal level in the Supreme Military Council and the Federal Executive Council, but not in state cabinets. The cabinet members we interviewed did speak to the issues of authority within a mixed civilian-military system; and they did address themselves to the characteristics and definition of a military regime. The civilian members of the cabinet did not see the military regime as simply another regime. Most of the civilian cabinet members distinguished between military and civilian rule, although at the same time they recognized that military governors had individual styles and treated civilian politicians differently.

Cabinet Government in a Military Regime

On June 3, 1967, the Nigerian Federal Military Government announced that civilians would be appointed to a Federal Executive Council. Executive authority would reside in both the Supreme Military Council and the Federal Executive Council. The only civilian on the Supreme Military Council was the then Administrator for the East Central State, the core area of the former Biafra. Members of the Federal Executive Council, however, consisted of both armed forces personnel and civilians. General Gowon chaired both executive organs from 1967 until his overthrow in 1975. Each of the twelve states from mid-1967 through 1974 had such executive councils with civilian commissioners. The civilian commissioners were formerly prominent politicians, technocrats, or professionals who had not been active in politics prior to the military period. The mix of civilians varied from state to state.

In Nigeria as a whole, the introduction of civilians into federal and state executive positions was interpreted by many as a move towards civilian rule. The mixed executive system was seen as a transition. Nigerian military leaders had on many occasions asserted their commitment to return to civilian rule. And these assertions were not atypical of military regimes in Africa.

However, Nigerian military leaders mades such announcements frequently. They also spelled out their plans for a return to civilian rule. And when the military government brought civilians into both the state military governments and the Federal Military Government, it was conceivable that at least some officers were considering a formal return to civilian rule. Indeed, on June 12, 1967, when General Gowon addressed the first meeting of the Federal Executive Council, which included civilian politicians, he said: "We are now embarking on the road back to full civilian rule. During this transition, however, we must continue with the political and administrative program of the Supreme Military Council."[10] And on the 30th of June, 1967, the Military Governor of the Western State of Nigeria, Brigadier R. A. Adebayo, appointed twelve civilian commissioners to his cabinet. The term "commissioner" was used because, according to General Gowon, many Nigerians:

> were not anxious to see those who in recent years participated in politics back in ministerial seats before the job of national reconstruction is completed . . . it will probably be better if civilian members of the Federal Executive Council are called Commissioners. This temporary nomenclature will not in any way detract from your departmental responsibilities.[11]

Commissioners held ministerial title when on overseas tours.

Once the commissioners had been sworn in, the Federal Republic and the states were governed explicitly by a mixed civilian-military system. Nonetheless, the regime was still understood by Nigerians as a military regime. In the Western State, both the military governor, General Adebayo, and the civilian commissioners made this clear. The late Alhaji D. C. Adegbenro, the senior civilian commissioner, addressed the Governor on behalf of his colleagues at the swearing-in ceremony of the commissioners as follows:

> We realize that yours is a Military regime and the fact that you have thought it fit to bring civilians into your cabinet shows the extent of your patriotism and love for the Yoruba people . . . The Western State has suffered a series of reverses in the past few years due to graft and inordinate ambition. The Military regime with the aid of civil commissioners must correct this unfortunate situation. . . .[12]

What did it mean to call the government a military regime? Brigadier Adebayo's government was defined as a military one because the head of government was in this position by virtue of appointment by the head of the federal military government, General Gowon. The authority came from the head of state and the Supreme Military Council which ruled by decree. The commissioners in Brigadier Adebayo's government, the highest level civil servants and governor Adebayo himself did not agree among themselves about the nature of this military government, or about their own roles in this government. They disagreed over whether the cabinet, a term used by both commissioners and the Governor, should be an executive body or merely advisory to the governor. Indeed, after the fact they disagreed as to whether it had functioned in an advisory or executive capacity. They differed over what representation was supposed to mean in a Brigadier's cabinet. They differed over the civilian commissioners' relationships to civil servants, again disagreeing over both what ought to be the case and what had been the case during 1967–1971. They also disagreed about how the military officers, aside from the governor, functioned politically.

The civilian commissioners were well qualified to consider the questions of civil service operations under a military regime, the nature of executive authority, and patterns of decison making in military as compared to civilian regimes because the cabinet in the Western State was not a cabinet of technicians or professionals. Although the cabinet included some professionals, it was a highly political body. Most of the commissioners had been prominent politicians during the 1960s, or even much earlier, and they were still major figures in the Western States political life. That there was some disagreement between them can be traced in part to long standing differences in political perspective as well as to the ambiguities of the situation itself. Patterns were not always clear because personal relationship between the Governor and his individual commissioners was also an important variable. Clear-cut guidelines were not layed down by the Governor. Individuals were also selective in what they recalled from cabinet meetings and how they interpreted these meetings. While there was no complete agreement on a number of issues, a number of themes did repeatedly emerge in the interviews.

The commissioners clearly saw themselves as political appointees.[13] They were people who had been federal cabinet members, members of the Western Region's cabinet, or prominent party leaders. Even the two "technocrats" were identified with particular parties in the civilian regime.[14] All the individuals interviewed noted the balancing act that Governor Adebayo had performed in appointing members by party, and by province and district.

Governor Adebayo consulted with the leaders of the banned parties before he made these appointments, although to say he cleared the appointments with party leaders would be to put the matter too strongly. Some individuals to whom the offer of cabinet appointment was made consulted with party leaders; others did not. And at least one cabinet member said he was instructed to enter the Military Governor's cabinet by the leader of his party. This same member said that when he, the commissioner, wanted to quit the cabinet over a particular matter, when he no longer wanted to be associated with an unpopular regime, Adebayo then went to the party leader to prevail upon him to keep this particular commissioner in the cabinet.

While commissioners agreed that the cabinet was political, they possessed a variety of views about the nature of the authority held by the cabinet. Let the commissioners speak for themselves. Each quote is the statement of an individual commissioner, unless otherwise noted.

> We were the Governor in Council. We were not just advisory to him. The majority did not feel this. The Attorney General told us differently that we were more than advisory.

Adebayo said the cabinet was pure advisory. We told him we have an executive council. A Governor in Council. The Secretary Odumosu (Civil Service Head in the State) told him we were right. The Attorney General did the same thing. He ignored this often, particularly where the profit margin was involved.

The distinction was made between legal and actual authority in the cabinet.

To some extent I would agree that commissioners did not have the old ministerial powers. Legally speaking we did not but practically speaking. As a military regime, [sic] the Governor is the final authority. A commissioner is his advisor. In practice he of course cannot see to everything. He allows you to take decisions on consultation. he invariably approves.

There was no difference between a commissioner and a minister. I had discretion. The federal scope was wider though. The commissioner could speak to the Governor. The Governor did not want the commissioners to act as politicians. There was no constituency representation.

The cabinet was an executive body; that's a correct view. It was not just advisory. Only once or twice did Adebayo try to assert his position as Military Governor, and then he reconsidered and took the consensus advice. There were no votes.

I resigned because I had responsibility without power. The military tried to say we had a constitution to operate. But they kept reminding us it was a military regime, and that we did not have to follow law. Decisions are not party decisions. The Governor says "X" and signs an edict. The edict is published and becomes law.

This last commentator also said that the cabinet met weekly and that there was the feeling of cabinet responsibility at least on noncontroversial matters. He and almost every other commissioner interviewed agreed that there was free, open, and even heated discussion. Not all cabinet members agreed, however, that all serious issues were openly discussed. This commissioner objected to how decisions were taken.

Adebayo looked outside the cabinet to his friends, to civil servants especially, not necessarily to military officers. He did not like going to officers. He did not have any confidence in the cabinet. He could get along with different parties.

A number of commissioners echoed the view that they had responsibility without power, that power lay with the military ultimately, although in the short run civil servants had wider scope for decision making in the military regime than in civilian regimes. At the same time, Nigerian politicians, the commissioners included, made judgments about the political skill of high-ranking military officers and distinguished officers in terms of their political styles. The commissioners generally felt that Governor Adebayo was a much more political person than his successor, Governor Rotimi, who served from 1971 to 1974. They said Governor Adebayo felt that he had political constituencies and that these constituencies were defined in party, district and institutional terms. In this respect, Adebayo was considered an unusual military leader.

The cabinet felt strongly that since the military regime was a hybrid one (a term used by three cabinet members), civilian-military relations were influenced by the personality of the officer who was governor. One cabinet member said: "What does a military government mean? In many ways it [the Western State Government] doesn't function as a military government. . . . The cabinet is different with different heads." Another asked, "Where does military end and civilian begin?"

Although the cabinet members saw the military government as a complex regime, they still recognized important differences between the military regime and a civilian regime. One cabinet member said:

> In the military regime there is no constiuency whatsoever. Anyone who wants to influence the Governor has no constituency to back him up in anything he wants. During the civilian regime the reverse takes place. The Premier would consider the influence of a person in the cabinet but also his influence outside the cabinet. . . . In military regime there is no question of being affected in judging cabinet members by how many people vote for them. If it is a civilian regime, the Prime Minister must always be alert to losing support of the most influential people.

In other words, cabinet members were overtly conscious of the problems of representation and constituency within the military regime. They were aware that party and region had been variables effecting the governor's choice of individual commissioners. At the same time, they saw a different relationship between the military and civilian regimes and political constituencies. And, importantly, they saw themselves in a different relationship to their political constituencies than when they were ministers in a civilian regime. This was in spite of the fact that many of them argued that the Adebayo cabinet was strong politically, that it had some local support, and that Adebayo himself had tried to keep in touch with the grass roots. Some of the prominent Action Group politicians who entered the Adebayo cabinet saw themselves as having independent political support. They mentioned their connections to Chief Awolowo, then the Action Group leader. But they also recognized the ultimate power of the military government over their decisions and their own short-run political fate. A commissioner could say: "We functioned as political appointees, and there were splits in the cabinet on a party basis. It was not a political regime." All commissioners believed that they had a responsibility to represent their local areas to the governor on questions of amenities. Even the commissioners who were least political, those who believed the needs of the Western State were clear cut, expressed their view.

The role played by the parties was awkward both for the commissioners and the military government. Parties had been banned in Nigeria since the first military coup in 1966. Yet in the Western State, the old parties were still political realities both for elites and for the masses in some parts of the state. The cabinet was a multiparty organization. One commissioner pointed out that separate meetings were held outside of the cabinet in party caucus. Another would stress that differences of opinion within the cabinet cut across party lines. Both views were correct. Some issues were highly partisan, or they brought out latent partisan cleavages within the cabinet. Struggles over the accession of chiefs and questions of patronage distribution were threatening to the military government, for while broad policy issues were not involved, partisan alignments came into play.

Struggles over succession to chieftaincy had long roiled the politics of the Western Region and the Western State. Among the Yoruba, struggles over chieftaincy positions involved lineage, factional and party alignments. The cabinet of Governor Adebayo had to deal with the issue of who would become the new Alafin, or traditional ruler, or Oyo. The Military Governor was caught in a no-win situation on this kind of issue. Since his own power base did not depend on cementing alignments with traditional groups, as in contradistinction to the former party politicians' base of power, he could only make enemies with the appointment. In the last analysis, factional politics among the Yoruba, and conflicts between clans and lineages, especially when those were mixed up with party politics, were not easy for a military leader to manipulate and control. We can be skeptical, perhaps, or the argument that military regimes in Africa resurrect a colonial pattern which not only emphasizes rule by civil servants, but also expands the authority and role of traditional leaders.[15] Military leaders may feel that they have a poor grasp of the intricacies of politics among traditional authorities. The possible political costs are not worth the potential benefit of trying to harness these authorities.

Military organizations put a high premium on corporate identity and cohesion. They may have to take up issues which divide them, as the Nigerian military could not avoid taking up the issue of state secession in 1966 and 1967. Local issues involving grass roots participation are potentially very messy, and the military may try very hard to avoid these issues. Indeed, the military may put a higher premium on avoiding conflict within itself than on settling certain kinds of political disputes. If the cabinet members feared having responsibiity without power, it can be said of the military that they wanted power without the responsibility of taking on many issues which could prove divisive and would have little pay off. Particularly, armed forces frequently have an aversion to representing constituencies because this means legitimating a constituency base of politics, and often this creates constituencies with ties to factions within the military. This, in turn, threatens corporate cohesion and unity.

One particular issue illustrated this dilemma for the military. It was also an issue which created great difficulties for the military government in the Western State, paralyzed the government for a time, and finally showed the military government's weakness in conflict resolution and decision-making. In 1968–1969, widespread rioting broke out in the Western State as opposition to tax collection spread. The riots, and the political movement associated with them, became known as *Agbekoya* (literally, "farmers reject suffering"). In the Western Region, there was a long history of peasant unrest associated with areas which had suffered the swollen shoot disease of cocoa plants. The riots of 1968—69, however, to use the words of Christopher Beer, "possessed distinctive characteristics which set them aside from many such earlier manifestations. First, they were essentially based on support of the peasantry . . . the riots were without doubt caused by the rise of specially *agrarian populism* . . . the 1968–69 riots were large in scale, materalized widely in dispersed geographical locations, whilst occurring almost simultaneously in time."[16] Indeed *Agbekoya* seems to have been a rebellion with overt class manifestations.

During the riots, farmers refused to pay taxes, and in many areas tax collection virtually ceased until July 1969. When the Government tried to resume tax collection, riots broke out again. Tax collection had not been restored in all places of the state in the 1970s. During *Agbekoya* leaders were attacked and murdered. Farmers entered Ibadan in September 1969 and in daylight, attacked the federal prison, freeing its occupants. Police disappeared from many of the towns (including Ibadan), where rioting occurred. Pitched battles occurred between army, police and farmers in some areas. For the most part, the military government seemed paralyzed. It did not attempt to crush the dissidence with overwhelming force. The military seemed to lack political institutions at the local levels through which the conflict could be mediated. The military government relied on ad hoc meetings between politicians and dissident leaders, while it occasionally used, and more often threatened to use, force.

In this case absence of regular, grass roots political contacts was consequential. The flow of information to the central policy-making bodies was poor, and the military government underestimated the discontent among farmers. Local government bodies persisted under military rule, but these bodies no longer had elected representatives on them. The military had appointed "sole administrators" to perform the functions previously handled by elected councillors. Because the sole administrators were usually not "locals" and frequently they lacked contact with local areas, they, in turn, surrounded themselves with local advisors. Party politics continued to infuse local administration under the military government and the military government got the worst of all worlds. Advisers were selected ad hoc, and they had no statutory accountability or functions. As a result there was a great deal of local discontent with the sole administrator system.

The cabinet discussed local representation and the tax riots. The Governor understood the rebellion to be politically instigated and he spoke of "unprovoked and premeditated attacks on police." Adebayo rejected the protest as one directed against the level of taxation. He argued that tax agitation was most rampant in better-off areas where people had basic services such as water and electricity, although he reproached traditional and local leaders for not showing more concern about their areas.[17] Some commissioners felt that with the Governor they shared responsibility for the riots by having been insensitive to local demands. The dominant view in the cabinet had been that district councils must balance their budgets and collect more taxes. The commissioner for Local Government and Chieftaincy Affairs who was close to the Governor, and had been his former school teacher, argued that public services could not be maintained if taxes were reduced.[18]

A number of commissioners stated that, although the Governor discussed the riots in the cabinet, and although he was personally influenced by his commissioner for local government, the Governor only reluctantly called cabinet meetings on the tax riots. One said:

> He (Adebayo) hadn't had a cabinet meeting in six weeks. By this time Awolowo had intervened. They [the military] were unresponsive to local conditions and frustrations. *Agbekoya* was an economic thing. Farmers were worse off. There was a feudal land tenure system. It was a peasant movement. The government felt politicians were trying to lower them. . . . They said we [commissioners] were politicians.

Another commissioner agreed that *Agbekoya* was discussed openly in the cabinet, but this commissioner felt that Adebayo looked for advice to his friends outside the cabinet, and to the civil servants, especially, when he made decisons about *Agbekoya*.

Some commissioners, and many former members of the Western House of Assembly were very critical of the army's role during *Agbekoya*.

> The military botched it . . . I told Adebayo he was not handling the farmers properly. Also, the military created no security. People were in thousands. We were told to hold a cabinet meeting [under these circumstances]. *Agbekoya* wanted to take over the government. The police were afraid. The army too.

One commissioner spoke of a failure in military intelligence as well as a failure to provide security. Another informant, a key civil servant at one time, agreed that military and police intelligence failed. This official said that while the government knew there were difficulties in the rural areas, it did not know *Agbekoya* was so well organized. The civil servant attributed this level of organization to the politicians. One commissioner, however, said that Adebayo himself unfairly blamed the army for *Agbekoya*.

> Rotimi was the commanding officer [in the Western State] when the prisoners were released from Agodi. Adebayo blames the army for this. We AG said this was not fair to the army. Omisade [a commissioner] told Adebayo not to go to Benin [capital of the Mid-Western State] that day. I called him in Benin and told him to come back. Rotimi was in Lagos. He came by road and crushed the rebellion. Rotimi insulted Adebayo at the cabinet meeting next day. He called him irresponsible and worse. Then Rotimi never came to another cabinet meeting. He gave a designate.

The *Agbekoya* crisis gave the politicians then in government a good chance to see the top military officers in serious disagreement with one another. In the localities, as well as in Ibadan, the breakdown of order was evident. Western State politicians could not see any unity of the military or its capacity for keeping order. Politicians became increasingly aware of the need to differentiate among military men who held political power. The military coups of 1966 had made politicians sensitive to factionalism inside the armed forces. Now tensions were evident over the way to respond to local dissidence.

Politicians' perceptions of the military differed depending on their individual vantage points. Commissioners at the center differentiated among officers. They viewed some as political and others as interested only in army matters—such as, pay, barracks, promotions, and the acquisition of military hardware. One commissioner said: "Only one or two officers were interested in government. Adebayo feared a coup, and he did not encourage them to be interested." This commissioner properly distinguished between policy interests in running a government and involvement in coups. Lower-ranking politicians on the other hand, felt that military officers were only concerned with narrow interest group demands, not with broad social, political, and economic issues.

Politicians who did not serve in the cabinet tended to feel civil servants and commissioners framed policies that they thought could be put forward without offending the sensibilities of the military.[19] Civil servants stressed their own importance in defining policies and implementing them, but they, too, saw the military clearly as the possessor of ultimate power. Military officers said that broader issues were discussed among themselves but not between themselves and non-military personnel. Formally, the officer in command in the Western State, who was based in Ibadan, was a member of the cabinet. Under Adebayo, this officer was Colonel Rotimi who succeeded Adebayo as Governor in 1971. The Commissioner of Police also served *ex officio* in the cabinet.[20] The view of some commissioners was that the Officer in Command and the Commissioner of Police sat quietly during cabinet meetings. A few commissioners deduced from this that these officers did not discuss political matters. General Adebayo himself did not share this view. Both these men were important figures outside the cabinet. Other military offices also saw Adebayo, and he explained governmental affairs to them. Military men were concerned with a wide range of issues.

Both cabinet members and former members of the Western House of Assembly thought that the great weakness of the military regime was its failure to represent groups. Those cabinet members who felt that the cabinet was politically strong, that its members had grass roots support, did not see the military as having local links. Individual commissioners mentioned over and over how "little people" were afraid to go and see military officers, because they had to go past a series of soldiers with guns. Nigerian politicians were often outraged that, although the officers and soldiers became rich, they spent money only on themselves and their close relatives. The money did not trickle down. One person we interviewed said, "The military is corrupt. Not less so than the old politicians. Even corporals and privates have money in my own town. They take part of what the colonels leave."

Conclusions

I have described aspects of the process of military government, largely as seen through the eyes of civilian active and inactive political participants. The accounts of participants and observers do not always agree. The difficulties this particular military government faced in handling issues of representation, in getting information from below, and in taking on locally divisive issues all unmistakably emerge. This case study of military government in one Nigerian state does argue that while the lines between civilian and military can become blurred, and while there can be various patterns of interpenetration and coalition between military and civilian actors, military takeover pre-empts the political process. In the Western State, the military was not *merely* another political actor. The distinction between military and civilian institutions and regimes was meaningful. Even if cross-national, aggregate data do not show us that a military regime determines parameters of development or foreign relations, or political stability or economic growth, we can at least point to differences between certain kinds of military regimes and certain kinds of civilian regimes.

Specific outcomes may not be related to the existence of military governments, but there may be good reasons for hypothesizing that military rule will make a difference in political processes. These reasons have to do with the nature of military organization, internal socialization processes within the military, and the kinds of relationships between military personnel and civilian political actors. These factors vary across systems, and the civilian-military relationship factor is especially variable.

In the Western State, and in Nigeria as a whole, the introduction of civilians into executive authority was a process controlled by the military. Even though civilian commissioners frequently had a great deal to say about the ways that their ministries were run, and even though civilian input into cabinet deliberations was important, the process of civilianization was always controlled or truncated by the military. Between 1967 and 1974 Nigeria operated with civilians in executive positions, and these civilians were politicians, not civil servants. During this period, however, neither the military nor the civilian participants were in any doubt as to the source of authority in the system. It was a military regime. The basis of civilian authority was appointment by military leaders. Civilians understood that they did not have an independent, popular, constituency base to their authority. They could be dismissed without cause by a military governor at any time. Civilians could make life difficult for a military governor, but they could not oust him. In the Western State, and in the Nigerian Federal Republic, civilians could not penetrate the military chain of command to enforce dismissals of governors, although individual civilians could have close ties to particular officers.

Civil servants had expanded roles under a military regime. Nonetheless, politicians were able to exert themselves in the cabinet of the Western State. At least some commissioners felt that they dominated their ministries. In a crisis situation the civilian politicians were required by the military to make contact with the grass roots. Indeed, the failure of the military to have their own grass roots links in Nigeria gave civilian politicians greater scope. This was true not only for commissioners. During *Agbekoya,* local level politicians were able to play political roles precisely because the military's weakness was its inability to represent and become involved in local politics.

Crisis situations weaken military rule once the military is in power. During a crisis, the military needs help from civilians. When the Western State Government had to deal with a fall in international cocoa prices, it ran into political difficulties with farmers as had the civilian government before it. These difficulties were exacerbated for the military government because of a lack of communication between the military regime and people at the grass roots. This problem has been ameliorated to some extent because the recent large increases in federal revenues have enabled the Government to provide new benefits to many people in rural areas. In the future the lack of grass roots contact may again become serious.

No large theoretical formulations emerged from this study. The aim was to provide information in an area where there is not enough empirical work on the military in developing countries, or on the military in industrial countries. The critical analytical points have already been sketched out by students of the military in developing countries. Now it is necessary to describe the precise ways in which civilian-military relationships operate in different contexts.

Military rule itself is a term which needs refinement. As we become aware of the complexities of military-civilian relationships, we ask: what kinds of political decisions are made in a military regime, by whom and through what processes? What political networks exist outside the military? In what way do these networks relate to the military's own factional networks and alliances? In Nigeria a mixed civilian-military system had a good deal of civilian input at central decision-making levels. Since politicians were prevented from operating openly at local levels and the military had not established its own political networks at local or middle levels of politics, a political vacuum existed. In some places, civil servants moved to fill this vacuum. Sometimes it was easier to co-opt civilians, both politicians and civil servants, and attach them to the military regime at the highest levels of politics. Perhaps civilians were easily co-opted because the central elites in Nigeria fundamentally shared the same values, irrespective of civilian or military allegiances. The military felt it could control central decision-making even when civilians participated in the process. Local politics, on the other hand, seemed to be harder for military elites to control and to understand.

The strength of Nigeria's political system from 1967–1974, a time of stress and even intermittent open warfare, lay in the ability of civilians and military to cooperate. The hostility felt by politicians for military rulers, however, does not bode well for continued institutionalized cooperation. Perhaps newer elites, including professional and technical elites, can be brought into central decision-making processes in Nigeria. Already the civil service is a substantial participant in the running of a system which the military could not run by itself. But even if technical and professional elites cooperate, and even if the Nigerian military develops its own technical and professional elite, the problem of forging ties to the grass roots and of handling the problem of representation will remain.

Military rule does not do away with politics or with the need for someone to play the role previously played by civilian politicians. From 1967 to 1974 Nigeria attempted to create a civilian-military relationship which would allow for cooperation and a sharing of power. The military, however, remained in authority. And under military rule, even if masses of people do not prefer civilian rule, political problems remain and must be coped with. And it is not, after all, *the* military which rules, but a group, or groups within the military, which can always be challenged by different factions. Thus for particular military leaders in any military government, civilian cooperation is not with the military at large, although the issue is often stated in that fashion, but cooperation is between sets of elites. Lack of elite support and mass apathy may not be dangerous for military rule, but for the rule of a particular group within the military. Thus, from the military leaders' own perspectives, the finding of a successful formula for civilian-military cooperation is a political necessity.

Notes

1. W. F. Gutteridge, *Military Regimes in Africa* (London: Methuen, 1975), p. 22.

2. Aristide Zolberg, "The Structure of Political Conflict in the New States of Tropical Africa," *The American Political Science Review* 62, no. 1 (March 1968): 70–87.

3. Case studies include: Robin Luckham, *The Nigerian Military* (Cambridge, Cambridge University Press, 1971); Thomas S. Cox, *Civil-Military Relations in Sierra Leone* (Cambridge, Mass.: Harvard University Press, 1976); Samuel Decalo, *Coups and Army Rule in Africa* (New Haven: Yale University Press, 1976); Anton Bebler, *Military Rule in Africa: Dahomey, Ghana, Sierra Leone, and Mali* (New York: Praeger, 1973), p. 194.

4. R. D. McKinlay and A. S. Cohan, "A Comparative Analysis of Political and Economic Performance of Military and Civilian Regimes," *Comparative Politics* 8, no. 1 (October 1975): 23.

5. Robert W. Jackman, "Politicians in Uniform: Military Governments and Social Change in the Third World," *American Political Science Review*, 70 (December 1976). Jackman reanalyzed the data used by Eric A. Nordlinger, "Soldiers in Mufti: The Impact of Military Rule Upon Economic and Social Change in the Non-Western States," *American Political Science Review* 65 (December 1970): 1131–1148.

6. These three points are taken verbatim from McKinlay and Cohan, *op. cit.,* pp. 22–23. McKinlay and Cohan have also written, "The Economic Performance of Military Regimes: A Cross-National Aggregate Data Study," *The British Journal of Politics* 6, no. 3 (July 1976): 291–310. In this work, the authors find that there is some better performance by military regimes than preceding civilian regimes, a finding not made by Nordlinger or Jackman. But McKinlay and Cohan also find that the main parameters of economic performance are set by existing levels of development and by previous performance levels.

7. Kurt Lang, "Introduction" to his *Military Institutions and the Sociology of War* (Beverly Hills: Sage Publications, 1972).

8. Barry Ames, "Rhetoric and Reality in a Militarized Regime: Brazil Since 1964" (Beverly Hills: Sage Professional Papers in Comparative Politics), pp. 01–042.

9. For studies of the Nigerian military see: Luckham, *op. cit.*; S. K. Panter-Brick, ed., *Nigerian Politics and Military Rule* (London: Athlone Press, 1970); Ruth First, *Power in Africa* (New York: Pantheon, 1970), especially pp. 144–168 and pp. 278–362; N. J. Miners, *The Nigerian Army 1956–1966* (London: Methuen and Co., 1971); Anthony Kirk-Greene, *Crises and Conflict in Nigeria: A Documentary Source Book 1966–1970,* vol. 1 (London: Oxford University Press, 1971); J. M. Lee, *African Armies and Civil Order* (London: Chatto and Windus, 1969); Gutteridge, *op. cit.*; B. J. Dudley, *Instability and Political Order: Politics and Crises in Nigeria* (Ibadan: University of Ibadan Press, 1973).

10. Kirk-Greene, *op. cit.,* pp. 453–455. In 1975, General Gowon later rescinded a decision to have the military withdraw from power by 1976.

11. From Gowon's address to the first civilian members of the Federal Executive Council in Kirk-Greene, *op. cit.,* p. 454.

12. Speech by Alhaji D. S. Adegbenro, Commissioner for Trade and Industry on the occasion of the Swearing-In Ceremony of the Civil Commissioners by the Military Governor, Brigadier Robert Adeyinka Adebayo, June 30, 1967, published in the booklet, *Our New Civil Commissioners* (Ibadan: Government Printer, 1967). General Adebayo defined his regime as a military one in Robert Adeyinka Adebayo, "Civilians in Government," statement of June 30, 1967, reprinted in the R. A. Adebayo, *Problems and Solutions,* vol. I (Ibadan: Government Printer, 1968).

13. Six of the twelve commissioners appointed in 1967 had clear ties to the Action Group (AG). Three were major leaders in the National Convention of Nigerian Citizens (NCNC) and three were men with ties to the Nigerian National Democratic Party (NNDP).

14. One was a professor of medicine and Vice Dean of the Lagos University Medical School, who had been Chairman of the Western Region's Nigerian Broadcasting Corporation from 1957–1963. One was a mathematician at the University of Ibadan but like many Yoruba academics he had ties to a particular party.

15. See Edward Feit, "Military Coups and Political Development: Some Lessons from Ghana and Nigeria," *World Politics* 20, no. 2 (January 1968): 179–193.

16. For description and analysis of the 1968–1969 riots I have relied heavily on two sources: Christopher Beer's "The Farmer and the State in Western Nigeria: The Role of the Farmers' Organizations and Cooperatives" (Ph.D. diss., University of Ibadan, Department of Political Science, 1971); and the *Report of the Commission of Inquiry into the Civil Disturbance which Occurred in Certain Parts of the Western State of Nigeria in the Month of December 1968* (Ibadan: Government Printer, 1969).

17. See Adebayo's "The Truth About Tax Riots: Governor Adebayo Speaks" (Ibadan: Government Printer, 1969).

18. Chief Benjamin A. Ajayi was the commissioner. While his portfolio did not include finance, he had responsibilities for local government.

19. This view was also articulated by Leo Dare, in *Military Leadership and Political Development in the Western State of Nigeria* (Ph.D. diss., Carleton University, Faculty of Graduate Studies, Department of Political Science, 1972), p. 186. .

20. One commissioner said Adebayo had an "extra constitutional cabinet because people came who were not entitled to attend." Among them was the deputy commissioner of police.

Chapter 10

Politicians under Military Rule
in Nigeria

Successful military coups often cut off politicians from power and its perquisites. Ministers from the civilian regime usually lose their jobs, their
government houses, cars and other fringe benefits. They may lose their assets
or even their lives. However, even in regimes where military personnel are
appointed to ministerial positions, public corporations, and district or provincial administrative posts, civilians continue to be crucial administrative
and political actors.

In Africa, military regimes rarely have appointed military personnel to key
positions formerly held by civil servants during the civilian regime. More
frequently, officers have taken over ministries. Even in these cases, civilians
often have been called upon in advisory capacities and have been placed on
consultative committees or advisory groups. Sometimes, formal arrangements
have been made to institutionalize civilian input into a military regime.
Civilians, including many former politicians from the old civilian regime, have
been brought back as ministers or as members of special commissions. Since
many African militaries have come to power explicitly promising a return to
civilian rule, and have continued to reiterate these promises even a decade
after military rule, demilitarization commissions have proliferated and civilian
politicians have played prominent roles on such groups.

Recently, attention has been given to civilian activities in military governments and increasingly observers have abandoned the dichotomy between
civilian and military regimes. They have focused instead on civilian-military
relations. Most of this attention has been given to the role of civilians at
national levels and in national institutions: cabinets, commissions, consu-
tative commissions, civil services. Less studied have been the roles played by
former politicians and would-be new entrants into political life who reconstruct old political networks or who try to build new networks outside of the
formal institutions the military creates for civilians. We know relatively little
about the operation of politicians under a military regime at middle levels or at

local levels. Information is presented below from the former Western State of Nigeria in order to case some light on civilian politicians' activities under a military regime.

The Activities of Former Members of the Western House of Assembly

In Nigeria, in 1967, civilians were brought into the Federal Executive Committee and the executive committees of the states. Between these cabinet members and local politicians, there was a group which was potentially significant for civil-military relations. These were former politicians who had played a role in federal or regional politics prior to the 1966 coups. Nigeria had a large number of elected politicians who were cut off from power by the abolition of parliamentary government and the banning of party politics in 1966. We were interested in finding out what those people were doing during the military regime. They had been active politically during civilian rule; they had the talents and resources to advance their own interests and the interests of others. What happened to them now in a military regime? Were they a source of active or potential opposition? Could they be harnessed or coopted by military elites? Were military elites interested in their cooperation or fearful of their opposition?

Nigeria provided a rare context for looking at former politicians. It was clear from casual observation and from reading the press that, of the large elite of former politicians, some had retired from the fray; some (including a number who had been incarcerated for a time by the military government) were still playing active roles, and others were biding their time. Since Nigeria was a place where one could carry out interviews freely, we determined to try and interview a large number of former politicians.

If we had construed "politicians" broadly it could have meant interviewing trade union leaders and leaders of other economic or associational groups. We decided to concentrate on elected politicians, those who had participated in party politics under the civilian regime and had successfully stood for office, and we decided to work in one state only, rather than interview a few politicians from each state. In the Western State, there were two potential pools of former elected politicians. One was the Western Region's members of the Federal Parliament. The other consisted of former members of the Western House of Assembly, the regional parliament. Here we report on the latter group who provide us with information on state and district roles of former politicians.

It is necessary to say something about the size, range and reliability of the sample. We interviewed 54 MHAs (MHAs will be used from now on to refer to former Members of the Western House of Assembly) out of 128 living MHAs.[1] We held 54 in-depth interviews, usually lasting two hours, often preceded or followed by more casual meetings.[2] Background information on the 54 MHA's is provided in Tables 1 to 6.

Table 1

Age of MHAs

	N	Percent
30–40	3	5.6
41–50	23	42.6
51–60	20	37.0
61 plus	8	14.5

Table 2

Highest Level of Education Achieved

	N	*Percent*
Primary	1	1.9
Secondary	15	27.8
Postsecondary but not university	16	29.6
University	8	14.8
Law	5	9.3
University/law	8	14.8
Don't know	1	1.9

Table 3

	Number[a]	*Percentage out of 54 respondents*
Occupation before becoming a MHA		
Teacher	18	33.0
Lawyer	12	22.2
Clerical	9	16.7
Large trader/contractor[b]	8	14.8
Headmaster/school proprietor	7	13.0
Manager	5	9.3
Civil servant (nonteacher)	5	9.3
Journalist	3	5.6
Petty trader[b]	5	3.7
Doctor	1	1.9
Farmer	1	1.9
Religious	0	0
Occupation after MHA (between 1966 and 1973)		
Teacher	11	20.4
Large trader/contractor[b]	11	20.4
Lawyer	10	18.5
Petty trader[b]	9	16.7
Political[c]	9	16.7
Headmaster/school proprietor	6	11.1
Farmer	6	11.1
Manager	4	7.4
Director	3	5.6
Civil servant (nonteacher)	2	3.7
Journalist	2	3.7
Doctor	1	1.9
Religious	1	1.9
Clerical	1	1.9
International Organization	1	1.9

[a]Some MHAs listed more than one occupation.

[b]We characterized a person as large or petty contractor after evaluating answers on the nature of business being performed. "Trader/contractor" includes owner of business which might be a lumber yard, laundry, appliance store, or insurance business.

[c]"Political" refers to anyone who served in the Federal Executive Council or the Western State cabinet after 1967 or who had headed a state corporation or commission.

Table 4

Position in Assembly[a]

	N	Percent
Backbencher	16	29.6
Junior minister	9	16.7
(Parliamentary Secretary)		
Minister	22	40.7
Whip	3	5.6
Speaker	4	7.4
(or Deputy Speaker)		
Federal minister	1	1.9
(at some time)		
Don't know	1	1.9

[a]If a man had been both minister and junior minister we coded minister only. But for someone who had been both speaker and a minister, we coded both, so the table sums to more than 54. However, percentages are based on the 54 people not the number of responses.

People shifted party membership in the Western House of Assembly through the period 1960–1965.

Table 5

Party Identification in the WHA
Postelection 1965, Preelection 1965, 1964, 1962[a]

	1965 postelection	*1965 preelection*	*1964*[b]	*1962*[c]	
N	73	58	31	—	United Peoples Party—NNDP
N	3	5	31	33	NCNC
N	15	27	26	83	AG

[a]Sources are *Nigerian Yearbook* (Lagos Time Press Limited) for the years 1963 (pages 193–194); 1964 (pages 255–256); 1965 (pages 178–179); 1966 (pages 178–179).

[b]There were four vacancies in 1964.

[c]The 1962 seats included constituencies which later became part of the Mid-West Region.

The decline in both AG and NCNC representation from pre- and post-election 1965 was from people "losing" at the polls or not running; there were no further shifts in party loyalty by AG or NCNC people in the WHA in 1965. A few of those who did become NNDP and who appeared in our sample sometimes did so directly; that is, they had no other party affiliation ever. One could also become NNDP after having been AG, or having passed through the brief UPP affiliation or from a sequence of AG-UPP-NNDP. There was also the NCNC route to NNDP. One could start as NCNC and become NNDP through the UPP or gò directly, bypassing the UPP stage. We even had two homerun hitters who touched all bases: NCNC-AG-UPP-NNDP.

Table 6

Respondents by Party Identification

Party[a]	N	Percent
AG	14	25.9
AG-NNDP	11	20.4
AG-UPP-NNDP	8	14.8
NNDP	1	1.9
UPP-NNDP	1	1.9
NCNC	5	9.3
NCNC-NNDP	8	14.8
NCNC-UPP-NNDP	3	5.6
NCNC-AG-UPP-NNDP	2	3.7
Don't know	1	1.9

[a]AG, Action Group; NNDP, Nigerian National Democratic Party (formed in 1964); UPP, United Peoples Party (formed in 1963 by Chief Akintola after the split in the AG, and later absorbed by the NNDP); NCNC, National Council of Nigerian Citizens.

By age, education, occupation, our sample appeared representative of the larger group of MHAs.[3] For most MHAs, politics had been a full-time profession. Less than a third of our sample had been backbenchers. The cabinets in the Western Region, like cabinets in the Nigerian Federal Republic and the other regional governments, were very large.[4]

We did not try to construct a sample which was representative by party identification. We tried to interview all the MHAs we could. There is something of an underrepresentation of Nigerian National Democratic Party (NNDP) MHAs if one takes the 1965 postelection Western House of Assembly, but not if one takes the Western House of Assembly prior to the October, 1965 election. The underrepresentation comes from our not being able to locate and interview as many newcomers to the 1965 House as we wished. Many of these people were, in Yoruba political terminology, "small boys." That is, they were not significant political figures. Thus we interviewed more of the NNDP leadership compared to NNDP backbenchers.

It was these NNDP former ministers who suffered most among party politicians in the Western Region during and after the military coups. While Action Group (AG) leaders had been jailed or intimidated before 1966, after 1966 it was NNDP leaders whose houses were burned and who suffered immediate losses of income. And it was NNDP leaders who faced the Somolu Commission which looked into the assets of public officeholders.[5] Party affiliation was an important variable for the roles politicians played and for the attitudes they held after 1966.

In January 1966 many politicians in the Western Region, especially leaders of the NNDP, went into hiding or fled to their home areas. Some feared that troops would seek them out and kill them; others feared the settling of old scores by their political opponents, and especially by supporters of the AG. Civilian politics in the Western Region was dominated after 1966 at first by former AG leaders rather than by NNDP people, because the NNDP had been discredited. Moreover, in the NNDP, there was no clear-cut leadership left after the January coup. The National Convention of Nigerian Citizens (NCNC) had been shattered when most of it had moved into the NNDP in 1964–1965 and it was seen by 1966, more than ever, as a party of the Eastern Region. Parties in any case were banned by Decree No. 33 of 1966, promulgated by the military government headed by General Ironsi. But even before his release from jail in August 1966, Chief Awolowo had been able to create unity in what was left of the AG leadership. He had been able to delegate nominal leadership of the AG to Alhaji Adegbenro. Without Awolowo, there would have been more fragmentation within the rump of the AG that was left after so many AG MPs and MHAs went over to the NNDP.

The AG, however, was not without problems. It had, after all, lost most of its elected representatives prior to the coup. And the NNDP had developed strength in certain areas of the Western Region. The intense factionalism within and between Nigerian political parties posed a problem for the Military Government headed by Colonel R. A. Adebayo in the Western Region after August 1966 because this government needed civilian support. When the military government banned parties and dissolved discredited native courts in the Western Region, it took very popular steps. On the other hand, military leaders had to either avoid civilian politicians completely or enter a very complicated set of factional alignments and relationships between politicians and their constituencies.

In the view of the national leaders, military and civil servants alike, who were committed to the maintenance of the Nigerian Federal Republic, the Western Region had to be kept in the federation. The Yoruba military leaders in the Western Region thus had special problems. They had to relate to fellow officers in the Supreme Military Council which was the national ruling body. At the same time, the new Military Governor of the Western Region, Colonel Adebayo, was not only responsible to the chain of command in the armed forces, but he also felt himself responsible as a Yoruba Head of Government, for the welfare of the Western Region. From his vantage point, it was necessary to unify a disunified Western Region, link military and civilian elites, and mobilize support from the populace. This meant for the military creating institutions in which the energies of politicians could be both used and controlled. And for the civilian leaders it meant using these institutions to build a base of power independent of the military which would give them leverage in a political system they no longer controlled. In the Western Region from August 1966 until May 1967, when civilians were brought into cabinets headed by military men, politicians had to operate as a group out of power; but they were a group essential to military leaders.

Civilians and military needed each other's support on many issues, above all on the question of secession of the Western Region from the Nigerian federation. Many issues were debated privately among military and civilians. It was necessary, however, to create forums in which issues could be discussed and policies could be explained to a wider audience. It was necessary to have these forums because many individuals had been involved at various levels in Yoruba politics. Support had to be mobilized from below in the face of a national crisis from 1966 to 1970. It also had to be mobilized among district elites in the Western Region. Because the Western Region had been so split from 1962 to 1966, civilian-military cooperation was necessary as the Western Region bargained with other units of the Federal Republic. But cooperation was also hard to achieve because factional politics among civilians were still rife and spilled over into the military.

Two regional forums for factional politics at the center of the Western State developed during 1967.[6] One was the cabinet of the Military Governor which came into being after June 1967, and which was discussed in Chapter 9; the other was the Leaders of Thought.

Leaders of Thought

I have suggested that the military leadership in the Western Region faced a mobilized population and a divided elite. While Awolowo remained in jail, large numbers of the Yoruba remained unhappy and not completely reconciled to the national military regime or to the military government in the Western Region. Thus General Gowon released Awolowo and greeted him on August 3, 1966 with the remark, "We need you for the wealth of your experience."[7] Within a few days, Awolowo had become "Leader of Yorubas"[8] and head of the Leaders of Thought in the West. The Leaders of Thought was not confined to the West. They were groups coopted by military and civilian leaders and summoned by Yakubu Gowon to debate issues involved in forthcoming constitutional reviews.[9] The Leaders of Thought in the West became a political group whose debates were to range beyond constitutional issues. It was a forum which allowed civilian politicians to meet under the auspices of a military regime.

It was Awolowo who dominated the Leaders of Thought. Awolowo made the first of a number of key addresses to the Western Leaders of Thought in August 1966. At that time he talked about reuniting the country and stressed the need for unity in the Western Region. He mentioned that Leaders of Thought throughout the land must eschew self interest. He never mentioned the military in this address.[10] Who was it that Awolowo addressed and how were they chosen? More than 80 percent of the 54 former Members of the Western House of Assembly whom we interviewed had been invited to be a Leader of Thought (see Table 7).

Table 7

MHAs Who Were Leaders of Thought

	N	*Percent*
No	6 (2AG, 4NNDP)	11.1
Yes	29 (11 AG, 15 NNDP, 3 NCNC)	53.1
Was invited but did not attend	16 (1AG, 15 NNDP)	29.6
Don't know	3	5.6

Of the 16 who were invited but never attended, all but one was NNDP. Some NNDP people remarked that they used to receive invitations one day after the meetings. Some of the MHAs said that they were personally invited by the Governor or a high civil servant. Others said that they received circulars from the Governor's office. The Leaders of Thought were not restricted to MHAs. Former national MPs from the Western Region and local politicians were invited also.

When we asked MHAs whether the Leaders of Thought were useful, 12, or 22.2 percent, said no; 7, or 13.1 percent said yes; 20, or 37 percent, responded that it was AG dominated.[11] But not only AG people came to meetings of the Leaders of Thought. One NNDP MHA said that, out of the 65 people at a Leaders of Thought meeting he attended, 10 were NNDP. Another MHA felt about 75 percent of those who came to the meeting were AG or NCNC. He added that NNDP people had been told not to attend by NNDP leaders. This MHA also said that 30 percent of the Leaders of Thought were Ijebu Yorubas. This was not true but some non-Ijebu Yorubas felt that the Leaders of Thought was dominated by Ijebus (Awolowo is an Ijebu).

About 200 people attended large meetings of Leaders of Thought that were held in Ibadan. Civil servants attended meetings. There were some restricted meetings that took place with Obas (chiefs). Also, rump meetings were held in the house of a civilian commissioner with a group of twenty in 1967. One respondent said he was a member of an "inner caucus" or advisory group which met on secret matters and had influence on matters discussed in the cabinet.

The term "dyarchy" describes the Western Region after Awwolowo's release from jail. During 1967–1969, both civilians and the military vied for power in the West as civil war went on in the country. Indeed, the very day that the Western State civilian commissioners were sworn in—June 30, 1967—the Biafran leader, Colonal Ojukwu declared that he would wage open war on Nigeria, and one day later, he was dismissed as Governor of the East Central State and dismissed from the Nigerian army. The civil war which proceeded during summer 1967 threatened the West itself as the neighboring Midwest was occupied by Biafran troops in early August.

Although Awolowo had threatened to lead the West to secession if the East should secede, he did not. On the contrary, Awolowo joined the Federal Executive Council in June 1967, as vice-chairman of the council and commissioner for finance in the federal government. But this post gave Awolowo a virtual prime ministership in the Federal Executive Council. While he had used the Leaders of Thought to constrain the military in the West, the federal military government and the Western military government had coopted Awolowo too. It is difficult, however, to reconstruct the relationship of Awolowo to the military leaders, and it is hard to describe with certainty the military leaders' attitudes toward the Leaders of Thought. One high Yoruba military officer felt that it was stupid for Awolowo to show his face and be the Leader of the Yorubas. "This should have been the Governor's position." This officer asserted that the Leaders of Thought was useless and was merely an AG forum.[12] But Adebayo himself used the Leaders of Thought as a forum; in October 1966 he addressed it in Ibadan and called on the Western Region to remain calm. The Leaders of Thought had visibility in the Western Region and later on in the Western State. How important its deliberations were is another matter.

Luckham asserts that it was the military leaders and their civil service advisors who took the final decisions at the end of 1966 and through 1967 that led up to the civil war.[13] This may be true at the national level. It is hard to know what the weight of individual opinions was. In the Western Region, however, the Leaders of Thought discussed the critical issues and civilians played a major role both there and in the meetings of the Ad Hoc Constitutional Conference which met in Lagos starting in September 1966. Kirk-Greene, at one point, describes the function of the Ad Hoc Constitutional Conference as being to consider resolutions of all the regional Leaders of Thought.[14] The delegates to the Conference were selected, according to Luckham, by Military Governors and by the Leaders of Thought.[15]

Awolowo used the Leaders of Thought as a forum in which to make important policy pronouncements. He announced to the meeting of the Leaders of Thought of November 1966 that the Western Region had been victimized by the loss of the Yoruba people with the excision of Lagos, Ilorin, Kabba, and Akoko-Edo from the homeland.[16] It was Awolowo who, at a meeting of the Leaders of Thought in Ibadan on May 1, made the famous announcement that if the federal government, by "acts of commission or omission," brought about the secession of the East, then the West would secede too.[17] At this time, Awolowo stated his responsibility for the physical, mental, and spiritual well-being of the Yoruba people, in particular, and Nigerians in general. He announced his opposition to the use of force to keep Nigeria one. He also announced his opposition to the disintegration of the federation. When he made this address, he was flanked by Colonel Adebayo, Lt. Colonel Olutoye, and Major Sotimi.[18] Adebayo was Governor, Olutoye was Area Commander of the West, and Sotimi was Commanding Officer, 3rd Battalion, Ibadan. The military command in the Western Region appeared to be giving its support both to Awolowo and to his use of the Leaders of Thought as a forum.

From November 1966 on, Awolowo exercised control over the composition of meetings of the Leaders of Thought.[19] Here was a military regime in which civilians had a great deal to say, publicly, about policies and appointments and where civilian factional conflict remained an important factor for military regime strategy.

In the Western State, the Leaders of Thought meetings had legitimating functions and they were also arenas in which Awolowo could consolidate his authority. They probably produced some give-and-take on policy questions, but do not appear to have been a place where policies were thrashed out. They were arenas in which civil servants, officers, and politicians came together. Officers addressed meetings and made their views known there.

The Leaders of Thought was most active in the Western Region and the Western State between August 1966 and August 1967. Most of our respondents agreed that it fizzled out in 1968 and that the last meeting was in 1968. Indeed, one man who was in charge of the arrangements for its meetings said the Leaders of Thought was cancelled. Yet a former cabinet member said that meetings were still going on in 1973. "We still meet. We were called up to Agodi or Mapo Hall (meeting places in Ibadan) and, while the permanent secretaries and commissioners pretend they are telling us about new policies, they are really asking for our help."[20] The confusion here probably arises because informal groups of leaders were still called together in the early 1970s and some seemed to think of these as convenings of Leaders of Thought. But the introduction of the civilian commissioners into a military governor's cabinet in mid-1967 made the Leaders of Thought less necessary for the mobilizing of both elite and mass support. Governor Adebayo was not reluctant to see the Leaders of Thought, dominated by Awolowo, replaced with a cabinet system in which non-AG leaders offset Awolowo's authority in the Western State. Awolowo was now playing a federal role as Commissioner for Finance, and his own attention was deflected somewhat from the Western State.

Local Channels for Political Participation

The Leaders of Thought was not the only channel for civilian political action in the West. Between 1966 and 1973 half of the MHAs had participated in some other governmental or informal body sponsored by government. Outside of self-help committees, the most common form of MHA participation was through local councils or school boards and education committees (Tables 8 and 9).

Table 8

MHA Participation in Governmental and Quasi-Governmental Bodies Since 1966[a]

	N	*Percent*
No participation	27	50
Advisory/local councils	10	18.5
School boards/education committees	9	16.7
Cabinet	8	14.8
Statutory boards	5	9.3
Don't know	1	1.9

[a]Some MHAs had multiple memberships.

Table 9

Involvement in Self-Help Committees

	N	*Percent*
Yes	27	50
No	9	16.7
Don't know	18	33.3

The various committees, councils, and special bodies facilitated civilian participation in political activities under the military regime. However, not all the committees and councils were established in order to institutionalize civilian participation. Nigeria had operated with a system of local government since 1952. While the military deliberately altered some of the local administrative and representative bodies, it also allowed some to continue. And the military regimes promoted certain activities like self-help organizations. The military wanted to promote administrative efficiency, and this meant getting information from below. It wanted to harness local energies and to provide channels for participation. But it did not want politicians to use the various organizations to promote their own political careers; it did not want to see local political bases established through functional organizations.

Local government was a constant and vexing problem for the military regime as it had been for the civilian regimes before it. Matters of local government reorganization were mixed up with the questions of tax reform, sites for administrative centers, internal Yoruba splits, and controversies over whom would be installed in traditional leadership positions. The military government had abolished elected local councils in 1966 and had appointed "sole administrators" who were civil servants, to constitute the local government. The breakdown of local government in the Western State was apparent in 1968–1969 during the *Agbekoya* riots discussed in Chapter 9.

One of the most striking things about the tax revolts of 1968–69 was the presentation of a coherent political program by organized movements such as the *Egbe Agbekoya* in Ibadan.[21] While some of the main politicians were involved in a few localities, many of the leaders of various *Agbekoya* movements in different divisions had not been prominent in Yoruba politics prior to the revolts.[22] The man who emerged as a folk hero, 'Tafa Adeoye, was not a well-known figure prior to *Agbekoya*. Nonetheless, the Military Governor, commissioners, and other important politicians went to Adeoye's headquarters to meet with him. As the violence escalated in 1969 Awolowo set out to portray himself as the savior of the peasantry, and he met with Adeoye in early October on Adeoye's home ground. Awolowo endorsed most of the peasants' demands in his recommendations to Governor Adebayo although Awolowo did not agree to the abolition of the district councils, then run by the sole administrators, and he favored a higher flat rate tax than the farmers wanted.[23] It is not clear what kind of a mandate, if any, Awolowo had from Adebayo but there was no doubt that negotiations during a crisis situation were in civilian and not military hands.[24]

Many former NNDP MHAs thought that *Agbekoya* had been fomented by the AG to embarrass the military government once Awolowo's close connection to Adebayo had been broken. But the AG had not been identified with low status and low income elements in Yoruba politics, although it had a wing of younger members who saw themselves as socialists. In Ibadan, the major leaders of lower class elements had come from the Mabolaje Grand Alliance (MGA) and later from the NCNC. According to one MHA who was extremely important in Ibadan politics, Governor Adebayo at first appealed to Awolowo and Adegbenro to head off the peasant movement. They replied that it was NNDP fomented. Indeed, in 1968, the government ordered the closure of publications that were reputedly organs of the banned NNDP.

The Governor himself, at least in retrospect, came to see *Agbekoya* as an AG plot. At least one commissioner agreed with him. This commissioner said:

> *Agbekoya* was hatched by politicians. They were in back of it to discredit the military regime. They tested the strength of the military. Then they arrested it and nipped it in the bud. Then they confirmed their own authority.

Another commissioner held that it was the old Mabolaje Grand Alliance and the NCNC politicians from Ibadan who were responsible for *Agbekoya*. Perhaps the most accurate assessment was from the commissioners who felt that AG and NCNC politicians had all been trying to use farmers' cooperatives and unions for political purposes. Politicians in the cabinet were included in his indictment. He said, however, that "*Agbekoya* was not a party thing. People wanted to use *Agbekoya* but they couldn't control them" Politicians had no liking for the violent methods and lack of political sophistication of the *Agbekoya* farmers.

One commissioner, A. Adisa, who had responsibilities for Lands and Housing and who also headed the Western State Marketing Board, believed that the Governor once thought him to be the head of *Agbekoya*. Adisa was a major Ibadan politician who had been in the MGA and in the NCNC. He insisted that the Governor, after meeting with *Agbekoya* leaders, came to understand that he, Adisa, had refused to support *Agbekoya*.[25] Adisa, among other politicians, went on tour with the Governor to disaffected areas. Mojid Agbaje, another old MGA politician in Ibadan who had fought with Adisa over the succession to leadership of the MGA after Adelabu's death, also toured with the Governor. Yet Agbaje was offering legal advice to farmers from Ibadan and many politicians considered him one of the town politicians with extremely close ties to *Agbekoya* groups.

Politicians in the cabinet, and some outside of it, like Awolowo and Agbaje, appeared to fill a political vacuum. The government looked to established politicians to make contact with, and possibly coopt, the leaders of the farmers' movement. Thus it is no surprise to find out that a number of MHAs were approached by the government to help it deal with *Agbekoya* (see Table 10).

Table 10

MHAs approached by Government on *Agbekoya*

Answer	N	Percent
No	10	18.5
There was no *Agbekoya* in my area	11	20.4
Yes	14	25.9
Yes, I would not help	4	7.7
I was approached by farmers	4	7.4
I told farmers it was wrong	1	1.9
I kept away from my area	1	1.9
No answer	9	16.7

The military government had not been sensitive to the farmers' plight, having tried to raise taxes at a time when farmers' income had fallen and government services to farmers were declining. The politicians were more sensitive to the real grievances. It was clear both to politicians and to the commission which inquired into the disturbances that there had been a failure in the representative function of government.

The military government recognized that a gap existed between local government officials such as district council secretaries, treasurers, rate clerks and the populace. The Ayoola Commission had argued that local government administrative officials were more suited to actual administration than they were suited to prior discussion with the people of measures to be taken. The suspension of locally elected councilors had created a communications gap.[26]

Governor Adebayo recognized the problem when he said: "Although this is a military regime, I strongly believe in the ability of members of the community to assist the military government in the affairs of the state."[27] He set about to establish local advisory councils to assist in local government administration. District officers sent out letters of invitation to individuals in each council area.

Adebayo insisted that politics should not creep into the advisory councils. Not party identification but only merit, was to be the criterion for appointment to advisory councils. No consultation with political leaders was to take place nor was lobbying for posts on the councils allowed. Appointments were reviewable every six months. The councils were to meet every three months or during emergencies. The district council officer was still to make decisions, but he was also supposed to take advice from the advisory councils. The military government was caught in a problem: it wanted nonpartisan representatives to carry out representative tasks in a highly partisan and conflict-ridden local environment. The politicians saw this conflict. Some said that local advisory councils fell into disuse as the farmers' revolt deepened in 1969 because farmers would have taken politicians' participation in advisory councils as a sign of support for government.

The military got the worst outcome. It continued to lack a set of institutions through which cleavage and conflict could be mediated at the divisional and district levels. At the same time, politicians did come back into local political life through the local advisory committees and through self-help committees. Moreover, politicians were involved in the government's attempts to reorganize local government. The Western State Government was bent on consolidating local government jurisdictions and it also wanted to change the traditional sites of certain local government centers. Some MHAs took an active role in lobbying for a specified number of councils in their division or for a particular local government site and they tried to organize support around these activities.

Self-Help Committees

Self-help committees constituted another sphere of activity open to politicians. In July 1968, Adebayo addressed the Obas, Chiefs and Leaders of Thought on the subject of economic development through self help.[28] The following September, the Western State Self-help Council was launched and in each of the 25 administrative divisions of the state, a 15-man divisional self-help committee was set up.[29] These committees were supposed to raise capital and to organize people for cooperative self-help activities. When they were established, Adebayo warned against politicians' "spreading the tentacles of political activities."[30]

Political figures became involved in self-help committees. Of the MHAs we interviewed, at least half had had some involvement with them. How political the self-help programs became depended on specific politicians and the politics of particular areas. Some MHAs said that they avoided self-help schemes because they were political and the MHAs did not want to get into difficulties with government. Some individuals avoided them because they were expensive, not for political reasons. Others said the self-help schemes were a call to service, not an opportunity for political contacts.

Self-help schemes provided an opening for politicians to be involved in local politics just as they also provided an opening for some military personnel, too. However, there was no systematic development of civilian political networks through self-help committies. They were localized in the same ways as school committees. Insofar as civilian political networks did extend beyond quite local levels, they depended on the old party and personal alignments, although new factions continued to be formed out of old factional arrangements.[31] The local networks were pulled together, insofar as they were pulled together at all, by major leaders who, except for a few prominent NNDP leaders, operated as Leaders of Thought.

Our interviews with the former MHAs provided information about more informal ways of "nursing a constituency" in a period of military rule. Table 11 sets out their answers to two questions.

Table 11

Question and reply	N	Percent
Do you still try to represent your people?		
Yes	29 (AG 11; NCNC 3; NNDP 14; No identification 1)	53.7
No	18 (AG 1; NCNC 1; NNDP 16)	33.0
No answer	7 (AG 2; NCNC 1; NNDP 4)	13.0
Do you do many favors now?		
Yes	29 (AG 11; NCNC 4; NNDP 14)	53.7
Yes but less than before	14 (AG 3; NNDP 10; No identification 1)	25.9
No	9 (NCNC 1; NNDP 8)	16.7
No answer	2 (NNDP 2)	3.7

When it came to doing favors and continuing to represent people, AG MHAs were more active on both counts than NNDP MHAs. Overwhelmingly, the AG respondents said that they continued to represent their people, but NNDP were about evenly split. This reflected the fact that some NNDP MHAs were forced out of politics, and it also reflected the greater activity of AG MHAs. Doing favors meant and means many things. It means giving money for gifts, handouts, and school fees. A number of our respondents said that people understood that politicians could not give money now but that they could still intercede for individuals and groups. The range of these intercessions was great both in intensity and scope. Some MHAs helped groups to organize petitions; some would lead groups to lobby civilian commissioners but they would not go to military people. Others were willing to deal with former contacts among civil servants, including technical personnel such as engineers as well as high-level administrators, but they were unwilling to go to military personnel. Others said they would go to military officers if they knew them personally, or if they were from their home area. There was more reluctance to go to military men than to civil servants. This was partly a matter of pride, but it also reflected the fact that many MHAs did not know military officers. Yoruba officers tended to come either from outside the Western State, that is, they were Yoruba speakers from what is now Kwara State, or they come disproportionately from certain Yoruba areas like Ekiti. Thus, there were large parts of the Western State which did not have many officers as native sons. In a system which relies heavily on personal contacts through which representations are made, MHAs were cut off from officers. This was clear from responses to direct questioning about the contacts MHAs had with officers as compared to contacts with civil servants and other MHAs (Table 12). We asked: Do you see officers, civil servants, and MHAs?

Table 12

MHA Contacts with Military Officers, Civil Servants, and Other MHAs[a]

Reply	Other MHAs	Military officers	Civil servants
Often	23 (42.6%)	9 (16.7%)	24 (44.4%)
Seldom	14 (25.9%)	16 (29.6%)	12 (22.2%)
Never	3 (5.6%)	19 (35.2%)	6 (11.1%)
As friends only	11 (20.4%)	8 (14.8%)	7 (13.0%)
No answer	3 (5.6%)	2 (3.7%)	5 (9.3%)

[a]Out of 54 respondents.

Despite a general antagonism that politicians seemed to feel for military personnel, politicians were able to distinguish among the military's performance in different policy areas. We asked MHAs to compare military efforts and civilian efforts in various policy areas.

Clearly, former MHAs were generally unfavorable to the military, and among themselves, they were in large measure of agreement as to the military's failure to be representative. The question about the military's ability to bring stability, on the other hand, split the politicians. They were most favorable towards the military on the national unity question. Those who felt that the military had created more stability in Nigeria pointed to the creation of a new federal system of twelve states, as did those who gave the military a high score on bringing about national unity. Those who thought that the military brought more stability did not attribute this to more efficient administration or to the possession of greater authority. Nor did they think the military

Table 13

Military Succees

	N	Percent (rounded)
Have the military been more successful than civilians in representing the people?		
Yes	5	9
No	40	74
They don't try to represent	4	7
Have a mixed record	2	4
No answer	3	6
Have the military been more successful than civilians in promoting economic development?		
Yes	9	17
No	19	35
They have oil	13	24
Their intensions are good	5	9
They follow old policies	4	7
No answer	4	7
Have the military been more successful than civilians in developing health and educational services?		
Yes	8	15
No	14	26
They follow old policies	7	13
Their intentions are good	3	6
They have oil	2	4
No answer	20	37
Have the military been more successful in bringing stability than the civilians?		
Yes	15	27
No	10	14
Stability of the gun	7	13
It's a surface stability	6	11
The military is itself unstable	4	7
It's too soon to say	1	2
No answer	11	20
Have the military been more successful in creating national unity than civilians were?[a]		
Yes	13	24
Creation of more states needed	27	50
The creation of states was the best thing they did	18	33
No	13	24
No more states needed	4	7
Too soon to say	3	6
No answer	4	7

[a]The responses sum to more than 54 and the percentages to more than 100 percent because we included responses about the need to create more states (or not to create more states). These responses were embedded in answers to the national unity question.

was less corrupt or more cohesive than the civilian government had been. Indeed, politicians were skeptical about the notion of "the" military. They treated the military as a differentiated group and tended to personalize military politics—as they tended to personalize all politics in Nigeria.

Conclusion

The focus here has been on those politicians who operated at high and middle levels in the Western State. Local ward politicians, former town councillors, are not dealt with; nor are trade union leaders or other associational group leaders discussed. This study itself demonstrates the need for more empirical work to be done on local politics under military rule. Just as studies of political parties in Africa suffered for too long from the lack of attention to local political networks, so studies of military rule neglect grass roots politics now. Our interviews in the Western State did provide, however, an unusual cut into politics under a military regime.

From the very inception of a military regime in the Western Region and then in the Western State there was a sharing of authority between civilians and military, although ultimate power rested with military leaders. Between 1967–1971, authority was shared between Adebayo, the Military Governor, and Awolowo, the civilian leader. Awolowo could call on his past party supporters and large numbers of people in the Western State who looked upon him as a martyr and great leader. (Awolowo also had the liability of having made party and personal enemies. He was widely thought of as a vindictive and uncompromising political figure.) Adebayo himself had liabilities as well as advantages. He had to take account, more than Awolowo, of the sensibilities of his armed forces colleagues. He had to deal personaly with enlisted men and officers. This was both an advantage for and a constraint on Adebayo. While some old politicians saw Adebayo as partisan, he played the game in such a way that he could not easily be identified with a particular factional group. He tried, after June 1967, to create more of a balance between the old parties so that there would be among the civilian leaders those who did not support Awolowo. Adebayo's own personality and political alignments thus came to be important factors in the politics of the Western State.

The evolution of the dyarchy in the Western State took place within the context of the civil war. The war influenced the ways that civil-military relations evolved. The army rapidly expanded. The very expansion of the army made the recruitment of Yorubas into the armed forces easier. While actual fighting allowed the military leaders to rule without feeling pressure for a return to civilian rule, the civil war made it necessary to mobilize civilian support. In order to do this, the military had to rely on old political and civil service networks. It did not have the time, and most officers did not appear to have had the inclination, to forge their own political networks, although individual officers became involved in civilian factions.

By focusing on politicians' participation in politics under a military regime, we mean to suggest that military rule is a term which needs redefining. As we recognize the complexities of military-civilian relationships, we can better ask: What kinds of decisions are made by whom, and through what processes? What political networks exist outside the military and in what ways and how do they relate to the military's own factional networks and alliances? Admittedly, this essay has spoken to some of these questions, and only in part. It has shown that military rule did not do away with politics or with the need for civilian politicians.

Notes

1. Between 1966 and 1972 at least seven MHAs died. One was physically incapacitated.

2. Since the range of interviewees was good by party background, geographical location, age, political status prior to 1966 and afterwards, the 54 completed interviews seem to us not too small a sample. But how reliable were the interviewees? Most interviewees were quite willing to be interviewed; only a few were reluctant. Most did not preface the interviews with warnings or make an interview conditional by being "off the record" or by stating their fear of consequences from the interview, although a few raised the question of confidentiality. We assured all the MHAs that no names would be used in reporting general or specific information. Some of the interviews were quite perfunctory, with MHAs responding to specific questions and hurrying through the interview. Other interviews were very rich.

3. It may be that among those we did not interview there were somewhat more traders in present occupation since we found that individuals who did not have have fixed abodes, and these were hard to meet, frequently were traders. But there were lawyers and managers who moved around a good bit too and we were unable to locate some of them. We did interview in 9 divisions. We interviewed in Lagos and in Ibadan MHAs from the 4 western divisions of the Western State where we did not do interviews.

4. An intricate game was played to give various geographic divisions and political groups a representative in the cabinet. When the cabinet was made up of different party coalitions in 1963–64 it was necessary to take party and factional alignment into account too. And since one could not legally be a minister or junior minister and also carry on a private occupation, a large part of our group were full-time paid representatives. Indeed, many of those who remained backbenchers said that they had been offered a cabinet position but had declined because they wanted to continue to pay great attention to business.

5. For a discussion of the intense factionalism of Western Region politics see B. J. Dudley, "Western Nigeria and the Nigerian Crisis," in Keith Panter-Brick, *Nigerian Politics and Military Rule: Prelude to Civil War* (London: The Athlone Press, 1970), pp. 94–110; also see B. J. Dudley, *Instability and Political Order* (Ibadan: University of Ibadan Press, 1974); and Anthony Kirk-Greene, *Crises and Conflict in Nigeria: A Documentary Source Book, 1966–1970* (London: Oxford University Press, 1971), Vol. 1.

6. We shall refer to the Western State instead of the Western Region for events after May 1967, since the Western State came into being with the promulgation of the twelve-state system on May 27, 1967.

7. Kirk-Greene, *op. cit.,* p. 55, citing *Daily Times,* August 4, 1966.

8. Dudley states that when Awolowo was made Leader of the Yorubas, by this the Yoruba intelligentsia (Dudley's term) meant not just the peoples of the Western Region but all Yoruba-speaking peoples. There was a territorial claim to include in a single political unit the Yoruba people of the Western Region, Lagos, Kabba/Ilorin in the North and Akoko-Edo in the Midwest; Dudley, *Instability and Political Order, op. cit.,* pp. 146–147.

9. In the East, an Eastern Nigerian Consultative Assembly was set up. See Robin Luckham, *The Nigerian Military* (Cambridge: Cambridge University Press, 1971), p. 311 ff. Lt. Col.

Usman Hassan Katsina, Military Governor of the North, had been meeting with the traditional ruling structure in the North for months. He himself was a son of the Emir of Katsina and moved easily within this structure.

10. Kirk-Greene, *op. cit.,* pp. 202–203, reproduces this address.

11. Thirteen people, or 24.1 percent, did not respond to this question.

12. Interview with high-ranking military officer, 1973.

13. Luckham, *op. cit.,* p. 311.

14. Kirk-Greene, *op. cit.,* p. 60.

15. Luckham, *op. cit.,* p. 313.

16. Dudley, *Instability and Political Order, op. cit.,* pp. 147–148.

17. Awolowo's address is reprinted in full in Kirk-Greene, *op. cit.,* pp. 414–418, and a report of it is reprinted in Panter-Brick, *op. cit.,* pp. 200–205.

18. Luckham, *op. cit.,* p. 320.

19. *Ibid.,* p. 333; and Dudley, in Panter-Brick, *op. cit.,* pp. 108–109.

20. Interview with former commissioner, Ibadan, 1973.

21. Christopher Beer, *The Farmer and the State in Western Nigeria: The Role of The Farmers Organizations and Cooperatives,* Ph.D. diss., University of Ibadan, Department of Political Science, 1971), p. 394.

22. The role of traditional leaders varied from place to place. The Shoun of Ogbmomosho was murdered. But in Egba division, the *Parakoyis,* or traditional chiefs, appear to have organized riots. These chiefs felt that their functions were being usurped by district council functionaries. *Ibid.,* p. 405; and the *Report of the Commission of Inquiry into the Civil Disturbances Which Occurred in Certain Parts of the Western State of Nigeria in the Month of December 1968* (Ibadan: Government Printer, 1968). This report is known as the Ayoola Commission Report after the Chairman, Mr. Justice Ebenezer Olufemi Ayoola. The Alake of Abeokuta, the major Yoruba Oba there, also opposed the district council and was thought to have surrounded himself with NNDP people. *Ayoola Commission Report,* p. 26.

23. Beer, *op. cit.,* pp. 482–483.

24. One commissioner said in an interview that it was Gowon who asked Awolowo to see 'Tafa Adeoye, the *Agbekoya* leader.

25. Interview with Mr. Adisa, in which he allowed these views to be reported.

26. *Ayoola Commission Report,* pp. 91–92.

27. From an address by Governor Adebayo to members of Advisory Commission for Local Government Councils entitled *A Call to Service* (Ibadan: Information Division, Ministry of Home Affair and Information, n.d.).

28. Address of July 17, 1968. See *Face to Face with Brigadier Adebayo* (Ibadan: Information Division of the Ministry of Home Affairs and Information, September 3, 1970), p. 11. See also *Self Help for Social and Economic Progress* (Ibadan: Information Division of Ministry of Home Affairs and Information, n.d.).

29. The Commissioner for Trade and Industry was named chairman of the Council.

30. See Adebayo, *Problems and Solutions, op. cit.,* p. 121.

31. A fascinating look into a group convened by Bola Ige, former Publicity Secretary of the AG and one of Awolowo's leading lieutenants, is provided by a list of those who attended Chief Awolowo at the burial of his Mother in February, 1970. Bola Ige sent a circular from the Ministry of Lands and Housing, of which he was Commissioner, to 106 people, requesting that they join in a procession from the home of the deceased into the church. While many of the 106 were former AG leaders at the national and Western Region levels, NCNC leaders like S. Yerokun and Chief Kolawole Balogun were there. A few former AG turned NNDP were there, too, as were some NCNC turned NNDP. But there were very few indeed, whereas almost all the MHAs and MPs who stayed loyal to the AG were present. All the AG members of the cabinet who were serving under Adebayo were present, but not all non-AG members of the cabinet were present.

Chapter 11

Civil Servants under Military Rule
in Nigeria

Military-Civil Service Alliance

The importance of civil servants in military regimes was overlooked in the early writings on the military in Africa. These writings tended to examine coups and military interventions, and they tended to focus on the internal characteristics of armed forces.[1] Subsequently, analysts became concerned with the relationship of military to society and with the broad effects of the military on the development process.[2] But processes of government were still not examined thoroughly. It is much more difficult to get information on how governments work than it is to try to isolate factors for intervention via cross-national aggregate data studies or to get information on size of armed forces, rates of growth of gross national product, etc. The ways that decisions are made by military regimes, the nature of deliberation processes, the ways that factional and institutional alliances are formed—all these usually remain closed to the outside observer.

Nonetheless a number of observers of military regimes in Africa did call attention to the role of civil servants and some observers began to refer to military regimes as coalition regimes of military personnel and civil servants.[3] Edward Feit referred to African armies as the "apotheosis of administration" and saw them as reconstructing an administrative-traditional order. Because countries are more complex than armies, the soldiers' solution was to abrogate political activity and to rule by administrative fiat in alliance with civil servants.[4] Feit saw the military-civil service coalition as one without a consensus or basic legitimacy in which both military officers and civil servants often have a reluctance to assume responsibilities through direct involvement in politics, even after a military-civil service allegiance has been established.[5] Soldiers look to civil sevants to help them establish legitimacy, whereas the latter look after their own personal and institutional interests.[6]

Anton Bebler also called attention to the military's sharing norms with the civilian bureaucracy and to the fact that African military governments often have been unwilling to commit the officer corp to active involvement in administration.[7] He stated that in Mali when a military government dismissed civilian mayors and *commandants de cercle* for being too closely connected with the former civilian regime, and appointed officers formally to fill those positions, actual business was carried out by civilian administrators.[8] African military governments rarely have used military personnel to fill more than a few public corporation posts and a limited number of regional and ministerial posts. When military governments have replaced traditional authorities, they have, as Feit pointed out for Nigeria, replaced them with administrative cadres, not with military officers.[9]

Bebler[10] concluded for Dahomey, Ghana, Sierra Leone and Mali that:

> Regardless of the formal organization of power the real impact of military rule on state administration seems to have been an increase in its autonomy. . . . The military removed or minimized party and "political" pressures on the bureaucrats without bringing in their own system of effective control.

Bebler went on to argue that the military juntas in these four countries espoused notions of the civilian administrations' corporate autonomy and apolitical nature. While sometimes relations were not cordial between miliary juntas and civilian administrators, "in the long run no junta changed anything of substance in the organization and functioning of the civil administration."[11]

The civil service has been seen as a net gainer from military rule in Africa. It is said that civil servants are glad to be free of political interference in their day-to-day work. It is said that civil servants share values with military men because they are like them in origin and education. Insofar as the military centralizes authority, the civil service benefits from the top down. Civilian ex-politicians seem to share with academic observers the view that the civil service has gained from military rule. Probably many civil servants may agree in the short run.

Events in both Ethiopia and Nigeria should give observers some pause. An Ethiopian military government, ruling by unwieldly committees and subcommittees, with its main executive body split by ethnic origin, ideology, specific policy commitments and rank, puts heavy burdens on its civil service. Imprisonment of high level functionaries has created reluctances to make decisions. Decisions get bucked up to the central military governing body. Initiatives cease to be made by civilians. It could be argued that this outcome is more a function of a revolutionary and chaotic situation than of a specifically military regime. The problem is of general relevance, however, when civilian administrators do not know what the lines of authority are. One of the presumed advantages of a military government is clarity in lines of authority. This does not exist in Ethiopia and in some other African military regimes. Moreover, military governments cannot enforce always, in a day to day way, decisions at local levels. And local military commanders operate sometimes with a great deal of autonomy.

In general, military regimes put heavy burdens on civilian administrators. The military devolves upon civil servants many tasks and decisions that it does not want to take. Then it reproaches, or in the Ethiopian case, does much worse things, to civil servants with whom military officers are unhappy. We can see African militaries both underinvolved and overinvolved with government as we examine civil service-military relationships.

The Nigerian Case

Nigeria provides an especially interesting example of civil service-military relations. Nigeria was one of the military regimes of which it was said that the civil service was a net gainer from military rule. As we shall see below, this view was shared widely by politicians we interviewed, and by civil servants themselves. Yet it was in Nigeria, after July 1975, that wholesale dismissals of civil servants took place. It is true that civil servants earlier had their activities investigated under Nigerian military regimes. In both Lagos State and in the then Western State, commissions had taken up the matter of possible corruption of civil servants as well as corruption among former politicians.[12] The Military Governor of the Western State, Brigadier Robert Adeyinka Adebayo, ordered an inquiry into the assets of those who held public office between October 1960 and January 1966.[13] But confiscations of property fell on former politicians, not on civil servants.[14] An inquiry into major civil disturbances which took place in the Western State in December, 1968, was undertaken and this inquiry was critical of local government structure and administration; it pointed to various civil servants' corrupt practices.[15] Nonetheless, significant purging of civil servants did not take place prior to September 1975 in the Western State or at the federal level, nor in other states of the Nigerian Federal Republic.

Soon after Brigadier Murtala Mohammed replaced General Yakubu Gowon, he announced that one of the factors in the ouster of Gowon had been the growth of official corruption. Many military leaders have pointed to corruption as a reason for their takeover, but they have had in mind the corruption of party politicians. In October 1975 Brigadier Mohammed stated his intention to carry out a purge in the military, civil service, and publicly owned corporations.[16] Nigeria's new military government had already dismissed over four hundred federal officials. By mid-October close to 600 civil servants had lost their jobs and the new regime had asked the past and present civil servants to declare their assets. Special state and federal tribunes were established.[17]

By the end of September 1975, more than two dozen federal and state permanent secretaries had been dismissed; heads of the civil service in four states were gone.[18] By November, over half of the secretaries to the military governors in the states were gone. These men had functioned as prime

ministers in the states since no civilian commissioners in the state governments had overall charge of all ministries.[19]

Other changes took place at the expense of civil servants. Permanent
secretaries at the federal level were no longer to participate in the deliberations
of the Federal Executive Council, which was, after the Supreme Military
Council, the highest executive body in Nigeria. Permanent secretaries were
told they could attend the Federal Executive Council meetings only at the
request of their commissioners and in an advisory capacity.[20]

In part, the military was continuing a centralization of authority that had
been going on in Nigeria under previous military governments. Military
governors of the then twelve states were not henceforth going to sit *ex officio*
on the Supreme Military Council as they had prior to July, 1975. They were
now considered officers posted to their service in a state, and they were not
going to be appointed to serve as governor of a state of their own origin. They
now were to be directly responsible to the Chief of Staff of the armed forces
who was to function as a prime minister to the Commander in Chief of the
armed forces, who was Head of State.

In the past, the civil service had been a chief beneficiary of centralization of
authority over functional jurisdictions like revenue allocation, taxation, direct
investments and the universities. After the Mohammed coup, both high- and
low-level civil servants were replaced, in a sweeping purge of the civil service.
No African military regime had retired or dismissed so many high-level
administrative officials. The purge reached into public corporations in the
states as well as into the federal service, and officials were hauled up before
state public service commissions on accusations of inefficiency, irresponsible
financial management, corruption.

Perhaps we can understand better the unprecedented magnitude of the
attack on the civil service by presenting information collected during a study of
civil-military relations in the Western State of Nigeria, now broken into Ondo,
Oyo, and Ogun states. Our interviews reveal the ways that civil servants were
perceived by former members of the Western House of Assembly and by
those who served in the cabinet of the military governor of the Western State
between 1967 and 1971.[21] They also reveal something about the processes of
deliberation under a military regime and the role of civil servants in those
processes.

Politicians' Views of the Civil Service

Very few former Members of the Western House of Assembly (MHA) had
themselves been civil servants either before becoming a MHA or after the
Assembly was dissolved in January 1966. Nine percent were civil servants
prior to entering the Assembly, and 4 percent became civil servants after
1966.

We asked these MHAs: Who gained most from the military regime? Do
most civil servants want a return to civilian rule? Do civil servants have

different relationships with officers than they had with civilians in the past?
The answers were all self-supplied; we made no suggestions regarding individuals or groups (see Table 1).

Table 1

Politicians' Perceptions of Civil Servants
in a Military Regime

Questions and replies	N	Percentage out of 54 respondents[a]
Who has gained most from the military regime?		
The military	10	19
The civil servants	13	24
The North	6	11
The West	1	2
The people	3	6
Women contractors	3	6
Minorities	1	2
No answer	21	39
Do most civil servants was a return to civilian rule?		
Yes	5	9
No	31	59
Don't know	3	6
No answer	18	28
Do civil servants have different relationships with officers than they had with civilians in the past?		
No	4	7
Yes[b]	6	11
They have more power	29	54
They had more power at first, not now	3	6
They have less power	1	2
Can't tell	1	2
No answer	10	19

[a]More than one answer was sometimes given.

[b]Most of the "yes" responses seemed to indicate that civil servants were more influential under
the military regime, but the response was not clear-cut, so we made a distinction between
"yes" and "more power."

The majority of MHAs felt that the civil service had gained in power during
the military regime and that civil servants did not want a return to civilian rule.

It was the cabinet members, however, who interacted with civil servants from day to day in their ministerial duties and who participated with key civil servants in cabinet deliberations. It was they who were involved in the sorting out of the relationships between political people, civil servants, and the Governor.

Cabinet Members' Views of the Civil Service

Some of the cabinet members stressed the personal aspects of their own relationships with civil servants rather than any change in basic system-wide authority relationships with the coming of a military regime. It is best to let them speak for themselves on their relationships. One said:

> It is not easy to categorize the civil servants. If commissioners were weak they took over. It all depended on how one dealt with civil servants. Mine were loyal to me. They did not go without my knowledge to the Governor. The Governor would occasionally see them. He was a clever and efficient man and could see people personally. Once I took exception to this [seeing civil servants directly] and he never did it again. In fairness to Adebayo, he did not bypass me. I stood by my civil servants too.

Another commissioner offered:

> The old ministers had much more power. Civil servants could do things to commissioners and get away with it. They were careful though in the way they dealt with us. They could go to the Governor. It was an invisible government. If a commissioner was strong he could override them. Real civil servants went to Odumosu [the Civil Service Head in the Western State]. When other civil servants went to the Governor, Odumosu called them to order.

One commissioner felt that the civil service was important but that this was more of a personal problem than one of general application:

> Civil servants tasted power before the commissioners were appointed, and did not want it taken back. I had experience of this. When I came in, I wasn't briefed. I took the initiative. I asked for a total review of my department. I worked from 8:00 a.m. to 9:00 p.m. Within a weekend I had made the queries. I wanted briefs in 48 hours on 48 items. The civil servants tested you. The permanent secretary might go to the Governor. It depended on his personal relationship to the Governor. But the Governor would not act without a commissioner. Adebayo dealt with you decently and on a cabinet basis.

Yet another commissioner said:

> The civil service relationships were different. Before the appointment of commissioners, the government had been by permanent secretaries. Some did not

feel that they needed civilian commissioners. They had been there from January 1966 to July 1967. They had power and ministerial responsibility too. But some felt that a revolt against government would hurt them. They saw the commissiones as buffers. They readjusted to commissioners. They knew the real power was with the Governor and they could go to him directly. He encouraged this but not in writing. They could also go to the Secretary to the Military Government [Odumosu]. There were many cabinet reshuffles and conflicts and resignations. But the civil service will obey any master. I can't speak for them but they prefer the present setup. They like the inexperience of military leaders.

And another commissioner:

Civil servants were far more powerful than in the civilian regime. If you could not master your subject, they ruled you. Civil servants played havoc on the Alafin issue [the appointment of a new Alafin of Oyo]. The Commissioner for Local Government did not even see the file. Permanent secretaries went to the head of the civil service or even the Governor if he called them without the commissioner's permission. But the commissioner had real power. It wasn't easy to wield it. The Governor could overrule you, and even overrule the cabinet. But he was cautious. He would advise you. We had frank and open cabinet meetings.

Another commissioner:

Civil servants felt they had to keep clearing with the Governor, not just their commissioner. In a civilian government only a major issue went to the cabinet as a whole. The civil servant is responsible to you as a commissioner, but all the same they work to the Governor. Many commissioners are young and inexperienced. [This commissioner was referring to the regime of Brigadier Rotimi, governor of the Western State from 1971 to 1974, not to the Adebayo regime, which had experienced commissioners.]

One commissioner, when asked who was influential in the cabinet, responded by saying:

I think it all depends on the issue; it all depends on the subjects. One would not say that any commissioner was the most influential. . . . I remember now when we first went into the cabinet, it was said that Adebayo was leaning too much on the senior civil servants, not even permanent secretaries, civil servants, the people lower down, and that he had his own purposes [for doing so]. So you can see the grievances of the commissioners now, and as a result of it we began to hold our meetings to see to it that what were our privileges were not taken away from us.

When this commissioner was asked whether the Governor tended to take advice directly from permanent secretaries or from the commissioners, he said:

It all depends on which ministry and which permanent secretary. As a whole we have a team of brilliant civil servants. There's no doubt about it and they are aware that their influence depends on the value of their advice, and if they give advice which proves wrong in the long run, they will lose influence. At the same time, I don't think the civil servants are easily affected by the circumstances and factors which affect a commissioner's actions. They [civil servants] don't have that element of distraction that this thing should be done as quickly as possible. This is where the commissioner undoubtedly sits on top. The only difference between a commissioner and a minister in the civilian regime is that the premier would hardly ever call on the permanent secretary. Information would always come through the minister. But with the Governor that is not necessarily so. If he feels that the commissioner would happen to know more about it or if he feels it would be better to go through the channel of the commissioner he would. But nothing inhbits him from approaching the permanent secretary directly.

When asked if this caused friction, the commissioner answered:

No, I don't think so because the first few months we spent there we made it clear that the information we gave the Governor and the permanent secretary was one and between them they could do whatever liked with it. But between us and the Governor is preeminence [vis-à-vis civil servants] and we would not like it usurped.

This commissioner also stated that civil servants did not attend cabinet meetings and that therefore if a civil servant wanted to send a proposal to the cabinet and the commissioner did not agree, that was the end of it. "He could go to the Governor but the Governor could only say that the commissioner had better bring this matter to the cabinet with the permanent secretary's view and his own."

It appears from the above that personal relations with permanent secretaries were very important. At the same time, the commissioners believed that they had to master their civil servants. Of course this is a feeling that ministers in civilian regimes have have too. But the fact that a military regime existed meant that commissioners did not have a direct constituency base and they felt this even though some of them believed that political criteria counted for their appointment. They felt that they had a lessened authority because of the lack of election and mandate. They also knew that civil servants had a different attitude in the military regime and would feel freer in going to the Governor directly, especially the three most powerful permanent secretaries who attended cabinet meetings.

Some of the civilian commissioners had been ministers in a civilian government. Two had been federal ministers; some were ministers in the old Western Region. One had been a junior minister in the Western Region. Thus they could compare cabinet government in civilian and military regimes. Only one of the people we interviewed thought the relationship was the same under both military and civilian regimes. For the rest, their words speak for themselves.

It would, of course, be extremely valuable to have had many interviews with civil servants to see how they understand their relationships with civilian commissioners. We did conduct some interviews with senior civil servants in the federal government and in the Western State. Since the permanent secretaries in the Adebayo Government were still functioning as permanent secretaries under Governor Rotimi, we felt it would not be possible to conduct wide-ranging interviews with all the permanent secretaries in 1972–1973. Still, it is worth reporting the sense of meetings we had with senior civil servants.

Civil Servants Speak for Themselves

One federal government civil servant said that the civil servant works to the commissioner. If the commissioner is strong, he can dominate. The civil servant, if he is a senior one, can go to the head of the civil serice. He denied that a permanent secretary could go directly to the Head of State or to one of his military secretaries or aides. If he did that and lost, the civil servant would be finished. This high level civil servant insisted that civil servants used to formulate policies too under the civilian regime. "Many ministers were uneducated. Who used to write their memos?" This civil servant said he personally did not trust the military, yet he recognized new roles civil servants played under a military regime. They had more operating leeway and they were more independent on state corporations and boards.[22]

A senior civil servant from the Western State said that permanent secretaries could go to Adebayo but it had been possible in the civilian regime for permanent secretaries to bypass ministers and go to the premier. He felt that Adebayo was a cunning politician but someone with whom you could speak freely. His own view of the commissioners was complex.

> The worse they were the better because you could do things then. Some were brilliant but wouldn't concentrate. It was an individual matter between a civil servant and the commissioner. Although the styles are different between Adebayo and Rotimi, in a way government functioned the same. It was a hybrid regime. It was military up to July 1967. But they appointed commissioners because they could not rule by themselves. Cabinet discussions were frank, although sometimes Adebayo had made up his mind already. The cabinet was advisory to the government. It is wrong to say otherwise. Three civil servants were in the cabinet as such. [These were the permanent secretaries for Finance, the Political Administration in the Governor's Office and the Secretary to the Military Governor.] Sometimes a commissioner had his permanent secretary present for discussions. A cabinet meeting was for enlightenment and thus a commissioner should not be embarrassed to have a permanent secretary present. Permanent secretaries were members of the executive councils but did not swear allegiance.[23] Some permanent secretaries talked at cabinet members although they were discreet on certain political things. They sometimes just kept asking and asking questions.

This high-level civil servant in the Western State believed that key civil servants in the federal government exerted vast power:

If you went to Lagos you could speak to civil servants there. The key ones run things. It is frightening they have so much power. If Gowon says something and Ebong or Ayida [former permanent secretaries for Economic Development and Finance respectively] don't agree, next day he changes it.

Indeed, civil servants at the federal level have been much more open about their power than their Western State counterparts. There are a number of documents which are quite extraordinary in that they reveal federal government secretaries speaking out openly on policy matters in Nigeria under the Gowon regime. In August 1970, a conference was held at the Institute of Administration, Ahmadu Bello University in Zaria. Both state and federal permanent secretaries were in attendance.[24] Mr. Phillip Asiodu, then permanent secretary to the Federal Ministry of Mines and Power, addressed this conference.[25] In his address, Ms. Asiodu noted a number of things that are undoubtedly true in Nigeria as well as in many other African countries but that are not usually said by civil servants:

The members of the civil sevice are often the only concrete manifestation of government for the citizens. . . . The effectiveness of a government is to a very great extent determined by the efficiency and competence of the civil service. The Higher Civil Service indeed plays a crucial role in that it participates fully in the formulation of policy and at the same time is responsible for the execution of agreed policy. This was always the case under the Civilian Regime. To some extent, moreover, it can be argued that the policy formulating role of the Higher Civil Service has expanded, or has been given greater recognition, under the Military Regime.[26]

One of the discussants of Mr. Asiodu's paper, Alhaji Yusuf Gobir, another permanent secretary in the federal government, noted that the military government raised the status and prestige of civil servants:

This is because when the military took over, the politicians were regarded with some suspicion and the only alternative source of advice they had was the civil servant. And because of this, one finds that in many of the states' executive councils, probably in all, the Head of the Civil Service is a member of the Executive Council.[27]

In November 1972, another conference was held at Ahmadu Bello University. The topic of the conference was "institutional and administrative perspectives for national development." It was billed as a conference on the future of Nigeria, and past and future institutional options were discussed. The delegates included academics, ministers, and permanent secretaries.[28] A number of civil servants spoke out on issues of military rule and civilian-military relationships.[29]

The conference reached a number of conclusions about the future of Nigeria and the high level civil servants were associated with these conclusions. These conclusions were themselves of interest, but the point is that civil servants participated in formulating ideas about constitutional and political issues and were publicly on record to this effect. Such politically important issues as whether or not there should be political parties during transition from military to civilian rule were discussed. It was decided there should not be parties. It was considered that the heads of state governments should be executive governors and that for the center a modified presidential system with a provision for prime minister would be appropriate. "After an extensive debate regarding the concept of accountability and the relationship between the political and civil service arms of government, it was agreed that there should be no conflict of interests because the two groups should be equally committed to national objectives."[30]

Perhaps the most striking public demonstration of a high level civil servant speaking out publicly on major issues was the address of A. Ayida to the Nigerian Economic Society's Annual Meeting in 1973. Mr. Ayida spoke on "The Nigerian Revolution 1966–1976." He was at the time the permanent secretary to the Federal Ministry of Finance. He spoke in his capacity as President of the Nigerian Economic Society:

> After some deep reflection, I have decided to share some of my inner thoughts on the past, present and future of Nigeria with you, by analyzing the social and economic forces which have determined the course of events in this country since 1966. One cannot analyze meaningfully economic and social determinants without making explicit one's assumptions about the future pattern of politics in the country. . . . Every Nigerian has the right to predict the likely course of events on the basis of knowledge at his disposal. . . .[31]

Mr. Ayida spoke out on the sensitive issue of creation of more states and on allocation of revenues as between states and the federal government. He also noted that there were five categories of advisers and pressure groups associated with the determination of policies since January 16, 1966: (1) public officers, notably senior civil servants; (2) political appointees, notably civil commissioners; (3) members of the armed forces; (4) the private establishment, such as chuch leaders, trade unionists, and captains of industry and employers; and (5) personal friends and confidants. Mr. Ayida came to the conclusion that, "Unfortunately, there is abundant evidence that the basis of civilian participation in the military administration is not abundantly clear even to some Civil Commissioners."

> If Civil Commissioners appear to exercise less power than the former Ministers, it is not because their functions have been usurped by Permanent Secretaries and other Senior Servants. It is because authority now resides in the military. Commissioners and senior civil servants are fellow advisers to the powers-that-be who sometimes receive their advice from outside the two groups, to their mutual frustration and suspicion. Commissioners were not appointed to run the government as political masters but as servants of the military, the new political masters.[32]

He went on to say that it was the barrel of the gun that determines the outcome of political controversy or personality conflict and that the ultimate distribution of power in a future civilian government may not be significantly different from the present Nigerian military government. "The political reality in Africa today is that the fact of the elective basis of government will not, *ipso facto,* remove the ultimate sanction in the hands of the military."

Mr. Ayida noted that although federal permanent secretaries headed ministries between January 15, 1966 and June 12, 1967, all ministerial powers were vested in the Federal Executive Council, and not in individual permanent secretaries. "When the military seized power, one of their first suggestions was to draw members of the Federal Executive from the military, the universities, and some federal permanent secretaries. We declined to serve and preferred to retain our role of advisers." But he also argued that modern governments depend on professional and technical advice in the formulation and execution of public business and thus the military recognizes this by permitting permanent secretaries and professional experts to participate in meetings of the Federal Executive Council.

Mr. Ayida believed that new ideas and policy reform proposals have tended to emanate from the civil service in Nigeria:

> The viability of the few politically determined ideas, such as free primary education, had to be worked out by the civil service machinery. The material difference between them and today is that there is no parliamentary forum under the military for Honourable ministers to deliver speeches and appear to be seen to originate new ideas and policy measures.[33]

We have quoted at length from Mr Ayida's address because it showed clearly the disposition of a high-level civil servant to comment on political matters, including the civil service's relationship with politicians and the military. The substance and tenor of the remarks were interesting too. For while Mr. Ayida specifically stated that the civil service should not be politicized and that it should not compose the vanguard he saw as necessary for the survival of the military revolution, he cast the civil service in a critical policy formulation and implementation role. And he saw it involved in sensitive political matters in the past, present, and future. In one part of his speech, Mr. Ayida stated that at the time of the July 1966 coup, civil servants volunteered to go to Ikeja Barracks to advise against seccessionist threats from northern troops:

> It was gratifying to note that while we were driving to the barracks, the troops in battle order, and hidden in the bush, stood up in a column subsequently known as the Rising Grass, to ask our escort in Hausa, "What is their tribe or nation?" Apparently our escort replied, "They are civil servants." There could have been no greater compliment to the public image of the Federal Civil Service in those dark days. That intervention probably had a decisive impact on the pattern of political events in the country.[34]

Mr. Ayida also suggested that the military was clearly masters over both politicians and civil servants. Many of those that we interviewed disagreed.

Some former MHAs suggested that the civil service had struck a bargain with the military. The military would get what it wanted on interest group demands, e.g., barracks, salary, and hardware. The civil service would determined substantive policy in areas outside of narrow military interest group concerns. The civil service was prepared to be vetoed on some issues to get what it wanted most of the time. By civil service, the MHAs meant senior civil servants at the state and federal levels.

One high-level civil servant basically agreed, although he had a somewhat different perspective.

> The military goes along with the civil servants. It wants to stay in. When the army wants something for itself it is adamant. It says, "That's it." But generally they do not come into policy matters. They don't want to administer and they can't. The military wants to be in politics but it is inept; it doesn't know how. It has no talent for politics. Adebayo was rare; and the army can't administer anything. So it makes a marriage of convenience with the civil service. It gives them substantive power and administration in exchange for being able to stay in. The military doesn't want to rule with the gun so it needs the civil service.

But this civil servant suggested that he personnally abhorred military government and wanted an elected government. He felt that many civil servants were "liberally educated" and shared this feeling. He did not know about lower level civil servants but believed that even the key civil servants in Lagos agreed with him, although he made the caveat that "Maybe power has gone to some of their heads."

The MHAs did not agree that most civil servants want a return to civilian rule. Certainly many of the civil servants had grievances against civilian politicians. The Deputy Police Commissioner of the Western State, K. O. Tinubu, put it this way:

> We all will recall how during the 1962–1966 crisis some of us were made scapegoats and sacrificial lambs for the inordinate ambitions and heart-rending atrocities of some of our politicians.[35]

While the police were in an especially difficult position in the Western Region during this period, grievances against politicians were shared and expressed by many civil servants. When civil servants themselves began to function in political roles under the military regime and became visible in those roles, they became vulnerable to being used as scapegoats once again. Indeed, because the military regime had special needs for the civil servants, and because civil servants were forced to confront politically organized demands, their vulnerability was heightened.

Civil Servants and Political Pressures

We do not have a large amount of information on the ways that civil servants have operated in the field, at district and subdistrict levels, under different military regimes in Nigeria. From the end of colonial rule up to military rule in 1966, divisional officers' authority weakened and their functions narrowed in the Western and Midwestern Regions. In those two states, divisional and district officers became known as local government advisers.[36] After the military banished parties and ended legislative bodies at the national, state, and local levels, it required mechanisms to make contact with the grass roots. Former politicians continued to play some linking roles in both formal and informal bodies such as Leaders of Thought, advisory councils, and as civilian commissioners. But at the local level especially, the military had a problem in getting information and in having representative functions performed. Local government bodies remained, but they no longer had elected representatives on them. The military appointed local government advisers who became known as "sole administrators" in lieu of elected local councils. I have already noted in Chapters 9 and 10 the breakdown of this system when large-scale tax riots broke out in the Western State in 1968 and 1969.

An investigatory report into the tax riots portrayed the confusion surrounding local government without elected councillors, and it noted how party politics continued to infuse local administration:

> The sole administrators, appreciating that they could not by themselves discharge their functions without local aid, have sometimes used their own initiatives to surround themselves with a body of advisers. . . . It is not clear to the Commission how these bodies of advisers were selected. . . . They had no statutory locus nor functions. Their powers and duties are not defined. Their identities are sometimes unknown to the local populace, and it would appear that they held their offices at the pleasure of the particular sole administrator who selected or made use of them. Without definite criteria to guide him, other than his own absolute discretion, the body so selected sometimes reflected a leaning towards this or that banned political party. . . . Where inconvenient measures are introduced, the sole administrator and his body of advisers . . . are accused of having brought them about by the local populace acting under the increased propaganda of the dissatisfied Party adherents. . . . The so-called ban which had been placed on political activities becomes a sham or dead letter.[37]

Sole administrators were not usually local people. Their difficulties in making contact with the populace were aggravated by civil service caution. One observer suggests that civil servants at first thought that the military had no mandate for radical reform in the localities.[38] Another observer says:

> This [civil service] echelon was, however, inert in the process of representation. Conditioned to the position of some subservience under the old ministerial regime, it took civil servants some time to realize that they might have a function to represent the people. It was hard for them to fulfill the broker function in the way that politicians could do it.[39]

We should distinguish between senior civil servants both at the national and the state levels on the one hand, and local government officials on the other hand. The state and national civil servants were often aggressive in moving to fill political vacuums. But at the local levels civil servants could not both administer and represent.

The civil servants' greater freedom of action in administrative and political spheres have made them more vulnerable to charges of corruption. Margaret Peil states that senior civil servants have used their freedom of action to provide decisions in the national interest, but some lower executive officers and clerks have found the opportunities for corruption to good to miss.[40] But Nigerian civil servants probably have no greater opportunity for corruption than they had under civilian regimes. Rather, the civil servants are no longer seen to be under politicians' orders,[41] and they are more visible and perceived more as independent actors. Indeed, this holds true more for senior civil servants than for junior ones. And large numbers of senior civil servants were dismissed after Murtala Mohammed's coup.

We are not on very solid ground when we speculate about mass opinions or the views of political groups concerning civil servants. It does appear that both military officers and civil servants came to be seen by significant political groups as representing various political and ethnic configurations. This was evident when different groups petitioned for the breaking up of the Western State into more states. Civil servants and military were identified with particular subdivisions within the Yoruba. Many high level civil servants were either Ijebu or Ekiti Yoruba and many Yoruba officers were from the Ekiti areas. Thus, when the Alafin of Oyo and the Chief of Oyo submitted a petition to General Gowon for the creation of more states they wrote: "Since the Army take-over, the harsh hands of neglect have gripped our area and we are choking under the throes of a ruthless Ijebu and Ekiti officialdom."[42]

There is some evidence that there has been fairly widespread dissatisfaction with civil servants at local levels especially. The military regime in Nigeria is perceived as not trying to be representative. Peil reports that respondents in a survey she did in 1971–1972 were largely in favor of civilian commissioners on the ground that military severity must be moderated by some representation of the people.[43] Our own interviews with civilian commissioners established that they saw their appointments as designed to link military and civil service to the people.

Conclusions

Politicians and civil servants in the Western State agreed on the important and expanded role that civil servants played under the military regime. Indeed, if we had conducted this study at the federal level or in other states, I think we would have found even greater importance attached to civil servants' roles. The federal civil service in Nigeria has attracted very high-powered people. While the Western State probbly had the next most highly trained set of civil servants in Nigeria, it also had vigorous party politicians who still were able to make their political will felt. At the national level, there was more of a political vacuum. And this is especially true in some of the new states that did not have political parties developed for contending primarily within the states' present boundaries. Some states have few native sons who are high-level military officers too. And the East Central State has seen the retirement or forcing out of the military of most of its top military officers. Thus civil servants play even a greater role in some states and in the Federal Military Government.

Civil servants, however, became more intimately linked in factional alliances with military officers from 1966 to 1975. Individual military leaders undoubtedly had grievances against individual civil servants all along. But the increasing visibility of the civil service and the perception among elites and nonelites in Nigeria that the civil service was a political actor made the civil service more vulnerable to the housecleaning that a new military leadership undertook. The civil service was now part of the political fray, and thus it was fairer game—a proper coup target. As some civil servants feared, the political activity of civil servants weakened the civil service as an institution. Some high-level civil serants who were closely linked with the Gowon regime were not tolerated by the Mohammed regime. Low-level civil servants and high-level ones too became convenient scapegoats for a military regime itself vulnerable to charges of corrupt practices.

Leo Dare had concluded prior to the third Nigerian coup that political power opened up vistas for the satisfaction of personal economic interests for soldiers.[44] Soldiers were able to exploit self-help schemes toward their own ends and they affected the siting of industries for their own personal and political interests.[45] Soldiers applied to development corporations for loans for their own projects.[46] Dare argued that there was a widespread perception of military corruption, at least in the Western State (see Table 2).

Table 2

Perception of Corruption in the Western State[a]

	Agree	Disagree	Don't know
From your experience of the past few years, do you agree with the following statements?			
Our soldiers have generally been honest people	61 (22.5%)	189 (69.7%)	21 (7.7%)
Our policemen have generally been honest people	29 (9.6%)	236 (87.1)	9 (3.3%)
Our soldiers are more honest than our policemen	146 (53.9%)	74 (24.3%)	51 (18.8%)

[a]See Leo Dare, paper presented to the Nigerian Political Science Association meetings held in Ibadan in 1973. "Political Orientation Towards the Military Regime of the Western State: A Preliminary Research Report." Dare reported the results from a randomly selected sample in nine major towns and cities of the Western State, about thirty people in each town.

Some civil servants who were interviewed insisted that civil servants could serve under a military or a civilian regime and that it was important for civil servants to have the politicians and the public perceive this. Civil servants have, however, become closely linked to the military, which is itself seen as corrupt. In this context, low-level civil servants, and high level ones also, became convenient scapegoats upon whom to displace feelings that corruption was increasing, income inequalities were growing, and things in general were not going well, despite the oil boom. True, military personnel were removed after the Mohammed coup, including the military governors of the states, but civil servants constituted the overwhelming number of public officials who were removed. By the time General Mohammed was himself assassinated in February 1976, as many as 11,000 civil servants were reported to have been removed.[47]

Between 1966 and 1975, military and civil service institutions needed each other and used each other. The civil service has turned out to be the more vulnerable institution, for the short run. Widespread dismissals of civil servants may weaken the civil service so much that administrative and economic efficiency is affected and the military regime in turn may suffer in performance and capabilities. Military government has not been possible in Nigeria without wide-ranging cooperation of the civil servants. Military government has been a mixed regime with civil servants continuing to be important actors. But we can expect that civil servants in the future will be more reticent and less visible politically. Any instability in the Nigerian armed forces will make civil servants more reluctant to form alliances with military actors in either military or civilian regimes. Civil servants will be more reluctant to take firm policy positions and will try to hedge their bets on different issues.

The Nigerian civil service has provided continuity of governance in Nigeria through civilian political crises and military coups and countercoups. It remains to be seen whether a civil service that became visible and prominent, and then was radically purged, can continue to provide the backbone of government in Nigeria.

Notes

1. For a review of the literature, see Samuel Decalo, "Military Coups and Military Regimes in Africa," in *Journal of Modern African Studies* 11, no. 1 (1973): 105–127; Henry Bienen, "The Background," in Henry Bienen, ed., *The Military and Modernization* (Chicago: Atherton/Aldine, 1970). Among the many studies of military intervention are J. Van Doorn and Morris Janowitz, eds. *On Military Intervention* (The Hague: Mouton, 1972); Henry Bienen, ed., *The Military Intervenes: Case Studies in Political Development* (New York: Russell Sage Foundation, 1968); Daniel La Touche, *Process and Level of Military Intervention in the States of Tropical Africa* (unpublished dissertation, University of British Columbia, 1973); Samuel Finer, *The Man on Horseback: The Role of the Military in Politics* (New York: Pall Mall, 1962).

2. See Samuel Huntington, *Political Order in Changing Societies* (New Haven: Yale University Press, 1968); Claude Welch, *Soldier and State in Africa* (Evanston: Northwestern University Press, 1970); Robert Dowse, "The Military and Political Development," in Colin

Leys, ed., *Politics and Change in Development Countries* (Cambridge: Cambridge University Press, 1969), pp. 213–246.

3. Decalo, *op. cit.*

4. Edward Feit, "Military Coups and Political Development: Some Lessons from Ghana and Nigeria," in *World Politics* 20, no. 2 (January 1968): 179–193.

5. Edward Feit, "The Rule of the 'Iron Surgeons': Military Government in Spain and Ghana," in *Comparative Politics* 1, no. 4 (July 1969): 485–497.

6. Edward Feit, *The Armed Bureaucrats* (Boston: Houghton, Mifflin, 1973), esp. pp. 1–21.

7. Anton Bebler, *Military Rule in Africa: Dahomey, Ghana, Sierra Leone, and Mali* (New York: Praeger, 1973), p. 194.

8. *Ibid.*, p. 192. William Gutteridge comments on this in the Ghanaian context in his *Military Regimes in Africa* (London: Methuen, 1975), pp. 76–77. Gutteridge notes that the Ghanaian military leadership was impatient with inefficiencies and unpunctuality of civil servants at the lower levels and unhappy with higher level civil servants' determination to remain politically neutral. But he notes the essential unity of the military and civil service elite in Ghana and the civil servants' lack of enthusiasm for a return to civilian rule.

9. Feit, "Military Coups and Political Development," *op. cit.* p. 100.

10. Bebler, *op. cit.,* p. 203.

11. *Ibid.,* p. 204.

12. See the *Comments of the Federal Military Government on the Report of the Tribunal of Inquiry into the Affairs of the Lagos Civil Council for the Period October 15, 1962–April 18, 1966* (Lagos: Government Printer, 1966).

13. A five-man tribunal headed by Justice Olujide Somolu and known as the Somolu Commission of Inquiry investigated 75 ministers, 186 corporation chairmen and directors, 51 members of the Western House of Assembly, and 246 senior civil servants, among others.

14. See *The Western State: A Review of the Achievements of the Military Government of the Western State of Nigeria* (Ibadan: Government Printer, 1968), pp. 54–55.

15. See the *Report of the Commission of Inquiry into the Civil Disturbances Which Occurred in Certain Parts of the Western State of Nigeria in the Month of December 1968* (Ibadan: Government Printer, 1969), esp. pp. 90–98. This report is known as the *Ayoola Commission Report* after its Chairman.

16. *The New York Times,* October 2, 1975, p. 11.

17. *The New York Times,* October 19, 1975, p. 11.

18. See *West Africa,* September 15, 1975, p. 1074.

19. *Ibid.,* November 3, 1975, p. 1302. In the absence of a military governor from a state, the secretary to the governor had been de facto deputized to act as head of government in a state.

20. *Ibid.,* August 25, 1975, p. 1006.

21. Our interviews have been described in Chapters 9 and 10.

22. Civil servants have played a critical role in the expanding state corporation system in Nigeria. As one commentator pointed out, with the exception of one member, all the others on the Board of the National Oil Corporation in 1972–73 were top civil servants and the chairman was the permanent secretary from the Federal Ministry of Mines and Power. [See Olu Akaragaogun, "Civil Servants Vital to Nation's Development," in *Daily Sketch* (Ibadan), December 20, 1972, p. 3.] In theory, the chairman of the National Oil Corporation is supposed to be responsible to the Ministry of Mines and Power at least for broad policy matters. The permanent secretary has something to say about the policies of this ministry, of course. It is also true, however, that a permanent secretary may not sit on all the boards for which he is listed. Thus, A. A. Ayida, former permanent secretary, Finance, noted that while he was a member of over fifty boards, he sat on only three of them and delegated the work to other representatives. (See A. A. Ayida, address to the Nigerian Economic Society's Annual Meeting, 1973, "The Nigerian Revolution, 1966–1976." This meeting was held at Enugu, East Central State, March 1973).

23. In the minutes of the Western State Executive Council meetings, permanent secretaries were listed as Executive Council members.

24. Among the former federal permanent secretaries were Mallam C. L. Ciroma, permanent secretary, Ministry of Information; Alhaji Yusuf Gobir, permanent secretary, Establishments; Mallam Ahmed Joda, permanent secretary, Education; P. C. Asiodu, permanent secretary, Ministry of Mines and Power. From the state governments, seven other permanent secretaries attended.

25. Mr. Asiodu was considered one of the most powerful permanent secretaries.

26. Phillip Asiodu, "The Future of the Federal and State Civil Services in the Context of the Twelve State Structure," in Mahmud Tukur, ed., *Administrative and Political Development: Prospects for Nigeria* (Kaduna: University of Zaria, 1970), pp. 124–146. Mr. Asiodu made clear his commitment to a strong federal government and to the dominance by the federal civil service of the state civil services.

27. *Ibid.,* p. 161.

28. Among the participants were Mr. Asiodu, then permanent secretary, Mines and Power; Mr. Ayida, permanent secretary, Ministry of Finance; Alhaji Gobir, permanent secretary, Establishments; Mr. Ime Ebong, permanent secretary, Economic Development; Alhaji A. Ciroma, permanent secretary, Ministry of Industry, the secretaries of the Western and North Central States' Military Government, P. T. Odumosu and Alhaji Garba Ja Abdul Kadir.

29. Ime Ebong produced a paper on "The Transition from Military Junta to Civilian Regime: The Case of Egypt." This is reproduced in the *New Nigerian,* November 25, 1972, p. 11.

30. A summary statement of the conclusions of the conference can be found in the *New Nigerian,* November 25, 1972, p. 11.

31. I am citing from a copy of the mimeographed version of Mr. Ayida's speech.

32. *Ibid.*

33. *Ibid.*

34. *Ibid.*

35. K. O. Tinubu, "The Dilemma of the Nigeria Police under the Civilian Regime" (unpublished paper, 1972). This is an interesting account of police powers and the way that politicians interferred with the police. We are grateful to Mr. Tinubu for making this paper available.

36. G. O. Orewa, "The Role of the Field Administrator in Midwestern Nigeria Under the Military," *The Quarterly Journal of Administration* 7, no. 3 (April 1973): 241. At the time of writing Dr. Orewa was permanent secretary, Ministry of Local Government, Midwestern State.

37. *Report of the Commission of Inquiry with the Civil Disturbances which occurred in certain parts of the Western State of Nigeria in the month of December 1968* (Ibadan: Government Printer, 1968).

38. Leo Dare, *Military Leadership and Political Development in the Western State of Nigeria* (thesis submitted to Carleton University, Faculty of Graduate Studies, Department of Political Science, 1972), p. 122.

39. Martin Dent, "The Military and Politicians," in Keith Panter-Brick, ed., *Nigerian Politics and Military Rule* (London: Athlone Press, 1970), p. 83.

40. Margaret Peil, "A Civilian Appraisal of Military Rule in Nigeria," *Armed Forces and Society* 2, no. 1 (Fall 1975): 41.

41. Peil herself makes this point in *ibid.* She does not cite any hard survey data from her sample on perceptions of corruption.

42. "Petition for the Creation of More States in the West," submitted by Alafin of Oyo and chiefs, people of Oyo, to General Gowon, June 20, 1967, published as Appendix F in Panter-Brick, *op. cit.,* pp. 267–268. "Petition for the Creation of a Yoruba Central State," submitted by

Oshun Representatives Committee to General Gowon, June 28, 1967, published as Appendix E in *ibid.*, pp. 269–271, made similar points.

43.   Peil, *op. cit.* Peil's sample consisted of 830 people, half of whom lived in Lagos. The sample was not representive of Nigeria by occupation or income.

44.   Dare, *op. cit.*, p. 181.

45.   *Ibid.*, pp. 149–156.

46.   *Ibid.*, p. 181.

47.   *The New York Times*, February 15, 1976.

Chapter 12

Conclusions:
Transitions from Military Rule

Military regimes are systems in which there are varying degrees of civilian participation. We should be interested in investigating how the mix of authority might shift more towards civilian authority and control. Welch has noted that military withdrawl from intervention in politics may occur as a result of four factors:

1. Voluntary withdrawal, due to division within the military and/or pressure from civilians
2. Disappearance or diminution of the conditions that initially brought about intervention
3. Conscious civilianization of the military government, making it indistinguishable, in the long run, from a government with more "ordinary" origins
4. Overthrow of the military-dominated regime, leading directly to a civilian-controlled government[1]

In my terms, the process that Welch calls military withdrawal from intervention in politics can be thought of as a transition to civilian rule. "Transition" ought to mean changes in formal and informal roles and relationships. There are different kinds of transition. The military in power may itself set a deadline by which it says it would like to see civilian rule restored. This means arriving at some new formula by which the head of state at least becomes chief executive by virtue of some process other than achieving leadership of the armed forces. It may mean holding of new elections for a parliament, as in Ghana before that country's second military coup in 1972. It may mean the calling of some kind of consultative assembly or constitutional convention. It may be that the military sets the rules of the game for this kind of transition, as in Nigeria from 1966 to 1977. It can happen that a military regime collapses rather suddenly from its own lack of will and capacity and from outside pressures, as happened in the case of the Sudanese regime under Abboud in 1964. In the Sudan, street demonstrators were backed by junior officers. In Thailand, military governments could not or would not overcome popular demonstrations and gave way in 1964 and again in 1973. In Thailand, too, there were cross-cutting military and civilian alliances.

It may be that the military is split about whether or not it should continue in office. There may be strong civilian pressures on it, with some civilians trying to get the military to transfer power while others want it to stay in to protect them against social and political change, as, for example, in Argentina before Peron returned to power. Foreigners sometimes can prop up or bring down a military regime. In Sierra Leone, a split officer corps was forced by non-commissioned officers to return power to civilians. Civilians then relied on troops from Guinea to stay in power.

Military regimes will also try to transform themselves. The transformation may be a modest one, as, for example, when the Thai military allowed a parliament to operate between 1969 and 1971. Power was maintained by the military during this period, and it was able and willing to abrogate the experiment. In Upper Volta, in 1970, the military regime permitted national elections and a National Assembly came into being along with a civilian-military cabinet. But in early 1974, General Lamizana abolished the Assembly and ended the experiment. The phased reimposition of overt civilian control is difficult because elements in both civilian and military sectors often reject the timing or the intent of the experiment. On the other hand, neither collapse of the military regime, as in Sudan, nor precipitous withdrawal, as in Dahomey, nor carrying out of deliberate plans for military withdrawl within a rather short time span, as in Ghana, are any guarantee of the maintenance of civilian rule.

The transformation from military rule may be a more radical one, as in the case of Turkey under Ataturk. Ataturk had insisted that Turkish officers who wanted to have a political role had to resign their commissions and enter into civilian politics by forming a new party. The South Korean military for a time seemed to be moving in this direction, only to revert to a rather "pure" military rule. African countries ruled by militaries have not undertaken what has come to be called the Ataturk or Kemalist model of civilian-military relations. Observers of militaries in developing countries have wistfully raised the Kemalist model as an appropriate one for recivilianization. Janowitz saw the Turkish experience as a model from which officers in developing countries could learn to play positive political roles.[2] Huntington later wrote: "Mexico and Turkey are two noteworthy examples where parties came out of the womb of the army, political generals created a political army, and the political party put an end to political generals. . . . In those countries which are less complex and less highly developed (than Mexico and Turkey) the military may yet play a constructive role, if they are willing to follow the Kemalist model."[3]

It is generally maintained that the Kemalist model is a "moderating" one in which a military oligarchy provides socioeconomic reforms. Janowitz, for instance, notes that Turkey under Ataturk "represented the one case in which a military oligarchy under an enlightened leader made fundamental contributions to social and economic modernization."[4] Similarly, Welch argues that "Ataturk envisaged nothing less than a total transformation of Turkish society."[5] The model also stipulates that change was gradual and stable and was facilitated by effective political institution building. Central political control was essential to regulate institutional innovation—so that changes would occur fast enough, but not so fast that social mobility would undermine political stability.[6] And, supposedly, the Turkish experience provided an example of increasing, if slowly rising, levels of political mobilization and participation of larger segments of the populace in politics. "His [Ataturk's] was not a self-serving military clique or junta but a government that built popular support by means of economic development, gradual mobilization of support as through the Houses of the People, and the charisma of Ataturk."[7] Perhaps the most significant aspect of the model is the alleged establishment and maintenance of civilian supremacy in the Turkish Republic. The distinct separation, upon Ataturk's initiative, of the military and political roles in the early years of the republic is cited as the basic factor in the establishment of civilian supremacy as well as in the maintenance of military cohesion.[8] Finally, reference is made to the evolution of multiparty competitive politics in Turkey after a tutelary period of nation building and political education of the populace.[9]

Whether or not those who have propounded the Ataturk model have accurately understood the Turkish experience is a matter for debate. Certainly, the army never ceased to be a critical factor in Turkish politics. It intervened in 1960–1961 and again in 1971. Perhaps most importantly, the social structures, historical circumstances, and different development of the state in Turkey must be taken into account in evaluating the relevance of the Turkish experience for other countries. The tradition of the powerful Ottoman state, to which rural elites owed allegiance, is not widely present in Africa. The Ataturk regime's dependence on rural notables was great, especially at the regime's inception. Though some have claimed that military regimes in Africa retraditionalize society and buttress traditional authorities,[10] it is hard to see an alliance between rural notables and the military in Africa. The traditional ruling structure of Northern Nigeria had made peace with some, but not all, military regimes in Nigeria. It does not seem to have a penchant for military rule per se. The military government in the Western State did not rely on Yoruba Obas. Where a traditional ruling structure was still partially in place in Bugunda, the Amin military regime broke with it quickly. Few African societies have cohesive and articulate rural elites. Some, like Kenya, have class differentiation on the land and a middle class and large rural property-owning class coming into being. Some have retained the impotance of local chiefs or notables. In parts of West Africa, one can find rural authorities who have intertwined religious, administrative, and economic roles with their political roles—for example, in Senegal and Northern Nigeria. But this is not characteristic of Black Africa.

The Ataturk model has been recommended because it is seen as providing for controlled political participation while institution building goes on apace. Civilian control is maintained while the army functions as a nation builder. African expriences have shown how difficult it is to create a party underneath a military. It is in part because African military leaders have a hard time finding political allies with whom to construct parties that they remain so ambivalent about the parties they do sometimes bring into being. Also, African officers have no confidence that they can operate within civilian political structures.

In the Nigerian study, we were interested in knowing whether officers and politicians thought that the military would opt for an Ataturk model, that is, whether soldiers would want to become directly involved in partisan politics and would leave the armed forces to do so. Some military officers stationed in the Western State thought that military governors, and more generally soldiers who wanted to opt for politics, would have to surrender their uniforms and vie with politicians.[11] One general thought few officers would stand.[12] Most cabinet members in the Western State believed that officers could run because they had money. Five of the former commissioners we interviewed stated explicitly that some officers would run but that only a small number would do so; General Gowon, then Head of State, and General Adebayo, former Governor of the Western State, were mentioned. Only one former commissioner said that none of them would run and that there was support for officers only while they were in uniform.

The members of the Western House of Assembly (MHAs) were asked about the likelihood of military men seeking election under a civilian regime. The results of this survey are in Table 1.

Table 1

Will Military Men Seek Election Under a Civilian Regime?

Replies	*N*	*Percent*
Yes	12	22.2
Yes, some, but they won't do well	10	18.5
Few will	10	18.5
It is their right; they are Nigerians	7	13.0
No	4	7.4
No answer	11	20.4

The MHAs, like commissioners, were conscious of the high costs of running for office in Nigeria. Officers were seen to have the financial resources to run. The MHAs believed that at least some officers wanted to run if elections were held. There was a view, widely held by politicians, that military men did not have strong local roots. They did not always build a large house back in their home area, as politicians had done. The military man's ties with a home area had become more attenuated through postings and barracks life. This view was supported by one general who said, "Why should the military spend money on the people. We have no constituency. Few officers will stand [for election]."[13] In the Western State, some officers did try to build themselves a local political base either through involvement in self-help schemes or in factional politics. One prominent Yoruba officer, Brigadier B. Adekunle, was given a traditional title and made the Ashipa of Ogbomosho when he was a colonel. Undoubtedly, many officers felt that a local base was unnecessary because the military would stay in power in any case.

The hostility politicians in Nigeria felt for military rule never boded well for continued institutionalized cooperation. They frequently cooperated with the military and recognized their ability to continue to rule. But party politicians did not see a formidable alliance between themselves and military officers. This was striking because army officers had made contact with elected officials in Nigeria even prior to the coups of 1966. And, civilian commissioners were serving with military men in the federal and state executives. But politicians did not see these contacts as creating a new set of networks of Nigerian politics. Furthermore, the politicians we interviewed were against continuing dyarchy of military-civilian rule. Looking to the future, they rejected the idea that the military should have a veto over a civilian regime (see Table 2).

Table 2

Should the Military Have a Veto over the Civilian Regime?

Replies	N	Percent
Yes	4	7.4
No	28	51.9
We have a mixed system now	1	1.9
No answer	21	38.9

The question in Table 2 was asked in a special context. On October 27, 1972, Dr. Nnamdi Azikiwe, the former civilian president of Nigeria, suggested that a military-civilian government should be established for a period of five years at the expiration of the military government. Dr. Azikiwe gave a lecture at the University of Lagos titled "Nigeria after Military Rule," in which he argued that civilian rule had been unsatisfactory.[14] He went through a catalog of sins of the civilian governments in the regions and at the federal level. He argued that in the light of civilians' denying rights of assembly, muzzling public opinion, and so forth, the military had proved to be a bastion of stability. Dr. Azikiwe maintained that "the military should ensure that would-be politicians place before the electorate a positive program of action that should inspire the people of Nigeria with respect for those who propose to rule them."[15] Before the transition to civilian rule takes place, he said, "adequate safeguards must be made to avoid transforming Nigeria into a regular battleground for staging bloody revolutions."[16]

At this point in his argument, Azikiwe proposed a dyarchy:

> The point is that civil rule depends upon the military establishment as a sanction for the maintenance and enforcement of the law. The two, being complementary, should coexist bilaterally. There is also the corollary that without the political wisdom and experience of the civilians, the military cannot rule democratically. Thus a *modus vivendi* must be devised to avert a clash of authority. . . .
>
> My view is that there should not be an immediate transfer of power to complete civilian rule; rather a *modus operandi* should be devised for a combined civil and military government that should rule this country, on a democratic basis, for five years, after which period the continuation of such a regime should be reviewed in the light of experience and reason.[17]

The basis for this proposal was that military leaders, too, had ambitions and were also citizens, a part of the body politic. They had equal stakes with civilians in good government. "Thus it would be criminal folly to expect a soldier always to be satisfied to take a back seat while the civilian glories in assuming his seat. . . ."[18] To make political life stable, Azikiwe suggested the incorporation of the military hierarchy "on a more active basis in civilian-based administration." The military should constitute a fourth arm of the state, along with the executive, legislative, and judiciary. He argued specifically that the head of the Nigerian army, the head of the Nigerian navy, the head of the Nigerian airforce, and the head of the Nigerian police should become ex officio members of the Council of Ministers, whose secretary should be a top-ranking civil servant.[19] He proposed that the four, if unanimous, have a veto over proposals affecting the rule of law, the democratic process, individual freedom, and the right of dissent. There were many other specific proposals, including making military members of the executive council ex officio but voting members of Parliament. In the states, there would be four nominees in each state from the army, navy, airforce, and police, and they would serve on state executive councils.

Shortly after Azikiwe's lecture was published, a storm of comment was raised in the newspapers, at university seminars around the country, and in private discussions among politicians. The Governor of the Rivers State, Naval Commander Alfred Diete-Spiff, supported the suggestion for a dyarchy after 1976.[20] Other military leaders did not openly respond, however, and the press was almost unanimously against Azikiwe's proposals.[21] Much later, a new acting Governor of the South-Eastern State, Colonel Olu Bajowa, spelled out his ideas on a gradual transition from military to civilian rule.

> I believe that the military should not hand over power in chaos. When it does hand over power we should try as much as possible to guarantee peace and stability.

The handover should commence in 1976 beginning from the state level to the federal and finally to the office of the President. It should be gradual, systematic, and smooth to ensure peace and stability. I can foresee turbulent political activities in 1976 and if the military were suddenly to step down, there may be confusion. I am not saying there will be, but we should not take chances. . . . However, if the three to four years' gradual handover is interpreted as a continuation of military rule, it should be seen against this background and not against the background that the military just wants to stay indefinitely. . . .[22]

Then Colonel Bajowa went on to say:

We should have either a purely military or purely civilian government. My own view is that the military should be kept out of politics as much as possible. Their continuous involvement in the day-to-day administration of the country will expose them to possible corrupt political influences.[23]

We started out interviewing shortly after Azikiwe had floated his proposals,[24] and we included a question on dyarchy to see how MHAs responded to Azikiwe's notions of a military-civilian regime. Many of them attacked Azikiwe personally for trying to ingratiate himself with the military, and some saw his proposals as a trial balloon floated by military leaders themselves. Over and over, MHAs said that a military government should be a military government and that a civilian one should be unfettered by the military. The cabinet members agreed, although Chief Kolawole Balgun, former federal minister and former commissioner under General Adebayo, argued that the executive offices of President of the Republic and governors of the state should be held by very senior army officers.[25]

Because civilians were operating in a military regime, because the military regime kept stating that there would be a transfer of power to civilian rule, and because many civilians already saw a mixed system operating, what the MHAs were saying was that the military should withdraw completely in a legal way. Indeed, they feared, as did many of those who commented on Azikiwe's proposals, that any discussion of a legally mixed system or a interregnum would give the military an excuse to stay in power. And the MHAs feared that the military would stay in power despite all of its claims to the contrary (see Tables 3 and 4).

Table 3

Do Most Officers Want a Return to Civilian Rule?

Reply	N	Percent
Yes	4	7.4
No	26	48.1
Not sure	3	5.6
If their interests are gratified	1	1.9
No answer	20	37.0

Table 4

Will There be Civilian Rule in 1976?

Replies	N	Percent
Yes	8	14.8
No	23	42.6
Military cannot be forced to go	5	9.3
Military does not want to go, but it will be forced to	4	7.4
Don't know	12	22.2
No answer	2	3.7

Politicians distinguished between those officers who they believed were committed to staying in power and those military men who wanted a return to civilian rule or who were at least not opposed to civilian rule. Politicians also confessed to be in doubt as to where many individual officers stood on the issue of return to civilian rule. In what ways the military would withdraw, if at all, was a major question for politicians. Their estimation of the future role of the Nigerian armed forces in political life was critical to the ways the politicians behaved from 1966 on. Whether and in what ways to make one's peace with the military, whether to form alliances with soldiers, whether to wait the military out, whether to surface politically and even overtly to oppose state governments or the federal government—these were questions that faced politicians. Future careers and even lives could be at stake depending on how these questions were answered.

The interviews we carried out in 1972–1973 on military withdrawal are ancient history, as is the debate prompted by Azikiwe's proposals of late 1972. Since that time, Nigeria had a coup in 1975 that replaced General Gowon. The coup leader, General Murtala Mohammed, committed himself to military withdrawl by 1979, after General Gowon had, in 1974, abrogated the military's pledge to return power to civilians by 1976.[26] General Mohammed put in motion the creation of a new Constitution, which was drafted after he was assassinated in 1976. The Draft Constitution, as put forward in October 1976, mentioned the military hardly at all. The armed forces were given no special right or duty to guarantee the Constitution, as is the case in states in which the military has built in a constitutional right to intervene. The armed forces of Nigeria are to defend Nigeria from external aggression, to maintain territorial integrity, and to suppress insurrection. Military officers do not sit ex officio on the National Security Council; the heads of the combined armed forces, head of army, navy, and airforce do sit ex officio on a National Defense Council.[27] No civilian-military dyarchy is constitutionalized.

The debate that surfaced in 1972–1974 over civilian-military relations in a transitional period and over the scope of the military's role in a civilian regime raised critical issues that were settled, prospectively, by the military's complete withdrawal, at least constitutionally speaking. Of course, deadlines for military withdrawal have been abrogated before in Nigeria. The present Head of State, General Obasanjo, is committed to withdrawal. But commitments have changed in Nigeria and conceivably officers could carry out a coup against his leadership.

Looking back at the period 1966–1976, we can say that civilian pressures mounted, especially after 1974, for military withdrawal. But conscious civilization of the military government did not come about through civilian pressure. The military's introduction of civilian commissioners in 1967 was a response to the need to mobilize support during crises and civil war. Subsequently, the creation of a new Draft Constitution and the carrying out of local elections were movements toward civilian rule by a military that was very concerned about its own corporate cohesion. Concern for military unity led significant numbers of officers to want to withdraw. Civilian politics remains very faction ridden, and ethnic-regional cleavages are still very intense, and thus the Nigerian context is not especially propitious for a return to civilian rule from the military's own perspective. However, Nigerian officers did not torture civilian opponents. There has been bloodshed within the Nigerian military and purges since 1975, but nothing on the scale of 1966 and the civil war period. On balance, Nigeria did not have an easy transition to civilian rule, and it may not be able to achieve civilian rule or persist with it once achieved, although abrogating the process again would risk mobilizing wider segments of the civilian population into active opposition.

The Nigerian case is certainly not an example of the implementation of the Kemalist model. Military elites did not develop their own networks for handling political cleavages and demands throughout Nigeria. The military did not create its own party as an auxiliary to the armed forces or as an organizational weapon of the armed forces. Nor have soldiers started resigning with a vew toward becoming politicians. The process of civilianizing a military regime by the military's creating a party has not occurred in Nigeria. Such a venture often splits the military and creates party officers and nonparty officers. Where strong parties already exist, as in communist systems, or in the Baath parties of Syria and Iraq,[28] army-party tensions exist but can be more easily handled than where the army creates a new party.

The African experience has so far not produced civilian-military alliances through party-army networks that have the viability of the Chinese or Cuban arrangements.[29] Different kinds of military regimes might evolve in Africa in countries in which guerrilla struggle has been significant for determining leadership after independence. In order to understand how Mozambique will be organized, it may make more sense to look at Cuba than at Tanzania. For we are not talking about a regime brought about by coups but by armed struggle. And Black Africa has not provided models for this pattern prior to the collapse of Portuguese rule and recent events in southern Africa.

A number of African military regimes have either put mass parties in place or talked about putting them in place. In Congo (Brazzaville) it is a "Marxist-Leninist" party, the Parti Congolais du Travail. In Mobutu's Zaire, where the intention to build a mass revolutionary party has received the most attention, it is the Movement Populaire de la Revolution (MPR). In Togo, it is the Rassemblement du Peuples Togolais (RPT). This party rejected the recommendation of its own Central Committee that power be return to a civilian regime.[30] Although the Togo regime, according to Decalo, has consolidated its rule, broadened its base, and utilizes a bargaining style in politics, the party is used for plebiscitary purposes; it is not a party of rule or of mobilization. Officers have not resigned in numbers to contend in a political arena. It remains a hollow structure, as does Mobutu's party. In the Sudan, the Sudan Socialist Union was created in 1972, and since then national and regional elections have occurred; there are lots of party branches and subbranches. Real contests took place under this party's aegis according to Kasfir.[31] But once again the phenomenon seems one of controlled participation rather than mobilization and transfromation. Moreover, Sudanese officers are not leaving the army to contend for political power in a new arena. Of course, controlled participation was the essence of most African one-party systems, and in this regard the army-created parties are not completely different. But the earlier African one-party systems did have more and deeper rural roots than the parties brought into being by military regimes, at least so far. Although one should not exaggerate the grass-roots presence of most of Africa's earlier one-party systems, it cannot be doubted that there was more representation of nonelites and more competition than within parties created by military regimes.

Where a party did seem to have life apart from the military leadership in Congo (Brazzaville), it was because junior officers staked out an independent role in the party[32] Militia and army factions tried to lead party elements against Marien Ngouabi.[33] Congo (Brazzaville) is an example, not of an independent party being built and a civilizing process taking place, but of a party that provided an arena in which military and nonmilitary factions make alliances against other military and nonmilitary factions.

The creation of parties under African military regimes thus far should not be seen as a civilizing process within the Kemalist model. That is, the military has not gone back to the barracks and created independent parties. We should not dismiss these parties created by militaries any more than we should dismiss the old single parties because they were not what they claimed to be. The old ruling single parties were not representative parties; they were not homogeneous embodiments of the nation; they were not strong, centralized, mobilizing parties. They did, however, perform many functions. They were involved in distributing patronage; they provided an arena for elite competition at various levels; they provided symbolic as well as material payoffs; they recruited personnel; in certain situations they legitimated bureaucratic power; and they provided channels for information flows, albeit imperfectly.

The creation of parties by military regimes is an attempt to carry out some of the above functions without direct use of the military. It is dangerous for military organizations to get involved in patronage distribution and to be the only political arena for elite competition outside the civil service.

In the African context, the development of parties underneath, and perhaps alongside, militaries in Zaire, Congo (Brazzaville), Togo, Benin, Burundi, Central African Republic, and Sudan should be seen not so much as a transition from military rule as the development of a new variant in civilian-military relations, with the military retaining dominance.

Futurology

We shall see in Africa a great deal of moving in and out of different institutional formulas and lots of variation in the civilian-military mixture. Obviously, the military will remain a critical source of power in Africa. At the same time, factional struggle within the armed forces, civilian pressures, and military needs in corporate and statist terms will force military regimes to experiment with ways to harness and control civilian institutions and to collaborate with civilian elements. There will be no military exit from power in Africa, but there will be complicated civilian-military systems of power.

The specific nature of the civilian-military system will depend on the same array of factors that have defied easy generalization about military initial interventions, continuing coups, and policy outcomes under military regimes. The kinds of officer corps, their scale of size, motives of officers, and relationships with noncommissioned officers will be one set of factors. We can understand the development of officer corps in terms of historical experiences, training programs, social and educational forces in society, and relationships to economic groups. But we should not get too hard a fix on an African officer corps, no matter how much we know about organizational and social variables internal to African armies. This is because the idiosyncratic element of individual style and personality of high-level commanders has special weight in African armies. Precisely because these armies are relatively uninstitutionalized, personal factors play a great role. There is no neat correlation between level of professionalization in African armies and scope for individual leadership. One could assume that the more corporate an African army, the more professional, the narrower the scope for individual idiosyncrasies. But leaders can affect corporate and professional levels. Armies can be purged or demoralized. Thus, although we can say that an army with certain organizational and social variables is more or less ikely to throw up an Amin, and although theories of organization can state the conditions under which we can expect certain leadership styles, we should allow for variation in these styles, even under similar conditions, between different armies and societies.

I do not believe that once we know whether some African societies are more or less middle class, or have a comparatively larger agricultural or industrial structure than others, we can move to an understanding of civilian-military relationships. Again, there is simply too much variation in subsystem variables within similar kinds of societies. What we can understand is the possibe scope for military action and authority. The levels of African economies and the structures of economies and societies set parameters on military rule in the same way that they set parameters on civilian rule.

I have tried to argue that knowing that a regime is a military one in Africa tells us something about the way it will operate. It tells us less about predictable policy outcomes. Once we know the reasons for military intervention, once we have understood specific organizational factors that pertain to individual armed forces, then we can begin to look at military relationships with civilian sectors and see the military in society as well as society in the military. In Africa, there are still severe limits on any regime's ability to centralize authority or carry out mobilization policies or squeeze resources for investment. Within the limits we can sketch, we shall find a wide variety of military regimes and interesting mixes of civilian-military authority expressed through different institutional formats. We can generalize about some aspects of these formats. Other aspects remain quite specific to time and place.

Notes

1. Claude Welch, "Cincinnatus in Africa: The Possibilities of Military Withdrawal from Poltics," in *The State of the Nations,* ed. Michael Lofchie (Berkeley: University of California Press, 1971), p. 217).

2. Morris Janowitz, *The Military in the Political Development of New Nations* (Chicago: University of Chicago Press, 1964).

3. Samuel P. Huntington, *Political Order in Changing Societies* (New Haven, Conn.: Yale University Press, 1969), pp. 258, 261.

4. Janowitz, *The Military in the Political Development of New Nations,* p. 104.

5. Claude Welch, "The African Military and Political Development," in *The Military and Modernization,* ed. Henry Bienen (Chicago: Atherton/Aldine, 1970), p. 220.

6. Daniel Lerner and Richard Robinson, "Swords and Ploughshares: The Turkish Army as a Modernizing Force," in *The Military and Modernization,* ed. Bienen, p. 124.

7. Welch, "The African Military and Political Development, p. 221.

8. See Henry Bienen, "The Background to Contemporary Study of Militaries and Modernization," in *The Military and Modernization,* ed. Bienen, pp. 1–35, and Nur Yalman, "Intervention and Extrication: The Officer Corps in the Turkish Crises," in *The Military Intervenes: Case Studies in Political Development,* ed. Henry Bienen (New York: Russell Sage Foundation, 1968).

9. I have greatly benefited from an unpublished paper by Daryal Batibay, "The Ataturk Model and the Turkey of Ataturk." This is an excellent review of the Ataturk model and its use by social scientists. Batibay argues against some of the historical specifics that purveyors of the model have seen, and he questions the appropriateness of the model for developing countries.

10. Ali A. Mazrui, "Soldiers as Traditionalizers: Military Rule and the Reafricanization of Africa," *World Politics* 28, no. 2 (January 1976): 246–272. Also Ali, Mazrui, "The Resurrection of the Warrior Tradition in Africa," *Journal of Modern African Studies* 13, no. 1 (1975): 67–84; Ali Mazrui *Soldiers and Kinsmen in Uganda* (Beverly Hills, Calif.: Sage Publications, 1975). Also, G. N. Uzoigwe, "Pre-Colonial Military Studies in Africa," *Journal of Modern African Studies* 13, no. 3 (1975): 469–482; Edward Feit, "Military Coups and Political Development: Some Lessons from Ghana and Nigeria," *World Politics* 20, no. 2 (January 1968): 179–193; Edward Feit, "The Rule of the Iron Surgeons; Military Government in Spain and Ghana," *Comparative Politics* 1, no. 4 (July 1969): 485–497.

11. These were the words used by Colonel Bajowa, then Governor of the Southeastern State, in an interview published in the *Sunday Times* (Lagos), July 14, 1974, p. 9.

12. Personal interview, Lagos, 1973.

13. Personal interview, Lagos, 1973.

14. *Sunday Times* (Lagos) October 19, 1972, pp. 5, 7–9, 16, and *Daily Times* (Lagos) October 28, 1972, p. 1.

15. *Ibid.*

16. *Ibid.*

17. *Ibid.,* p. 9.

18. *Ibid.,* p. 16.

19. *Ibid.*

20. Diete-Spiff's comments were reported in the *Sunday Times* (Lagos), November 5, 1972, p. 24.

21. Many comments in editorials suggested that Azikiwe bore personal responsibility for Nigeria's past ills. Substantially, it was argued that Azikiwe's proposals were unworkable compromises, (*Sunday Times* (Lagos) editorial opinion, November 5, 1972, pp. 1, 24); that they built in instability (*New Nigerian,* as reported in *Sunday Times,* November 5, 1972, p. 5). A long rejoinder was written by Tai Solarin in the *Nigerian Tribune* (Ibadan), November 13, 1972, pp. 4–5; and the *Tribune* ran a series of front-page editorials from November 8 to November 10, 1972. One of the things the *Tribune* objected to most strongly was Azikiwe's questioning of whether politicians had "learned their lessons," because this suggested that the politicians who would take over would the same ones who had been prominent before 1966. The *Tribune* also reacted strongly to what it called the "sickening sycophancy" with which Azikiwe treated the military.

22. *Sunday Times* (Lagos), July 14, 1974, p. 9.

23. Ibid.

24. Dr. Azikiwe continued the debate by making rebuttals to those who had responded to his initial lecture. Dr. Azikiwe's "First Rebuttal" was published in the *Sunday Times* (Lagos), November 12, 1972, pp. 6–7, 19, 21. In the same issue of the *Sunday Times,* there were other comments on the initial lecture by Dr. Owodion Idemeko, pp. 9–10; by Dr. Ayodele Awojobi, pp. 10–11; and by the New Left Study Group, pp. 11–17. A long rejoinder to Azikiwe was published in the *Sunday Times* of November 5, 1972, by Dr. Obarogie Ohonbamu, pp. 6–7, 17. Dr. Azikiwe published a "Second Rebuttal" in the *Sunday Times* on November 19, 1972, pp. 11, 14–15, 19, and a "Final Rebuttal" in the *Sunday Times* of November 26, 1972, pp. 12–15. In these rebuttals, Dr. Azikiwe responded to personal attacks and to individual points, but he did not extend his argument to make new points.

25. *Sunday Sketch* (Ibadan), November 10, 1972, p. 3.

26. As early as January 1966, General Ironsi had talked about the military government as "interim." In 1967, a phasing of stages for return to civilian rule was announced that included preparation for elections in early 1969. This phasing was not adhered to. However, the military government still insisted that it wanted civilian rule, and on October 1, 1970, it announced a Nine-Point Program for return to civilian rule by 1976. In the aftermath of controversy over a new census—a controversy reminiscent of the one that raged in the 1960s over an earlier census—General Gowon announced the military government's intention to stay in power beyond 1976 on October 1, 1974. General Gowon said that the nation's military leaders had decided it would be "utterly irresponsible to leave he nation in the lurch by a precipitate withdrawal." He stated that the military had not abandoned the idea of a return to civilian rule, but he maintained the ban on political parties that had been in effect since January 1966.

27. The Draft Constitution can be found in the *New Nigerian* (Kaduna) October 10, 11, 12, 1976.

28. For a discussion of Syria and Iraq, see Gabriel Ben-Dor, "Civilianization of Military Regimes in the Arab World," in *Political Participation Under Military Regimes,* ed. Henry Bienen and David Morell (Beverly Hills, Calif.: Sage Publications, 1976), pp. 39–49.

29. For a discussion of the Chinese case see Ying-mao Kau, *The People's Liberation Army and China's Nation Building* (White Plains, N.Y.: International Arts and Science Press, 1973);

Ellis Joffe, *Party and Army Professionalism and Political Control in the Chinese Officer Corps* (Cambridge, Mass.: Harvard University Press, 1968). For a general discussion of civilian-military relations, see Eric Nordlinger, *Soldiers in Politics: Military Coups and Governments* (Englewood Cliffs, N.J.: Prentice-Hall, 1977).

30. Samuel Decalo, *Coups and Army Rule in Africa* (New Haven, Conn.: Yale University Press, 1976), p. 177.

21. Nelson Kasfir, "Civilian Participation Under Military Rule in Uganda and Sudan," in *Political Participation Under Military Regimes,* ed. Bienen and Morell, pp. 66–85.

32. Decalo, *Coups and Army Rule in Africa,* p. 161.

33. Ngouabi was assassinated in an abortive coup in 1977.

List
of
Publications

Center of International Studies
Princeton University
List of Publications (available from publishers)

Gabriel A. Almond. *The Appeals of Communism* (Princeton University Press, 1954).

William W. Kaufmann, ed. *Military Policy and National Security* (Princeton University Press, 1956).

Klaus Knorr. *The War Potential of Nations* (Princeton University Press, 1956.).

Lucian W. Pye. *Guerrilla Communism in Malaya* (Princeton University Press, 1956).

Charles De Visscher. *Theory and Reality in Public International Law,* trans. by P. E. Corbett (Princeton University Press, 1957; rev. ed., 1968).

Bernard C. Cohen. *The Political Process and Foreign Policy: The Making of the Japanese Peace Settlement* (Princeton University Press, 1957).

Myron Weiner. *Party Politics in India: The Development of a Multi-Party System* (Princeton University Press, 1957).

Percy E. Corbett. *Law in Diplomacy* (Princeton University Press, 1959).

Rolf Sannwald and Jacques Stohler. *Economic Integration: Theoretical Assumptions and Consequences of European Unification,* trans. by Herman Karreman (Princeton University Press, 1959).

Klaus Knorr, ed. *NATO and American Security* (Princeton University Press, 1959).

Gabriel A. Almond and James S. Coleman, eds. *The Politics of the Developing Areas* (Princeton University Press, 1960).

Herman Kahn. *On Thermonuclear War* (Princeton University Press, 1960).

Sidney Verba. *Small Groups and Political Behavior: A Study of Leadership* (Princeton University Press, 1961).

Robert J. C. Butow. *Tojo and the Coming of the War* (Princeton University Press, 1961).

Glenn H. Snyder. *Deterrence and Defense: Toward a Theory of National Security* (Princeton University Press, 1961).

Klaus Knorr and Sidney Verba, eds. *The International System: Theoretical Essays* (Princeton University press, 1961).

Peter Paret and John W. Shy. *Guerrillas in the 1960's* (Praeger, 1962).

George Modelski. *A Theory of Foreign Policy* (Praeger, 1962).

Klaus Knorr and Thornton Read, eds., *Limited Strategic War* (Praeger, 1963).

Frederick S. Dunn. *Peace-Making and the Settlement with Japan* (Princeton University Press, 1963).

Arthur L. Burns and Nina Heathcote. *Peace-Keeping by United Nations Forces* (Praeger, 1963).

Richard A. Falk. *Law, Morality, and War in the Contemporary World* (Praeger, 1963).

James N. Rosenau. *National Leadership and Foreign Policy: A Case Study in the Mobilization of Public Support* (Princeton University Press, 1963).

Gabriel A. Almond and Sidney Verba. *The Civic Culture: Political Attitudes and Democracy in Five Nations* (Princeton University Press, 1963).

Bernard C. Cohen. *The Press and Foreign Policy* (Princeton University Press, 1963).

Richard L. Sklar. *Nigerian Political Parties: Power in an Emergent African Nation* (Princeton University Press, 1963).

Peter Paret. *French Revolutionary Warfare from Indochina to Algeria: The Analysis of a Political and Military Doctrine* (Praeger, 1964).

Harry Eckstein, ed. *Internal War: Problems and Approaches* (Free Press, 1964).

Cyril E. Black and Thomas P. Thornton, eds. *Communism and Revolution: The Strategic Uses of Political Violence* (Princeton University Press, 1964).

Miriam Camps. *Britain and the European Community 1955–1963* (Princeton University Press, 1964).

Thomas P. Thornton, ed. *The Third World in Soviet Perspective: Studies by Soviet Writers on the Developing Areas* (Princeton University Press, 1964).

James N. Rosenau, ed. *International Aspects of Civil Strife* (Princeton University Press, 1964).

Sidney I. Ploss. *Conflict and Decision-Making in Soviet Russia: A Case Study of Agricultural Policy, 1953–1963* (Princeton University Press, 1965).

Richard A. Falk and Richard J. Barnet, eds., *Security in Disarmament* (Princeton University Press, 1965).

Karl von Vorys. *Political Development in Pakistan* (Princeton University Press, 1965).

Harold and Margaret Sprout. *The Ecological Perspective on Human Affairs, with Special Reference to International Politics* (Princeton University Press, 1965).

Klaus Knorr. *On the Uses of Military Power in the Nuclear Age* (Princeton University Press, 1966).

Harry Eckstein. *Division and Cohesion in Democracy: A Study of Norway* (Princeton University Press, 1966).

Cyril E. Black. *The Dynamics of Modernization: A Study in Comparative History* (Harper and Row, 1966).

Peter Kunstadter, ed. *Southeast Asian Tribes, Minorities, and Nations* (Princeton University Press, 1967).

E. Victor Wolfenstein. *The Revolutionary Personality: Lenin, Trotsky, Gandhi* (Princeton University Press, 1967).

Leon Gordenker. *The UN Secretary-General and the Maintenance of Peace* (Columbia University Press, 1967).

Oran R. Young. *The Intermediaries: Third Parties in International Crises* (Princeton University Press, 1967).

James N. Rosenau, ed. *Domestic Sources of Foreign Policy* (Free Press, 1967).

Richard F. Hamilton. *Affluence and the French Worker in the Fourth Republic* (Princeton University Press, 1967).

Linda B. Miller, *World Order and Local Disorder: The United Nations and Internal Conflicts* (Princeton University Press, 1967).

Henry Bienen, *Tanzania: Party Transformation and Economic Development* (Princeton University Press, 1967).

Wolfram F. Hanrieder, *West German Foreign Policy, 1949–1963: International Pressures and Domestic Response* (Stanford University Press, 1967).

Richard H. Ullman. *Britain and the Russian Civil War: November 1918–February 1920* (Princeton University Press, 1968).

Robert Gilpin. *France in the Age of the Scientific State* (Princeton University Press, 1968).

William B. Bader. *The United States and the Spread of Nuclear Weapons* (Pegasus, 1968).

Richard A. Falk. *Legal Order in a Violent World* (Princeton University Press, 1968).

Cyril E. Black, Richard A. Falk, Klaus Knorr and Oran R. Young. *Neutralization and World Politics* (Princeton University Press, 1968).

Oran R. Young. *The Politics of Force: Bargaining During International Crises* (Princeton University Press, 1969).

Klaus Knorr and James N. Rosenau, eds. *Contending Approaches to International Politics* (Princeton University Press, 1969).

James N. Rosenau, ed. *Linkage Politics: Essays on the Convergence of National and International Systems* (Free Press, 1969).

John T. McAlister, Jr. *Viet Nam: The Origins of Revolution* (Knopf 1969).

Jean Edward Smith. *Germany Beyond the Wall: People, Politics and Prosperity* (Little, Brown, 1969).

James Barros. *Betrayal from Within: Joseph Avenol, Secretary-General of the League of Nations, 1933–1940* (Yale University Press, 1969).

Charles Hermann. *Crises in Foreign Policy: A Simulation Analysis* (Bobbs-Merrill, 1969).

Robert C. Tucker. *The Marxian Revolutionary Idea: Essays on Marxist Thought and Its Impact on Radical Movements* (W. W. Norton, 1969).

Harvey Waterman. *Political Change in Contemporary France: The Politics of an Industrial Democracy* (Charles E. Merrill, 1969).

Cyril E. Black and Richard A. Falk, eds. *The Future of the International Legal Order.* Vol. I: *Trends and Patterns* (Princeton University Press, 1969).

Ted Robert Gurr. *Why Men Rebel* (Princeton University Press, 1969).

C. Sylvester Whitaker. *The Politics of Tradition: Continuity and Change in Northern Nigeria 1946–1966* (Princeton University Press, 1970).

Richard A. Falk. *The Status of Law in International Society* (Princeton University Press, 1970).

Klaus Knorr. *Military Power and Potential* (D.C. Heath, 1970).

Cyril E. Black and Richard A. Falk, eds. *The Future of the International Legal Order.* Vol. II: *Wealth and Resources* (Princeton University Press, 1970).

Leon Gordenker, ed. *The United Nations in International Politics* (Princeton University Press, 1971).

Cyril E. Black and Richard A. Falk, eds. *The Future of the International Legal Order.* Vol. III: *Conflict Management* (Princeton University Press, 1971).

Francine R. Frankel. *India's Green Revolution: Political Costs of Economic Growth* (Princeton University Press, 1971).

Harold and Margaret Sprout. *Toward a Politics of the Planet Earth* (Van Nostrand Reinhold, 1971).

Cyril E. Black and Richard A. Falk, eds. *The Future of the International Legal Order.* Vol. IV: *The Structure of the International Environment* (Princeton University Press, 1972).

Gerald Garvey. *Energy, Ecology, Economy* (W. W. Norton, 1972).

Richard Ullman. *The Anglo-Soviet Accord* (Princeton University Press, 1973).

Klaus Knorr. *Power and Wealth: The Political Economy of International Power* (Basic Books, 1973).

Anton Bebler. *Military Rule in Africa: Dahomey, Ghana, Sierra Leone, and Mali* (Praeger Publishers, 1973).

Robert C. Tucker. *Stalin as Revolutionary 1879–1929: A Study in History and Personality* (W. W. Norton, 1973).

Edward L. Morse. *Foreign Policy and Interdependence in Gaullist France* (Princeton University Press, 1973).

Henry Bienen. *Kenya: The Politics of Participation and Control* (Princeton University Press, 1974).

Gregory J. Massell. *The Surrogate Proletariat: Moslem Women and Revolutionary Strategies in Soviet Central Asia, 1919–1929* (Princeton University Press, 1974).

James N. Rosenau. *Citizenship Between Elections: An Inquiry Into The Mobilizable American* (Free Press, 1974).

Ervin Laszio. *A Strategy For the Future: The Systems Approach to World Order* (Braziller, 1974).

John R. Vincent. *Nonintervention and International Order* (Princeton University Press, 1974).

Jan H. Kalicki. *The Pattern of Sino-American Crises: Political-Military Interactions in the 1950s* (Cambridge University Press, 1975).

Klaus Knorr. *The Power of Nations: The Political Economy of International Relations* (Basic Books, Inc., 1975).

James P. Sewell. *UNESCO and World Politics: Engaging in International Relations* (Princeton University Press, 1975).

Richard A. Falk. *A Global Approach to National Policy* (Harvard University Press, 1975).

Harry Eckstein and Ted Robert Gurr. *Patterns of Authority: A Structural Basis for Political Inquiry* (John Wiley & Sons, 1975).

Cyril E. Black, Marius B. Jansen, Herbert S. Levine, Marion J. Levy, Jr., Henry Rosovsky, Gilbert Rozman, Henry D. Smith, II, and S. Frederick Starr. *The Modernization of Japan and Russia* (Free Press, 1975).

Leon Gordenker. *International Aid and National Decisions: Development Programs in Malawi, Tanzania, and Zambia* (Princeton University Press, 1976).

Carl Von Clausewitz, *On War*, edited and translated by Michael Howard and Peter Paret (Princeton University Press, 1976).

Gerald Garvey and Lou Ann Garvey. *International Resource Flows* Lexington Books, 1977).

Walter F. Murphy and Joseph Tanenhaus. *Comparative Constitutional Law Cases and Commentaries* (St. Martin's Press, 1977).

INDEX